DYING FROM IMPROVEME

Inquests and Inquiries into Indigenous Deaths in Custody

No matter where in Canada they occur, inquiries and inquests into the deaths of Indigenous people while in state custody often tell the same story. Repeating details of fatty livers, mental illness, alcoholic belligerence, and a mysterious incapacity to cope with modern life, the legal proceedings declare that there are no villains here, only inevitable casualties of Indigenous life.

But what about a sixty-seven-year-old man who dies in a hospital in police custody with a large, visible, purple boot print on his chest? Or a barely conscious, alcoholic older man, dropped off by police in a dark alley on a cold Vancouver night? Or Saskatoon's infamous and lethal starlight tours, whose victims were left on the outskirts of town in subzero temperatures? How do we account for the repeated failure to care evident in so many cases of Indigenous deaths in custody?

In *Dying from Improvement,* Sherene H. Razack argues that, amidst systematic state violence against Indigenous people, inquiries and inquests serve to obscure the violence of ongoing settler colonialism under the guise of benevolent concern. They tell settler society that it is caring, compassionate, and engaged in improving the lives of Indigenous people – even as the incarceration rate of Indigenous men and women increases and the number of those who die in custody rises.

Razack's powerful critique of the Canadian settler state and its legal system speaks to many of today's most pressing issues of social justice: the treatment of Indigenous people, the unparalleled authority of the police and the justice system, and their systematic inhumanity towards those whose lives they perceive as insignificant.

SHERENE H. RAZACK is a professor in the Department of Social Justice Education at the Ontario Institute for Studies in Education, University of Toronto.

Dying from Improvement

Inquests and Inquiries into Indigenous Deaths in Custody

SHERENE H. RAZACK

UNIVERSITY OF TORONTO PRESS
Toronto Buffalo London

Toronto Buffalo London
www.utppublishing.com
Printed in the U.S.A.

ISBN 978-1-4426-3737-5 (cloth)
ISBN 978-1-4426-2891-5 (paper)

Printed on acid-free, 100% post-consumer recycled paper with vegetable-based inks.

Library and Archives Canada Cataloguing in Publication

Razack, Sherene, author
Dying from improvement : inquests and inquiries into Indigenous deaths in custody / Sherene H. Razack.

Includes bibliographical references and index.
ISBN 978-1-4426-3737-5 (bound). – ISBN 978-1-4426-2891-5 (paperback)

1. Indian prisoners – British Columbia – Death. 2. Indian prisoners – Saskatchewan – Death. 3. Coroners – British Columbia. 4. Coroners – Saskatchewan. 5. Discrimination in criminal justice administration – British Columbia. 6. Discrimination in criminal justice administration – Saskatchewan. I. Title.

E78.B9R39 2015 365'.6089970711 C2015-900940-5

University of Toronto Press acknowledges the financial assistance to its publishing program of the Canada Council for the Arts and the Ontario Arts Council, an agency of the Government of Ontario.

Canada Council for the Arts Conseil des Arts du Canada

University of Toronto Press acknowledges the financial support of the Government of Canada through the Canada Book Fund for its publishing activities.

For Paul Alphonse, Frank Paul, Anthany Dawson,
and all those who died in custody

Contents

Acknowledgments

The research and writing of this book was an exceptionally long process for me. While I would like to blame the delay on the demands of academic life, the truth is that the closer I got to the state and settlers' role in Indigenous death, the more I felt unable to write about it. I am very much in debt to those who understand the violence at the heart of settler colonialism and who encouraged me to carry on trying to name it. This book is dedicated to all those who died in custody. My debt begins with the family of Paul Alphonse and especially with Kristy Palmantier, who was generous beyond measure. Alphonse's community, including former Chief Nancy Sandy, Amy Sandy, Elder Jean Alphonse, and Kiddo Alphonse, took the time to meet with me and share their thoughts about Paul Alphonse's death in custody. Nancy Dawson spoke to me candidly of her son Anthany's life and death. Peggy Clement did not hesitate to give me her support when I asked her how Frank Paul's family would feel if I wrote about his case. Saskatchewan, for many the epicentre of Indigenous deaths in custody, would not have been possible for me to begin to grasp without my late friend and colleague, Patricia Monture-Angus, to whom chapter six is dedicated. Trisha not only drove me to meet with those who could help me understand Indigenous deaths in custody, but she also inspired and supported me with her own remarkable courage and unflinching attention to colonial violence that I could not do without and that I continue to rely on. I wish to thank Cynthia Callison, Stephen Keliher, Cameron Ward, Laurie Wilson, and Don Worme, the legal professionals associated with some of the cases I discuss, who shared their files and their thoughts. Research assistants are really the foundation of this book. Leslie Thielen Wilson, Carmela Murdocca, Lynn Caldwell, and Gada Mahrouse, while still doctoral students, kept pushing me to write this book and were caring enough to berate me when I could not find the courage to do it for a few years. When they became professors, they continued to think about deaths in custody and sustained me with their encouragement. More than this, however, their stellar anti-colonial scholarship has deeply enriched my own. Kate Milley took over where they left off as students and gave me the full measure of her research skills, compassion, and insight into colonial violence, as well as years of experience working with marginalized groups. I am particularly grateful to Kate for continuing to remind me, even as the book went to press, that I track not only Indigenous death but Indigenous resistance. Shaista Patel, Nashwa Salem, and Louise Tam gave unsparingly of their intellectual gifts. They, along with virtually every graduate student whose path crossed mine at the Ontario Institute for Studies in Education of the University of Toronto, contributed research, ideas, and an abiding commitment to anti-colonial work. I am forever grateful.

No book like this sees the light of day without plenty of dress rehearsals. I have often felt uneasy giving lectures on the research, hazarding analyses that were too preliminary, forgetting to think about the pain I cause in speaking of this violence, and sometimes speaking too confidently about something I could only sense. The scholars of the West Coast and the Prairies – at Simon Fraser University, the University of British Columbia (UBC), UBC Okanagan, Mount Royal College, and the University of Saskatchewan – have all been gracious and insightful. I owe special thanks to Jiji Voronka, Rod Michalco, and Tanya Titchkosky, who helped me explore the parallels between colonialism and the oppression of people with disabilities. I thank friends and colleagues who read drafts, offered help, and enriched this work with their own, among them Brenna Bhandar, Mark Harris, Jon Goldberg Hillier, Tasha Hubbard, Donna Jeffery, Carmela Murdocca, Honor Ford Smith, Bonita Lawrence, Sarah Keenan, Suvendrini Perera, Joseph Pugliese, Denise Ferreira da Silva, and Nadera Shalhoub Kevorkian. At the end of the writing during time I spent on a fellowship at Curtin University, Suvendi's intellectual gifts, including her work on racial and colonial violence, and her friendship gave me the last push I needed to bring the book into the light of day. My thanks to the three anonymous reviewers and to Doug Hildebrand and the team at the University of Toronto Press for their support and for the care they gave this manuscript. Carolyn Zapf was a remarkable copy editor, and she improved this work immeasurably. Angela Pietrobon prepared a superb index.

Two people have had an extraordinary impact on this book. My dear friend Barbara Buckman walked alongside me, and like a good friend always reminded me to think about what I knew and didn't know concerning violence against Indigenous peoples. My initial understanding that I had immigrated to a settler society began when I met Barb in a university dorm and learned that while she and I were both called Indians, we came out of very different colonial histories. Thank you Barb for a forty-year-old friendship, and especially for holding my hand in Williams Lake. Chapter four is dedicated to Chaz (Chester Patrick), Gitxsan artist and Barb's partner, who died the kind of death the chapter describes and who shared with me his own analysis of Indigenous deaths in custody shortly before his death. Leslie Thielen-Wilson is the second person who walked alongside me through every step of this journey, not only from footnote to footnote, but throughout the analytical process. Leslie's acute understanding of what in her own work she calls "white terror" always pushes me further than I think I can go. I rely on her anti-colonial instincts and scholarship and on her capacity for deep friendship to get me through most of my scholarly projects, but none more so than this one.

I have never been able to get by without my family. My sister, my brothers, and their families shared their homes when I needed a place to write and took over my share of family responsibilities. My sons, Ilya and Benjamin, and my partner Larry are the reasons I could begin and finish anything. Their love sustains me. It is an added bonus to benefit from their understanding of violence and law.

I am grateful to the following journals for permission to reproduce in whole or in part my work already published in the following articles:

2014. "'It Happened More than Once': Freezing Deaths in Saskatchewan." *Canadian Journal of Women and the Law* 26, no. 1: 51–80.
2012. "Memorializing Colonial Power: The Death of Frank Paul." *Law and Society Review* 37, no. 4: 908–32.
2011. "Timely Deaths: Medicalizing the Deaths of Aboriginal People in Police Custody." *Law, Culture and the Humanities*. Published electronically before print, 30 June. doi:10.1177/1743872111407022.
2011. "The Space of Difference in Law: Inquests into Aboriginal Deaths in Custody." *Somatechnics* 1, no. 1: 87–123.

A Note on Names

Any discussion of deaths in custody brings pain to family members and friends. A death in custody is especially painful because it is untimely, and because, more often than not, families and friends do not ever learn why their loved ones have died and who is responsible for their deaths. I can only hope to bring a dimension of justice to the overall issue of Indigenous deaths in custody, deaths that occur more frequently than any one of us should accept. While the research for this book was based on publicly available transcripts of inquests and inquiries, I have tried to lessen the invasion of privacy and the circulation of painful accounts by using the initials of those who died in the body of the text. In the case of deaths where I have had an opportunity to speak with family members or where deaths have already been too widely discussed in the media and elsewhere to preserve anonymity, I have used the full names.

DYING FROM IMPROVEMENT

Inquests and Inquiries into Indigenous Deaths in Custody

Introduction

Boot Print on the Chest: Disappearing "Indians" in Life and Law

dis·ap·pear (dĭs′ə-pîr′)
v. **dis·ap·peared, dis·ap·pear·ing, dis·ap·pears**
v.intr.
1. To pass out of sight; vanish.
2. To cease to exist.
v.tr.
To cause (someone) to disappear, especially by kidnapping or murder.[1]

Colonialism survives in a settler form. In this form, it fails at what it is supposed to do: eliminate Indigenous people; take all their land; absorb them into a white, property-owning body politic.

Audra Simpson, Mohawk scholar[2]

The cover of this book is the gravestone that marks the burial place of Paul Alphonse, an Indigenous[3] (Secwepemc) man whose death sparked the beginning of my research into Indigenous deaths in custody. Paul Alphonse's family located him in hospital in police custody after looking for him for a few days. His niece noticed that there was a large purple boot print on his chest. Alphonse died shortly after his family found him, and an inquest into his death was held in 2001–2. Reading through the transcript of the inquest, I was surprised to find that the boot print seemed to be a peripheral issue. Instead, the inquest was taken up with discussing Alphonse's alcoholism and the difficulties he posed for police and health-care professionals. Alphonse, a sixty-seven-year-old man, was one of a group known locally as the troopers, senior Indigenous men and women who are survivors of residential schools and who now spend some of their time drinking in the parks, the mall, and other public spaces of Williams Lake, British Columbia. Family and community members express a strong sense of responsibility towards this group, and the younger generation is taught to go to Boitanio Park to check on the troopers and ensure that they head home safely to the reserve before dark. Walking the nine kilometres from the town to the reserve along a dark highway poses a risk of being hit by a car or picked up by police.[4] The inquest's focus on Alphonse's alcoholism effectively deflected attention away from police/Indigenous relations, although the band and the family tried hard to bring these relations, both past and ongoing, into the picture.

In numerous inquests and inquiries into Indigenous deaths in custody, such as the Wright inquiry into the freezing death of Neil Stonechild in the prairie city of Saskatoon and the Davies inquiry into the death of Frank Paul who was left by police in an alley in the city of Vancouver, I encountered the story of alcoholism and dysfunction rather than an interrogation of the violence against Indigenous people committed by state actors. Significantly, this dynamic was present even in inquests and inquiries that are counted as the most progressive in terms of the attention paid to the actions of state officials. In every instance, state accountability receded the more that details about physically and emotionally ravaged Indigenous people came into view. This unvarying pattern prompted the central question of this book: "Why is Indigenous death nearly always considered a timely death, a death that no one could prevent or cause?" Coronial inquests and inquiries consistently produce the story of the Indian on the brink of death, repeating the narrative of the vanishing Indian that has been dear to white settler societies from the time of their inception. Inundating us with details of fatty livers, mental illness, alcoholic belligerence, and a mysterious incapacity to cope with modern life, legal records tell the story of a premodern people encountering and losing out to a more advanced and superior race.

The narrative of a dying race, perhaps the oldest settler colonial story, can be found elsewhere in law. For example, rejecting the land claim of the Gitksan and Wet'suwet'en of northwestern British Columbia, Chief Justice Alan McEachern of the British Columbia Supreme Court commented on "the relentless energy" of Europeans, with which Indigenous people "would not, or could not, compete," concluding that if Indigenous people were conquered, it was not by dint of force but simply through the superior capacities of a more resilient group.[5] Triumphalist narratives abound and are the dominant stories in contemporary settler colonial societies such as Canada, Australia, the United States, and Israel. A. Dirk Moses suggests that the argument according to which Australia's Indigenous peoples were victims of their own pathologies fulfilled an important function. The "rhetoric of Indigenous decline also served to mask choices open to policy-makers, choices they were not prepared to entertain because they fundamentally approved of the civilizing process in which they were engaged."[6] When inquests and inquiries instruct us in the pathologies of Indigenous peoples, states provide themselves with alibis not only for inaction but also for crimes of overt violence. The idea of a disappearing race is also productive for settler subjectivities. Through it, settlers are able to feel Indigenous disappearance and to imagine their own superiority. Perpetually needing assistance into modernity from an enlightened and compassionate European race, Indigenous people are scripted in these moments as remnants, while settlers see themselves as pioneers. As Lorenzo Veracini writes, the definition of a successful settler project is when the Indigenous population has been reduced to a "manageable remnant."[7] The road to settler success is lined with legal decisions and reports which declare what settlers hope to make true on the ground, namely that they have become the original citizens through their enterprising spirit. It is the aim of this book to track and to understand the manifestly colonial story of the disappearing Indian told in Canadian inquests and inquiries into Indigenous deaths in custody. If settlers must so unfailingly tell the story of a dying race, the question that must be asked is, "What does the story do?"

Mapping the Official Story

My interest in this book is the official story a white settler society tells about Indigenous deaths in custody. What do inquests and inquiries reveal about how and why Indigenous people die in custody? What is said about a sixty-seven-year-old man who dies in a hospital in police custody with a large, visible, purple boot print on his chest, a mark no one in the hospital or among the police notice? How do we account for the police dropping off a barely conscious, alcoholic older man, Frank Paul (Mi'kmaq), in a dark alley on a cold Vancouver night, a man who could be seen on a video recording being dragged into the police station, presumably unable to walk on his own? What sense are we to make of the patterns of these deaths – patterns involving a repeated failure to care, a systemic indifference and callousness, and sometimes, outright murder? Examining inquests and inquiries into Indigenous deaths in custody for two Canadian provinces, British Columbia and Saskatchewan, I advance the argument that the violence state actors visit on Indigenous bodies imprints colonial power on the skin, as much as the branding of slaves or the whipping and abuse of children in residential schools once did. Such a branding declares Indigenous bodies, and crucially their lands, to be settler property, and simultaneously announces that Indigenous people are subhuman, the kind of human one can only deal with through force. Importantly, the power imprinted on bodies need not take the form of a boot print. The failure to provide care, indeed *to* care, marks the body as a lower form of humanity, one that is already in between life and death. Legal processes such as inquests and inquiries endorse the racial hierarchy that a boot print produces through routinely declaring such actions as lawful, necessary, or inevitable. Through a legal performance of Indigenous people as a dying race who are simply pathologically unable to cope with the demands of modern life, the settler subject is formed and his or her entitlement to the land secured. The settler and the settler state are both constituted as modern and as exemplary in their efforts to assist Indigenous people's entry into modernity. In this way, killing becomes saving, and murder brings redemption. Law is absolutely crucial to this alchemical transformation.

In the face of such a damning indictment, many readers will immediately point out that inquests and inquiries are particular kinds of legal sites. An inquest is a legal process conducted by a coroner. Its purpose is to determine cause of death, and, as such, it is not a criminal trial in which suspects defend themselves. The aim of an inquest is to identify what would prevent death from happening under the same circumstances. An inquiry, while it shares with the inquest an investigative rather than an adversarial function, reviews deaths that have given rise to public concern. Typically led by a judge, an inquiry is a more public and broader judicial process than an inquest. As coroners and commissioners never fail to say, these processes are not trials, and thus they are not concerned with establishing innocence or guilt. Instead, they are devoted to the prevention of deaths, an apparently Sisyphean task. But if inquests and inquiries are structured to have little time for the past, they cannot get to the future without going back in time. The fiction, therefore, that they cannot attend to the matter of "who did it," brackets the involvement of state professionals in acts of murder or neglect, and keeps the discussion in the more abstract realm of devising better systems of care and vigilance over dysfunctional bodies and a dying race. The inquest or the inquiry is tailor-made to present both the story

of the disappearance of a race *and* the story of white settlers assisting Indigenous people into modernity. They occupy a specific site in colonial law, one devoted to that most quintessential of colonial activities: the improvement of the colonized, or, in an old phrase, the civilizing mission.

Critical scholars have long noted that states defend their reputations and the actions of police and medical professionals in inquests and inquiries. As Phillip Scraton and Kathryn Chadwick put it, inquests, defying the injunction of the proverb, generally turn on speaking ill of the dead.[8] Those most vulnerable to police violence are transformed into individuals who are blamed for their own deaths. Simon Pemberton shows, for instance, that inquests construct victims and police dialectically, establishing the former as authors of their own demise and the latter as heroes as well as victims of a hard-to-police population.[9] Are Indigenous deaths in custody any different from other deaths where the dead are blamed for their own demise? In this book, I argue that while non-Indigenous people are also often thought to have caused their own deaths, in the case of Indigenous people, it is important to identify what is secured both by the practices of policing that lead to death and by the state's response to such deaths in inquests and inquiries. Indigenous people stand in the way of settler colonialism, contesting settler entitlement to the land and throwing into question settler legitimacy as the original and rightful owners. The settler is not legitimate. The land is occupied and continues to be stolen. Colonialism continues apace. How can settlers come to believe in their own legitimacy when Indigenous people enter the spaces deemed civilized and contest the colonial order by their very presence? Perhaps more than any other group, that is, the myriads of the impoverished, the criminalized, and the psychiatrized, whose presence also disrupts, Indigenous people challenge the settler's claim to modernity. Is it any wonder that violence is directed at them and that a strenuous policing of Indigenous bodies in the settler city end in death for some?

In pursuing the official story about Indigenous death in custody, this book does not expand upon how Indigenous communities live with disappearances. Indigenous resistance to violence and to the official story is, however, a crucial stream running through all inquests and inquiries. Those who are declared to be the last vestiges of a dying race have interrupted more than one inquest or inquiry, insisting on their voices being heard and offering a clear and compelling analysis of the colonial violence visited on their communities in the past, and crucially, in the present. I think, for example, of the family of Lawrence Wegner who never stopped asking questions about their son's freezing death; of Nancy Sandy, chief of the Sugar Cane Reserve, who made connections for the coroner between Paul Alphonse's death, dispossession, and police/Indigenous relations in Williams Lake; of the troopers who battled their own ill health and fear, and came to the inquest to testify about the violence they saw meted out to Paul Alphonse; of Cree Elder Andrew Yellowback who reminded the inquiry into Frank Paul's death that one can die of improvement; and of Nancy Dawson, the mother of Anthany Dawson, who told the jury that no one should die the way her son died and that he was a brilliant artist who in his life had encountered unrelenting police racism. In each of these instances, Indigenous families and communities tirelessly pursued justice, often waiting years before having a chance to ask their questions in a legal forum. Coroners and commissioners often declare such Indigenous interventions out of bounds, either by silencing them outright or by allowing Indigenous presence only in tightly scripted moments of ceremony. In the wake of a legal system dedicated to the story of disappearing Indians, it can be difficult to recognize these moments of resistance, coming as they do as interruptions. Audra Simpson, writing of the Mohawks of Kahnawà:ke, suggests that such moments amount to a politics of refusal, the refusal "to stop being themselves."[10] As a "political and ethical stance that stands in stark contrast to the desire to have one's distinctiveness as a culture, as a people, recognized," refusal is a direct engagement with a colonial legal system, a daring to ask, "Who are they to do so?"[11] What it costs to ask such questions should not be underestimated. Simpson describes "the labor of living in the face of an expectant and a *foretold* cultural and political death ... the hard labor of hanging on to territory, defining and fighting for your rights, negotiating and maintaining governmental and gendered forms of power."[12] Remnants are not expected to contest their disappearance. Amidst the details meant to convey and indeed accomplish Indigenous disappearance, it can be difficult in legal settings to track the hard labour of Indigenous refusal, and not least because it is so relentlessly suppressed, both by legal rules and by the tide of information about damaged and dysfunctional Indigenous bodies. It may be that an ethnography of interruptions is required to understand and fully illuminate the history of refusal. As Leanne Simpson reminds us:

> The story here, the real story, is virtually the same story in every Indigenous nation: Over the past several centuries we have been violently dispossessed of most of our land to make room for settlement and resource

development. The very active system of settler colonialism maintains that dispossession and erases us from the consciousness of settler Canadians except in ways that is deemed acceptable and non-threatening to the state. We start out dissenting and registering our dissent through state-sanctioned mechanisms like environmental impact assessments. Our dissent is ignored. Some of us explore Canadian legal strategies, even though the courts are stacked against us. Slowly but surely we get backed into a corner where the only thing left to do is to put our bodies on the land. The response is always the same – intimidation, force, violence, media smear campaigns, criminalization, silence, talk, negotiation, "new relationships," promises, placated resistance and then more broken promises. Then the cycle repeats itself.[13]

What have inquests and inquiries determined about Indigenous deaths in custody? Are police merely present when it happens, as many inquests conclude? Are some police corrupt? Are medical professionals overburdened? If, as I maintain, the legal processes I examine here all tell a version of the same story – that Indigenous people who die in custody are the detritus of modern society, the remnants of a dying colonialism – then we must conclude that a central function of inquests and inquiries is the making of remnants. The claim I make is that Indigenous peoples are first treated as remnants – as people who are dying anyway – and their bodies are then legally staged as bodies already in their final stages of decay. Legal processes are in the first instance pedagogical. Through them we learn about superior races and inferior races, and about who is fit to enter modern life. In a more sinister way, we also learn that when death comes to Indigenous people, no one is to blame, and thus no one can be called to account. It is of course true that the bodies which inquests and inquiries examine with such care are (for the most part), in life, on the edge of death, bodies weakened by ill health, addiction, and disease as a result of colonialism. What the law establishes is that there is no duty to care, either because it would be hard to know how to care for bodies at this stage of decay, or because care is superfluous. Who can stop the march of history and progress? In their staging of Indigenous pathology and dysfunction, inquests and inquiries also install white settler superiority through the expert evidence of men and women of science. If these experts establish that Indigenous people are hard to care for, or beyond care, they also confirm that settler society nevertheless tries hard to save the dying race. A settler society defines itself as benevolent, a quality that inquests and inquiries seek to showcase.

Law and Disappearance

As a transitive verb, "to disappear" Indians means to commit an act that results in disappearance. For Indians to disappear, law must actively produce their disappearance as independent sovereign nations. Indigenous leaders and scholars have long understood this reality and concluded that the answer to genocide and ongoing occupation cannot be found in the law that authorized it. Mohawk legal scholar Patricia Monture-Angus presents this position powerfully, emphasizing that the colonial project is above all legally authorized:

> Think about everything that First Nations people have survived in this country: the taking of our land, the taking of our children, residential schools, the current criminal justice system, the outlawing of potlatches, sundances, and other ceremonies, and the stripping of Indian women (and other Indian people) of their status. Everything we survived as individuals or as Indian peoples. How was all of this delivered? The answer is simple: through law. For almost every single one of the oppressions I have named, I can take you to the law library and I can show you where they wrote it down in the statutes and in the regulations. Sometimes the colonialism is expressed on the face of the statute books, and other times it is hidden in the power of bureaucrats who take their authority from those same books. Still, so many people still believe that law is the answer. The reason why Canadian law just does not fully work for resolving Aboriginal claims – including those fundamentally concerning Aboriginal women – is quite simple. Canadian courts owe their origin to British notions of when a nation is sovereign. It is from Canadian sovereignty that Canadian courts owe their existence. Courts, therefore, cannot question the very source of their own existence without fully jeopardizing their own being. Courts cannot be forced to look at issues about the legitimacy (or, more appropriately, the lack thereof) of Canadian sovereignty as against the claims of Aboriginal sovereignties.[14]

The decisions in land claim cases bear out Monture-Angus's assertion that law libraries are filled with evidence showing that the law is premised above all on settler sovereignty. Anishinaabe legal scholar John Borrows, commenting on *Delgamuukw v. British Columbia*,[15] the 1997 Supreme Court of Canada ruling that many have taken to be a positive and landmark decision for Indigenous peoples, has cogently analysed the same bind Monture-Angus recognized.[16] When the Gitksan and Wet'suwet'en peoples went to court claiming Aboriginal title and self-government over approximately 58,000 square kilometres of land in northwestern British Columbia, they relied on their own oral histories and ceremonies, as well as on the accounts of European traders, to show that they had been the owners of the land for centuries. As mentioned earlier, lower courts, notably the Supreme Court of British Columbia in its 1991 decision by Chief Justice McEachern, were not satisfied with the evidence presented as proof of ownership. Declaring that the two nations did not own the land in any European sense of the word (McEachern famously relied on Thomas Hobbes to declare that life for the Gitksan and Wet'suwet'en in the years before Europeans arrived was "nasty, brutish and short" in communities that did not even have horses), Chief Justice McEachern simply reaffirmed the sovereignty of the Crown. As Leslie Thielen-Wilson, drawing on C.B. Macpherson, has brilliantly argued, in the European ideology of possessive individualism, property is central to what it means to be human.[17] Chief Justice McEachern merely relied on Enlightenment notions of the connection between property and personhood, understanding a property owner as an individual who cultivated the land as Europeans did. When the case reached the Supreme Court of Canada, this fundamental assertion of settler sovereignty (and the connection between European notions of property and personhood) remained undisturbed, even as the court granted that oral histories had to be taken into account when establishing ownership and that the two nations had successfully established a degree of ownership. In reaching its decision to expand the rules of evidence to include oral histories, Crown assertions of sovereignty remained the standard against which all Aboriginal rights were measured, its illegitimate and violent basis notwithstanding. As Borrows pithily sums up, the court considered Indigenous peoples as serfs who work Crown land.[18] Winning the right to the use of some of their land, providing the land is used in traditional ways, the Gitskan and Wet'suwet'en had to prove the basis of their ownership under conditions set by the court. As Dakota scholar Phillip Deloria has shown, the emphasis on tradition is simply a variant of "vanishing Indian ideology." Where the only real Indian is a traditional Indian, white society can maintain that few Indians have survived and that settlers are perfectly positioned to salvage the little that is left of Native culture and to become authorities on who is an Indian.[19] The traditional Indian, Scott Lyons observes, possesses a timelessness that effectively removes Indians from history, positioning Indians as things rather than as social actors.[20] If not regarded as things, Indigenous people are present in colonial law only as acted-upon beings. They do not exist in settler law as sovereign subjects. The Crown, Borrows notes, bears none of the burdens that Indigenous peoples do in the law. The settler state is always presumed to legitimately possess the land, and Aboriginal title and Aboriginal rights are, by definition, restricted and diminished. Legal rules guarantee that this premise continues to operate. In *Delgamuukw*, for instance, Indigenous legal systems were considered subordinate to common law, and the court gave itself the right to authenticate Indigenous traditions. Pre-existing land-use regimes were all ignored, and, most significant of all, the Crown was declared to have the power to extinguish Aboriginal rights. Borrows, recalling the words of George Watts, chairman of the Nuu-chah-nulth nation, soberly observes that you have to destroy a people before you can extinguish their title: "For many Aboriginal peoples, extinguishment is genocide."[21]

The racial basis to the doctrine of discovery forever haunts law, as Peter Fitzpatrick has long argued. The discoverer remains the subject with whom time began, while the discovered are the object that acquires definition only upon contact, possessing neither a history nor autonomous personhood.[22] The moment of discovery is never named as violence, and law will insist henceforth that Aboriginal rights are contained within the story of settler sovereignty, as Borrows argued. From the Gitksan and Wet'suwet'en to Mabo in Australia,[23] even when the settler state is at its most expansive in acknowledging Aboriginal rights, the premise remains that history begins with the sovereignty of the settler state. The discovered enter into the arrangements of European legal regimes forever subordinate, awaiting improvement, an invitation always deferred, to join the nation state. Perniciously, as Fitzpatrick observes, the Indigenous, positioned as incompletely modern, are also measured by yardsticks that already define them as irrevocably outside of modernity and beyond improvement.[24]

Land and Boot Prints

The origin story of settler sovereignty, that a superior, modern race inevitably triumphed over a pre-modern and dying race, persists intact in land claims through the decades. In 1989, the Tsilhqot'in (Chilcotin) nation, to which Paul Alphonse belonged, found itself trying to prevent the harnessing of timber on lands it claimed it owned in the Nemiah Valley. In what appeared to be at least a partial victory in 2007, British Columbia Supreme Court Justice David Vickers found that the Tsilhqot'in had rights to the lands they use and that the logging companies infringed upon these rights.[25] The court nevertheless stated it was unable in the context of the proceedings to make a declaration of Aboriginal title (although it offered an opinion that Aboriginal title does exist inside and outside the claim area). The court held that Tsilhqot'in people had the right to hunt and trap birds throughout the claim area. However, only the federal government has the right to authorize forestry activities or any other use or control of natural resources on Aboriginal title land.[26] On appeal by the government of British Columbia to the British Columbia Court of Appeal, the court rejected even the limited reading of the meaning of Aboriginal title declared by Justice Vickers, ruling that title cannot be established over broad areas of land and always has to be demonstrated for specific sites and for tracts of land actually occupied by the Tsilhqot'in at the time of sovereignty. The Tsilhqot'in were semi-nomadic at that time, and therefore could not show that their village sites were occupied throughout the year.[27] On appeal to the Supreme Court of Canada, the Tsilhqot'in introduced evidence concerning the Chilcotin war, when some of their chiefs were hung and for which they received an apology from the government in the 1990s (in response to the recommendations of the Cariboo-Chilcotin Justice Inquiry discussed in chapter three). The Chilcotin war and the subsequent apology confirmed that the Tsilhqot'in nation had a long pattern of land use and defence.[28] On 26 June 2014, the Supreme Court of Canada ruled that the Tsilhqot'in held Aboriginal title and that the government of British Columbia had breached its duty to consult. The government is required to consult on land that is potentially subject to Aboriginal title. Thus, the court clearly recognized Aboriginal title, but emphasized that the test to establish title continues to be a demanding one, with application only to specific tracts of land. It stopped short of requiring Aboriginal consent, even as it appeared to increase requirements for consultation.[29] The limits to what appeared to be a Tsilhqot'in victory soon became apparent. The Songhees and Esquimalt nations of British Columbia found that the ruling in the Tsilhqot'in case concerning the duty to consult did not enable them to claim the government had a duty to negotiate. As the Supreme Court of British Columbia ruled,[30] the Tsilhqot'in decision offered only a requirement to consult and accommodate but not one compelling negotiation. As the Songhees and Esquimalt nations concluded, Indigenous nations will simply be forced to go to court again and again to establish land title.[31] As adept as any First Nation becomes in proving land ownership (and the test remains one of European land usage), the possibility always remains that land title and Aboriginal rights will be qualified at best to mean the right to hunting and fishing, and not the right to determine how the land should be used. Further, courts are likely to continue to assume the authority to declare who is and is not "Indian," and to insist that the only real Indian is a traditional Indian. As in *Delgamuukw* and *Mabo*, land title can only go so far as the stakes get higher. Taseko Mines Ltd., for example, is currently seeking to develop a billion-dollar gold and copper mine on Tsilhqot'in ancestral grounds in the area, subject to the land claim. The site has been assessed as the tenth largest underdeveloped gold-copper deposit in the world, with approximately 2.4 billion kilograms of copper and 377,000 kilograms or 13.3 million ounces of gold. The Tsilhqot'in have submitted to a Federal Review Panel that the mine would result in significant environmental damage and in the contamination of a sacred ceremonial site.[32]

British Columbia: The Spatiality of the Colonial Project

The histories of both Paul Alphonse and Constable Irwin, who arrested and detained Alphonse, begin with boot prints – the boot prints of the first colonizers to set foot in Western Canada. Following the colonial trail takes me ultimately to the 4,000 acres set aside for the reserves of the Williams Lake Indian Band, and to the Sugar Cane Reserve, where land claims disputes are still in progress. The residential school, St. Joseph's Mission, made infamous by the cases of physical and sexual abuse documented for over a century, has now disappeared, but as a child and young adult, Alphonse endured its violence and contributed his labour to the building of the ranches of the Oblate order. White settlers, preempting much of the arable land in the nineteenth century, now own the area's ranches, places that Alphonse also helped to build as a ranch hand until the 1980s. Although Constable Irwin's own blood relations cannot be tracked along the same geographies as Paul Alphonse's, it is possible to connect him professionally to white police officers before him, men tasked with controlling the movements of the Indigenous peoples of the Cariboo. From its inception as a colonial police force, the Northwest Mounted Police, which would become the Royal Canadian Mounted Police (RCMP), assisted in securing the territory, ultimately transforming its largely military function into a domestic policing of the settler's town, a town surrounded by reserves. Colonial policing, as I show in the chapters that follow, persists into the present. Keeping order in public space still largely means mostly non-Indigenous police controlling the movements of Indigenous peoples in city space.

Colonial policing emerges from and maintains a colonial project, begun a century and a half earlier, which has a very distinctive spatiality. The work of Cole Harris, among others, confirms this observation for British Columbia, one of the two provinces examined in this book. Harris dedicates his book *Making Native Space* to the memory of Gilbert Malcom Sproat, "a colonizer who listened." Acknowledging that there were both good and bad colonizers, Harris ends his description of Sproat's arrival in British Columbia in 1860 and his confrontation with the Nuu-chah-nulth, whom he called the Aht, with the clear pronouncement that whatever else we might say about what went on that summer when Sproat planted his (likely booted) feet on the ground, it "came down to a forced displacement of a people."[33] Sproat made clear to the chief of the Nuu-chah-nulth that regardless of what he felt about selling his land (an invitation Sproat made with cannons pointed at the village), whites would come and would keep on coming. Harris is centrally concerned with the mechanics of forced displacement: how the colonial project took shape, making land available for colonists and managing displacement carefully in order to ensure that the Natives would not resist and rise up to murder the colonists in their beds.

The confinement of Natives to reserves provided a solution to both the colonists' material needs and to their anxieties about the proximity of those whom they had displaced. The line separating Indian reserves from the settlers, "the primal line" in Harris's words, took a quarter of a century to lay out and to form the axis of colonial geography in British Columbia. As Harris observes:

> In various ways in different parts of the province, Native life came to be lived in, around, and well beyond these reserves, but wherever one went, if one were a Native person, the reserves bore on what one could and could not do. They were fixed geographical points of reference, surrounded by clusters of permissions and inhibitions that affected most Native opportunities and movements.[34]

Colonial cartography – large reserves or small reserves – and its moral impulses (a liberal humanitarianism, or a pragmatic self-interest) were varied and contradictory. Some colonizers listened and others did not, as Harris shows. James Douglas, for example, the first governor of British Columbia, thought that reserves should be set aside for the Natives before the settlers came in large numbers, since settler interests would inevitably clash with the interests of Natives. In contrast to this pragmatic approach, one that recognized Native people had to have land for their own survival, both the bureaucracy and subsequent governors saw little need to manage or placate Natives in this way, assuming they would soon either assimilate or die off.

As Sproat anticipated, the lands of Paul Alphonse's ancestors, the people of the Cariboo Chilcotin, were quickly claimed by white settlers by the second half of the nineteenth century. Small reserves with few acres of arable land were set aside for the nations of the Cariboo, but only after protracted wrangling between Ottawa and Victoria. Seven Shuswap chiefs petitioned the Crown in 1874 that their people were starving and needed land. Sproat, who became a commissioner of the newly created Indian Reserve Commission in 1878, advocated for forms of Indian sovereignty, but, as Harris shows, by the time his successor Peter O'Reilly took over, settlers had already pre-empted much of the arable land. At Williams Lake, O'Reilley was able to make a reserve allocation of 4,100 acres. From the start, Cariboo Chilcotin reserves could not provide stable livelihoods. Harris suggests that a Foucauldian-inspired analysis of colonial practices in British Columbia would have to start with residential schools and missions, and he draws on the remarkable work of Mary-Ellen Kelm to show the connections between the size and quality of reserve land and disease and mortality rates in these institutions.[35]

Settler colonials often think of colonialism as existing in the distant past, if it is acknowledged at all. The idea that colonialism is ongoing is widely considered fanciful, if not downright malicious. It is best, then, to be as specific as possible about stolen land. In March 2006, the Indian Claims Commission reported its decision on the claim made by the Williams Lake Indian Band that two village sites had been stolen by white settlers through the process known as pre-emption. (The band's claim had been submitted to the Specific Claims Branch of the Department of Indian Affairs and Northern Development in 1994, and was rejected one year later.) The pre-emption policy, formalized in Proclamation No. 15 in 1860, allowed settlers to acquire unoccupied, unreserved, and unsurveyed Crown land in British Columbia. Conversely, settlers were prohibited from acquiring land reserved for Indians. British colonialism clothed the thefts of land and the ensuing death and destruction of Indigenous communities in a mantle of law. That fiction persists today.

The Williams Lake Indian Band "traditionally used its lands according to 'seasonal rounds' that saw band members use specific areas of land for specific reasons at specific times."[36] This rotating method is understood in law as indicating that the band had no claim to specific land. The band introduced archaeological evidence to prove that it had long occupied the lands in question. For example, bones have been uncovered in what is now Boitanio Mall and Boitanio Park (areas where the troopers, Paul Alphonse and his generation, went to drink and where Alphonse was arrested), where Williams Lake Band members who were executed in the 1860s for treason were buried. Elders recall that once the settlers started coming, they found themselves running into fences on lands that used to be theirs. White settlers began to claim the land belonging to the Williams Lake Band by 1850–60. They did so even when it was clear that the band lived there. The Williams Lake Indians found themselves forced off their lands almost immediately, and already by 1861, the gold commissioner and magistrate reported that the Williams Lake Band Indians were starving. He asked that lands be reserved for them, but although the governor of British Columbia instructed the gold commissioner to allocate four to five hundred acres, this was not done. When Chief William wrote a letter to the newspaper in 1879 describing the land thefts and stressing that his people were starving, several colonial officials responded, either recognizing the oversight or blaming the other side of government. In 1881, the band received some allotments, although the federal government did not move to strike out the illegal pre-emptions. The disputed land was owned by William Pinchbeck, a settler who is celebrated today as a pioneer of Williams Lake. As time went on, more settlers arrived, and the Williams Lake Band found itself having to pay to use parkland on which its people had camped for hundreds of years. Dams were built that flooded land. As Kristy Palmantier, Paul Alphonse's niece, testified to the Indian Claims Commission, in her own parents' generation, the Williams Lake Band was forced to move to the St. Joseph's Mission because white settlers had by then occupied all the land.[37]

Self-destructive Peoples

The activity of clearing settler spaces of Indigenous bodies becomes morally defensible if Indigenous people can in fact be turned into debris, a transformation that is accomplished by viewing the Indigenous body as sick, dysfunctional, and self-destructive. In her book *Colonizing Bodies*,[38] Mary-Ellen Kelm begins by reminding us that, in contrast to the views held by settlers, for Indigenous peoples the current state of Indigenous bodies must be seen as an outcome of colonization. She notes that characterizing Aboriginal bodies as inherently sick and dysfunctional has a two-hundred-year history, one that I suggest is actively maintained by inquests and inquiries. Medical surveys, beginning in the early twentieth century in British Columbia, sustained the persistent impression that Indigenous people were, by nature, sick. (Statistics and notions of population have long functioned to create pathologies.) Commentators early in the twentieth century tended to attribute poor conditions to a "natural" tolerance for, and even a predisposition to, dirt among the First Nations. In Kelm's words, colonizers "claimed hygiene, both figuratively and literally, as Aboriginal territory to which, like the land itself, they had inalienable rights."[39] Residential schools were predicated "on the basic notion that the First Nations were, *by nature*, unclean and diseased[;] residential schooling was advocated as a means to 'save' Aboriginal children from the insalubrious influences of home life on reserve."[40] In fact, rather than preserving the bodies of the children who were entrusted to their care, the residential schools tended to further endanger them through exposure to disease, overwork, underfeeding, and various forms of abuse. Kelm offers historical statistics on high numbers of infectious diseases caught in schools and high incidence of morbidity and mortality. At St. Joseph's Mission, for instance, school officials responded to department-imposed economic restraints in the early 1890s by selling agricultural and manufactured products at low prices to local settlers. Yet, by the turn of the century, hunger among the students was widespread, prompting some students to run away. In the winter of 1902, a Shuswap boy, Duncan Sticks, fled into the night and froze to death. The inquest that ensued showed that while the farm was a success, students were given very little to eat, and even the little they got was often spoiled.[41]

In her study of St. Joseph's Mission (the Williams Lake residential school), a book published in 1992 and well before the events leading to Paul Alphonse's death, Elizabeth Furniss uncovered a pattern of child deaths going back to the school's inception in 1891. Three generations of Native people endured its ill effects, including Paul Alphonse. The school had a history of dead eight-year-olds found in the snow, bodies with wounds coroners could not explain. Perhaps even more to the point, the school also had a history of inquiries, where children bravely testified about the violence inflicted on them. As Furniss documents in *Victims of Benevolence*, Indian Affairs conducted three investigations in 1899, 1902, and 1920 into allegations of mistreatment of students. She writes that "the overwhelming majority of students recall their time as a traumatic one dominated by feelings of fear, loneliness, and unhappiness," adding that students were "often hungry, being strapped for

speaking their own language, and being taught to feel ashamed of their Indian culture and heritage."[42] In 1981 the Mission school closed, bringing about the end of an institution which has had a profound influence on three generations of First Nations in the Cariboo region. Soon thereafter, allegations of sexual abuse began to emerge. For example, in 1989, a priest, Harold McIntee, pleaded guilty to sexually assaulting thirteen boys at the Mission during the 1950s and 1960s, and in 1991 there were six sex-related charges against Bishop Hubert O'Connor, a former principal of the school.[43] Although the residential school has now been demolished, the nearby gravestones of those who killed themselves or died of addictions suggest an enduring legacy of violence in the community that is at least partly linked to the school. Paul Alphonse himself is remembered as someone bearing a terrible pain from the Mission, a school where he received very little education. Beverly Sellars, former chief of the Soda Creek Band, has written movingly and with great insight about the school's destructive impact on her community over generations, and about the Tribal Council's efforts to examine the multiple ways in which the school damaged community members.[44]

Saskatchewan: "Clearing the Plains"[45]

The spatialities and mythologies of the settler colonial project are comparable across geographic regions, although some details vary. We find their resonance in the inquests and inquiries discussed in this book. For example, the most pernicious myth that inquests and inquiries install is the idea that Indigenous peoples possess a mysterious incapacity for modern life. The genesis of this idea is that Indigenous peoples, upon contact, found they were genetically unable to withstand disease and simply began to die out. If occasionally inquests and inquiries acknowledge that colonialism produced some of the ravages on Indigenous bodies which these legal processes so meticulously document, acknowledgment does not extend to responsibility. Recording the impact of alcohol abuse on the body, for instance, by entering on record the multiple times that Frank Paul or Paul Alphonse ended up in hospital and noting the conditions of their lungs, livers, and limbs, inquests and inquiries may connect these bodily failings to residential schools but only insofar as colonial histories made these two men vulnerable. Those same histories are not imagined as making the colonial state accountable. Although Indigenous people repeatedly register the connection between colonial violence and accountability, their voices are seldom heard. Because we are so familiar with the idea of Indigenous people as a vulnerable rather than an oppressed group, and because the sickness and dysfunction that fill the pages of legal record threaten to reify the colonial condition as one of a mysterious incapacity, it is important to connect what happens in inquests and inquiries to the historical record. For Saskatchewan, the second site of research, the history of the loss of Indigenous life on the prairies provides one way of denaturalizing the Indigenous body as a sick body, in the way that Mary-Ellen Kelm's exemplary work, quoted earlier, described. James Daschuk's *Clearing the Plains* enables us to trace the histories out of which emerged Neil Stonechild, Rodney Naistus, and Lawrence Wegner, the three men whose freezing deaths are discussed in chapter six (among others from Saskatchewan), and, more importantly, the histories of white state actors such as the police officers, coroners, and judges whose responses to Indigenous people on the prairies are tracked in the following chapters.

Setting out to focus on the material conditions rather than the ideas that fuelled the marginalization of the reserve population, Daschuk begins *Clearing the Plains* by noting that when industrial capitalism supplanted the fur trade, Indigenous peoples on the prairies lost a viable economic base and were plunged into an economic system that had an enormous impact on their health and well-being, to say nothing of the impact on the land itself. Lest we are tempted to imagine that the First Nations of Western Canada simply lost out in the march of progress, as Justice McEachern considered to be the case with the Gitksan and Wet'suwet'en peoples, it is important to note that the Cree, for example, resisted control by fur traders for some time, as the work of Paul Thistle shows, and that the historical record is not simply a seamless story of victimization.[46] Importantly, Indigenous resistance notwithstanding, Daschuk carefully shows how disease and starvation, which came with the change in economies, and the corresponding decline of First Nations' health was the direct result of both economic and cultural suppression. We might also consider the impact of colonial pressures on the capacity to withstand disease.[47] If, for many reasons, the terrible epidemics of the fur trade period had an extraordinary impact on First Nations communities in the West, wiping out many and prompting others to flee or amalgamate, the fault lay not only with their first exposure to European diseases but also with the conditions of trade. An equestrian trade network served as "a disease vector," as the Cree people, among others, struggled to survive in the new economies.[48] By the time the Dominion of Canada came into existence and a formal colonial project began, the stage was set for considerable devastation. Disease and the disappearance of the bison population prompted many First Nations to respond to the Dominion's push for treaties, legal arrangements that would in the end cement their subordination. Cree negotiators of Treaty 6, for example, negotiated for medical aid and famine relief, all too aware of the food and disease crises that loomed. With the treaties, food became a major weapon, and overcrowded and malnourished reserve populations faced not only hunger but disease. By the early 1880s, for instance, tuberculosis became the main killer of reserve populations.[49] Food aid, provided inadequately and only to those who signed treaties, paved the way for confining the vast majority of First Nations to reserves, while starvation forced the dispersal of reserves. Facing extreme reductions in food rations, a withholding of rations until young girls were procured for government officials, and increasingly harsh living and climactic conditions, Indigenous and Métis people rebelled.[50] Punishment was swift and extended: chiefs were hung or imprisoned, a pass system was instituted to keep Indians away from white communities, and a relentless surveillance (involving policing and a suppression of religious practices) was instituted. By 1886, Daschuk reports, all Indians found off reserve were questioned.[51] The devastation of this period was extensive. By 1889, less than half the pre-rebellion population of the Battleford reserves, for instance, survived.[52] At the same time, the government encouraged those with part white ancestry to renounce their Indian status, and many chose this option to avoid starvation on reserves. The Onion Lake registry, for example, where the ancestors of Rodney Naistus originate, declined by half.[53] Laws prohibited reserves from selling their produce in towns, thereby protecting white farmers and excluding Indigenous peoples from the white economy. The drastic cutting of food rations, openly acknowledged by Ottawa as causing suffering, brought a recalcitrant population into line, and disease did the rest (such as the high mortality rate from measles). It is no small irony that having deliberately impoverished and weakened the First Nations, settlers who began to flood into the prairies by the 1890s viewed the people they had dispossessed as a threat to property and as a dying race.[54] The death toll for the 1880s and 1890s on the reserves of the prairies was enormous. Daschuk comments that in the modern period, Europeans would not experience a comparable death rate from disease until the Warsaw Ghetto, when incarcerated Jews experienced high mortality rates from disease.[55] We can gain some insight into the meaning of Indigeneity for the settler state when we consider Daschuk's example of an Indigenous prisoner who was so weak and riddled with disease that he could not walk to the gallows. Indians, he concludes, were "punished to death."[56]

The colonial spatialities and the material conditions described for the late nineteenth century and produced through a series of factors, chief among them "state sponsored attacks," most certainly haunt us still, as Daschuk suggests.[57] Their legacies are visible in the patterns of Indigenous deaths in custody today. As I have shown elsewhere, Indigenous women on the prairies are still widely considered "squaws," whom it is permissible to violate with impunity, violence the law often condones.[58] There is even a Canadian phenomenon labelled "missing and murdered Indigenous women." The twelve hundred missing Indigenous women, some of whom are presumed murdered, can be connected historically to the Indigenous women whom settlers, colonial police, and officials considered sexually available and expendable.[59] Policing, as the following chapters show, remains devoted to evicting Indigenous bodies from the prairie city, and the imprinting of colonial power on both Indigenous men and women continues apace and in gendered ways. In an ongoing colonialism, where conquest must be inscribed on the ground, we can expect more deaths in custody.

The Chapters

Each chapter in this book represents an iteration of the colonial story about disappearing Indians, a story that law sustains. In chapter one, I show that the police dumping of Frank Paul in an alley in the city of Vancouver, where he was left to die, is the outcome of a long history of what Samira Kawash has described as marking the body as placeless, that is, as not belonging to the spaces of respectable citizens and thus having no place.[60] In his lifetime, Frank Paul could not be allowed to rest, to heal, or to thrive in settlers' spaces. Instead, his body had to bear the imprint of colonial power, first forcibly confined to reserves and to residential schools, and then denied bodily integrity as he moved through the city of Vancouver. Branded as bestial, as a man who could only crawl and whose life was lived on the edge of existence, Frank Paul was a presence that law establishes as only an absence, that is, barely human, barely alive, and thus reduced to the status of bare life. The inquiry into his death tried its best not to confront the meaning of Indigeneity, retreating instead into long meditations on wasted lives and wounded flesh. Chapter two continues with the inquiry into Frank Paul's death, showing that inquiries do the work of colonial governance by establishing a central colonial truth: the most that colonial society can ever be guilty of is not knowing how to care. Inquests and inquiries are tailor-made for redemptive gestures, establishing settlers as caring in the moment when the very opposite is true. The inquiry into Frank Paul's death establishes that he was first and foremost an alcoholic who carried within him the seeds of his own demise. The best the settler state can do is to improve its capacity to care for such damaged bodies, bodies that, paradoxically, are already declared to be beyond improvement. The inquiry resolves settlers' anxieties that they have in fact failed to care by announcing a commitment to improving Indigenous lives through understanding cultural differences.

In chapter three, I consider the death of Paul Alphonse. In the city of Williams Lake, British Columbia, we see that the relationship between police and Indigenous peoples is one of regular, intimate, and violent contact, a relationship in which the Indigenous body itself is treated as the frontier. The police enact daily the racial hierarchy that structures the colonial city, kicking and slapping the bodies they know only as the dying remnants of a bygone era. There can be no encounter more typical in settler colonialism than the encounter between a police officer and an Indigenous person arrested for drunkenness. The parks and streets where Indigenous people are to be found become a frontier, a place where law has authorized its own absence, and where the police can violate Indigenous peoples with impunity. The police hold down the fort in such spaces, a metaphor of colonial origin that captures what is imagined, projected, and enacted there. At the frontier, it is impossible to establish if the law is being broken. The inquest into Alphonse's death reveals that however insurmountable the odds, Indigenous people contest their dispossession, naming the violence that secures settler sovereignty whenever it is possible to do so.

The inquest is a place where it is established that care is wasted on bodies too damaged to survive. Indigenous death, when it comes, is only ever timely. Continuing with the case of Alphonse and considering other deaths, chapter four shows how Indigenous people who die in custody are considered to have died an ordinary and non-controversial death. By striving to establish Indigenous people as pathologically fragile, bent on living a dissolute life, the inquest teaches us that we can expect no less of these people. The persistent medicalizing of Indigenous death, an insistence that death is nothing but the end point of a body in decline, obscures the striking indifference that doctors, nurses, guards, police, and others display towards Indigenous people in their custody. In chapter five, by examining the inquest into the death of Anthany Dawson, I explore a full-blown medico-legal alliance that operates in inquests; I show that where mental frailty and dysfunction prove difficult to establish, they must simply be invented. When Dawson, who ran screaming through the streets of Victoria, dies as he is being forcibly restrained (labelled positional asphyxia), it can only be because drugs in his system weakened his heart. When no drugs can be found, his death is attributed to a rare genetic abnormality, a biological convenience that enables the inquest to blame Dawson for his own demise.

In chapter six, I consider what is perhaps the most iconic of Indigenous deaths in custody: freezing deaths. The bodies of Indigenous men found frozen to death on the outskirts of the city of Saskatoon, all of whom had documented encounters with police shortly before their deaths, raise the spectre of extreme police misconduct, if not manslaughter and murder. Deaths that earned Canada the condemnation of the United Nations Special Rapporteur on Human Rights, freezing deaths reveal at a glance a recurring theme of this book, the racial/spatial economies of the colonial city. To mark and maintain their own emplacement on stolen land, settlers must repeatedly enact the most enduring colonial truth: the land belongs to the settler, and Indigenous people who are in the city are not of the city. Marked as surplus and subjected to repeated evictions, Indigenous people are considered by settler society as the waste or excess that must be expelled. The daily routines of policing the prairie city have long been devoted to inscribing this truth on the ground. Freezing deaths are the outcome of dumping, a literal and deadly eviction from city space to the fields and isolated spaces beyond the city. These colonial lines of force, as Frantz Fanon memorably described them, are maintained in law through the inquest and the inquiry, where we learn that those who are unable to bear the stresses of modern life, those whose difference is an insurmountable challenge, end up frozen to death in fields just outside the city limits. The inquest reveals that the streets of the prairie city are militarized zones for Indigenous peoples, sites of surveillance and danger. In the conclusion, I survey the landscape of Indigenous deaths, asking what the high rates and patterns reveal. Settler society has typically viewed statistics (which, in any event, are scant) of elevated rates of death as evidence that "Indians" really are disappearing, an organic process rather than a disappearance that is the outcome of settler practices of neglect and overt violence. I suggest we read between the lines, exploring what the numbers tell us about a systematized dehumanization that is everywhere, yet rendered invisible by settler law and ways of life.

Conclusion: "They Want It All"

In his introduction to the first anthology on genocide in Australia, A. Dirk Moses rehearses the polemic over the meaning of genocide, noting that the debate over Polish-Jewish jurist Raphael Lemkin's definition of genocide as the criminal intent to destroy or permanently cripple a group has typically focused on the Nazi holocaust.[61] Moses suggests three ways in which the genocide concept may be usefully applied to settler societies. First, we can consider the nature of intention in colonial contexts; second, we can reflect on the structure of settler colonialism; third, we can examine how settler colonial societies progress to reach their "genocidal moments."[62] Regarding the first, intention, Moses recalls the expanded definition of intent in nineteenth century English law, where a person who could reasonably have inferred the outcome of his actions must be considered to have intended the consequences of his actions. He unpacks what this capacious notion of intention might mean in the case of settler colonialism. The colonial office often warned settlers and governors not to exterminate the Aborigines. Further, the Indigenous population declined drastically because of disease, starvation, frontier violence, and intra-Indigenous conflict. Yet the authorities in London cannot be absolved of responsibility for the consequences of British settlement in Australia, since they were unwilling to cease or amend the colonial project to avoid the consequences. Although it was certainly true that London could not easily halt the colonial project, Moses makes an important argument that European colonial powers knew the outcome of their settlement projects, most desired it, and, importantly, law aided and abetted it.

If the multiple ways of engaging in a genocidal project are our focus, then we must think of what Patrick Wolfe has termed "the logic of elimination"[63] and Andrea Smith calls "the logic of genocide"[64] as a complex project in which there are genocidal moments. Historians, among others, have protested the use of the word genocide to describe such a multifaceted process as we see in settler colonialism, and the contributors to the Australian anthology more or less agree with Moses that murder is not really the same as assimilation. It is best, Moses concludes, to consider when and how the settler colonial system "radicalizes from assimilation to destruction."[65] Genocides may happen over time, but if we understand the genocidal or annihilative impulse at the heart of settler colonialism, we can track where and when genocidal moments become full-blown genocides. Are we in a moment now in Canada and in other settler societies where we have moved from assimilation to destruction?

Barbara Perry, who conducted 278 interviews with Native Americans concerning their experiences of what she called "hate crime" and which I prefer to call racial or colonial violence, reports what she believed was a significant finding. Hate crime escalated whenever Native peoples protested the theft of their land and resources. As one interviewee speculated, there seems to be a "jealousy" about the land: "Our reservations are just a sliver of our former land holdings, but they want it all. We have to be forever vigilant about that."[66] Kristy Palmantier, the niece of Paul Alphonse, reminded me of the popular saying that it takes seven generations to get over residential schools.[67] How many generations does it take for colonizers to get over their own genocidal fantasy of wanting it all? As long as the racial logic of accumulation continues apace, the Indian must always be disappearing, as Andrea Smith argues.[68] There is no sign that colonialism's rapacious practices are changing.

Today, state-sponsored attacks on Indigenous communities continue unabated. As Brenna Bhandar notes, such attacks range from the standoff between police and Elsipogtog Mi'kmaq First Nation (Frank Paul's nation), as the latter attempt to protect their lands from a Houston-based company doing shale gas explorations, to the Canadian Conservative government's omnibus Bill C-45, which, among its many targets, makes it easy for communally held reserve land to be alienated and privatized.[69] The omnibus bill also sets new minimum sentences that will mean Indigenous people remain in prison longer.[70] From the forced starvation policies of the 1880s to now, there are many ways to commit genocide. As the stakes grow higher, and gold and oil still remain to be taken, will settler society make true on the ground what it so deeply desires: a dying race to whom nothing is owed? In her examination of cruelty in contemporary Latin America, Jean Franco writes that the Indigenous are everywhere seen to have no place in the modern.[71] Standing in the way of resource exploitation, and indeed of modernity itself, the Latin American regimes Franco describes engage in various genocidal measures, announcing with each new massacre that the country has been cleansed of all that holds it back. Franco speculates in her afterword about the subjectivities that require violence, thinking for instance of the masculinities of military regimes that go on to become the masculinities of drug cartels.

My own speculation concerns settler subjects who require disappearing Indians. When we think of settler and police violence, for example, the act of driving an Indigenous man out of the city in the depths of winter and leaving him to walk back without shoes or coat, it is natural to consider intentionality. The individual policeman who performed this deadly act may have been intending to commit murder, or he may have believed in his own mind that his actions would not result in death and so were merely mildly punitive. What I argue throughout this book is that intentionality is beside the point. The settler/police subject comes into his own personhood through these acts, becoming a settler through the control and regulation of the Indigenous subject. That is, the settler becomes the original citizen who is entitled to dispose of the remnants of prehistoric life in ways that preserve his domain. By focusing on what it takes to become the settler, an active psychic and material disposal of Indigenous life, I propose that we understand colonial violence as a project into which settlers are repeatedly interpellated. It is clear that the Indian must disappear if settlers are to have their land, oil, diamonds, and gold, but many will not see themselves as participating in the cruel modernity Franco describes, particularly when we believe ourselves to be engaging in practices of reconciliation and improvement.

Leslie Thielen-Wilson writes that settlers must be able to imagine when they are leaving, by which she means renegotiating what is fundamentally an illegitimate subject position.[72] This suggestion nearly always provokes anxiety and resentment when it is advanced, with even seasoned anti-colonial scholars announcing that they have come to stay and will not be driven out. An added twist to this response comes from people of colour who make the point that they have already been driven from their lands of origin and cannot be considered to be settlers. Rather than focus on our individual histories of dispossession and migration, and thus handily avoid the question of what it means to live in a settler colonial state, people of colour and white settlers alike must confront our collective illegitimacy and determine how to live without participating in and sustaining the disappearance of Indigenous peoples. I take Thielen-Wilson's invitation to leave as a call to confront head-on the premises of modern life, at the heart of which is the banishment of the racial and the cultural to the outside of humanity.[73] In order to respond to this challenge, we must understand and acknowledge Indigenous relationship to the land. As Andrea Smith has argued, responsibility and care for the land and its inhabitants, both human and animal, necessitates an expansion of the concept of Indigeneity to include an ethics and practice premised on stewardship over the land and the interdependency of all. If we begin with modernity as a cultural paradigm that has produced and required the death of Indigenous and racialized peoples and, simultaneously, the destruction of the land, it is clear that no change will come until we can conceptualize an alternative way of being in the world. To do so, it is imperative to begin by confronting what settler colonial societies do to make Indigenous peoples disappear, the annihilative impulse that is the beating heart of modern life. Such a project requires both a deeper, anti-colonial level of inquiry and the daring to imagine another world.

Chapter One

The Body as Placeless: Memorializing Colonial Power

Imagining politics as a form of war, we must ask: What place is given to life, death, and the human body (in particular the wounded or slain body)? How are they inscribed in the order of power?

Achille Mbembe[1]

To talk of land and displacement, particularly in a place like Vancouver's Downtown Eastside, and not to consider colonialism is to commit an unforgivable, but not unprecedented oversight.

Nicholas Blomley[2]

Introduction

On 5 December 1998, Frank Paul was taken into custody for being drunk in a public place and placed in a drunk tank. He was released a few hours later, but subsequently taken into custody again that same day. This time, when the driver of the police van, Constable David Instant, brought him in to the fifth floor lock-up, Sergeant Russell Sanderson decided not to accept him into jail and directed Constable Instant to return him to the police van and deliver him to an area he was known to frequent (Broadway and Maple). A police video shows Frank Paul being dragged in and out of the police station, seemingly unable to walk. Consulting with a senior police officer whom he encountered when driving two other men to the Vancouver Detox Centre, Constable Instant was told that Frank Paul was in fact homeless and should not be taken to Broadway and Maple. Instant was advised to leave Frank Paul in an alleyway that led to the detox centre. He was found dead a few

…ours later, and death was attributed to hypothermia due to acute alcohol intoxication. Sanderson and Instant each received a one- to two-day suspension without pay. No inquest was ordered, and although five separate opinions were sought as to whether to lay criminal charges against Sanderson and Instant, each concluded that there was insufficient evidence to meet a criminal standard of proof. Finally on 9 March 2007, a public inquiry into the death of Frank Paul was convened with the Honourable William Davies serving as commissioner.

A significant aspect of the relationship between Indigenous peoples and white settlers in contemporary colonial cities such as Canada's cities is the seeming paradox that an astonishing indifference or callousness marks the settler's response to Indigenous people, but this indifference occurs within intense, often daily, encounters between state officials (police and health-care professionals) and Indigenous populations in the city. It is an indifference practiced alongside a familiarity, and even an intimacy, with the Indigenous Other. Struggling to explain indifference amidst almost daily routines of health care and policing, coroners and commissioners of inquiries called on to investigate the event of an Indigenous death in custody often acknowledge instances of neglect displayed by individuals but dance around the idea of racism and colonialism as its root cause. Dehumanization is never a part of legal explanations.

Despite Indigenous overrepresentation in the justice system and elevated rates of deaths in custody,[3] and the unflagging efforts of many Indigenous and some non-Indigenous scholars to show that colonialism is a central explanation for these statistics, the plight of Indigenous people in Canada is seldom officially connected to colonialism. Inquests, commissions of inquiry, and royal commissions, places where the state defines "the Aboriginal problem" and articulates strategies for reform, have only rarely acknowledged that colonialism had, and (even more rarely acknowledged) continues to have, a profound impact on the status of Indigenous people and their experiences in the criminal justice system. Two exceptions are the Manitoba Public Inquiry into the Administration of Justice and First Nations People[4] and the Royal Commission on Aboriginal Peoples.[5] In the latter case, however, as Monture-Angus argues, the commission acknowledged past injustices such as residential schools but gave less attention to the effects of an ongoing colonialism.[6] While colonialism often remains a shadowy event in inquiries and royal commissions, official accounts generally stop short of acknowledging the virulence and persistence of racism. Instead, they reiterate that somehow indifference prevails among the police and the health professions, an indifference attributed to systems that have not been properly organized to respond to the problem Indigeneity poses in cities. With respect to Indigenous men, this problem is nearly always thought to concern alcohol. Inquests and commissions of inquiry thus turn endlessly on the best ways to treat Indigenous alcoholics. For instance, the inquiry into the death of Frank Paul, a Mi'kmaq man and the subject of this chapter, concluded that society simply did not know how to treat homeless chronic alcoholics with mental health problems. Inquests and inquiries have mapped indifference and abandonment in the same ways for 150 years. How do we understand this indifference and abandonment, whether of the individual, systemic, or societal kind, an indifference that pervades the routines of policing and medical care with respect to Indigenous peoples and ultimately pervades the inquests and inquiries into their deaths?

A man whose physical capacities were well known to police and who was largely unable to walk the night he died was dragged by police to an alley on a cold, wet night and left to die. His death was of little concern to the authorities, and for several years the state refused to call an inquiry into his death. Confronted with this puzzle of familiarity but also indifference, the commissioner of the inquiry, William Davies, comments on the police officers who exhibited what he considers to be bad judgment. While Davies forgives the junior officer who abandoned Frank Paul on the grounds that he had naturally relied on the judgment of a senior officer, in the commissioner's view, both police and health professionals appear to treat chronic, mentally ill alcoholics who live on the streets in ways that are less than efficient. The commissioner finds bureaucratic failings, but no racism and little colonialism, although he is reminded by Indigenous individuals and organizations to look for them. I follow him on his journey, asking all the while what happens to the story of colonization. I first find the colonial story in its omission, that is, in the inquiry's determined looking away from it. In the construction of Indigenous people as (inexplicably) vulnerable, rather than colonized, the story's principal players come into view: the Indigenous body as bestial and as human waste, and the white body as the maker of order, the modern subject of the settlers' city. Zygmunt Bauman writes of this relationship:

> The production of "human waste," or more correctly wasted humans (the "excessive" and "redundant," that is the population of those who either could not or were not wished to be recognized or allowed to stay), is an inevitable outcome of modernization, and an inseparable accompaniment

> of modernity. It is an inescapable side-effect of *order-building* (each order casts some parts of the extant population as "out of place," "unfit" or "undesirable") and of *economic progress* (that cannot proceed without degrading and devaluing the previously effective modes of "making a living" and cannot but deprive their practitioners of their livelihood).[7]

Order-building first requires dispossession. In settler societies, dispossession is ongoing. Bauman's comments are a reminder of how invested the modern city is in rendering Indigenous bodies out of place. While Indigenous bodies haunt settlers, a too-present reminder that the land is indeed stolen, these bodies must also serve to remind settlers of their own modernity and entitlement to the land.

What then is the relationship between the settlers and those whom they have dispossessed and continue to dispossess? As I argue throughout this book, it is a relationship that is spatially and racially organized as one between modern subjects and those who must be assisted into modernity. Law, in the form of an inquiry, serves to confirm these arrangements. Mandated to resolve problems of governance, inquiries offer a wealth of information about how the state engages in the management of populations and how that engagement is accomplished, resisted, and contested by individuals and communities.[8] Adam Ashforth proposed that commissions of inquiry are not simply or even principally policy-making instruments. Rather, they are best considered "as symbolic rituals within modern States, theatres of power which do 'make policy' but which do much else beside."[9] Inquiries are "ways of speaking about social life which makes possible the work of organizing political subjection."[10] Summoning "archival power" by what they accumulate around them, "inquiries mirror, even as they produce a colonial common sense," suggests Ann Stoler.[11] Observing that inquiries in colonial regimes utilize stock and formulaic phrases which "are faithful to the truth-claims of racialized rule," Stoler reminds us, as does Ashforth, of the pedagogic value of inquiries: inquiries instruct us in the "truths" of the state.[12] In this chapter, I explore how the inquiry into Frank Paul's death constructs a particular truth about Indigenous alcoholics who live on the streets, one that concerns the mysterious inability of Indigenous people to survive modern life and the challenges their incapacities pose to a caring society.

I organize my reflections around the theme of memorializing, a term which means quite simply "to leave a memory of." The term has multiple meanings in the context of the death of Frank Paul. What is the memory of colonialism left on Frank Paul's body? What marks are left on the territory, in this case Vancouver's Downtown East Side where Frank Paul ended up, land belonging to Coast Salish peoples until the last village was relocated in 1923?[13] What is the memory of Frank Paul offered by the inquiry into his death? And finally, how do I propose that we remember him? The argument proceeds in five parts. In part one, "Redemption," I begin with the inquiry, where Frank Paul is transformed from the violated and dispossessed into the intrinsically vulnerable. There can be no one fully to blame for what happens to an imperiled population. In part two, "Memorializing," I unravel Frank Paul's story, showing the imprinting of colonial power on his body. In part three, "Cleansing," I show that when the Indigenous body is marked as one pathologically unable to enter modernity, it must be repeatedly evicted from the civilized spaces of the settler. The colonial city is endlessly engaged in cleansing itself of bodies considered unfit for modern life. Displacement is embodied in the case of Frank Paul, and the emplacement of the settler is secured through the routines of policing and social service provision. Paul is transformed into the bestial body, the body that must be expunged in daily rituals of cleansing. These rituals confirm that there are two levels of humanity. In part four, "Abandonment," the cleansing ritual proves lethal; Frank Paul is left to die in an alley, an outcome that is declared comprehensible, given the body's incompatibility with modern life. Inquiries confirm the diagnosis, performing in the bargain the "moral righteousness" Bauman notices about humanitarian initiatives among the excluded of improving care for those already declared to be beyond help.[14] In part five, "Death-Worlds," I consider the Downtown East Side where Frank Paul lived as a death-world, Achille Mbembe's description of places under late modern colonial occupation where whole populations are reduced to the status of the living dead.[15] My objective throughout is to contest the colonial common sense of the inquiry that Frank Paul was simply vulnerable, and to argue that he must be understood and remembered as an Indigenous man whose body bore the imprint of an ongoing colonialism.

Part One. Redemption

In his interim report,[16] Commissioner William Davies enjoins us not to think of Frank Paul only as a "homeless chronic alcoholic" but to see the man behind the photos. Certainly it is difficult to see the man in the grainy videotape of a body being dragged to and from an elevator on a floor of the Vancouver Police Department (VPD). In the sparse details of his life, it is tempting, as well, to see Frank Paul as someone who was simply not up to living modern life. If it matters to the inquiry into his death that Frank Paul was a Mi'kmaq man, it is only so that we note his special vulnerability. It is not so that we settlers consider our own relationship to him as one that is also shaped by the colonial context. Davies takes note of Frank Paul's colonial history but not, as we see below, of how this same history affected those professionals who responded to him.

> It also matters that Frank Paul was a Mi'kmaq man. The circumstances of his life and death are an account in miniature of the risks and struggles faced by many First Nations people of his generation. It is not surprising to learn that Frank Paul was burdened with having been sent to residential school, losing members of his family to alcohol abuse and struggling from his early childhood to make sense of a world in which his family was fragmented and fractured. It is not surprising that he came to Vancouver and isolated himself from his family and community for the last two decades of his life. We cannot know when the psychic injuries of childhood were compounded by the addiction and mental illness of his adult years. We must acknowledge, however, that the tragic arc of his life was that followed all too frequently by members of the First Nations in our community and that his death speaks out yet again of our need to revisit and refashion the important relationship between the First Nations peoples of Canada and the general community.[17]

Elsewhere, the commissioner makes clear how he understands the bearing that Aboriginality had on what happened to Frank Paul. Rejecting the submissions of the First Nations Leadership Council that the way Frank Paul was treated by dominant society was a significant aspect of what happened to him, the commissioner reasons: "Whether his Aboriginal status is the governing reason why he died cannot be known on the evidence. What we do know is that it was his Aboriginal status that put him in a place of vulnerability."[18] Not surprisingly, when the Aboriginal Legal Services of Toronto submits to the inquiry that there is a troubled history between Aboriginal peoples and the police, this issue is not considered to have a significant connection to the death of Frank Paul. Vulnerability restricts the extent to which anyone can be culpable; it is a condition connected to colonialism but not to colonizers. Inquiries and inquests remind us that it is a difficult task to respond to individuals who have been so damaged. If, as the commissioner maintained, the inquiry had to revisit the relationship between

First Nations peoples and the general community at the time of Frank Paul's death and address the question of how it could be changed, this relationship was considered to be about how a society responds to the needs of its most vulnerable population.

Commissioner Davies observes: "Homeless chronic alcoholics (of whom Frank Paul was representative) are a clearly identifiable sub-cohort of 50–200 individuals in Vancouver's Downtown East Side with predictable patterns of behavior and unique needs."[19] Frank Paul belonged to a special subset that resorts to rice wine or mouthwash to get drunk because they have no money for anything else. They are more frequently characterized as "nuisances" rather than as hardened criminals.[20] Perhaps forty per cent of this group on Vancouver's Downtown East Side is Aboriginal. One study estimated that the state can sometimes spend up to $55,000 per year per adult when responding to homeless chronic alcoholics, an amount that could potentially be decreased to $37,000 if adequate housing and support or a livelihood were to be provided instead.[21]

If the state generally does not know how to respond to homeless chronic alcoholics, it knows even less how to do so when they are Indigenous. Ardith Walkem, who prepared a study for the inquiry, opens her report with a sentence the commissioner felt compelled to quote: "There are no Aboriginal organizations in the Downtown Eastside (DTES) equipped to provide comprehensive services to chronic alcoholics in a similar position to Frank Paul."[22] This situation, Walkem reports, arises in spite of a desire (and several long-standing attempts) by Aboriginal organizations to operate in the Downtown East Side. Walkem documents jurisdictional disputes between various levels of government, conveying what is essentially a never-ending and intrinsically colonial dispute over who has charge of Indians. She describes the difficulties that Aboriginal organizations face when presenting the specific needs of Aboriginal peoples, and notes that they receive less funding than other organizations, based on the rationale that Aboriginal peoples make up a smaller percentage of the Canadian population than other peoples. Their overrepresentation in the Downtown East Side is ignored. The Aboriginal Front Door Society, for instance, has only one full-time staff member, yet it is the one organization where someone like Frank Paul might have gone.

Walkem's answer to the question "Does it matter that Frank Paul was Aboriginal?" is different from the commissioner's. Aboriginal peoples are the most vulnerable of the vulnerable, not only because they have difficulty accessing services but also because they have "personal histories of dislocation from their home cultures and communities or through the Indian Residential School (IRS) or child welfare systems that make it both more likely that they will end up with chronic addictions in the DTES, and less likely that they will be able to seek help than their non-Aboriginal peers."[23] Ultimately, Walkem concludes, "The 'why' for Aboriginal people is often quite different than for other people. Concurrent substance abuse and mental health issues, poverty and homelessness among Aboriginal peoples cannot be separated from the historic racism and inequities Aboriginal people have experienced."[24] Importantly, Aboriginal peoples have good reasons for not seeking help. Walkem found that instead of seeking help or protection from the VPD, "Aboriginal people were frightened of the VPD and tried to actively avoid VPD officers for fear of harassment or violence."[25] In a footnote, she adds that people she interviewed were even fearful of a particular team of plain clothes VPD officers who were known to practice extreme brutality.[26] For Walkem, then, strategies had to be Aboriginal centred and land based in order "to help people recover their connections to land and Aboriginal communities, including access to traditional foods or medicines."[27] Her recommendations are quite specific: culturally appropriate services run by the Aboriginal community, a healing centre, sustained, targeted funding, mandated safe spaces for Aboriginal peoples in general service organizations, a twenty-four-hour drop-in, a wet shelter, an Aboriginal Housing First strategy, mental health services, and a monitored process to improve the relationship between Aboriginal peoples and the VPD, including the creation of a watchdog position.

The commissioner paid attention to Walkem's report, among others, but came to his own conclusions about the Downtown East Side and the group to which Frank Paul belonged, ignoring Walkem's message about the colonial and racist roots of the problem and concentrating instead on its cultural dimensions.[28] Nonetheless, appreciating the high cost and the futility of policing, if not the brutality of it (he contents himself with referring to the police as a paramilitary group unsuited to the tasks of caring for chronic alcoholics), Davies is sufficiently provoked to take a stand. He refuses to propose any improvements to procedures of the Vancouver Police Department, announcing that he does not want to run the risk of perpetuating the current regime.[29] How else to respond to the 1996 informal research of Inspector Kenneth Frail, who was working on streamlining fire, ambulance, and police responses? Commissioner Davies notes that Frail documented four thousand "man down" calls annually for the Downtown East Side, almost half of which involved inebriation. Half of these involved Aboriginal men drunk on rice wine.[30] Davies accepted Walkem's analysis that

> the underlying causes for Aboriginal addiction arise from unique historical and social circumstances, including cultural loss and disconnection as a result of moving from reserves to the Downtown Eastside, then impacts of the Indian residential school system, and the impacts of provincial child welfare systems. Third, most non-Aboriginal facilities do not offer the cultural safety many Aboriginal people need in order to confront and deal with the many complex issues they experience.[31]

These factors enable Davies to make the case that Aboriginal people need culturally sensitive services in which they have a hand in devising and running.

If he is able to believe that the police are not suited for the role of caring for chronic alcoholics and that services ought to be Aboriginal sensitive, Commissioner Davies nonetheless stops short of interrogating more fully what in fact is the current relationship between Indigenous people and those charged with caring for them. Walkem's plea that the state's response to Aboriginal alcoholics on the Downtown East Side should be Aboriginal centred and land based is heard only insofar as the commissioner recognizes a need for cultural sensitivity when dealing with a vulnerable and culturally different (from the mainstream) population. In this respect, Commissioner Davies, who is arguably more attentive to police brutality than many in his position, nevertheless repeats the colonial common sense that Stoler suggested inquiries reproduce: the colonized are uniquely vulnerable. The emphasis on vulnerability entirely obscures its production: how do bodies become and remain vulnerable? The inquiry reveals this context as one in which police and health professionals engage in the Sisyphean task of clearing the city streets of homeless chronic alcoholics. Conceived as a removal of Indigenous peoples from city streets when they become nuisances, the task of responding to homeless chronic alcoholics inevitably reduces Indigenous people to objects, an objectification so complete that we come to understand Indigenous peoples as debris to be cleared from the landscape.[32] The best that a caring society can do, then, is to determine how to do this more humanely. In part two, I trace "thingification,"[33] Aimé Césaire's term, and a process which, as Andrea Smith notes, is driven by the idea that Native bodies are "a pollution from which the colonial body must constantly purify itself."[34] Considered dirty and inherently violable, Native bodies are not entitled to bodily integrity.[35]

Part Two. Memorializing

How do colonial powers trace their sign on naked flesh? Frank Paul's body was one that had to be in constant motion. Sick, he nevertheless could not rest against a wall or a doorframe. He had to be picked up and dropped off in a seemingly endless shuttling between the street, the jail, and the shelter. In the violent shuttling back and forth, he becomes the abject body against whom the settler defines himself as respectable. Ultimately, the shuttling kills. The body gives out, whether through a violent kick (as in other cases), a dragging through the cold, rainy night, or not. Give out it must, and then we recognize it only as a body that has destroyed itself through drinking. A vulnerable body. Law provides the place where this explanation is rehearsed.

How do we give the activity of clearing the streets of Indigenous people a history, literally fleshing it out, as it were, by asking about the body that is produced through the routines and practices of past and ongoing colonialism? Hortense Spillers writes of the imprinting of power on the body as branding. Spillers notes that the socio-political order of the New World is written in blood. That order "represents for its African and indigenous peoples a scene of *actual* mutilation, dismemberment, and exile. [The process begins with a] *theft* of the body – a willful and violent (and unimaginable from this distance) severing of the captive body from its motive will, its active desire."[36] Speaking of African slaves and their descendants, Spillers makes an important distinction between flesh and body, remarking that the theft of bodies from Africa is preceded by "crimes against the flesh as the person of African females and African males registered the wounding. If we think of the 'flesh' as a primary narrative, then we mean its seared, divided, ripped-apartness, riveted to the ship's hole, fallen, or 'escaped' overboard." On the slave plantation, the wounding continues "as the calculated work of iron, whips, chains, knives, the canine patrol, the bullet."[37] Marking and branding continues from one generation to another, long after the abolition of slavery. Up to the 1930s, "sick negroes" were used for medical experimentation. There was no question of ethics, since these "procedures adopted for the captive's flesh demarcate a total objectification, as the entire captive community becomes a living laboratory."[38]

The captive's body, even when liberated, is "murdered" over and over again, an endless branding.[39]

The forced confinement to reserves and the later carceral regimes of residential school and prison mark the severing of the Indigenous captive's body from his will. Frank Paul came to Vancouver from his reserve in New Brunswick as a person already branded from the violence of residential school and the alcoholism and mental illness it has so often produced in its wake. Once there, the destruction continued apace, a power once again written on the body. In the inquiry, one is confronted with things that are done (and not done), both in the past and in the present, to Frank Paul, things so routinized that it is hard to recognize such practices as inhumane. They become simply the way the state deals with Indigenous peoples on the streets, in hospitals, and in jails. Bodies on the street are prodded, poked, and dragged, establishing their status as barely living and their condition as dying. These are bodies without bodily integrity; others may violate their boundaries with impunity. Herding these bodies from one location to another (from the street to the jail, from the jail to the hospital) is calculated work to spatially contain their dying presence, to ensure that their deaths do not inconvenience, but that their slow dying confirms the settler's own possession of himself and the land. As inquiries show, bodies must be constantly evicted from settler space, rituals which establish that the state is able to control public space and civilized life. When police and medical professionals "treated," detained, or evicted Frank Paul two or three times a week, were they doing the calculated work of branding, marking the line between modernity and pre-modernity, between subject and object, and staking the claim of white settlers to the land?

Objectification is fed by intimacy. The man who loved to draw on canvas ended up on the streets of Vancouver's Downtown East Side, and by the early 1990s, he no longer phoned home. Described as a "powerful man" who had grand mal seizures and was unable to walk easily, Frank Paul had 2,024 pages of medical records documenting his many encounters at Vancouver General Hospital, most of these in emergency owing to seizures, head traumas, alcohol dementia, broken bones, and various symptoms classified as "mental illness." Frank Paul's "extraordinary use of medical and police services" is striking, and the statistics gathered by the inquiry bear repeating: "He was taken into custody by the VPD on more than a dozen occasions in the months leading up to his death. The BC Ambulance Service responded to 121 calls between

April 1996 and December 1998. He was treated at, or admitted to, Vancouver General Hospital 93 times. He was treated at, or admitted to, St. Paul's Hospital 63 times by June 1997... He had been to the Vancouver Detox Centre 82 times since 1983."[40] As the commissioner observed:

> [P]rofessional responders working in the Downtown Eastside knew Frank Paul well. Almost all those who dealt with him in the last days of his life had dealt with him before. He had been for at least 15 years, part of a small core of homeless chronic alcoholics of less than 100 people. Most of these people are men, and many of them are of First Nations descent.[41]

The inquiry affords us an opportunity to consider the quality of these frequent encounters from the point of view of the professional responders working on the Downtown East Side. When asked to describe the characteristics of the men from Vancouver's Downtown East Side, Jim Douglas, a paramedic with the BC Ambulance Service, commented:

> The overall characteristics of that group were they were all living a lifestyle that involved alcohol consumption to a large degree. I would say without exception all of them were chronic alcoholics. Some would also be abusing recreational drugs, elicit [*sic*] drugs. A portion of that might also have underlying medical conditions, mental health issues, but that they were seen on a regular enough basis.[42]

Pressed further, Douglas acknowledged that "a significant portion" of this population was Aboriginal. We might note here what the concept of "lifestyle" accomplishes. Alcoholism can be seen as a choice, a bad choice made by people unable to cope with the demands of life. Aboriginality is entirely occluded in Douglas's description, perhaps to avoid an allegation of racism.

Paramedics such as Douglas usually encountered Frank Paul after a third party telephoned emergency services to report a person who appeared to be intoxicated lying down on a sidewalk, parking lot, or public area.[43] Police were called to remove Paul, testified Joseph Albert, an apartment building manager, after tenants complained there was "a real bad smell from someone outside ... who had urinated on himself and [had a] body odour."[44] Frank Paul, Albert recalled, annoyed people because of his smell. Frank Paul was a "regular" in the sense that he was arrested on numerous occasions and transported almost daily from the street to the jail or to detox, and then back again to the street. Barry Conroy, a driver with Saferide, a free transportation service run by a non-profit organization and catering to people with chronic alcohol and drug problems, described these circular activities in detail:

> Normally we'd pick him up and we would take him to the sobering unit and then after four or five hours we'd get a call to come and pick him up again from the sobering unit, and usually Frank didn't have an address so we would take him to the Lookout shelter, and my experience with Frank is that he would normally – he would normally – I also worked at the lookout shelter at times. Frank would normally come in and he'd stand by the desk and when the Saferide van drove away he'd wander off and go his own way.[45]

For Conroy, Frank was a person "who was acclimatized to living outside." As he opined, "For people that have become that way, it's hard to live inside a building, it's too hot for you."[46] In the following exchange, Conroy described a typical encounter with Frank Paul:

> Q Tell me more about that.
> A I mean, I'm trying to be as respectful to people as I can, but Frank would be – his hygiene wasn't good and he was probably urinary incontinent.
> Q How would you notice that?
> A Because he would be soaking wet.
> Q How would you know it was urine?
> A Because we would smell it. You'd pick him up and help him into the van and he's a heavy guy, so when you picked him up – we'd have to get quite close to each other. A lot of times our clothes would also get – would not smell good when we were done. He would be usually not speaking clearly, but he would be co-operative. He would be co-operative and help us. Some people when you went to pick them up they would be dead weight. They would play dead on you. Frank always had – Frank had a dignity about him and he would try – he was a strong guy and he would get up and he would try to help himself as much as you were trying to help him.
> Q How would he handle himself in terms of how he could stand or move around?
> A Well, he would stumble but, I mean, not all the time. I would say with him, once we got him on his feet with a minimum of support, he could usually walk.

Q Did you notice anything about how he walked?
A Yeah, he kind of – he was kind of hunched over a little bit, especially near the end there. Sometimes he had a hard time. I think his feet hurt him or something. He had a hard time walking sometimes.[47]

Familiar with Frank Paul, ambulance workers and community van drivers came to know him personally and testified that they had strategies for dealing with him. For example, they sometimes bribed him into their vehicles by bringing him snacks, coffee, or cigarettes.[48] Paramedics described how they routinely approached Paul. Finding him lying down or sitting against a wall, they noted that a verbal exchange was usually ineffective since he wouldn't respond. It was usually necessary to use "pain stimuli" to elicit a response. Jim Douglas of BC Ambulance Service described it as follows: "The classic method of a pain response on a person in this condition would be to squeeze the trapezius muscle at the base of the neck hard enough to install some pain."[49] Attesting to the same technique, police officer Sanderson clarified that the objective was to determine if a person was unconscious or merely passed out, something that could be done by "applying pain by either rubbing a knuckle on the breast bone, a thumb behind the ear in the little hollow or under the jaw, … [which] would elicit a large pain response but … would not injure the person, and … would arouse the person from their stupor so that you could make sure that they were actually just physically passed out."[50] It is difficult to imagine that this encounter with a body to be prodded and poked for response through the infliction of pain had any other meaning for the police than clearing the city streets of people who were waste.

Most of the professionals interviewed described themselves as deeply familiar with Frank Paul – the word "regular" was employed often. Currie Low, a nurse at the Vancouver Detox Centre, testified that she would see Frank Paul up to ten times a month starting in the mid-1980s.[51] Each professional believed that he or she had been humane. For instance, one police officer noted: "I believe that I can stand proud of some of the things I did for Mr. Paul."[52] Yet, this same officer did not think to call Frank Paul's family with any information about his death. A correctional officer, Kevin Low, believed that if you gave food to the homeless, they would only keep coming back for more. Frank Paul asked for food, and this officer fed him but felt that Frank Paul only got arrested so he could get more food.[53] During the inquiry, the family of Frank Paul asked their lawyer to thank Constable Jean Prince for giving Frank Paul a toonie (a two dollar coin) to buy coffee, a single act of kindness during the last hours of his life.[54] Compassionate or not, professionals engaged in moving Frank Paul from one location to the next do not appear to have considered either the practical or the ethical import of their daily activities.

Part Three. Cleansing

Mbembe writes of the racial city and its economy. Under apartheid, where Black people did all the work, the use value of Black labour had to be obfuscated and repressed, and the Black body rendered both indispensable and expendable.[55] Similarly, in the contemporary colonial city, the Indigenous body, so inextricably linked to the stolen land, must also be repressed, rendered simultaneously indispensable and expendable in the settler's psyche. Mbembe captures this dual structure of disjunctive inclusion, which he aptly describes as delirium, when he observes that "the native as an object had to be slightly human and as a human slightly 'thing-like.'"[56] The colonizer must both manage his fears and produce the material arrangements upon which his entitlement lies. The right of Blacks to live in the city had to be constantly undermined, even as their presence could not be eliminated altogether. Mbembe's racial city engages in segregation, jailing, eviction, and "floating spots" where dehumanization could be immediately practiced, a tracing of power on the naked flesh of the Black body.[57] Frank Paul endured these intimate rituals through which the settler comes to know himself.

The ritualistic character of Frank Paul's encounter with the police and service providers, an almost daily shuttling from one space to another, suggests the productive function of cleansing city streets of their urine-soaked bodies. Samira Kawash has brilliantly argued that we must consider such rituals with respect to homeless people as constitutive acts which serve to embody placelessness. In "The Homeless Body," Kawash begins by describing the way in which subway passengers avoid a homeless body curled up on a seat.[58] She remarks that the body, absolutely inert and non-threatening, nonetheless exerts a powerful effect on the other riders. For Kawash, the effect must be understood through the oppositions of public and homeless. The public must be protected from the homeless, as the police made clear about Frank Paul. Further, Paul must also be protected from himself. Public space is configured as a space that belongs to the public and one in which the homeless are intruders. The homeless are not us, an opposition that is ideological and material; through laws and policies, public space is constituted through the exclusion of the homeless body. Making the important point that the homeless body is not the same as the homeless person, she notes that the homeless body is "an event that marks the exclusion of the homeless from the public."[59] Frank Paul was often constituted as the event of which Kawash speaks – the event that was his eviction from public space and, simultaneously, the constitution of the public itself. His eviction from public space is an important way in which we come to know what public space is. The latex-gloved prodding of Frank Paul's body and the repeated transport from one location to another function as marks upon the territory itself, to use Mbembe's phrase.[60] That is to say, such events consolidate not only public space but the space of the nation. As an Indigenous man, Frank Paul was evicted from the public, which signals that the city belongs to the settlers. How else are we to understand pointless arrests that do not solve a "security" problem and do not help Frank Paul, if not as productive acts that constitute the nation?

It is instructive, Kawash tells us, that the homeless exist in a perpetual state of movement. Frank Paul cannot rest in one place: "homelessness is not only being without home, but more generally without place."[61] Significantly, "the condition of placelessness is marked on, or more accurately *as* the homeless body itself."[62] In other words, placelessness must be embodied if it is to perform the work of constituting the public. Drawing on the work of Rosalyn Deutsche, Kawash notes that it is the homeless person's body that stands as a barrier to the unity of the public sphere. It is as a body with material needs, an abject body that smells and urinates on itself, that Frank Paul could mark the settler's domain, yet it is a body that haunts. The homeless body challenges the abstraction of the public subject, and thus it must become the site of endless regulation. Kawash explains:

> The closure of society that is the aim of securing the public requires that a public place for the homeless be denied. The resultant contradiction between a material body that most certainly occupies space and the denial of a place for such a body cannot be resolved; nonetheless an attempt at such resolution is continually enacted through violent processes of containment, constriction and compression that seek not simply to exclude or control the homeless but rather to efface their presence altogether ... If the homeless population cannot be eliminated or erased, then at least it can be shrunk down, isolated, and contained so that the public need not feel the pressure of its presence.[63]

Importantly, the containment, through police harassment, "bum-proof" bus benches, overcrowded shelters where too many people are packed into a small space, the scanty provision of food in "soup" kitchens, the withdrawal of toilets, ensures that the homeless cannot be in control of their own bodily functions. And it is as uncontrolled bodies that the homeless must be excluded from civilized space.

Kawash speculates that the homeless body threatens to expose the fiction of the official meanings of public space, a possibility that "is the danger against which the public seeks to secure itself."[64] She concludes that "public security is not the unambiguous good that it appears to be. Rather, public security is necessarily paradoxical. It is security, a security of body, property, and self, that is promised as the reward for belonging to the public. But the violence necessary to secure such a public ensures that security is always illusory, always haunted by its violent condition."[65] It is this constitutive violence of which Kawash writes that I wish to expose in the death of Frank Paul, a violence I connect to colonial dispossession and one that remains unnamed in the inquiry.

To consider the processes of embodying placelessness specifically as colonial processes, we must recall the colonial city's routines of governance, including law and policing, that are deeply embedded in the theft of land and the management of Indigenous populations. Native people are simply not seen as real people; what distinguishes them is that they can be violated with impunity. If this relationship extends to other marginalized populations, its specificity in the case of Indigenous peoples remains connected to the theft of land and the ongoing displacement this theft both requires and produces. Perhaps this specificity is nowhere more visible than in the degree of violence meted out to Indigenous peoples, but it is also evident in the refusal to consider that colonialism happened and continues, and has a profound bearing on the lives of Indigenous peoples today.

Part Four. Abandonment

If cleansing rituals speak of intimacy and disjunctive inclusion – the settler experiences his emplacement through the ritualized and repeated eviction of the Indigenous body – there is also abandonment, a final expunging of the Indigenous body. The inquiry considered that two police officers failed in their duty to care. One of these, Sergeant Sanderson, was indicted as having exhibited a callous indifference; the other, Constable Instant, was merely considered to have failed in his duty. On the last days of his life, Frank Paul had engaged the services of the following: a Saferide van driver (4 December), a shelter (4 December), emergency health services (5 December), and the Vancouver City Police (5 December at 11:18 a.m. and again at 8 p.m.). On 5 December, an apparently routine day of extensive contact with the state, Sergeant Sanderson, although he knew that Frank Paul was often unconscious and unable to move, did not trouble to find out if Frank Paul, who had to be dragged into the station, was well enough to be taken back to the streets. Sanderson did not request a medical assessment. He made his own assessment in less than three minutes, while Paul was in the elevator. Challenged about the indifference demonstrated towards a man whom others felt was near comatose and deeply intoxicated (something confirmed by the pathologist who also believed that Frank Paul was already hypothermic), Sergeant Sanderson maintained that Paul was simply being Paul – a man who was often unable to walk. Steadfast that Frank Paul could take care of himself when he last saw him alive, Sanderson could not bring himself to acknowledge that his assessment of Frank Paul was, as a lawyer suggested to him, "the biggest mistake of your policing career." Asked whether he agreed that his action with respect to Frank Paul was the biggest mistake of his career, Sanderson replied, "That's a hard question. I don't think I can really answer that question without a lot of deep thought and without going back over my career. There's a lot of things I've done."[66]

Rejecting Sergeant Sanderson's defence that he believed Frank Paul to be sober and capable of caring for himself, the commissioner explored the reasons for the police officer's behaviour. He reasoned:

> Sgt. Sanderson testified that when Cst. Instant arrived with Frank Paul, he believed Mr. Paul was capable of caring for himself. It seems to me that there are three views that may be taken of this assertion:
>
> - he was lying, and did not actually believe this;
> - he was indifferent, and did not take appropriate steps to answer the question; and
> - he did, in fact, believe Mr. Paul was sober and capable of caring for himself.
>
> I have concluded that the evidence establishes the second proposition, but does not go so far as to prove that Sgt. Sanderson was lying.[67]

While Sanderson is indicted as failing to care and exhibiting a "callous" indifference,[68] Constable Instant and others are viewed more charitably.

Opining that everyone was simply tired of caring for Frank Paul (tired enough to send a man to his possible death), the commissioner noted that they were faced with doing an "unpleasant job that may seem without great moment or value, in a setting where the decision makers sit at the bottom of the paramilitary hierarchy."[69] For his part, Constable Instant is assessed as someone who knew little of the "alien" world to which Frank Paul belonged.[70] Questioned as to why he did not think that Paul needed medical attention, Instant explained that not only did he rely on the judgment of a more experienced officer but more significantly, he assumed that what he was seeing was normal for Frank Paul. It is here that we can locate the source of callous indifference in both police officers. Frank Paul was simply not in the same category as other humans, for whom an inability to walk and speak would be regarded as unusual. Indeed, both Sanderson and Instant acknowledge that their responses would not have been the same had Frank Paul been someone in a suit and tie. For Instant, the Downtown East Side was not a normal place, and its inhabitants could not be assessed using the same criteria as elsewhere. Instant's exchanges with Steven Kelliher, counsel for the family, are particularly revealing in this regard:

Q What did you think could account for his appearance and disability?
A What I felt accounted for his appearance and disability was years and years and years of hard living and ingesting I'm not sure what, and from living on the street.
Q So did you think you were witnessing a permanent state of inability to care for oneself?
A No. What I felt I was observing was Mr. Paul's normal day-to-day state of affairs.
Q That he was as he presented himself to you on that night virtually all the time?
A Yes.
Q Do you think that a person who was in that state required medical care and treatment and shelter?
A Yes. Ideally, yes. However, medical attention was available in the jail, and it wasn't accessed. Shelter? Mr. Paul lived on the street day to day, and yes, he was a mess, but the fact is, and my belief was, that this is how he functioned day to day.
Q But, sir, you could see from the time you set eyes on him that he was totally incapable of caring for himself. He couldn't walk. He could barely

move. He could barely speak. Isn't that a person that should be seen medically, if even briefly, by someone?

A Yes, I agree, however, I relied and defaulted to an individual with far more experience than I had to conduct an assessment of what I was seeing and the observations I was making.

Q Mmm. Right.

A Now, and to put that into context, the backdrop to this situation was the day-to-day reality of working in and being exposed to the Downtown Eastside.

Q Meaning?

A As a new officer to be put in this position of working in this area, there wasn't a lot that you'd encounter day to day that would be considered or that I considered to be normal. So I was as a new officer trying to work your way through a number of situations where what you think is normal and what you believe to be how things should be in fact aren't. It's not normal where I grew up that people sleep on the street in the middle of December, but the reality was we did have people sleep on the street in the middle of December. We had people walking around with all sorts of disease and disabilities, in various states of being catatonic. So to put that in respect, in context, what I was seeing in Mr. Paul, yes, he had significant problems, and I don't know how he survived day to day, but my belief was that he did survive day to day. And I got that belief from my previous experiences of dealing with other people that were in circumstances similar to Mr. Paul, and based on the information I received from a very experienced, senior member on the department who was seeing the exact same thing and conditions that I was observing. Looking back on it, it was wrong. He obviously was in need of assistance, but my mind-set that evening dealing with this situation was that what I was observing was – was what I was being – what I considered what was normal for Mr. Paul.[71]

As Instant concluded, his was a "subjective decision," one based on "what we felt we were dealing with."[72] And what they thought they were dealing with was someone who could withstand what other human beings could not, someone for whom a comatose state and crawling were normal conditions, yet someone defined as intrinsically vulnerable. Only the idea of Indigenous people as sub-humanity, that is, as a lower species, resolves this contradiction.

Instant's indifference to Frank Paul's condition, the commissioner speculates, was born of "deference to an organizational model that discouraged his questioning a superior officer that was Frank Paul's undoing that evening."[73] Troubled nonetheless by this systemic explanation for callousness, the commissioner relies on the report of Dr Lohrasbe, a forensic psychiatrist, who suggests that systems can govern an individual's response and cause him or her to behave unethically under pressure. (It is of interest that the United Native Nations Society accepts Lohrasbe's reasons, perhaps because they at least recognized that the police officers had behaved unethically.) If Instant dehumanized Frank Paul and exhibited a callous indifference to him, Davies concludes, quoting Lohrasbe, it could only be because in "an extraordinary or cruel situation within a powerful system, you would probably not behave as your 'familiar' self."[74] Instant was simply "persuaded by his training and superiors to behave as if his natural sympathies and sense of humanity were out of place and inappropriate."[75] Police officers had to be trained, then, to put human dignity first, presumably no matter what their superior officers ordered. Instant sincerely believed that Frank Paul possessed an unusual resistance to cold and wet.[76] Satisfied "that neither ethnic discrimination nor overt hostility motivated Frank Paul's arrest, and that his Aboriginal status was not a factor in Sgt. Sanderson treating him with callous indifference,"[77] Davies ultimately concludes that the Vancouver police did not intend to cause harm to Frank Paul nor were they seeking to accelerate his death. In this respect, Davies agrees with the Vancouver Police Department's statement that "[t]he most important reality emerging from the evidence is the complete absence of racism, malice or bad faith on the part of police officers, and the complete absence of evidence of an orchestrated 'cover-up' of Mr. Paul's death … Mr. Paul's death was simply the result of errors of judgment by two police officers."[78]

Callous indifference is a tricky diagnosis, because it requires that we understand its origins. If indifference did not stem from racism or from a more generic dehumanizing, if indeed the police were simply caught in systems that dehumanized or dulled their own capacity to be compassionate, then no one is to blame. Davies finds it hard to exonerate the police altogether. He indicts Sergeant Sanderson in particular, finding, in contrast, that the ambulance services workers exhibited "real concern" for Frank Paul.[79] Ultimately, however, Davies locates indifference in systems. Indifference, callousness, and failure to care all have their origin in societal responses to alcoholics. Accordingly, these systems must be reformed to provide for better care. But how systems are also people who exhibit an enduring indifference to Indigenous life is not something the inquiry explores.

The callous indifference so marked in police officers was so deeply embedded in the routines of the criminal justice system that it continued to be exhibited well after Frank Paul's death. The Vancouver Police Department conducted both a criminal investigation and a professional standards investigation. Because the police carried out deeply flawed forensic investigations (gathering very little forensic evidence, failing to examine Frank Paul's clothes, failing to interview witnesses, and so on), their report did not recommend that criminal charges be laid. The professional standards investigation was also cursory, and, in the commissioner's view, hampered by the inadequate forensic investigation and by the fact that the police in effect investigated themselves.

A month after his death, the family of Frank Paul were called by the Vancouver Police Department and informed of his death. The family testified that the police told them Paul had died as a result of a hit and run, something the police say may have occurred due to a mix-up. They were not told the truth until three years later. Two years later, Dana Urban, a senior lawyer with the BC Public Complaints Commission, called the family to say that he felt the case was not being looked into properly. As Frank Paul's cousin Peggy Clement testified, Urban said "he kept seeing an image of garbage being put out for the night," a comment which made her recall that when Paul's body was eventually shipped home for burial, a bag of still-wet clothes in a black garbage bag was shipped along with it.[80] Years of questions raised by Indigenous groups, the BC Civil Liberties Association, and the provincial office of the Public Complaint Commissioner ultimately provoked the BC government to call a public inquiry into Frank Paul's death. During this time, memos indicated that the government feared the public would see in what police termed a "breaching" of Frank Paul in an alley on a cold, wet night a parallel to the cases in Saskatchewan where Indigenous men were driven by the police out of the city and left to freeze to death. As the deputy commissioner of the Public Complaints Commission opined, "It is unavoidable in this matter not to give additional weight to the fact that the deceased is a Native person."[81]

Indifference hardly describes the response of Chief Constable Jamie Graham when he defended the police department's actions towards Frank Paul. Frank Paul, he explained, was simply someone who crawled. The police often dealt with people who were smelly, with feces, and who were belligerent and hard to control. It was a tough job, and one often had to drag a man and accept that "he had to crawl on occasion."[82] As the chief constable expanded, "Since he was a large man he was sometimes moved about by being dragged. This might seem like an unconscionable method and manner of handling an intoxicated person, but occasionally, it is necessary since it is the safest manner for all concerned."[83] These comments shed light on the nature of the callous indifference, so amply demonstrated but nonetheless un-interrogated, as something that merely lives in the systems of care practiced towards alcoholic homeless men. The denial of bodily integrity towards Indigenous peoples is so completely naturalized as a response, so integral to the relationship between Indigenous peoples and the state, that there is no need to ask questions about men who are dragged into the cold, wet night and left to die. It is what it is.[84]

In his opening remarks to the inquiry on behalf of the Paul family and the First Nations Leadership Council of British Columbia, Grand Chief Stewart Phillip, president of the Union of British Columbia Indian Chiefs, remarked that what had happened to Frank Paul was not an isolated event. Naming several other cases of death in police custody, Grand Chief Phillips summed up his organization's position that the case of Frank Paul revealed "an astonishingly callous disregard for the safety, health and well-being of Mr. Paul, who was obviously not in any condition to look after himself and was left in an alley in this city in inclement weather to suffer the final and fatal effects of hypothermia."[85] Reciting a long list of names of Aboriginal people who were failed by the justice system, Cameron Ward, the lawyer representing the United Native Nations Society, suggested that systemic racism was clearly in operation.[86] Counsel for the police, George Macintosh, acknowledged "perceived racism" and the view held by some of "systemic indifference" on the part of the police. Citing a Vancouver police report which acknowledged that the "Aboriginal community at large understandably perceives that [their] past colonization, with its assault on their cultural fabric, and at times on their existence, may be continuing," Macintosh grudgingly conveyed that the past left at least a perception of a problem.[87]

Inquiries or inquests involving the deaths of racialized groups in police custody are typically framed as above, that is, as either involving systemic racism (rarely) or simply about the complexities of policing and providing care to a difficult and culturally different population, perhaps one with a perception of perceived racism. They often get bogged down in concepts such as systemic racism, oscillating between the idea that systems oppress as do people and generally failing to find any straight line of accountability linking the actions of individuals to the deaths of Indigenous men in custody. In proposing a focus on how Indigenous bodies must bear the imprint of colonial power, we avoid such morasses. People who can be treated as garbage to be put out for the night, people whose incapacities do not need to be questioned, people whose dying and whose wounds are taken for granted, yet people with whom we interact on an almost daily basis, constitute our sense of self and place. If ordinary care proves to be so persistently beyond us as a society, then we must ask questions about our relationship to Indigenous peoples and what the current state of affairs sustains.

Part Five. Death-Worlds

In an essay on the fiction of Amos Tutuola[88] and in a much-quoted article titled "Necropolitics,"[89] Achille Mbembe sought to consider "extreme forms of human life, death-worlds, forms of social existence in which vast populations are subjected to conditions of life that confer upon them the status of living dead (ghosts)."[90] With Frank Paul and Vancouver's Downtown East Side in mind, I am drawn to the description Mbembe offers of death-worlds and the living dead, and especially to the question he poses concerning the place that is given in politics to the wounded or slain body. Reading inquests and inquiries into the deaths of Indigenous people who die in police custody, one is saturated with details of wounded or slain bodies: head wounds, lungs filled with pneumonia, disordered minds, legs that can only crawl, a boot print on the chest of an alcoholic old man, men with mysterious handcuff marks on their wrists who are found frozen to death on the outskirts of town, intoxicated or drug-addicted men and women left to die in cells in their own vomit or discarded as "garbage put out for the night," as one lawyer felt had been the case in the death of Frank Paul. These are not, however, bodies that are unimportant in the order of power. While living, such Indigenous bodies can consume the attention of two or three state officials, including police officers, health-care professionals, social service workers, and so on, sometimes up to two or three times a week. Extremely well known to their jailers and to medical professionals, Indigenous men and women who die in police custody nevertheless are not people on whom considerable care has been lavished. To Mbembe's question, "What place is given to the wounded or slain body," then, the response is that a very prominent place is given to wounded or slain Indigenous bodies in Canada. It is the dying, more so than the death, of Indigenous peoples that is clearly inscribed in the order of power of the Canadian white settler state. A strange and brutal truth lies at the heart of this prominence. While Indigenous people are literally the business of the state in certain locations, they are not its concern. Settler entitlement rests on a conviction of one's capacity to be a modern subject and the corresponding incapacity of an Indigenous person to enter modern life, a relationship that must be confirmed through multiple interactions. When state actors engage with Frank Paul daily, without attending to his needs, they confirm his alterity and simultaneously their own legitimacy. Is it for this reason that the colonial state and settlers maintain a compelling interest in dying as well as dead Indigenous bodies?

In pursuing the colonial story, I take seriously Mbembe's proposal that late modern colonial occupation combines the disciplinary, the biopolitical, and the necropolitical, the latter accounting for "the various ways in which, in our contemporary world, weapons are deployed in the interest of maximum destruction of persons and the creation of *death-worlds*."[91] Offering Palestine as an example of a death-world, Mbembe suggests that infrastructural warfare – control of water, air, and space – performs a kind of "invisible killing" to which is added "outright execution": "The extraction and looting of natural resources by war machines goes hand in hand with brutal attempts to immobilize and spatially fix whole categories of people or, paradoxically, to unleash them, to force them to scatter over broad areas no longer contained by the boundaries of a territorial state."[92] The indifference and callousness so evident in the inquiry surely amount to invisible killing. The spatial fixing of whole categories of people, so that they either stay on reserves where life is so often not tenable or they scatter to skid rows where dying is the order of business, suggest that we understand places like the Downtown East Side as something more than simply a space where the marginalized congregate.

Dara Culhane observes that the Aboriginal character of Vancouver's Downtown East Side surprises people who expect the cosmopolitan but majority European Canadian population of Vancouver.[93] In 1997, the city of Vancouver declared a public emergency in the Downtown East Side because HIV infection rates among residents exceeded those anywhere else in the developed world. Culhane argues that both public health and law enforcement authorities treat the Downtown East Side as a containment zone rather than a zone of enforcement, a place where there is an open market for drugs and illicit sex. Paradoxically, she adds, when public space is taken over in this way, it masks that the majority of the residents are first and foremost exceedingly poor. What their poverty has to do with their Aboriginality is even more obscured by the emphasis on the prevalence of addiction, mental health issues, and prostitution. For instance, seventy per cent of children in care in Vancouver are of Aboriginal descent, and seventy per cent of street prostitutes working in the most dangerous parts of the city are Aboriginal. As Culhane concludes, men who seek out Aboriginal women working as prostitutes in the Downtown East Side are "buying license to commit violence, to degrade, and to demean women considered disposable by 'Johns' and by society as a whole."[94] Nothing conveys the anomalous character of the area as a space of violence more than the hundreds of Aboriginal women from that part of the city who have gone missing and are presumed murdered. Amnesty International formally indicted Canada for its failure to investigate these deaths.[95] As of 31 March 2009, the Native Women's Association of Canada (NWAC) reports 520 cases of missing and murdered women in its database (sixty-seven per cent homicide or negligence, eight per cent suspicious deaths, and twenty-four per cent missing). Twenty-six per cent of these cases are in the province of British Columbia, a number NWAC suggests may be due to the information available about murders and disappearances on Vancouver's Downtown East Side and Highway 16 (the Highway of Tears).[96] The girls and women whose lives are described in NWAC's report come from loving as well as dysfunctional families. Among the latter are girls who ran away from foster homes or residential schools and ended up on the streets, addicted to alcohol and drugs and working in prostitution.[97] Courts and police have a record of treating murder as a natural outcome for Indigenous people who pursue a "violent life style."[98] In 2014, the RCMP updated the number of missing and murdered Indigenous women to twelve hundred, a conservative estimate in the eyes of many observers.[99]

Less attention is paid to Indigenous men in the Downtown East Side, and thus less information is available about their deaths in custody. As Vancouver's skid row, the area is often described as the end of a journey for men fleeing poverty and violence, men whose lives spiral into addiction and mental illness.[100] Little attention has been given to the role of colonial dispossession in bringing Indigenous men to the Downtown East Side. With the exception of Walkem's 2008 study, no study has examined the role that Indigeneity plays in the state's response to the problems of the area. Indeed, some scholars insist that the problems evident among Indigenous populations only have to do with individual education, employment, and migratory patterns, and not with colonial displacement. The histories that inform the men's and women's

journeys to Vancouver's Downtown East Side and, equally, the state's and individual settlers' violent responses are not considered in such works.[101] Quite specifically, however, as Nicholas Blomley shows, "endemic poverty and a lack of a land base on the reserve compel the relocation of many native people to the city."[102] Many Indigenous people end up as the urban poor, and their bodies continue to be the site of tremendous violence.

Conclusion: Reminders

How does one track colonialism in today's Canadian cities? Critical geographers have written about the development of postcolonial cities and shown how the colonial encounter continues in urban spaces. In *Unsettling the City*, Nicholas Blomley distinguishes between dispossession and displacement.[103] Dispossession for Blomley "refers to the processes through which settlers come to acquire title to land historically held by aboriginal people," whereas displacement, "while related, refers to the conceptual removal of aboriginal people from the city, and the concomitant 'emplacement' of white settlers."[104] Place making and enactments of claims to land, Blomley points out, are "partial and incomplete." Indeed, treaty negotiations with Aboriginal nations in British Columbia (the province where Vancouver is located) only began in 1991 with a partial acknowledgment of Aboriginal claims. Thus the city has to be repeatedly "made into a white place through physical settlement and occupation."[105] As Blomley succinctly puts it, "For a settler society, displacement is a social achievement, but also an aspiration; it is an accomplishment, and also an assertion."[106] This chapter has focused on the ongoing making of the city as white, and on the same processes of dispossession and displacement that Blomley describes, but with an emphasis on bodies. What must be imprinted on Indigenous bodies to make the city and the country white and to emplace white settlers? How is ongoing dispossession embodied? Can its processes be traced in what is enacted on the bodies of chronic alcoholics on Vancouver's Downtown East Side? Its tracks, I suggest, are evident in the dragging of Frank Paul into an alley where he is left to die. Ongoing dispossession is also evident in the Downtown East Side as a whole, an area virtually cordoned off as a space of violence, a space where few services exist for its desperately poor, displaced, sometimes addicted and ill population, many of whom are Indigenous. Significantly, colonialism is also evident in the inquiry's persistent remembering of Frank

Paul as vulnerable and not as colonized. Mbembe describes the inhabitants of death-worlds as

> human shapes that are alive, to be sure, but whose bodily integrity has been replaced by pieces, fragments, folds, even immense wounds that are difficult to close. Their function is to keep before the eyes of the victim – and of the people around him or her – the morbid spectacle of severing.[107]

He has in mind the severed hands of Africans in contemporary warfare. The settler, I suggest, feels his own modernity most intensely at the moment when he confronts the spectacle of severing, those human shapes missing limbs, shapes without bodily integrity. Can we consider alcohol and drug addiction and what is usually termed mental illness but so often resembles trauma, rampant in dispossessed Indigenous peoples on the streets of urban centres, as instances of severing, a visual reminder of the wounds of war and occupation? When we see sick Indigenous men and women who live under conditions of considerable violence and ill health on the streets of Vancouver, are we looking at late modern occupation where, for the colonized, to live "is to experience a permanent condition of 'being in pain'"?[108] When inquiries emphasize vulnerability and elide the colonial condition altogether, when Commissioner Davies uses words like ethnic discrimination and decorates his report with eagle feathers, the persistent history of neglect and abandonment remains, in the end, mysterious – perhaps an enduring feature of bureaucracies, perhaps a cultural conflict. Reflecting on Frank Paul's death, the commissioner is insistent: "We can, and should, learn from the past."[109] But we learn only that it is difficult to deal with wasted bodies. We do not learn what produces waste in the first place and who is produced by it.

Chapter Two

Dying from Improvement

[I]t's only a matter of degree that separates what happened to Frank Paul from what the governments of Canada have done with aboriginal people in this country from the beginning. That Canada and Canadians are inured, anaesthetized to the suffering of aboriginal people. And that's part of who we are ... To say is it relevant that Frank Paul was of aboriginal heritage, that he was an Indian, most certainly. And in part did he die as a result of it? Yes, he did. And in my submission we have to have the courage to see that and say it. The devaluation of his life is inextricably tied to his status as an Indian man.

Steven Kelliher, counsel for the Paul family[1]

Introduction

As chapter one discussed, on 5 December 1998, Frank Paul, an intoxicated Mi'kmaq man, was taken into police custody (for the second time that day) but soon released. Unable to walk, Frank Paul can be seen in a police surveillance videotape being dragged in and out of the police station, his clothing leaving a wet stain on the floor. He was dropped off by the Vancouver police in an alley on a cold, wet night, where he died several hours later. No inquest was held, and five separate legal opinions concluded that no charges should be laid against the two officers, Constable Instant and Sergeant Sanderson, involved in what the police term "a breaching" of Frank Paul.[2] It took nine years of lobbying by Indigenous groups, the BC Civil Liberties Association, and the BC Public Complaints Commission before there was a public inquiry into Frank Paul's death. Learning about the circumstances of Paul's death and viewing the videotape immediately give rise to the question, "Was Frank Paul left in circumstances where he could not fend for himself and where he was at risk of dying?" If so, and whether by negligence or intent, was Frank Paul's life devalued because he was Aboriginal, as Steven Kelliher, counsel for Paul's family suggests? Despite its haunting presence, the question never becomes a central one during the inquiry. Instead, alcoholism takes pride of place as the key to unlocking how and why Frank Paul died. In his report *Alone and Cold,* William Davies, commissioner of the inquiry, explores the conduct of the two officers and finds that one of them exhibited a callous indifference towards Frank Paul. The question of Frank Paul's Aboriginal status surfaces only insofar as the commissioner identifies a need for culturally sensitive services for homeless chronic alcoholics on Vancouver's Downtown East Side, many of whom are Aboriginal. Davies concludes that no one was to blame for what happened to Frank Paul. Rather, Canadian society simply did not know how to deal with homeless chronic alcoholics.[3] If Canadian society is guilty of anything, the inquiry concludes, it is guilty of not knowing how to care. It is not guilty of having failed to care. Race and colonialism can only enter the inquiry as complications of the main condition under investigation: alcoholism.

The inquiry into Frank Paul's death brought the issue of Indigenous deaths in custody a public attention it did not have before. In this chapter, I focus on the specific work that an inquiry does, exploring how it contributes to the colonial processes traced throughout this book, processes that I have suggested are given over to the project of making "Indians" disappear. It is not surprising that the inquiry should have focused on the systems in place for treating homeless chronic alcoholics and on the procedures for investigating deaths in custody. Inquiries do not concern themselves with guilt or innocence as trials do. Inquiries are structures of governance, however, and as such, they commit to law things that then acquire names, names which shape how these things come to be known. Frank Paul's death in an alley becomes a social problem called "homeless chronic alcoholics," and the failure to properly investigate Paul's death becomes the problem that the police investigate themselves in British Columbia. In examining what happens to the story of race and colonialism, the story, that is, of whether Frank Paul was devalued because he was an "Indian," I show how inquiries do the work of colonial governance in contemporary Canada, largely through a medicalized framework that masks ongoing violence.

In part one, I explore the challenge that Indigenous people and their advocates pose to the inquiry, a challenge encapsulated in the question, "Why did you fail to care?" When police and medical professionals respond to this question by emphasizing that Frank Paul was the kind of person who was hard to care for, they unwittingly confirm their belief that an intoxicated Indigenous man is not the same as others. In the responses of professionals, one can trace the devaluation of Indigenous life about which the Paul family lawyer Steven Kelliher spoke, the conviction, that is, that Frank Paul's suffering and the prospect of his untimely death were not things to worry about. Just as his physical incapacities provoked no grave concern on the night he died, so too his death in an alley failed to arouse alarm on the part of legal professionals and other state bureaucrats that he had been wrongfully treated. I suggest that the failure to care, documented by the inquiry, indicates a dehumanization of Indigenous peoples, practices born of the belief that there is no moral or legal duty to care for such abject beings. The historical and contemporary construction of Indigenous peoples as "drunken Indians" organizes the dehumanization discussed here.

In part two, I explore the inquiry's focus on alcohol addiction as the framework of the state's explanation for the failure to care. I suggest that the inquiry's focus on addiction is best understood as a redemptive gesture, which endows the state with moral authority but can only ultimately fail, given its side stepping of the everyday dehumanization of Indigenous peoples. The inquiry legitimizes settler colonialism and produces settlers as caring, civilized, and modern, persons with the moral authority and knowledge to save Indigenous peoples from themselves. Indigenous suffering becomes something non-Indigenous peoples will ameliorate, and public discourse shifts from land claims to rescue. At the inquiry's end, a metaphorical genocide is accomplished. There are no "Indians" left, only alcoholics. Steven Kelliher's words form the outline of the analysis offered here: It is only a matter of degree separating what happened to Frank Paul from what happens to Indigenous people collectively; non-Indigenous Canadians have become indifferent to Indigenous suffering; Frank Paul died as a result of the dehumanization of Indigenous people. Viewed as abject bodies always on the brink of death, Indigenous people can be imagined as less than human, a dehumanization that gives birth to the settler as fully human and as having emerged from the state of nature in which Indigenous people are thought to be trapped. Finally, we must find the courage to name and confront dehumanization.

Part One. Dehumanization

> I hear the question, How does social scientific knowledge justify the murder of people of color. My reply is, How does its arsenal explain it?[4]

Of what does dehumanization consist? The answer begins with conceptions of the human. In *Race and the Crisis of Humanism*, Kay Anderson offers a powerful argument: Aboriginal Australia provoked a rupture in the Enlightenment idea of what it meant to be human. Enlightenment theorists defined the human as separate from nature; all humans could be placed on a scale of development, defined as their gradual emergence from the state of nature. Cultivation (the subduing of nature), and the domination of mind over body, defined and separated the human from the animal. For John Locke, the American Indian represented the least developed human on the scale. Yet, as Anderson reminds us, "the western human–nature relationship has been no simple process of self-definition by negation."[5] Europeans doubted their own constructs, and their mounting insecurities of what it meant to be human were exacerbated by their encounter with Australian Aborigines, humans who were not human-like. Thought to be without agriculture and systems involving individual ownership of the land, as well as without clothing and other hallmarks of the civilized man, Australian Aborigines were deemed to be unable to progress into civilization. Indigenous intransigence (the refusal to be improved) prompted a crisis among Europeans; perhaps humans were not in fact different from animals. The nineteenth century turn to innatism, a new paradigm of innate and irredeemable human difference, could be seen as a response to these anxieties. Since European self-making was intrinsically a hierarchical project, the imperative to place Indigenous people off the scale, as it were, was fundamentally about re-asserting the humanity of Europeans. As such, the European–Indigenous encounter was not simply about racism (a belief in the inferiority of others) but also about a process of evicting racial Others outside of civilization, an eviction that formed the basis of European identity. Indigeneity posed a considerable challenge to European self-constitution and to the idea of man's exceptionality, a crisis resolved by innatism. Unable to emerge from the state of nature, Australian Aborigines were considered doomed to extinction. The nineteenth century idea that all "primitive" races were doomed to extinction, Patrick Brantlinger shows, underlined the view that an innate savagery was the reason for Indigenous disappearance, a view shared by humanitarians, scientists, and colonial propagandists alike.[6] Anderson's thesis suggests that while a great deal of work must go into marking Aboriginality as the limit of the human, uncertainty and fear always accompany this project.[7] To this argument, Denise Ferreira da Silva adds the never-ending need of Europeans to obliterate those who are understood to be at the limit of the human.

As with Anderson, Ferreira da Silva stresses that the Enlightenment idea of man as a self-determined subject, as rational and emerging from a state of nature, requires for self-definition a constitutive outside, a subject who cannot progress out of nature: "while the tools of universal reason (the 'laws of nature') produce and regulate human conditions, in each global region it establishes mentally (morally and intellectually) distinct kinds of human beings, namely the self-determined subject and its outer-determined others, the ones whose minds are subjected to their *natural* (in the scientific sense) conditions."[8] In this founding ontological moment, the racial is born as a constitutive human attribute that marks a different kind of human, one reduced to body and unable to progress out of nature. Notably, the racial derives its political force from its role in dividing humans. The racial is "deployed to explain away the violent deaths of people of colour as endless social scientific evidence renders them not only expected (as the outcome of juridical and economic exclusion) but also justified (as the forecasted end of the trajectory of an outer-determined consciousness)."[9] We cannot understand and end violence without confronting the logic that installs different kinds of humans on a scale of development and demands the obliteration of the Other as the condition enabling the self-determining subject's emergence. Identified with nature, the Indian has always signified the frontier, the space on which American subjects would inscribe their "civilization."[10] Ferreira da Silva's emphasis on violence against racial Others as constitutive of modernity yields the question that is central to her book *Toward a Global Idea of Race*, namely, how are modern subjects produced who can be excluded from the universal "without unleashing an ethical crisis?"[11] It bears emphasizing Ferreira da Silva's point that to be excluded from the universal is to be placed at a social and moral distance from the European. Violence can be directed with impunity at those outside the domain of justice.

If in the nineteenth century Aboriginality unsettled the schema of humanity on which the Enlightenment rested, in ongoing colonial and imperial regimes, Aboriginality continues to provoke a crisis. As untamed nature, Indigenous peoples must be subdued in the name of civilization. Colonial regimes unselfconsciously announce their relationship to Indigenous people as one of tutelage, subduing savagery by force, if necessary, and assisting (often without success) Indigenous people into civilization. However, the colonial project is inherently unstable. As several Indigenous scholars have argued, Indigeneity threatens to expose what Audra Simpson has described as "settlement's secret," the secret, that is, of Indigenous sovereignty. Settlers must always forget the source of their state's existence, the dispossession of sovereign nations (and the obliteration of human beings it requires). Forgetting requires the disappearance of the Native, since the settler never leaves.[12] Disappearance is both symbolic (disappearance from the scale of humanity) and concrete (violence marks the limit), the violence of outright extinction as well as slow death.

For Simpson, the disappearance of the Native is often and paradoxically accomplished through a gesture of inclusion, the moment when the settler state announces that it has not forgotten its Indians and means to assist them into modernity. As Peter Fitzpatrick remarked in an early essay on racism, discovery, and the grounds of law, from at least the late eighteenth century, when the doctrine of discovery changed from one in which full title could be claimed only for uninhabited land to one in which title could be claimed for inhabited land where inhabitants were manifestly unable to properly occupy it, Indigenous populations were categorized as chronically inadequate. Such peoples were thus rendered in a permanent state of tutelage.[13] Gillian Cowlishaw remarks for the Australian context that "there exists a widespread narcissistic desire, often muted and pressed into unconsciousness, to improve the Indigenous population."[14] The settler state governs through the idea of rescuing Indigenous communities from self-inflicted violence; rescue displaces the fact of colonial violence and pre-empts discourses of land rights, heritage, and culture, a feature Dian Million has shown for the Canadian context.[15] If the settler state "worries" about Indigenous populations, Cowlishaw argues, it does so to insist on its moral authority to rule over (to improve) an abject population, one that haunts the settler state. Improvement in this view functions to reinstall European settlers as having successfully remained within the boundaries of civilization. It resolves some of the anxieties about which Kay Anderson wrote, namely the anxiety that the line between civilization and the state of nature was not an absolute one.

Inquests and inquiries have a central role to play in colonial governance, providing the stage for such redemptive efforts. We might even think of them as spectacles, the way Audra Simpson thinks of the film *Avatar*. *Avatar* tells the story of an Indigenous people about to be annihilated but saved by an outside force. The saviour no longer occupies

Indigenous territory unjustly. *Avatar* thus "offers a representative foil for the guilt, shame, horror, and hope that gets shuttled someplace else when the matters of settlement and genocide are contemplated."[16] Such spectacles "redirect emotions, histories, and possibilities away from the means of societal and historical production – Indigenous dispossession, disenfranchisement, and containment."[17] Inquiries do not perform the political work Simpson describes for *Avatar* seamlessly, however. Instead, they work hard to suture the ruptures that have given rise to them in the first place. That is to say, inquiries must resolve the contradiction between rescuing Natives and suppressing the evidence of settler and police violence towards people who are assumed to be less than human.[18]

Frank Paul: A Man Who Crawled

Frank Paul's disappearance as a human being, his confinement to the category of the lowest form of human evolution, is evident in the testimonies from the professionals who encountered him several times a week, testimonies that he smelled, was likely incontinent, and was always drunk. There are people, Chief Constable Jamie Graham told the press, who can only crawl, that is, whose natural condition is a near bestial existence.[19] When asked, for example, whether Frank Paul's crawling in the police station bothered her, Constable Pamela Dawes replied that she didn't see it as "a horrible thing": "I guess I was happy that at least he wasn't going to hurt himself when he's staying close to the ground."[20] Corrections Officer Janet Ross, who signed Paul into jail the first time he was brought to the station the day he died, expected that drunk persons such as Frank Paul might simply crawl and lie down; Frank Paul's everyday state of being was quite simply animal like. Although this happened rarely, Ross did not consider the sight of Frank Paul crawling as "overly surprising."[21] Constable Elizabeth Jean Prince, who noted that it was a particularly cold day and that she gave Frank Paul money for coffee when he asked her for it, remembered most Frank Paul's gnarled hands and his inability to fully function.[22] This image conjures a different kind of human, one closer to nature and intrinsically imperiled: one on the brink of extinction. The professionals testifying about their encounters with Frank Paul offered countless images of him as someone who shuffled, someone whose movements and physical attributes marked him as belonging to another (earlier) stage of human development.[23] Seen as unable to emerge from a state of nature, yet always reminding settlers of the precariousness of the developmental schema in which Europeans understand themselves as more human than others, Indigenous people provoke anxiety that is often resolved through violence. For example, health professionals can deny treatment to Indigenous alcoholics on the grounds that ill health and addiction are normal conditions for Indigenous people and not worth attending to. As more than one study has shown, the standard response to intoxicated Aboriginal people is simply "so what – he's only Aboriginal."[24] The sick, self-destructive Indigenous body confirms the settler's emplacement as original citizen.

Perhaps because it could have lent weight to Sergeant Sanderson's defence that he thought Frank Paul was not drunk but was simply crawling as he normally did, the inquiry heard much discussion about Paul's physical attributes. Pathologist John Butt speculated that Frank Paul may have had Wernicke-Korsakoff syndrome, a condition related to alcohol abuse and its accompanying vitamin deficiencies that causes a type of gait he described as "crabbing," that is, moving like a crab. (The Korsakoff component involves a form of mental derangement, a problem with thinking and short-term memory loss). Dr Butt acknowledged that he arrived at the descriptor "crabbing" when he heard the account offered by Sergeant Sanderson of how Paul usually moved.[25] Confirming that Frank Paul's inability to walk would have been significant nonetheless, in that it suggested a human being who needed considerable care, and noting that Frank Paul may have been more vulnerable to hypothermia because he was an alcoholic, Butt concluded that "there could have been a concern that Frank Paul was not able to look after himself on the day he died."[26] Professionals could not summon the concern that Butt supposes should have been there because they could only see Frank Paul as someone beyond care. For most of those who came into frequent contact with Frank Paul – the constables, wagon drivers, health-care workers, and guards – the fact that he was "down on all fours"[27] and crawling was entirely normal, and there was little one could do about it. The ubiquity of this response underlines how difficult it was for Frank Paul's family and for Indigenous groups to insist at the inquiry that Frank Paul was human, and that he did not deserve to die as he did. As Ferreira da Silva and Anderson both point out, little is due to those who are not self-determining and who cannot progress from the state of nature.

While Frank Paul's body, his inability to fully function, underscored whose lives were worth living, it also revealed who had the power to decide between those who live and those who die. Peggy Clement, Paul's cousin, outlined the family's position that "only the creator has the power to decide who is to live and who is to die" and that "those [Paul] turned to in his need … ignored their responsibilities."[28] Her challenge stands alongside the tide of details about a man whose physical appearance (race and disability) marked him as someone whose life was neither worth living nor saving. Clement names the heart of the matter: who decides who must live and who must die? In law, Giorgio Agamben reminds us, where there is no common humanity, there is no common law. Frank Paul, evicted from humanity, is necessarily evicted from law, and those who take his life commit no crime.[29] In answer to Clement's question about who decides who must live and who must die, law responds that taking Frank Paul's life was not illegal. How it comes to be so has to do with what kind of human he was imagined to be.

What Any Reasonable Person Might Do

Who would leave a man who could not walk, a man who was severely intoxicated and known to be unwell and possibly mentally ill, a man who could only crawl, in an alley on a cold night? Who would find these actions reasonable? When the inquiry considers the actions of those police, medical, and legal professionals who failed to investigate Frank Paul's death, in particular the decisions of the Criminal Justice Branch not to prosecute Sanderson and Instant, it hears answers to these questions that have coherence only if one already accepts that there is a category of human whose daily life cannot be measured the same as the daily life of others.

Noting "the frightening power" of the Criminal Justice Branch to charge or not to charge, counsel for the family, Steven Kelliher, itemized the "evidentiary hooks" upon which the Branch relied to make its decision not to charge the two officers. He noted that the Branch's decision not to charge was based on the idea that a reasonable person would have difficulty determining the needs of a person as abnormal as Frank Paul.[30] Crown counsel Cullen, who made the first recommendation that the officers not be charged, determined that "the general evidence of Mr. Paul's life on the street" and the fact that he was "enthralled to alcohol on a daily basis" meant that it would be difficult to ascertain why he died. Paul's "life on the street" marks him not as someone who is dispossessed and homeless, but as someone already in a state of existence beyond salvaging. Ewert, Cullen's superior, following the trail of Cullen's line of reasoning, was more explicit. For Ewert, Frank Paul was a man on the brink of death anyway (the logic Anderson shows applied to Australia's Aborigines[31]). Taking the logic of the "disappearing Indian" to extraordinary lengths, Ewert argued that Paul may well have died on the vegetable stand where he was found passed out and taken to the jail. In a strange twist of logic, Ewert then concluded that the officers may have saved his life. Since Frank Paul's life was not in fact saved, Kelliher could only wonder out loud at this logic ("What in the world was this man thinking?").[32] As Kelliher observed, the legal arguments offered in these multiple decisions not to charge the two officers were "loose, rambling, incomplete, unstructured and almost casual documents in their nature."[33] Indeed, as the months and years go by and errors accumulate in the file, it is hard not to agree that the Branch displayed a stunning indifference to Frank Paul's death. Kelliher was particularly outraged by Ewert's assessment of Frank Paul's file. It is "shocking," he charged, that this very senior Crown counsel should have gotten his facts wrong. Ewert maintained that the police file indicated Sergeant Sanderson believed Frank Paul would be cared for by his buddies if he were taken to the Maple and Broadway area. He also noted evidence from other officers that Frank Paul always had to be dragged. (Neither fact can be found in the file.) Characterizing Frank Paul as someone known to be "a hard ass that has been physically deteriorating"[34] and considering that Sergeant Sanderson was known "as a nice guy," Ewert made the decision not to charge the two officers, concluding that no one could have foreseen the harm.[35] Indeed, how can you know for certain if you have killed someone when he was already dying?

Confronted with the same Orwellian logic of the Criminal Justice Branch, namely that it is impossible to kill a man who is dying, counsel for the United Native Nations, Cameron Ward, also highlighted the Crown's argument that a reasonable person could not easily determine what endangers a man who lived as Frank Paul did.[36] Putting the matter as bluntly as did Kelliher, Ward argued that Instant and Sanderson were not charged because Frank Paul was not seen as the same kind of human being as others: "I submit, with respect, that that's really just a polite or flowery way of saying Mr. Paul's death doesn't matter. He was just a drunken Indian."[37] Driving home his point, Ward asked the commissioner what would have happened if police had left an intoxicated teenaged girl to die in an alley.[38] He does not specify race, but goes on to list the cases (many of whom are Indigenous men) dying at the hands of the police.[39] What is revealed in these exchanges between the commissioner and counsel for Frank Paul's family and for Indigenous groups is the paradox that lies at the heart of the encounter between Indigenous peoples and Europeans: how is it possible to acknowledge the humanity of those who must be excluded from humanity if Europeans are to know themselves as self-determining individuals? Further, what would an acknowledgment of Frank Paul's humanity entail? Would it require acknowledging that his condition was one inextricably linked to colonial violence as well as a more general recognition that he was ill and deserved care?

What happens when individuals are confronted with the defence's argument that Frank Paul's life was devalued because he was an Indian? State officials pressed to explain their own decisions offer barely rational responses. "You've seen the stills, the jail stills of Mr. Paul being dragged in and dragged out, obviously grossly intoxicated and unable to care for himself?" Kelliher asks former chief coroner (and former mayor) Larry Campbell, questioning whether or not he accepted that Frank Paul was abandoned when, as the videotape shows, Paul obviously could not care for himself. Campbell advances the unlikely theory (since Frank Paul was known to be frequently intoxicated) that Frank Paul could have been sober when he left the jail and was later offered alcohol by people on the streets who were passing by in the dark alley that night. Why, Kelliher asks, does Campbell still "prefer Constable Instant's account that Frank Paul was able to care for himself when he left him, when the videotape shows otherwise?" Campbell can only erupt defensively to Kelliher's insistent questioning, announcing: "But I will not sit here and have you accuse me of being racist or of not doing my job or the Coroners Service." Cautioned by the commissioner that he was arguing with the witness, Kelliher in the end receives no response to his question.[40]

That Frank Paul was Indigenous was something everyone involved in his case knew and took notice of, but the full meaning of Paul's Indigeneity cannot be explored without risking the conclusion that Frank Paul was treated as he was *because* he was Indigenous. Above all, witnesses cannot acknowledge that they know about other Indigenous people dying in custody. Acknowledging that she knew Frank Paul was Aboriginal, former coroner Jeannine Robinson must then consider whether this had any bearing on her own response to the case. It is not surprising that Robinson, the coroner on duty in 1998, reacted angrily when Kelliher asked whether "the fact of the less than ideal relationship between the Aboriginal people of this province and the Vancouver City Police Department" was a factor in her decision not to pursue an inquest into Paul's death. Responding that she was "offended" by his question, Robinson nevertheless acknowledges that the inquiry has now raised some questions in her mind about the wisdom of that decision in 1998.[41] Reminded by Cameron Ward that just one month before Frank Paul's death, a coroner's verdict was rendered on the death of an Indigenous man taken into police custody who died in the police wagon (a death attributed to positional asphyxia and chronic alcohol abuse), remarkably, Robinson responds that she had been taught to treat each death as an individual matter. She would not have thought to consult the recommendations offered in a case having many similarities to Frank Paul's case, and such deaths would not have raised a red flag in her mind.[42] Such responses express the individualism that pervades law, and they amount to a willful denial of the pattern of violent responses to Indigenous peoples. To bring the violence into view requires attention to what *collectively* happens to Indigenous people, a shift that advocates for the family and for Indigenous groups try hard to accomplish.

It was the job of counsel for the family and for the United Native Nations to probe what the connection might have been between Frank Paul's Aboriginality and how professionals responded to him and to his death. Counsel consistently sought to explore the connection between witnesses' awareness of other Indigenous deaths and the conclusions they drew about Frank Paul. Cameron Ward, for example, noted that the death of Neil Stonechild in Saskatchewan and "starlight tours," where Indigenous men were driven by the police out of the city and left to freeze to death, as well as the deaths of Indigenous children in foster care in the city of Vancouver, should have alerted officials to a burgeoning issue of police brutality towards Indigenous peoples. Thus confronted, witnesses had little to say in their defence.[43] Terry Smith, chief coroner in 2001, who was asked about his own response when he became aware of the Frank Paul case in 2001 and 2004, acknowledged his awareness of Stonechild and the deaths of Indigenous children in foster care, but maintained that he did nothing about Frank Paul's death because he did not believe the matter was best dealt with by the coroner's office. Presumably, he believed that Frank Paul had not technically died in police custody, having been released into the alley. Reminding the former chief coroner that he had been criticized for his handling of the cases of Aboriginal children who died in foster care, and pressing him to offer an apology for failing to contact Frank Paul's family about his death, counsel ultimately was only able to put on record a strange but consistent failing over several years on the part of the coroner's office to investigate the circumstances of Aboriginal deaths, whether of children or grown men. While it is clear, as Cameron Ward opined in an interview, that it is never a good idea to bring up racism, owing to the defensive responses it produces, it is nevertheless obvious from these exchanges that witnesses could offer no explanation for why they acted as they did. Few could have been unaware of the collective implications of Frank Paul's death: that Indigenous peoples were dying in custody across the country and that such deaths often had the pattern of abandonment evident in Frank Paul's case.[44]

The colonial encounter is marked by a particular conception of the human that assigns to the colonized the status of the incompletely human. While the colonized must be assisted into modernity, confirming the settler's ethical position, the settler is certain that little can come from improvement. Although the encounter continually alternates between annihilation and improvement, in practice it can be difficult to tell the difference between the two. Police officers and medical professionals who fail to help are not easily distinguished from the murderer who sets out to kill. Each is governed by a sense of the racial Other's sub-humanity; each sees a life that is not worth living. The inquiry, confronted with the dehumanization that marked Frank Paul's encounters with police and helping professionals, and later, after his death, with the justice system, must confront what Frank Paul's Indigenous status had to do with how he was treated. In looking away from racism and colonialism, the inquiry was doomed to repeat the triumphalist logic of the colonial imaginary: a vanishing race is replaced by a stronger one.

Part Two. Improvement and "A Rough Attempt at a Circle"

Through inquiries, the state defines "the Aboriginal problem" and articulates strategies for reform, practices described by Adam Ashforth as symbolic rituals rather than policy-making instruments that instruct us in the truths of the state and organize political subjection.[45] As rituals or pedagogies, inquiries stage their truths, often through a performance of colonialism's compassion and commitment to the rule of law. Radhika Mongia provides a concrete example of how nineteenth century British colonial inquiries defined indentured Indian labour as legitimate, but did so paradoxically through a discussion of the failings of the system of indentureship. Inquiries function as regimes of truth as Michel Foucault defined them (rules that separate true from false, thereby restricting what could be recognized as true), Mongia argues, but an inquiry is also a site of anxiety, the stage for a restless and uneven performance of empire. British colonial inquiries into Indian indentureship revealed a constant anxiety around the freedom of colonized populations.[46]

In the same vein, Ann Stoler observes that

> the colonial archive pulls on some social facts and converts them into qualified knowledge that attends to some ways of knowing while repelling and refusing others. In no small part it inscribes the authority of the colonial state and the analytic energies mobilized to make its assertions. But it also registers other reverberations, crosscurrent frictions, attractions, and aversions that worked within and against those assertions of imperial rights to property, persons, and profits that colonial regimes claimed as their own.[47]

At these moments of contestation and unevenness, we can see the inquiry constructing what Stoler describes as "sentimental space," managing sentiments and making us feel through the "pathos of vignette" and through "stock and formulaic phrases" the rightness of a colonial common sense, even as we are also disturbed and unsettled by it.[48] The game is not won from the outset. We are, after all, in the midst of a colonial encounter, and if inquiries announce the "limits of care,"[49] they can also be disrupted by Indigenous peoples themselves who refuse to stay confined to the realm of the miserable.[50] In those brief moments during the Frank Paul inquiry when Indigenous people and their advocates ask, "Why did you fail to care?," there can be no answer. Improvement rushes in to smooth over the moment when a chasm appears between the dispossessed and those who have dispossessed them.

The inquiry stages the colonial encounter as one between experts and Indigenous people, the latter squeezed into the spaces of the spiritual, the communal, and the emotional, the former, more often than not, men (and sometimes women) of science. As Dian Million has argued with respect to the Canadian state's response to the recommendations of the Royal Commission on Aboriginal Peoples, the state works hard to shift the focus from political self-determination to healing, where healing "becomes intertwined with state-determined biopolitical programs for emotional and psychological self-care informed by trauma."[51] Only one Indigenous experience, the abuse of children in residential schools, garners attention, an experience that is then seen to require measures of self-care. Bracketed as an abuse of the colonial past, the residential school experience is uncoupled from the colonial present and individualized.

Alcoholism has a starring role in this scenario of individualized pathology, and non-Indigenous doctors and academics are enlisted in the project of managing damaged individuals. When healing is collectivized, Indigenous communities become the subject of large-scale healing projects, and the deliberate, ongoing impoverishment of Indigenous communities is consigned to the sidelines. In Million's words, community healing is "a little like accepting being bandaged by your armed assailant while he is still ransacking your house."[52] The therapeutic move of which Million writes is one that is eminently compatible with inquiries, enabling a vigorous pursuit of redemption.

During phase four of the inquiry, a number of experts were invited to make presentations relating to alcohol addiction.[53] As counsel for the inquiry explained, the work of phase four was not "theoretical." The day would be devoted to the practical matter of how society should respond to homeless chronic alcoholics; specifically, the commission set out to explore the decriminalization of intoxication. Commissions often place stock in their informality, relaxing rules and seemingly intent on canvassing many opinions. Under the guise of inclusiveness, Indigeneity remains very much in parenthesis. To raise it is always to skirt dangerously near the edges of racism and colonialism, and thereby to confront the possibility of encountering colonizers around every corner. Indigeneity must therefore remain confined to the realm of culture and spirituality, and enclosed firmly in anachronistic space and time, if it is not to disturb the idea that Indigenous people are dead and dying. For all that they are constrained, Indigenous peoples and their advocates nonetheless find ways to resist and to put racism and colonialism on record.

The phase four presentations were chaired by Jonathan Rudin, the legal director of Aboriginal Legal Services of Toronto, who began the day by introducing an Indigenous elder invited to offer the opening prayer. Confined to spiritual matters, ninety-three-year-old Andrew Yellowback began his prayer by noting that Cree culture pays attention to changes, the coming together of things and their disintegration.[54] Announcing that he heard it had been many years between Frank Paul's death and the inquiry (and getting to the heart of the matter immediately, namely that it has been difficult to call anyone to account), Andrew Yellowback then offered a story:

> So I remember the doctor going – passing by. The old lady was just sitting there, used to see the doctor going by. And [s]he says, "How is my neighbor doing," he said. "Oh," he says, "[s]he's improving." This kept

> going for a few weeks until one week the doctor told the lady, he says, "Did you hear she died last night?" So the lady went in, told her husband. She says, "Did you know our neighbor died last night?" He says, "I didn't know that. What did [s]he die from?" So the lady said, "I think she died of improvement." So this assembly I'm sure will not die.[55]

Amidst the confusion of he and she, and Andrew Yellowback's informal style, a cautionary tale emerges about projects of improvement. The moment stands out, marked by the irrefutable presence of Indigeneity both culturally and politically. The inquiry is reminded about how long it took to get the state to investigate, a tale is told about improvement, the Cree language is spoken, and Yellowback closes with a prayer that the inquiry will have the "courage to make the changes that will mean healing, freedom and hopefulness."[56] Using the very place where he has been marked as the spiritual Indian, Elder Andrew Yellowback reclaims the political, and the tension of the day begins.

Not yet finished with the spiritual and Indigenous part of the day, Rudin invites participants to consider the medicine wheel as a paradigm for the day and instructs the gathering on how the wheel applies.[57] Participants are invited to reflect on the vision to create a healthy community, on the relationship between the state and those individuals who find themselves intoxicated, as well as on the relationship between extreme intoxication and medical conditions. They are enjoined to consider "best practices" with respect to alcoholics and to explore future directions. Wrapped up in its Indigenous cultural packaging, the day as outlined by Rudin is nevertheless not about Indigeneity but about alcoholism. The person who was Frank Paul is replaced by a disease, but his ghostly presence continues to trouble the proceedings, emerging at uncanny moments.

Alcoholism as Addiction and the Narrative of White and Black Addicts

In her book *Inventing the Addict*, Susan Zieger explores cultural constructions of the addict, noting that narratives of addiction "have important things to tell us about changing conceptualizations of Anglo-American selfhood, freedom, and identity."[58] Peter Ferentzy also suggests that the United States has been preoccupied with addiction since the early twentieth century, when it led the global drive to ban narcotics, a preoccupation he speculates originates in its history as a colonizing and slave-owning society: “A stronger middle-class ethos, wild frontiers, and fear of races considered to be primitive or even animal-like (such as blacks and natives) all made for greater concern with self-control, autonomy, and freedom.”[59] Zieger, Ferentzy, and Marianna Valverde[60] trace the idea of addiction as a disease of the will, noting that the emergence of the concept of addiction as self-enslavement was anchored in the idea that self-control and self-domination were central to what it meant to be human. As discussed earlier, this Enlightenment conception of the human has always provoked European anxiety that rational man was at risk both internally from the forces of savagery within and externally from racial Others. It is not surprising, then, that the nineteenth century concern with addiction as a disease of the will should have emerged as “an exceptional story of white, masculine, middle-class self-making gone awry, ironically confronting its own embodiment as a mode of compulsion rather than freedom, habituation rather than spontaneity, dependency rather than autonomy, and disease rather than health.”[61] Through addiction, the white man became “figuratively black, disempowered, static, and emasculated.”[62]

What, then, of the addict who is not white? Because the addicted individual has a defective will, addiction is isolated from its social context.[63] Ferentzy shows how scientific explanations of alcohol addiction consistently sideline its social and economic roots. It is thought to be crack, and not poverty and homelessness, for instance, that most imperils Black “crack-babies.”[64] Zieger adds: “Because addiction unfolds as an ironic narrative of self-loss, it requires subjects who have much to lose – socially, financially, and psychologically; in the racist imagination of the nineteenth century, this meant white men and, increasingly, women.”[65] Describing “the ambivalent racialization of addiction and its imperial discontent,” Zieger shows, however, how the eugenic imagination of the late nineteenth and early twentieth century began to categorize addicts as “habitual criminals and racial defectives, denizens of a shadowy, parasitic underworld.”[66] The racialized addict was reconfigured as flirting with death and always on the brink of dying in his underworld. Indigeneity, not discussed by these scholars, fits easily into the history Zieger and others describe. Always imagined as beyond rationality and as a member of a dying race that exists (literally) on the margins of civilized society, the Indigenous addict simply fulfills the destiny of his race and is in this way indistinguishable from it. It becomes impossible, then, to separate societal responses to Indigenous alcoholics from responses to Indigenous peoples generally. While alcoholism comes to be seen as a problem of the race, the alcoholic's situation is not connected to dispossession and to ongoing colonial processes. It remains at the level of a cultural incapacity, mysterious in origin if somewhat loosely connected to past historical events.

The racialization that runs through cultural constructs of the addict surfaces in several ways during the inquiry, giving rise to gaps and inconsistencies. The inquiry spends time on harm reduction approaches to alcohol addiction, the cutting edge of treatment for addicts and an approach that is not popular with conservatives.[67] Dr Tomislav Svoboda begins his testimony to the inquiry by noting alcoholism's fearsome character. Svoboda, an expert in harm reduction programs for men who are homeless and suffering from severe problems related to mental illness and alcohol use, offers a graphic description of the effects of alcohol abuse, noting that the homeless chronic alcoholic population use the emergency room as their prime source of health care. Describing swollen organs, seizures, an elevated death rate, and a high incidence of depression, he recommends a harm reduction approach where, for instance, some shelters would permit alcohol, thereby enabling an addict to have shelter while learning how to stop abusing alcohol. Noting that many alcoholics in this group have come from "generations of alcohol dependency" and suffer many concurrent disorders, he stresses that what is most lacking for this group is supported housing.[68] There is institutionalized poverty, Dr Svoboda insists, which makes it imperative to provide housing where a harm reduction approach is adopted. People have "a moral kind of distaste" for providing help of this kind, sometimes believing that they would make things too easy for the homeless chronic alcoholic.[69] Daring in his insistence that housing is key to solving the problems of homeless chronic alcoholics, Svoboda's testimony points the inquiry in the right direction. The discussion does not get to dispossession, however, as individualized self-help remains the framework. Svoboda does not speculate about social responses to Indigeneity and therefore misses an opportunity to consider the barriers that stand in the way when harm reduction programs and housing are offered to Indigenous chronic alcoholics. The moral distaste of which Svoboda speaks is intensified when alcohol is provided to Indigenous people in shelters. With a long colonial history based on the idea that Indigenous people are innately unable to control their will and are prone to alcohol abuse, few Canadians accept such a proposition. As Indigenous people are already viewed as dependents of the state, the provision of housing to Indigenous alcoholics also provokes social outcry. In this way, a solution that appears promising may end up failing.

When alcohol abuse is considered by criminologist Dr Neil Boyd, the overall focus on the generic chronic alcoholic sits uneasily alongside his intent to consider the political, economic, social, and historical context and to focus on First Nations as well as the Australian experience. Beginning with the history of public intoxication laws, and reviewing the history of the temperance movement and the relationship between public drunkenness and policing, Boyd notes that vagrancy laws were connected to policing alcohol abuse, so that the offence was not drunkenness per se but a prohibition on being drunk and disorderly in public. Into this generic history of alcohol, Boyd then introduces First Nations, public intoxication, and the *Indian Act*, noting that Canada has long had policies targeting First Nations people and alcohol. Describing these laws but not attempting to analyse them, Boyd acknowledges, however, that the research clearly shows an overrepresentation of First Nations people arrested for alcohol-related offences. For example, a 1977 study of Regina showed that two-thirds of persons arrested for public intoxication were First Nations.[70] Since these patterns are the same for Australia, Boyd suggests that we learn from the Australian Royal Commission on Aboriginal Deaths in Custody. Offering no explanation for the overrepresentation in arrests or deaths in custody, he suggests that the heart of the matter is that we treat drunkenness as an offence and have "cultural blinders" on, which prevent us from understanding alcoholism as a disease. The coroners' inquiries Boyd reviews suggest that Indigenous people continue to die in custody at elevated rates in spite of repeated coronial recommendations for better monitoring. Discussing the typical patterns of such deaths, where severely ill prisoners die from lack of medical treatment, Boyd stresses that "our deficiency as a culture" is that we respond to a medical problem with a custodial/police-centred approach.[71] He notes that Europe has better responses to intoxication. Boyd is obliged to concede, however, that "location" complicates how the police respond in Canada. Where someone is picked up often determines whether they will receive medical care.[72]

If we are, as the criminologist Neil Boyd argues, "moralistic" towards people who abuse alcohol, there still remains the question posed by Steven Kelliher whether moralistic social attitudes are directed towards all individuals who abuse alcohol or are directed "ethnically," as Kelliher delicately put it. Refusing to consider ethnicity (used here as though a less confrontational word than race), Boyd is then asked by Cameron Ward to expand on his earlier acknowledgment that individuals in different locations are not treated in the same way. Attempting to keep the discussion off the topic of race and hoping to address the over-policing of certain populations, Boyd first offers the example of how the police ticket (presumably white) suburban mothers who drop their kids off to school and don't carry their licenses. Perhaps acknowledging the inappropriateness of the example, he finally concedes that, unlike his example of how police treat suburban mothers, "there are differences [in policing] we would not feel comfortable about."[73]

In what reads as a moment of rupture in which an unspeakable truth is named, Andrew Yellowback (sometimes erroneously referred to in the transcript as Yellowknife) interrupts this dance around the word "ethnicity" and the difference between how Indigenous people are treated by the police as compared to suburban and presumably white mothers.[74] He comments:

> I thought I'd want to share with you this. You said that Indians are treated differently in the community, and for me, I carry 93 winters on my back. I've always been an Indian. I think I will be an Indian till I die. And I think that only an Indian can express the reality of Indian life and culture. And also to articulate this, recently I had a friend who came from Europe, made a tour. An Indian – she lives – he lived right here. Anyway, we were talking about alcoholism, and he said, "You know what," he says, "the funniest thing," he says, "when I was in Europe, I seen a lot of this, a lot of prostitution, but, you know, everywhere I looked around," he says, "I never saw one Indian."
>
> So it tells you a lot of things, eh. So I think in reality what we're dealing with is the big word R, racism, discrimination, and all those other definitions we have, and I think society is incapable of addressing that issue. And I have been talking about this. I try to speak from here, from the heart, because it never works if you speak from here or from here. So it would do a disrespect. It would respect. I want to tell this assembly that it's time we address this issue, racial issue, because we cannot do anything and move forward unless we address it. And I've tried my best to give this healing, eh. And it's part of our culture. As you grow older you have to have respect, honesty, humility, bravery, and this is something that we forgot.
>
> As an Indian, I've been sober for 39 years. Maybe I share this with you now. I was raised in an institution, educational institution. I went to school when I was five years old, and like I told Jonathan this morning, what do you teach a child when he's young. You teach him where he comes from, his culture, his language, his very essence. And what did they teach me? Just the opposite. They physically abused me, sexually abused me, mentally abused me, and I remember all those details, but at my age again, when I look back, I look at my values. So what do we do? As an Indian I forgave the past. And when I talk to my people, I say we have to forget the

> past, and I say some people say you cannot forget, which I agree, because the past is with you, but you have to forgive. For me, I found out in my own time that forgiveness is the greatest healing force of all, and I've learned this, and I want to go further. You know, when you allow an elder to speak, he's not going to shut up, so while I have this opportunity, this is an opportunity to share with you my people will not speak up because the deplume [*sic*. Phonetic spelling of an Indigenous word] is in us. That story, we say noninterference, eh. It plays a great role in our society.[75]

Race and colonialism enter the room at these unscripted moments of unease, having been excluded by definition. Through stories of violence, and a powerful reminder of the consequences of white "interference" in the affairs of sovereign Indigenous nations, Andrew Yellowback once again interrupts the process of improvement. As he concludes his intervention, there is little left for the inquiry to do but to adjourn for lunch; as the commissioner concluded, "[T]he gathering you see today is our rough attempt at a circle."[76]

Addiction is everywhere severed from its history and context, and preserved as an individual failing. Even those who attend to history and social context miss the mark when they do not fully consider colonialism. Had criminologist Neil Boyd, for example, relied on a different history other than the story of morally condemning and punitive attitudes to alcohol, the inquiry would have been invited to walk down a road where uncomfortable questions about responses to Indigenous peoples could be asked. As Penelope Edmonds has demonstrated in her study of colonial Victoria, British Columbia, and Melbourne, Australia, attitudes to urban Indigenous peoples and alcohol have their origin in an altogether different history than the one related by Boyd. Attitudes to alcohol and First Nations have their origins in the making of the colonial city and in settler society's need to produce Indigenous bodies as bodies out of place. These same attitudes, attitudes that are fundamentally about the Indigenous presence in the city, survive in the contemporary policing of men like Frank Paul.

Perhaps because the "R" word had been uttered, the inquiry's afternoon session on the topic of homeless chronic alcoholics continues to strike discordant notes that threaten to bring out what lies beneath the surface. Inspector De Haas, who once worked on the Downtown East Side, strangely notes:

> [I]f there was any suggestion that the driver [of the wagon that dropped Paul in the alley] was biased by the police, we also need to recognize true

> aboriginal history, and I was very grateful for your comments about racism and discrimination for decades, if not centuries, that have resulted in a very difficult state for the aboriginal people, which is very much the underlying cause of overrepresentation, and it's going to take a lot of work to change the social context of the situation to remedy that, and I think that was kind of missing from what I heard this morning.[77]

It is unclear whether Inspector De Haas hears Yellowback's intervention only as an explanation for why Indigenous people are destroyed by alcohol and not as a reminder of the brutality of colonialism, but he is clearly driven to defend the wagon driver from the charge of racism. Community worker Jim Hauck expresses his belief that some people suffer from post-traumatic stress, presumably from colonialism.[78] These interventions open the way for Chris Livingstone, a Nisga'a First Nations man working with the Western Aboriginal Harm Reduction Society, to name the issue of First Nations governance and to point out that no funding comes to urban Aboriginal people.[79] When asked by Kelliher what could be done to reduce the number of urban Aboriginal people who need services, Livingstone replies:

> Well, it's a Canadian problem. It's all about entitlements. It's – I mean, when – there was somebody earlier talking about the Hudson's Bay Company coming in here and trading furs for alcohol, and they were talking about alcohol being – or prohibition being introduced, and really that's what it is, is that Canada has had a – it's a culture of exploitation and raping and pillaging and stealing. So, I mean, if that's the way that society is, I mean, health-wise, if you think of it from a health perspective, is it healthy or is it non-healthy. I think that true, like, jurisdiction has to be given back to the First Nations people. As a person that's from here, I see the Canadian government giving away this country. They're – it's up for sale. It's up for immigrants who have money. Any company, you can be bought by foreign interests. So to me it seems that the Canadian government is not practicing due diligence.[80]

The inquiry ends its day hearing that people are continuing to "disappear" on Vancouver's Downtown East Side and that "aboriginal children are still being removed by the social welfare system at rates in some cases exceeding what they were during the '60s too." As Hauck concludes, "it's a terrible, terrible thing."[81]

A problem is defined, wrapped, and sealed as a particular kind of problem, with specific solutions: the problem of homeless chronic alcoholics and the problem of societal attitudes to alcoholism. Terrible silences remain. They are only penetrated at inopportune moments, as jokes, anecdotes, and passionate asides, but these moments enable us to trace what has been declared out of bounds: dispossession, sexual and physical abuse in residential schools, disappearing Indigenous people and disappearing Indigenous children, raping, pillaging, and a culture of exploitation. Settlement's secret seeps out at the inquiry, disturbing the order of the proceedings. What happens to such moments at the end of the day, when "rough attempts at a circle" are concluded?

If nothing else, Indigeneity, in the form of cultural difference and not in the form of oppression, must be emphasized. Commissioner Davies makes clear that he has indeed paid attention to Aboriginal peoples.[82] He decorates his final report with eagle feathers in the margins, an inadvertently appropriate gesture of inclusion, given that the final recommendations relegate Aboriginality to the periphery. Commissioner Davies clearly paid attention to witnesses who described the ineffectiveness of contemporary approaches to homeless chronic alcoholics, and he recommends that there should be a medical rather than a police approach to the problem.[83] Accepting the proposal that services should emphasize a harm reduction approach and that housing is a key component of any strategy, Davies also insists that services should be culturally sensitive. Recognizing the urgency of the problem, he suggests that an ombudsperson be appointed who could oversee and coordinate the activities of various agencies. In the recommendations addressing police practices, Davies is clear that the police should not continue to investigate themselves, and he proposes a number of measures to ensure better police accountability.[84] Through these recommendations, the commissioner indicates that he was troubled by what he heard about the treatment Frank Paul received, and that he was deeply critical of the police and administrative practices which led to Paul's death going unnoticed. Commissioner Davies was not prepared to suture over what happened to Frank Paul. Where does Aboriginality go in this account? Put more specifically, where does the banality or ubiquity of the dehumanization of Indigenous people go? Never expressly named, Indigenous people simply remain on record as individually damaged people with whom the state must take special care, exercising cultural sensitivity. Settlers remain, for the most part, compassionate. Confronted with the intractable problem of alcohol addiction, for which the inquiry provides images, statistics, and "thick" description, settler society must simply dedicate itself anew to improvement.

Conclusion: The Compassionate State

Observing that many people could not understand why the two police officers, Sanderson and Instant, should be held responsible for Frank Paul's death when he was dying anyway and when Aboriginal people are not like everybody else, Steven Kelliher suggests that Aboriginal people are even "outside the concept of racism."[85] He shares with Denise Ferreira da Silva the idea that the racialized body is so completely beyond humanity that racism is not so much a question of treating some groups worse than others but of completely failing to recognize the humanity of the Other.[86] Kelliher recalls how puzzled his peers were that he would pursue accountability for Frank Paul's death. "You have quintessential Canadian people," Kelliher reflects, "whose racism is so deep and so perfectly melded with their person that it's not identifiable."[87] The responses to Frank Paul by professionals testifying at the inquiry seem to confirm Kelliher's observations. Few could see the man who was Frank Paul, even as they minutely examined his broken body and sometimes exhibited a charitable impulse. Yet unease persisted. Witnesses tried hard to assume a neutrality, one that would permit them to deny Frank Paul's Indigeneity and, most especially, to deny its social meaning, namely that Indigenous people are known to encounter a considerable and sometimes lethal police brutality and professional indifference. The inquiry both produced and colluded with the unspeakability of racism and colonialism, confining Indigenous people to moments of ceremony and to spaces of informality where their voices competed with experts, experts who carefully spoke not of racism or colonialism but of alcoholism. The sense that so many had of Frank Paul, that he was a man without mind, reduced to body and therefore outside of their ethical world, remained undisturbed.

Indigenous insistence that the inquiry examine whether or not Frank Paul was murdered is consistently displaced through the idea that Frank Paul was first and foremost a disease. Frank Paul's transformation from a dispossessed Indigenous man to the disease of alcoholism is a useful one for the settler state. Through a focus on a hard-to-serve population, the settler state is constituted as generous. It exhibits the compassionate imperialism Ann Stoler describes in her analysis of the colonial archive.[88] As a technology of governance, the inquiry contributes to the management of Indigenous peoples as a collection of individuals, a sick, dysfunctional population, rather than a dispossessed collective against whom violence is authorized. This individualizing and medicalizing move has long been central to settler colonial societies because it confirms that Indigenous peoples are simply people unable to progress from the state of nature. Inquiries confirm, in this way, who are the legitimate owners of the land and who are simply the pre-modern remnants with which a modern society must deal. Determining how this colonial legal agenda can be interrupted is not easy, although Indigenous witnesses and organizations consistently try. The politics of recognition are fraught, as Elizabeth Povinelli shows in her exploration of Australian liberal multiculturalism. The state recognizes Indigenous Australians only insofar as they fit the category of multicultural difference, a requirement that successfully preempts Indigenous land claims, even as it holds Indigenous people to state-defined standards of authentic traditional culture.[89] The price of recognition in an inquiry is often too high, yet it is difficult to see how it would otherwise be possible to uncover and name colonial violence.

In Simpson's words, sovereignty is "the uncitable thing," and it must remain secret because it calls up the illegitimacy of the settler state. What was supposed to be settled is not settled, and what has been declared uncitable nevertheless erupts. It is hard work to keep the lid on race and colonialism. Indigeneity "fundamentally interrupts what is received, what is ordered, what is supposed to be settled."[90] A ninety-three-year-old elder warns about improvement as a process that ends in death. Indigeneity also disturbs. Former coroners and Crown attorneys sputter about being accused of racism. The settler state has need of scholars whose science enables them to paper over these moments with theories of harm reduction and medical approaches to alcoholics, useful in their own right but limited if they do not confront the full meaning of Indigeneity. Science bolsters the case for a pathological Indigenous inability to become modern. There are gestures of inclusion: prayers are said, and the medicine wheel and circles remind everyone that the settler state is just and respectful of cultural difference.[91] But not for long are we permitted to wonder how it comes to be that a man who was very intoxicated, ill, and could not walk was left in an alley on a cold night. We are not permitted to hear why this event was of so little concern to anyone. The recommendations for change cannot then come, as Audra Simpson wishes, with "a radically different historical consciousness, one that is deeply cognizant of the means of its own societal production so that it may afford Indigeneity (and the conditions of many others) a robust present as well as a vigorous, variegated past and future."[92]

Chapter Three

The Body as Frontier

I sure wish you could give us our land back.

Chief Nancy Sandy to Coroner S.A. Cloverdale at the Coroner's Inquest into the Death of Paul Alphonse[1]

The moral landscape of the Frontier Myth is divided by significant borders, of which the wilderness/civilization, Indian/White border is the most basic.

Richard Slotkin, *Gunfighter Nation*[2]

Introduction

On 19 April 2000, Paul Alphonse, a sixty-seven-year-old Secwepemc (Shuswap) man of Sugar Cane Reserve, Williams Lake Indian Band,[3] British Columbia, died in hospital while in police custody. Although the hospital records state that Alphonse died of pneumonia and alcohol withdrawal, a pathologist concluded that a significant contributing factor to his death was that he had been stomped on so hard there was a boot print on his chest and several ribs were broken. The pathologist believed the stomping had probably occurred just prior to Alphonse's arrest and may not have been due to the actions of the police. The family of Paul Alphonse, who had tried to locate him and finally found him in the hospital shortly before he died, alleged police brutality. They felt that prior to his arrest, Alphonse had not shown signs of the pain that normally accompanies broken ribs. Untypically for an inquest, the jury concluded that Alphonse's death had been a homicide. Alphonse had been killed by "blunt force trauma" and pneumonia, but the jury was unable to establish a connection between police actions (specifically booking officer Constable Bob Irwin's treatment of Alphonse) and Alphonse's death. The Alphonse inquest offers an opportunity to explore the contemporary relationship between Indigenous people and Canadian society, and, significantly, how law operates as a site for managing that relationship. I propose to consider the boot print on Alphonse's chest and its significance at the inquest in these two different ways. First, although it cannot be traced to the boot of Constable Bob Irwin, we can examine the boot print as an event illustrating Indigenous/police relations in Williams Lake, both the specific relation between Alphonse and Irwin, and the wider relations between Indigenous people and the police. I characterize these relations as frontier relationships of regular, violent contact. Second, the response to the boot print at the inquest sheds light on how, through the idea of Indigenous difference read as nature, law is a site for obscuring the violence in Indigenous people's lives and for rendering Indigenous peoples as too abject to be owners of the land.

In the first of a trilogy of books exploring the myth of the frontier in American literary fiction and popular culture, Richard Slotkin writes:

> The Myth of the Frontier is our oldest and most characteristic myth, expressed in a body of literature, folklore, ritual, historiography, and polemics produced over a period of three centuries. According to this myth-historiography, the conquest of the wilderness and the subjugation or displacement of the Native Americans who originally inhabited it have been the means to our achievement of a national identity, a democratic polity, an ever-expanding economy, and a phenomenally dynamic and "progressive" civilization.[4]

The American subject of the frontier (both the historical place and the mythic representation) comes to know himself (women have their own version of this) through violence, understanding the encounter with Native Americans (and later other racialized groups, both domestic and international) as a savage war through which an American civilization comes into being. The savage war is a war of extermination. It is only through vanquishing Indians that the American subject can come into being. Slotkin is at pains to point out that while such violence is not peculiar to the history of the Americas, what is unique is the mythic significance assigned to it: "Although the Indian and the Wilderness are the settler's enemy, they also provide him with the new consciousness through which he will transform the world."[5] Regeneration through violence, Slotkin's phrase for the process through which Americans become national subjects, requires that the American must regularly cross the border into "Indian country," since the encounter with Indians is the means through which the settler comes to know himself.[6] Indian country is both a place and a body, as I have argued elsewhere, and it is through these violent journeys into personhood that settlers become owners, both materially and psychically.[7]

In part one, I suggest that for the police, as for other settlers, the Indigenous body is the frontier, the site on which a savage war is fought. Considered as bestial, close to nature, and a threat, the Indigenous body must be violated if the border between wilderness and civilization is to be maintained. In part two, I show that these frontier relations persist in the law. They are evident in how Indigenous witnesses are treated, and most of all in how violence against Indigenous people is defended as necessary. It is difficult to contest frontier logic, although Indigenous counsel, leaders, and family persistently try to do so. Inquests, with their focus on individual pathology and insistence on taking events out of historical context, make it difficult for Indigenous peoples to interrupt the narrative of their dysfunction and to put on record the historical relations of settler colonialism. I conclude that the Indigenous body remains the frontier as long as the material relations of settler colonialism persist. In the province of British Columbia, where Paul Alphonse died, there continues to be heated conflict over land and resources, struggles both in courts and outside, and the province continues to resist acknowledgment of past wrongs. If acknowledgment of colonialism is strenuously resisted, the idea that it is ongoing is even more so, although its processes are visible for anyone who cares to look.[8]

Part One. The Boot Print

The story of the boot print on Paul Alphonse's chest comes to an abrupt and disquieting end at the inquest. By the time of the second set of inquest proceedings in March 2002, after hearing the evidence in the fall of 2001 that the print on Alphonse's chest did not match Constable Irwin's boot, Paul Alphonse's niece, Kristy Palmantier, asked that the pathologist examine Paul Alphonse's own boot. Recalling the clear purple boot print she saw on her uncle's body at the hospital and her thought, "Who could do something like that?" and why, Palmantier offered a theory:

> And you know – and they ruled out the cops' round-toed boots and I said if they were taking Paul's boots and if that constable was angry, you know, he could have – without even thinking, he could have just took that boot that he took off and just banged it there on Paul's side, on his ribs while he was down. Could have done that so easy. That's – you know, it doesn't take 10 seconds to do something like that, and that's – that's what I thought and that's why I asked that you take a look at my Uncle Paul's boots.[9]

As she guessed, the boot print on her uncle's chest matched his own boot. Dr Jennifer Rice, the pathologist at the inquest, opined, however, that wielding the boot as a weapon, as suggested in Kristy Palmantier's theory, simply wouldn't produce the kind of injury sustained by Paul Alphonse, especially not through a layer of clothes. Dr Rice stated categorically: "This to me is a stomp. It is not somebody wielding the boot, as they might, say, a baseball bat."[10] The possibility that the boot's owner could have been Lee Alphonse, a nephew of Paul Alphonse who reportedly had had a quarrel with his uncle on the morning of 11 April, also led nowhere, since Lee Alphonse did not wear boots and could not be shown conclusively to have had a violent encounter with his uncle. Since Paul Alphonse could not have stomped on himself (although as a chronic alcoholic, the role he played in his own death became the main line of inquiry pursued at the inquest, something I take up in chapter four), there remained only the sinister possibility that someone deliberately stomped on Alphonse while wearing his own boot. The matter of who stomped on Alphonse is startlingly peripheral throughout the inquest. The goals of the inquest were to determine the cause of death, to consider what might prevent such deaths in the future, and finally, to satisfy the community that the death was not "overlooked, concealed, or ignored."[11] As the coroner reminded the jury, the inquest was not a trial. If the matter of the boot print was considered resolved once it was established that the boot in question was not Constable Irwin's, there remained, however, other sources of violence, namely the broader issues of how Alphonse was treated by police, including Irwin.

The Colonial World: A World Divided into Compartments

As Frantz Fanon has shown, the colonial world is a Manichean world, a world divided into compartments.[12] In *Wretched of the Earth*, Fanon points to the geographical layout of the colonial world to track its lines of force. Reminding us of the existence of native quarters and European quarters, schools for natives and schools for Europeans, the "well-fed" settlers' town and the "hungry" native's town that is a town "on its knees," Fanon noted that the dividing line between the two worlds was the policeman and the soldier. The "world cut into two" reveals the "lines of force" that create it. It is a world inhabited by "two different species":

> The originality of the colonial context is that economic reality, inequality, and the immense difference of ways of life never come to mask the human realities … [W]hat parcels out the world is to begin with the fact of belonging to or not belonging to a given race, a given species.[13]

As Fanon concluded, "The cause is the consequence; you are rich because you are white, you are white because you are rich."[14] The resolute spatialized hierarchy of the colonial world, the policing required to maintain its boundaries, and the habits of domination visible in the everyday treatment of the conquered population are all evidenced in police/Indigenous relations in Williams Lake. As Slotkin reminds us, the settler colonial world is one in which frontier men confront wilderness. The bodies of Indians become the site at which civilization must win over savagery.

It was acknowledged at the inquest that Alphonse was a member of a very specific group of elderly alcoholic men and women of the Indigenous nations of the Cariboo Chilcoten (Shuswap, Carrier, and Chilcotin), who were the last generation to attend residential school. Alphonse and his contemporaries were known locally as the "troopers," described officially as "a population described as displaced by society, phased out of employment by technology, and negatively affected by residential school and similar historical events."[15] The vagueness of the official description does not begin to reference the violence of colonial dispossession (the seizure of lands, the starving of communities, the confinement of Indigenous children to schools where they were frequently sexually assaulted and forcefully deprived of their culture and language, the violent policing of the boundaries of the settlers' town, and so on).

Some of the troopers walk the nine kilometres from the reserve into town daily, drinking in Boitanio Park (reportedly the site of an old Secwepec graveyard), near to the mall and the picnic table under which Constable Irwin found Alphonse. The inquest reveals the minutiae of how Indigenous bodies are inscribed in the present colonial order. Marked as different, a difference that is in essence a lower level of humanity, a species at an earlier, pre-modern stage of development, Indigenous bodies become violable as damaged bodies which can only be managed through force. It is possible to kick, punch, and drag Indigenous bodies with impunity, depositing them in cells with cold concrete floors; these are bodies for which the normal rules do not apply, a distinction so built into everyday routines that it often goes unremarked upon. Violence is not visible when it is meted out to bodies whose difference means that they can and, in fact, must be violated (if order is to be preserved).

The policeman, as agent of the state and as settler, encounters Indigenous bodies as bodies through which his own legitimacy is secured. It is likely that Constable Bob Irwin experienced his encounter with Paul Alphonse as one between two different species, to use Fanon's words, in as literal a way as possible. For Irwin, Alphonse was a person one neither touched nor communicated with, at least not in the normal way. Their encounter began in perhaps the most classic way encounters between Indigenous peoples and the police begin in the urban setting – with a phone call from a resident or business owner complaining of an Indigenous person's behaviour and the subsequent arrest of the Indigenous person for drunkenness. On 11 April 2000, a female employee of the grocery store Overwaitea telephoned the RCMP detachment and complained that a man was lying drunk and apparently passed out under a picnic table in front of the store. Constable Irwin was dispatched to the scene to undertake what he described as something he had done hundreds of times in his career, which was "to deal with impaired people."[16] If the phrase "impaired people" is a racially neutral one, Irwin's statement reveals that he understood his encounter with Paul Alphonse more specifically. Irwin described how he knew Paul Alphonse:

> Q Have you had any dealings before or were you familiar with him ah.
>
> A I know him as a, as a trooper and as a, as a frequent flyer. Like, we deal with him all the time but personally or, no. I don't remember him any more or any less than any of the others. I just knew him to see him around.[17]

Irwin knew the man he found lying underneath the picnic table in front of the grocery store as like "the others," the troopers, an otherwise undifferentiated group of Indigenous individuals routinely arrested for being drunk in the Boitanio Park area.[18] Alphonse had been arrested for being drunk in a public place more than seventy times.[19] Interested in establishing how Constable Irwin saw Alphonse, counsel for the band asked if Irwin also knew that the troopers were once the cowboys who built the ranches and farms around Williams Lake. Irwin replied that he did know, but added that he saw the troopers as people nobody wanted to bother with. He did not know that Alphonse had "a large and caring family" and a home on Sugar Cane Reserve, that he suffered from arthritis and osteoporosis, and that he was sixty-seven years old, facts put to him by counsel for the family.[20]

For Irwin, Alphonse was someone who required specific policing strategies, someone, that is, who could not respond to verbal communications. As Irwin told Corporal Holmes, the investigating officer, he first called to Alphonse, and when he received no response, took Alphonse's baseball cap and went back to the truck with it. As he explained, "A lot of times if you take ah take their hats or whatever, one of their effects and you put it in the back of the, the vehicle, they want their kit. You know, they want their, they want their hat so they'll comply."[21] Alphonse belonged to a group that had to be baited,[22] as elementally as dangling a worm before a fish. When Alphonse did not respond to the bait, Irwin was obliged to drag him out from under the table, grabbing him by the pant leg, taking hold of his arm and shoulder, and walking him over to the truck. (For Alphonse, this was the second time in two days that he was rounded up and taken to the drunk tank.) Irwin did not recall using his feet to nudge Alphonse, as a few witnesses attested, but conceded that he would certainly have done so in similar situations in the past. It is not clear if Alphonse resisted Irwin, or else found it difficult to walk. He stopped every few steps on the journey to the truck, in Irwin's words "sorta stuttering, not stuttering but sorta half kind of stopping every few steps."[23] For all his incapacity, once at the door of the truck, in Irwin's account, Alphonse was apparently able to lift himself up on to the back seat of the truck and bring a leg up to kick Irwin in the chest. The kick did not hurt. It only "made a contact mark" on Irwin's body "armor." Irwin related that he then pushed Alphonse into the truck, roughly enough that he fell into it and landed on the floor of the vehicle.

At the station, Irwin began to book Alphonse while other police officers and guards (who knew Alphonse) stood outside in the guard room. Constable Sullivan stood on one side of the booking desk, while Irwin stood on the other side. This is when an "altercation" occurred. In Irwin's words:

> He then ah tried to ah mule kick me in the testicles. I was standing right beside, or behind him and I could ah feel it coming up so I blocked his ah, blocked his kick and I trapped the leg between my knees and my legs with my legs and at that time I slapped him along, it'd be his right side with my right hand ah a couple of times. I told him to quit fuckin' around. Then I ah pinned him up against the ah pushed him up against the wall, pinned him against the wall with my left hand and reached down and grabbed his boot still between my legs and ah pulled it off. As I pulled it off, his ah right leg, which he tried to kick me with, went forward and then he turned counter clockwise and fell down. When he fell down, I could hear ah a sort of a "counk" sound which I have become familiar with over the years and it's a sound of ah bone ah striking concrete. I ah checked his eyes, and his eyes, opened his eyelids up and his eyes had rolled right back. Len then called the ah the paramedics and ah we just ah watched him and monitored him until the paramedics came.[24]

Irwin did not elaborate why Alphonse had to be slapped twice and ordered to behave. The inquest does not explore the feasibility of the idea that in pulling off Alphonse's boot, Irwin would also have had an opportunity to use it as a weapon, as suggested by Alphonse's niece, Kristy Palmantier. At the inquest, Irwin's fellow officers, Sullivan and MacMillan, who both knew Alphonse, said that in their own experience Alphonse posed no threat, especially given that he was a "very" small-statured man.[25] Steadfastly maintaining, nonetheless, that Irwin "behaved like a real gentleman," Corporal Sullivan speculated that perhaps the slap he saw was Irwin responding instinctively to Alphonse's slapping him.[26] For his part, when asked whether he saw disciplining and punishing prisoners as part of his job, Irwin replied in the negative, insisting that the slaps were merely his response to Alphonse's kick.[27] A startled response to a kick or an angry disciplining? It is not possible to establish which. If the latter, where might this impulse to discipline originate? Victoria Freeman speculates that her own colonial ancestors got into the habit of whipping Aboriginal peoples in residential schools because they themselves knew this kind of harsh discipline as poor people in Ireland.[28] Freeman does not explore whipping as a colonial technology of rule, the disciplining through practices of violence of those who are presumed to understand nothing but brute force. As historian Anna Haebich observes in the context of Australian settler colonialism:

> The power of wounding the body was well understood by Australian colonists familiar with the practice of breaking the human spirit and branding

> wrongdoers as outcasts at the end of a lash. It was a tragic irony that Western notions of savagery, difference and white superiority drove many to impart "civilization" to Aboriginal people in the same way.[29]

If, as Chief Nancy Sandy believed, both the RCMP and the white people of Williams Lake don't know the history of the troopers and see them only as dirty, alcoholic, street people and not as human beings, "useless people," in her words, then the chances of the slap as discipline increases.[30] Irwin did not recollect how hard he hit Alphonse, but felt sure that it was not hard. He insisted that Alphonse, much shorter than he was and intoxicated, was nevertheless able to kick backwards and to reach Irwin's testicles, an act that counsel for the family tried to suggest was physically impossible.[31] A video camera that would normally record the booking process was obstructed due to construction, so no visual records exist to confirm Irwin's account.[32] It was not established whether Irwin was ever alone with Alphonse in the booking room, and he could not remember if he had removed Alphonse's clothes, thus leaving a naked upper body upon which a boot would have left an imprint.[33]

If the encounter described by Constable Irwin in his statement has aspects of the mundane about it, notably the physical difficulty involved in getting a severely intoxicated man out from under a picnic table, attempting to get his boots off while booking him, and then attempting to get him back to the station from the hospital while, presumably, he remains somewhat belligerent, there are also some ominous or troubling aspects to the picture that only emerge if we consider the size, age, physical capacities, and histories of the individuals involved. Paul Alphonse was a short, 120 pound, sixty-seven-year-old man, someone with a reputation in most quarters for being quiet and gentle, although police descriptions suggest Alphonse could be belligerent. Constable Irwin thought Alphonse was in his fifties, twenty pounds heavier than he actually was, and slightly taller, at five feet, five inches. Irwin was Alphonse's physical opposite, a martial arts expert in Hap Quon Do (a Korean martial art characterized by kicking), who was said to be over six feet tall, 240 pounds, "hefty," and powerful (in the eyes of several witnesses), a man who had considerable experience arresting and booking intoxicated persons, and specifically, troopers. One witness to the arrest, a cabdriver, described Irwin as "large, bald and wearing black gloves."[34]

Irwin's relationship to Paul Alphonse's body, a body that he prods with a foot, baits, pushes, slaps, drags, and shoves, establishes Alphonse as outside the sphere of humanity that is Irwin's. It is not as though Alphonse is a dirty dog lying in Irwin's (or the grocery store's) way, since the kicking of dogs is not regarded as a civil act. Alphonse can be slapped, prodded, and dragged with impunity; this is simply how one deals with the troopers. The encounter reduces Alphonse to a thing, depriving him of bodily integrity, and, simultaneously, it enlarges Irwin to the status of owner of public space, the man appointed to clear public space of its unsightly objects. Alphonse is not passive in this encounter. He resists Irwin, stopping often on the way to the police van, turning his face away from Irwin at the hospital, possibly kicking Irwin. For all the distance it establishes between two bodies, the policing encounter is nevertheless an intimate one, providing Irwin with a daily sense of self (and Alphonse with his abjection). Discussing Fanon, Radhika Mohanram notes that if "the corporeal/bodily ego provides perspective for the white man," the Black man "functions to grant perspective to the white man."[35] Reduced to body, indeed the bestial body, both in representation and through material practices, the Black body is the "constitutive condition, enabling Western epistemology as well as Western ontology."[36] Other police officers, less violent in their responses, nonetheless preserve the circle of humanity from which Alphonse is excluded through the idea that Alphonse is culturally different and from the reserve. Alphonse is always experienced as Other, as outside. He is understood as culturally different, a type of human who does not speak and/or is not easily understood. Each police officer who testifies at the inquest confirms that Alphonse was someone one did not treat normally.

The Treatment of Witnesses

The relationship between the Indigenous community and the police was a strained and politically charged one. On 18 April 2000, a few hours before Alphonse died, after having observed the bright purple boot print on her uncle's chest, Kristy Palmantier went to the RCMP detachment with Chief Nancy Sandy and Gregory and Hazel Alphonse, Alphonse's brother and sister-in-law. A police record of the meeting notes that Chief Sandy spoke about members of the RCMP being insensitive to the troopers and to other members of the Williams Lake Indian Band. Sandy is also noted to have mentioned reports of police brutality and killings of Aboriginal peoples elsewhere, including "the Chilcotin Enquiry [*sic*] and the Saskatchewan investigation with street people left in the cold and of a mistrust that the police do not investigate these matters thoroughly."[37] Clearly, the history of Indigenous police relations intruded at the outset, but it did so in an RCMP investigation report as the opinion of a chief who was clearly characterized as unreasonably confrontational.

Although the police steadfastly maintained there was no particular history of tensions between the police and the Indigenous community in Williams Lake, it was nevertheless clear that for the troopers police power loomed large. Witnesses recanted or left town. In addition, many were unable to remember or were confused. The police made no accommodations for the population they already knew to have specific needs, and they easily intimidated witnesses. The family informed the police that a number of street-involved people had reported Alphonse had been kicked around by the arresting officer. They provided the names of Nora Tenale, Joey Haines, and Lily Michel. An investigation into the family's complaint began the following day when a police team arrived, including members of the Kamloops Special Crimes Unit, and met at the detachment to discuss the investigation. Soon after, the interviews of witnesses began, with the RCMP cruising the area around Boitanio Park, the area the troopers frequented. As the RCMP investigation report records:

> On 00.04.19 at 1823 Hrs, Nora Tenale was located by Cst Tucker and Cst Krebs and returned to the detachment to provide a KGB audio/video recorded statement. Nora did not display any signs of intoxication and provided a response to all questions.[38]

Nora Tenale was first given a lengthy and formal statement, known as the KGB warning, emphasizing that her statement was considered to be made under oath and that it was a criminal offence to make a false statement. Tenale was informed that she could be prosecuted for lying to the police.[39] The officer, Constable Krebs, seemed to guess at the effect of his ominous and legal-sounding words, because he announced to Tenale, "I don't mean to scare you," and "All I want is the truth." In her statement, Tenale mainly replied to his questions with "Uh hum." She nevertheless stuck to her story about seeing Irwin treat Alphonse roughly: "I just was sitting on that bench and seen him getting throwed in the cop car and then I seen the cop kick him a couple of times, to kick his legs in the car I guess."[40] When asked if the kick was a hard one, she said yes and described that she saw Alphonse falling back on the seat. "Paulsey" shouldn't have been treated that way, Tenale stated. When asked how this arrest was different to any other she had seen, Tenale answered, "I don't know, the way he was handled, I guess, 'cause he's an old man to be pushed over and kicked, so that was unusual than any other ones I seen."[41] Tenale's statement is the only one that suggests the possible use of excessive force, but even her account was less certain than the one she initially gave to Kristy Palmantier.[42] Joey Haines, contacted in Boitanio Park at 4 p.m. on 19 April said that he didn't see the arrest. Lily Michel, interviewed the same night, described an arrest in which Alphonse was kicked, but she was insistent that the arrest she witnessed was not in front of the Overwaitea grocery store but instead near the chain-link fence at the entrance to the park. As Sergeant McIntosh reported to Kristy Palmantier on 25 April, all three witnesses who were drinking with Paul Alphonse on 11 April recanted the story she had presumably heard, an outcome Palmantier felt was because the witnesses were afraid of the police.[43]

The band, acting with the family, felt that difficulties arose (especially but not limited to the ominous-sounding KGB warning) whenever the police attempted to interview the troopers without providing them with support.[44] Asked to do so by the band, a Native court worker and a victims' assistance worker began to contact witnesses to offer support. Chief Sandy recalled that the police were angry about what they perceived to be interference in an investigation, a hostility they carried into the inquest itself.[45] Indeed, the investigation report confirms that when Constable Mike Lesage found Lily Michel in the park behind Boitanio Mall, he felt that she was being "interviewed" by the two support workers, and he reported this to Constable Krebs. The two workers then accompanied Michel to the police station, where they stayed outside the detachment as she was being interviewed. They were not allowed to go into the interview room. At the inquest, Corporal Krebs (who was a constable at the time of the investigation) confirmed he did not feel that the troopers or other Indigenous witnesses needed any kind of special support, or that they might have had difficulties understanding him. Except for one witness, he did not see evidence that the troopers were afraid of the police. In fact, Krebs was staunchly opposed to providing support, believing he could not obtain an untainted interview if support workers were present. He felt that the band was trying to influence the investigation.

Unwilling to grant that there might be any specific needs, the police used their power to the fullest during the investigation. Corporal Krebs described how he picked up two witnesses, Clara and Etienne Bob, whom he saw hitchhiking. In an unmarked car and out of uniform, Krebs was not sure whether Clara Bob recognized him from when he had interviewed her earlier. He was also unsure if he had conveyed his intention to transport the two to the station after they sat down in his car. Confident of his police techniques and cross-cultural knowledge (he felt, for example, that Asians were better at deception than others), but unaware of the Cariboo-Chilcotin Justice Inquiry which detailed cases of police brutality, Krebs remained adamant at the inquest that he had conducted an investigation in which witnesses were neither intimidated nor tricked into being interviewed.[46] As with Irwin, Krebs displayed a confidence in his authority to deal with Indigenous witnesses as he deemed fit, notwithstanding unmarked police cars, non-English speakers, and a people with a history of police brutality.

Trust was definitely not in evidence as the investigation proceeded. Indigenous witnesses reported that they felt harassed by the police, who told them to leave town. Under these conditions, some refused to talk altogether. Accounts changed from one moment to another. Although Native court worker Amy Sandy wrote in her notes that a witness who worked for the Nenquanyi Treatment Centre had seen the arrest and was disturbed by it, as were two other individuals from the centre, little of their disquiet survived in their official statements. Douglas Reiling of the treatment centre told police he saw Irwin use his foot to nudge Alphonse, but that there was no excessive force.[47] His client confirmed that she too saw Irwin use his foot, but indicated she felt nervous about the KGB warning and about talking to the police.[48] The RCMP's investigation report itself describes at least two fearful witnesses. Albert Lacroix, who was visiting a friend in Alphonse's room at the hospital, heard Alphonse say that he got beat up for his money and that he didn't know who was responsible. Lacroix refused to go to the station to give his statement. He provided a recorded statement though the police cruiser window, fearing that if he got in the vehicle he would be taken off to jail.[49] Louie Billy, who shared a room with Paul Alphonse at the hospital, was very reluctant to talk to police, and the investigation report notes that he said Chief Sandy had advised him not to talk to police without the band. Billy remembered that Alphonse said he was beat up by the cops, something Alphonse also told the doctors and anyone else who would listen. Loraine Toby, who was visiting Louie, told Chief Sandy she heard Alphonse repeating to anyone who walked by that the cops beat him up. Sandy alerted McIntosh to this information in writing at Alphonse's funeral. On 16 June, Toby did not show up for her interview with the police. Etienne Bob, who was nearly blind and had to be escorted to the station by Clara Bob in Kreb's car, said that he saw nothing. Clara Bob, who had been drinking with Paul Alphonse earlier on the day he was arrested, could not recall the exact date of the arrest or the drinking incident. Although she denied being violent herself, Clara Bob's credibility was low since Sarah Stump, who ran a shelter for the troopers, told police that Clara Bob herself had been aggressive in the past and had beaten up both Alphonse and Etienne Bob before.

The encounter between a police officer and an Indigenous person who is being picked up and arrested for drunkenness in a public place is one that is overdetermined by colonial histories involving both the regulation of the movements of Indigenous peoples and the tremendous damage that alcohol has wreaked in Indigenous communities.[50] Australian scholar Mary Edmunds insightfully describes its significance, starting with what brings each party to the encounter.[51] Dispossessed and then divested of control over their own economic, political, and social life, Aboriginal peoples are never incorporated into settler society as full and equal members. Rather, they are incorporated as conquered peoples, under surveillance. In Roebourne, Australia, the site of Edmunds' study, Aboriginal peoples, first dispossessed and then shut out of pastoral (ranching) and mining activities, find themselves drawn into a web of state relations around funding and surveillance. The white town becomes for them a total institution, a space in which they enter, not as citizens, but as inmates, in the sense that Aboriginal bodies become highly visible bodies on which normalcy must be inscribed. The police act as the warders or guardians of the settlers' social order; they are "frontline agents, not just of law and order, but of white domination."[52] The public nature of Indigenous life, such as drinking in parks, itself an outcome of dispossession and colonization, becomes punishable in law. Edmunds points out that although we can read drinking in parks as a defiant, if temporary, re-appropriation of the land, the end result is the same as if there had been no intent of resistance: "Day after day, people drink there. And day after day, the police arrest them, lock them up, and charge them."[53] The park operates as a frontier, "a place of confrontation between two values and acceptable practices, two histories that have interlocked so often at points that underline the dependence of one group on the benevolence, the permission, formal or informal, of the other."[54]

The park Mary Edmunds describes as operating like a frontier, a description that fits Boitanio Park where the troopers go to drink, is also usefully understood as a space of exception, a place where law operates as a force of non-law. Anna Secor, drawing on the work of Pasquale Pasquino (who in turn follows Foucault), makes the important point that such spaces, which are also the bodies of the marginalized, are the outer limits of state power.[55] These spaces and bodies are points of the greatest disorder, that is to say, points that contest the state's official story of the social contract merely by their existence but also by open acts of resistance. Summing up Pasquino and writing on Kurdish migrants in Istanbul, Secor writes:

> Like Benjamin, Pasquino situates police at the limits of existing order. The police operate to guarantee the aims that the legal system fails to achieve, to exert control and to hold territory at the outer limits of state power. This is the zone of indistinction that the poor and the marginal find themselves inhabiting *everywhere and anywhere* [in the city of Istanbul] … Within this territory and its fantasy, its gathering thunder-heads of violence and half-glimpsed topography, it is impossible to tell if the law is being broken or upheld, whether chaos or the normal order reigns, whether we are outside, within, or below the police station.[56]

Applying Secor's points, Indigenous spaces and bodies can be seen as territorial challenges, a material as much as a symbolic provocation that is answered by acts of violence. The park, and the space that is the Indigenous body itself, are the outer limits, and when policing actions in these spaces come under scrutiny at the inquest, it is impossible to establish what is legal and what is not. What, after all, is the limit in spaces of exception? In the void created by the central paradox of the outer limits, that it is a place neither inside nor outside the law, the idea of Indigenous difference rushes in to give sanction to the theft of land and to the violence required to do so.

Part Two. Frontier Justice

At the Alphonse inquest, police and thus state power is obscured, first of all, when it proves difficult to enter on record Irwin's professional history with Indigenous people. Sergeant Forgues, who headed the police investigation, confirmed that he did not examine Irwin's service record in order to determine whether or not there had been other complaints of excessive force because he wished to keep an open mind. Acknowledging that in other investigations he would routinely check into the records of suspects, Forgues noted illogically that he had no reason to check Irwin's record as he had failed to uncover any evidence that Constable Irwin was responsible for the assault on Alphonse.[57] Trying and failing to have Irwin answer questions as to whether he had previously been the subject of a complaint, counsel for the band was only allowed to ask whether Irwin had been disciplined for excessive force, to which he replied no.[58] The matter of Irwin's record was definitely closed when Kristy Palmantier, Paul Alphonse's niece, told the inquest that even white people were scared of Irwin in Williams Lake, and the coroner instructed the jury to disregard the comment because it had no basis in fact.[59] (We might speculate here whether Palmantier's comment was an alternate way to get Irwin's reputation on the record.)

If Irwin appeared to occupy an exalted place in law, Indigenous people remained confined to the space of their difference, the space Denise Ferreira da Silva has aptly called "the other side of universality."[60] They never transcend their particularity. They entered the inquest proceedings as less than rational, outsiders to law, trapped forever on the wilderness side of the border in the frontier myth. The dynamics apparent during the investigation when police asserted their power over Indigenous people bore fruit during the inquest, and some Indigenous witnesses failed to appear. Those who did were constrained by the English-speaking, adversarial tone of a quasi-judicial process.[61] Witnesses remained fearful, vulnerable, and confused, and little of what they had to say made it intact into the inquest proceedings. Since no effort was made to accommodate them, key witnesses such as Lily Michel, who had been drinking with Alphonse shortly before his arrest, appeared confused when they testified. Michel's difficulties remembering events, combined with her language difficulties, worked to undermine her testimony. She said she could understand the proceedings in English providing that simple words were used. She maintained she saw Alphonse being arrested on 14 April, a date when he would have been in hospital. From this moment of confusion, little else could be done with her testimony that she saw the police being rough with Alphonse.[62] Michel was also unable to hear easily on the stand. The entire process proved too much for her, and she did not have the strength to continue her testimony beyond a few minutes.[63] Similarly, Clara Bob repeatedly answered that she did not recall details surrounding the last time she saw Alphonse, even though her statement noted otherwise. Invited several times by RCMP counsel, who perhaps knew that Bob was illiterate, to review her statement, Clara Bob refused, undermining her credibility.[64] Attempting damage control, counsel for the band, Jean Teillet, suggested that Clara Bob did not intend to contradict herself but was simply being asked overly long questions, which confused her.

She urged the coroner to insist upon simpler language, something that the jury agreed with in their recommendations.[65]

Contesting Difference

Seeking to contest the individualizing and pathologizing of Paul Alphonse's life, and in light of difficulties with the troopers, the band and the family relied on witnesses who were not troopers to introduce details about both the historical and the contemporary context. Since these witnesses worked on behalf of Indigenous peoples and were themselves Indigenous, their own credibility may have been undermined in a forum where the expert is understood as someone scientific, impartial, and, above all, unconnected to the victim – in effect, someone white. Experts connected to the state, however – for example, white professionals such as the pathologist – were not imagined to possess their own biases. No one questioned, for instance, the pathologist's findings that the boot print occurred just prior to Alphonse's incarceration.[66] Only another scientific expert could credibly question the pathologist's account, and the band was unable to supply one. In contrast, Indigenous experts were far less strongly shielded by their expertise; their accounts were easily seen as merely anecdotal and unscientific.

In describing what she did as a Native court worker and listing the difficulties Indigenous peoples had with the justice system, including language and cultural issues, Amy Sandy explained that as soon as she started her job in 1995, she began hearing complaints, initially about how Indigenous people were treated in the hospital and later about treatment by the police. By June 1997, she had recorded ten complaints concerning excessive force, among them what she described as complaints about "really, really excessive force," only a few of which went through a complaints process. Many complainants refused to go to the RCMP station to file a complaint, maintaining that if they did so, the next time they were picked up by the RCMP for being drunk in a public place, things would go much worse for them. Since they nonetheless wanted someone to know about these incidents, Amy Sandy began recording complaints in collaboration with the Nenqay Deni Yajelhtig Law Centre. They began using a form they developed, which was then sent on to the RCMP complaints commission. Feeling overwhelmed by the number of complaints, Amy Sandy organized an RCMP complaints committee involving several detachments in the area, the Law Centre, and the Cariboo Tribal Council in an effort to get complaints resolved.

By the time she left her position in March 2001, she had received forty-seven complaints. (In 2002, the committee's funding was cut.)[67] Sandy felt that people trusted her because she had already set up a protocol for dealing with hospital issues. They soon began to develop some protocols with the RCMP detachment. Sandy noticed that delinquent police officers, who were often the same ones named in complaints, were simply transferred out, and that complaints which were officially lodged would sometimes be investigated by officers who had once worked at the detachment, something that happened in the Alphonse investigation.[68] Confirming Amy Sandy's account describing Indigenous people's experience of the complaint process and noting that the five formal complaints in which she was involved were dismissed, Sharon Taylor, a victims' assistance worker who provided court support and other services to Indigenous peoples, described the fear she often encountered in Indigenous peoples who complained about police actions. The fear was real, she asserted. She observed that her First Nations clients feared the police, afraid they would not be believed because they were Indigenous, in the same way that victims who report spousal assaults fear they will not be believed.[69]

Amy Sandy's account was unceremoniously rejected. John Bethell, counsel for the coroner, interrupted a juror's question to Amy Sandy about whether the incidents she described were primarily concerning one detachment. Bethell complained that Sandy's evidence was not relevant. The coroner agreed, and the juror ceased his line of questioning.

> MR. BETHELL: Excuse me, Mr. Coroner, these questions and answers are very interesting. We're a long way from the death of Mr. Alphonse. We're talking about the process and the systems and with respect, I don't think that we can get into statistics of where and what. It's too far.
>
> THE CORONER: Thank you. We have certainly allowed a lot of discussion about R.C.M.P. complaints that Miss Sandy has received, and you have to be aware that Mr. Bethell is quite right, that we need to remain, as much as we can, within the realms of the facts regarding Mr. Alphonse's death, and I know there's some issues here we wanted to have discussed and brought forward and I think Ms. Teillet has done a very fine job of that and I think Ms. Sandy has added a great deal of enlightenment to that, but I would caution you that we want to be careful that we don't dwell in that area too deeply because it's removed from the facts of the case to a certain degree. If we start getting involved in individual complaints that occurred over a period of time, they're not related to this particular case.

> So I just want to help you understand what Mr. Bethell is talking about. He's the lawyer, I'm just an ordinary person like you, so try to interpret.[70]

With police brutality considered too far removed an issue for the inquest, there was little else that counsel for the family and the band could do to bring to the inquest's attention the relationship between the police and Indigenous peoples in Williams Lake.

The inquest also had an opportunity to hear from professionals about how the troopers, and Paul Alphonse in particular, lived their lives in Williams Lake, lives of hardship that involved frequent contact with the police and medical professionals. While these witnesses found a more sympathetic hearing, their testimony served paradoxically to confirm the police's argument that the troopers present society with a number of intractable problems which neither the police nor others can easily solve. Sarah Stump, who ran a lodge for street-involved people in Williams Lake and had been working on their care for more than three decades, knew Paul Alphonse well. She remembered him as frail and old, and she described him as someone who wasn't a complainer but who would cry, sob, and chant for hours after she picked him up from the police station. About the troopers, she noted that when she first met them, she was shocked that they ate out of garbage cans and tried to keep warm with sleeping bags held together with clothespins. Caring for them by providing beds, picking them up from the police station, and transporting them back to the reserve or to her lodge, Sarah Stump noted that she had attended eight funerals in the last ten days and that she was burning out. The RCMP would sometimes bring the troopers directly to her lodge, something they once did with Alphonse, but the problem was clearly too big for her to manage.[71]

Violet Stump, a coordinator of the First Nations Health Liaison Program (a position developed in response to the Cariboo-Chilcotin Justice Inquiry's recommendations) whose responsibilities included advocating for First Nations people who come into contact with the health-care system, also knew Paul Alphonse to see him around town and had come into contact with him professionally when the band complained in earlier incidents about how he had been treated in hospital. On one occasion, Alphonse was released from hospital in wet clothes. On a second occasion, he was sent by mistake to the hospital in Kamloops, and his clothes went missing in the process. Violet Stump was unaware that the family of Paul Alphonse had not been contacted about his hospital stay until 17 April.[72] Hazel Alphonse, the sister-in-law of Paul

Alphonse but also the person paid by the band to look after elders, described seeing Alphonse at breakfast on 10 April. He climbed her stairs and sat down to eat at 8 a.m., she noted in her diary, kept as part of her job. Significantly, he had no pain that day. When she did not see him for several days, she and her husband, Alphonse's brother Kiddo, went looking for him in Dog Creek on 17 April. She did not learn of Alphonse being in the hospital until later that day when Kristy Palmantier called to tell her. The family's counsel, Cynthia Callison, attempted to have Hazel Alphonse's diary entered as an exhibit for the jury in order to "balance the written record," since the RCMP had entered sixty pages of notes. The RCMP's counsel objected to the diary's inclusion, and the matter was dropped. Among other things, however, the diary confirmed that the band actively looked after its elders and that they were affected by the hospital's failure to inform them of Alphonse's whereabouts. It also suggested that Alphonse did not have broken ribs prior to 10 April.

Either because of legal rules or because of an informal but no less powerful thrust to confine Indigenous people's narratives to the space of difference and to limit the extent to which their lives could be understood within a historical, social, or political framework, it was difficult for the band and the family to materialize Alphonse as someone other than an alcoholic who posed a nuisance to himself, the public, the band, and his own family. Questioning Chief Sandy about the band's care of its alcoholic members, RCMP counsel sought to establish that it was the band's responsibility to look after its members, a responsibility that even the band found difficult to bear, especially if alcoholics became aggressive and violent. Sandy's response – that one approached the matter on a case-by-case basis and it only happened very rarely (twice) that the RCMP called requesting the band pick up a member and she decided the person was being so belligerent it was best he or she stay in lock up – provided an opening for the RCMP counsel to highlight the difficulties everyone had looking after alcoholics. Sandy offered considerable detail about how the band attempts to do just that, earning the rebuke of Hayes, counsel for the RCMP, that nevertheless Paul Alphonse fell through the cracks, his own community being one of them.[73] In these acrimonious exchanges, the figure of the "drunken Indian" beyond help circulates, fuelling the RCMP's argument that no one was to blame for Alphonse's condition.

If stories of police brutality were considered too far out of range to be germane to the Alphonse case, the matter of the history of Indigenous/

police relations in the Chilcotin region stood even less chance of being considered relevant. The band nevertheless sought to enter on record that colonization entails a long history of violence and police brutality, something that counsel for the band tried to capture by asking each witness if they had ever heard of the Cariboo-Chilcotin Justice Inquiry. In the spring of 1993, the three First Nations who inhabit the Cariboo Chilcotin area (Shuswap, Carrier, and Chilcotin) offered over fifty days of testimony in which they detailed more than two hundred incidents involving the police, the justice system, social service workers, and private security guards. The testimony before Judge Anthony Sarich confirmed that First Nations peoples felt strongly that they frequently experienced police brutality, racial abuse, and contempt from all sectors of the justice and social service systems.[74] The inquest offered little space to pursue this history lesson, however, and the shorthand in which such a history was introduced, "Are you familiar with the Cariboo Chilcoten Inquiry? [*sic*]" simply could not fill in the gaps sufficiently so that we might be able to connect colonization to the circumstances surrounding Alphonse's death. Significantly, the band's counsel often followed up her questions about the Cariboo-Chilcotin Justice Inquiry with a question about cultural competence, thereby limiting the issue to a cultural relationship and not a political one. Inviting the state to recognize Indigenous peoples as cultural groups, the band ran the risk of merely confirming the state's power of recognition.

Struggling to walk the balance between recognition and an acknowledgment of colonization, Chief Sandy, in her closing testimony, itemized for the coroner what she thought was the heart of the matter: "It's the years that we've lost in our pride and our dignity from the abuses that happened at the residential school. It's the years of resources that we've lost from our lands."[75] Describing why she felt there had to be political power applied to both the investigation and the inquest, Sandy explained that she feared the situation would not be taken seriously because of the troopers' lifestyle. It would become, she explained, a situation analogous to that of the many missing and presumed murdered Indigenous women of Vancouver's Downtown East Side, whose murders she felt the police ignored because the women were Indigenous and working as prostitutes.[76] The police response, she implied, emerged from a history in which Aboriginal people were not persons deserving of respect and care, but merely damaged human beings who were responsible for their own predicaments. Just as Irwin viewed the troopers as people nobody cared about and saw Alphonse as a man without family and community, so too the police might think they need not care that a man was stomped on so hard he died with a boot print on his chest. Towards the end of the inquest, Nancy Sandy commented to the coroner, "I sure wish you could give us our land back," a wish she ruefully acknowledged was not within his power to grant.

Inquests into the deaths of Indigenous people who die in police custody often unfold along the narrative lines we can trace in the Alphonse inquest. The police, health-care professionals, and the coroner establish that a damaged population (damaged by alcohol and sometimes by colonization, the latter understood as a shadowy event of the distant past) experiences untimely deaths. The best we can do is to try to have more compassionate responses and better procedures. No one is to blame. Indigenous people who invoke history, a history that in their view both causes the problems of ill health and dysfunction and affects relations between Canadian society and Indigenous peoples, do not succeed in puncturing the notion that the violence in Indigenous people's lives and the failure of policing and health-care institutions to care more effectively for them remain mysterious – as mysterious as how Indigenous people come to be so damaged in the first place.

Coroners' inquests are charged with the task of determining cause of death. The jury came to the conclusion that Paul Alphonse's death was a homicide, a finding that the family considered a victory.[77] Alphonse had not killed himself, nor had his lifestyle killed him. Rejecting the storyline of a rough life, the jury's conclusion appears to pay heed to the details that had emerged about police/hospital/Indigenous relations. In their recommendations, the jury suggested that the hospital develop guidelines for dealing with the troopers. The jury then addressed its recommendations to the police. They reminded the RCMP that there should be working surveillance cameras and secure seating in booking areas, and that mattresses and blankets should be provided to elderly, Indigenous prisoners. Incidents involving prisoners needing medical attention should be documented. Further, the RCMP should learn how to deal with First Nations populations, and in particular populations such as the troopers. Amidst the many recommendations that spell out specific advice, for example, allowing witnesses to be accompanied by a support person or conducting an independent investigation of a complaint rather than relying on an RCMP internal investigation, one thing becomes obvious. There was little new to say since so many previous recommendations, many of them part of the Cariboo-Chilcotin Justice Inquiry, had been blatantly ignored. The jury's succinct recommendation to the Williams Lake detachment simply states: review existing inquiries and protocols.

By virtue of having to spell out the simple routines of care and responsible policing, the jury unintentionally confirmed that something persists in the relationship between Indigenous peoples and Canadian society, something deadly that resists change. What this something is, however, was never directly linked to colonization. The indifference to Indigenous life demonstrated in the everyday routines of health care and policing are frontier practices, that is, practices born of the belief that Indian wars continue and that settlers have an obligation to subjugate Indians. In an inquest, can the death of Paul Alphonse be read otherwise? Can the outcome go beyond another injunction to chart all bruises and install video cameras? I suggest that unless the failures of policing and health-care practices towards Indigenous people are put into the context of an ongoing colonialism and understood as one of the ways in which dispossession is accomplished, they are doomed to be repeated.

It is possible to consider the patterns noted in the Paul Alphonse inquest, specifically the confinement of Indigenous peoples to the space of difference and pre-modernity, as somehow endemic to inquests, and perhaps even more so to inquests into the deaths of marginalized populations. Certainly scholars have noted these patterns in other contexts, notably inquests into the deaths of racialized populations.[78] With respect to Indigenous peoples, the regularity with which inquests itemize what Chris Cunneen called "the violence of neglect,"[79] coupled with the signs they offer that a colonial, that is to say, a hierarchical, relationship prevails between police and other professionals and the marginalized population, invites us to consider what is at stake in such performances. We can only make sense of what happens in policing and in inquests, where recommendations faithfully and fruitlessly enjoin settlers to treat Indigenous people more humanely, when we consider the material project such processes and practices sustain – specifically, the ongoing project of settler colonialism – and the colonial subjectivities required to sustain it.

Land and Law

How might it be possible for Chief Sandy's cry, "I sure wish you could give us our land back," to make sense in an inquest? When they confront the contemporary violence of incarceration, Cunneen observed, Indigenous peoples in Australia remember "massacres, containment on reserves, the forced removal of children and a discriminatory criminal justice system."[80] Inquests are quintessential sites for naturalizing this violence. The move to convert violence into Indigenous dysfunction and pathology is classically demonstrated in the Cariboo-Chilcotin Justice Inquiry to which the band's counsel so frequently referred during the inquest. Although the inquiry served to record that Indigenous peoples had a number of justified complaints against the RCMP and it indicted police for their arrogance and contempt of Indigenous peoples, Commissioner Anthony Sarich stuck resolutely to an analysis that cast Indigenous peoples in the role of a conquered and pre-modern people awaiting assistance into modern life. The manner in which this is accomplished mirrors the inquest. First, the violence of colonialism, considered safely in the past, is recognized, although it is often described not as violence but as misjudgment. Second, Indigenous peoples are considered to have been deeply damaged and rendered dependent by colonialism. Third, the police and others respond to the damaged populations they deal with professionally, but also inefficiently and arrogantly. Fourth, Indigenous peoples have to be helped to recover from colonization, and the police have to be more culturally sensitive as they assist them to do so. Under this scenario, colonialism becomes something that happened to Indigenous peoples, in much the same way that small pox decimated the Shuswap, through no direct fault of the colonizers. Colonization is not understood as something that also produced white settlers and their entitlement to the land, and the most settlers can be guilty of is not understanding the historical situation into which they haplessly wandered. What this narrative leaves out, of course, is ongoing settler violence and its source in an ongoing white supremacist colonial project.

From the start of his report, Commissioner Sarich adopts a folksy tone, describing the community halls in which the inquiry conducted hearings, the "toddlers in jolly jumpers" and the stray dogs, as well as the people telling their stories with the aid of an interpreter. If the report plunges us into an anthropological encounter with a pre-modern people, this is also the direction of its analytical frame, as is made obvious by the chapter title, "Clash of Cultures." For Commissioner Sarich, the fifty days of testimony about police brutality and the history of colonial relations, particularly what was revealed concerning the residential school St. Joseph's Mission near Williams Lake, leads to the conclusion that the source of the problem can be traced to government officials who "were unable or unwilling to accept that the community- and family-centred cultural values of the native people were irreconcilable with the values of a free-enterprise, individual-oriented, self-acquisitive society."[81] A modern capitalist society clashed with a tribal, collective one, and the result was that a once proud and independent people were reduced to a state of complete dependency.

If colonialism rendered native people "angry, confused and lost," however, and brought with it "alcoholism, family destruction and self-abasement,"[82] this analysis opens the door for a full-blown culturalist explanation of the state of Indigenous/police relations, whereby the problem that exists between Indigenous people and the police is understood to originate in cultural misunderstanding. The police have "an attitude problem" and see Indigenous people as dependent. For their part, Indigenous people are "confused and frightened," "handicapped by a cultural and language barrier."[83] When confronted with police "arrogance, disrespect and contempt," native people

> didn't complain because they were taught not to do so. They repressed their emotions, and many did in fact accept that they were inferior and inevitably would be treated differently than non-natives.[84]

Commissioner Sarich describes police conduct towards Indigenous peoples as ranging from "indifference, through arrogance and disrespect, to bordering on contempt."[85] Police overreact, abuse their authority, and have little communication with Indigenous peoples. There is a "remote and obdurate bureaucracy and the frightening and incomprehensible justice process."[86]

It is ironic that alongside this portrait of a frightened and abject Indigenous population, the inquiry records that "the people brought up land claims, resource management and control of their own lives."[87] The people also brought up history. Chief Beverly Sellars of the Soda Creek Indian Band recalled residential schools and specifically named St. Joseph's Mission as having an enormously destructive impact on the lives of the Indigenous peoples of the Cariboo Chilcotin area. Testimony was also offered about the Chilcotin war in 1864, when seven chiefs were unjustly hung for defending their lands. The treatment of Indigenous peoples by road builders (hired by Alfred Penderill Waddington for the gold rush) provoked resistance, as did the deadly effects of smallpox brought by the crowds of white men searching for gold. The epidemic wiped out one-third of the Shuswap. The Chilcotin war is the only war said to have occurred in Western Canada, and the Cariboo-Chilcotin Justice Inquiry becomes the first time the hanging of the chiefs was publicly acknowledged as unjust and the men officially pardoned.

Incongruously, Commissioner Sarich concludes that colonialism led to "an abysmal misunderstanding."[88] The commissioner is able to recognize police misconduct in the stories he hears, but in attributing the problem to a colonialism safely in the past and to the resulting cultural conflict and misunderstanding where police remain "essentially strangers to native people," he can only end with the need to provide Native people with help on their path to cultural recovery and modernity.

> In revitalizing their societies, natives will be searching for their cultural roots. All of them have lost contact with their history – some more than others, and will be rebuilding their societies at a different pace. In their own good time, they will develop a justice system suitable to themselves.[89]

Fully devoted to the idea of Native-controlled solutions, Commissioner Sarich accepts that in the meantime, the police ought to learn to be more culturally sensitive.

It is remarkable that after days of testimony in which Indigenous people recounted stories of not being able to obtain police help in highway accidents, in cases of missing persons, or in cases requiring the retrieval of dead bodies; stories of pregnant women being left by police at the side of the road in bitter cold weather, of police forcing their way with guns drawn (and without warrants) into homes, of police using excessive force; and stories of the detention of Indigenous people without charge, Commissioner Sarich concludes:

> These complaints are longstanding and insistent. They are the product of a conflict of cultural values and beliefs and are driven by the past and present conduct of non-native authority figures ... Native people have not been well served by the process of justice of non-native society. Cultural differences have left a wide chasm that will not be easy to bridge.[90]

Specifically of police practices, the commissioner has this to say:

> There have been many complaints against the RCMP during the course of this inquiry. The determination of their validity is somewhat like a philosopher's search for objective proof or absolute truth. The conduct the natives complain of is viewed in one light by them and in a different light by members of the RCMP.[91]

If it is impossible, then, to pursue absolute truth, if there are no wrongdoers, what is to be done?

The inquiry's recommendations can be grouped into four areas. Untypically, the first set of recommendations concerned land. The commissioner advised the government to negotiate and to stop the illegal use of disputed land. He also advised that the chiefs hung in the Chilcotin war be pardoned and their burial ground located to where they could be properly buried. The second set of recommendations acknowledged police abuses and recommended that there be an investigation of excessive force, the formal complaints process, and the operation of due process throughout the justice system. The commissioner also offered the idea of a Native police force or Canadian peacekeepers, an implicit if not an explicit recognition that the current arrangements are all but fruitless. As in the Alphonse inquest, a third set of recommendations suggested that there be programs for alcohol abuse and violence, and that search and rescue efforts be made available to Indigenous people, because as a people they need to have their dead recovered quickly. Marking Indigenous people in this way as strangely culturally different (and begging the question which peoples do not like their dead to be recovered quickly), the inquiry launched into its final set of recommendations about training white people to be culturally sensitive and kind. Ambulance personnel, coroners, pathologists, and the RCMP all should be instructed in such matters.

In her excellent analysis of the cultural myths that structure the Cariboo-Chilcotin Justice Inquiry (and the McEachern decision in *Delgamuukw*), Elizabeth Furniss identifies the operation of the frontier myth, which so profoundly shapes how the extensive testimony of the violence visited upon Aboriginal people came to be transformed largely into a matter of cultural difference. Furniss suggests that the narrative line underpinning the inquiry is the progressive version of the frontier myth, the version Richard Slotkin described as the populist myth. The hero of the populist myth, in this case Commissioner Sarich, "knows Indians" and acknowledges that they are victims of colonial conquest. He recognizes their struggles for recognition. Although unlike Chief Justice McEachern's decision in *Delgamuukw*, where, in a version of the frontier myth, Indigenous peoples are considered to have simply failed to emerge from the pre-modern era and to have been defeated by the forces of nature, the Cariboo-Chilcotin Justice Inquiry nevertheless draws on some of the frontier myth's main assumptions. As Furniss argues, Commissioner Sarich believes in an essential, immutable cultural difference between Aboriginal peoples and white people, and the extensive testimony he hears about racial violence only confirms for him that an enormous cultural divide exists.[92] The commissioner is sympathetic, and he writes glowingly of his own positive experience with the people of the region, peoples he recognizes as noble savages, in contrast to McEachern's ignoble savages. Cultural differences account for Aboriginal "confusion" about the justice system. As Furniss points out:

> In both the Sarich and McEachern reports, the idea of "confusion" is one-sided. Euro-Canadians are represented as having a privileged superior vantage point from which to view the real nature of Aboriginal/non-Aboriginal relations. It suggests the automatic burden of paternalism, reinforces the image of the Indian as childlike, fearful and semi-rational and upholds the responsibility of those who presume to understand the nature of the problem to take charge. In McEachern, this presumed omnipotence translates as the need for Euro-Canadian society to treat Aboriginal people with a paternalistic stiff hand. In the Sarich report it translates as the need for Euro-Canadian society to make a benevolent accommodation to Aboriginal people, who are imagined of as trapped within a rigid and unchanging culture.[93]

Sarich is able to condemn colonial actions on the evidence that noble savages have now been reduced to a state of confusion and dependency, concludes Furniss. The violence of colonialism, despite being so forcefully described and documented, remains invisible. Sarich is able to recommend autonomous justice systems, but the emphasis on the cultural difference that justifies such arrangements only serves to establish white innocence. To unsettle that most quintessential of settler stories about Indigenous peoples needing assistance into modernity, it is imperative to recognize that colonialism is, as the dictionary acknowledges, primarily a system in which one country rules another.

Dispossession of the Indigenous population is not accomplished once and for all at the time of conquest, and it requires a number of institutional strategies, both material and symbolic. It also requires settlers who come to understand and perform their own entitlement to the land, something that policing accomplishes, and law manages.

Conclusion. "There's Lots to Steal"[94]

The gravestones in the small cemetery on Sugar Cane Reserve tell the story of Indigenous death as a colonial story. Close to Paul Alphonse's grave lie the graves of his three brothers, Isadore, Peter, and Bucksy. Of the five Alphonse brothers, only one is still alive. In 1959, after returning to Williams Lake from a sanitorium (for TB patients) in Prince Rupert, Isadore, the oldest brother, died shortly after being held in police custody. Described by his brother Kiddo as someone who didn't drink that much, Isadore had bruises on his arm when he died. Peter and Bucksy both suffered from alcoholism. Bucksy died of hypothermia in Boitanio Park a few years after Paul Alphonse, while Peter died of alcohol-related complications at home.[95] The graveyard records the suicides of young men. As one moves from the graveyard towards the empty space where the residential school once stood, barns and tunnels are barely visible, places where children remember being taken and abused. The reserve itself is a small community with a church and a collection of small houses. Paul Alphonse lived in one of these, the former house of the priest who serviced the church. Sugar Cane Reserve, a place that has had a boiled water advisory for decades, is nine kilometres away from Williams Lake, the nearest place to purchase goods. The walk into town along the highway, a walk Nancy Sandy described as a walk that is "okay if you can defend yourself," is increasingly dangerous, the danger coming from cars, cops, young white boys, and other Indigenous people.[96] The mall, containing a few stores and the Overwaitea grocery store, is regularly patrolled. As though to shrink the spaces where Indigenous people can congregate in town, its food court was closed, and only a few benches for sitting remain.

Colonialism as a material project remains at the edges of any explanation about the boot print on Paul Alphonse's chest. To return to the description of the troopers offered in a press release jointly signed by the RCMP, the Williams Lake Indian Band, and the Ministry of Health, "a population described as displaced by society, phased out of employment by technology, and negatively affected by residential school and similar historical events,"[97] Indigenous people are, in this listing of factors, simply overtaken by modern life and damaged by a historical event. Never simply workers whose productive value has disappeared nor victims of a deliberate and brutal disciplining, Indigenous people haunt settlers in ways that other abject populations may not. The land is their land, and taking it continues apace. Dispossession is as much a psychic as a material project. The expulsion from settler society must be continuous – Irwin must slap and prod Alphonse daily, as must the state – if the settlers are to become the original inhabitants. Policing provides the site of this becoming, and the inquest offers us the chance to experience this becoming ourselves. To say that land lies at the basis of the boot print, the reason why surveillance cameras don't work, seats are not provided in the booking area, bruises aren't charted, and boot prints are not noticed, is to interrupt this becoming. Land offers the key to the mystery each inquest into an Indigenous death in custody confronts: why violence against Indigenous people persists and goes unrecognized in law.

Chapter Four

"People Die": A Killing Indifference

For Chaz (Chester Patrick), Gitxsan Dancer and Artist

Only man dies. The animal perishes.

Martin Heidegger[1]

Introduction

Many deaths in custody occur because the police or medical professionals will not touch, examine, or closely monitor Indigenous people in their care. This indifference kills. The pervasiveness of indifference among hospital, police, and prison personnel suggests a shared belief, an understanding that care would be wasted on Indigenous prisoners. The refusal to touch or be touched by another is indicative of the distance that professionals feel between themselves and their Indigenous prisoners or patients, a distance measured on a scale of humanity. Writing of prisoners tortured at Black sites and populations killed by drones, Joseph Pugliese remarks that those tortured and killed lose their status as humans and become *corpus nullius*, a "non-body that is merely animal carcass."[2] In Western societies (in contrast to many Indigenous societies), little is owed to animals and animal carcasses, and a body (human or animal) treated as a carcass is understood as an "object-thing that will not be liberated or redeemed."[3] Those imagined as non-human do not die; they only come to an end. Invoking Heidegger, who noted that to die, one must be thought capable of death (in contrast to animals, who in the Western view are without dignity and therefore just perish), Pugliese shows that torture and drone victims in the war on terror are deemed incapable of embodying the human, and so do not die.[4] In the same way, I suggest that for many prison, police, and medical professionals, Indigenous people are seen as animals (in the European view, animals are typically regarded as without the capacity for dignity). Incapable of embodying the human, their bodies do not require care in the same way as humans do, and when death is the result, it is only the outcome of a process set in motion long before an Indigenous prisoner is taken into custody.

How do inquests understand this professional indifference and negligence towards Indigenous people on the part of state actors? As previously mentioned, inquests for the most part consider the death of Indigenous people as timely rather than untimely. The story of timely death gains coherence through representations of Indigenous people as possessing a pathological frailty that is more often than not associated with alcohol abuse. If Indigenous people are a dying race of chronic alcoholics, then they are people that no one can really harm or repair. Each inquest reinforces this racial logic that Indigenous people are beyond saving because they are not the same kind of human as others. At the same time, as chapter two showed, inquests repeatedly offer the same suggestions for improvement, recommendations for change that are seldom implemented and do not address issues of neglect, but rather function to redeem the settler collective. Custody and the inquest are in this way a ritual of neglect and redemption. The ritual begins with the state ostentatiously performing the arrest for being drunk in a public place, and it proceeds with the booking, the filling out of forms, and the routines of custodial and medical care. At the inquest, protocols and policies are hammered out to describe the things we must do as a civilization when confronted with flesh that has decayed and minds that are presumed to have lost their rationality. Left untreated, wounded bodies give out, and their owners' demise is seen as natural and inevitable. It goes without saying that a people seen as damaged and dying cannot be entrusted with self-governance and stewardship over the land. Custody and the inquest therefore both bear an intrinsic relationship to continuing colonial occupation.

To illustrate the micro interactions that characterize colonial regimes, in this chapter I review several moments of indifference and neglect in medical and custodial settings, with the aim of exploring their complexity and considering the diverse ways settlers express their conviction that Indigenous lives are lives not worth living. In part one, I return to the case of Paul Alphonse who died in hospital while in police custody, showing how the Indigenous body is considered by healthcare professionals as so deeply destroyed by alcoholism that nothing else can destroy it, a situation that renders the body one that is not worth caring for and one that can be neglected with impunity. In part two, I discuss cases of Indigenous people who die while being held in jail cells, exposing the banal indifference of agents of the settler state towards Indigenous people. Since a jail cell is not a hospital, the expectation that prisoners should be monitored for illness and injury is low. Nonetheless, I explore how even this low threshold is crossed when guards and police officers treat the Indigenous body as a carcass. In part three, I examine deaths by suicide. By far the easiest situation for the settler state to refuse responsibility, cases of suicide nonetheless suggest that Indigenous people are driven to take their own lives when prison conditions close off possibilities for living. In those rare moments when Indigenous people are able to insert their views on the legal record, the colonial processes implicated in self-harm and suicide are revealed. In the conclusion, I discuss why settler societies display such a killing indifference towards Indigenous people. While other marginalized groups may experience dehumanization, notably other racialized groups, poor people, and people with disabilities, the violence that is meted out to Indigenous people in settler societies is a paradigmatic and foundational violence.

Part One. The Hospital: Medical Indifference

As the previous chapter discussed, Paul Alphonse, a sixty-seven-year-old Indigenous man, was arrested for public drunkenness. During the booking process at the local RCMP detachment, a scuffle ensued and he fell. He was taken to hospital, found to have no injuries, and returned to the cells. A short time later, Alphonse complained of chest pains, and in a second trip to the hospital, it was determined that he had several fractured ribs. He remained in hospital until his death eight days later. This sequence of events, related by the coroner at an inquest into his death, omits several important details related to Alphonse's medical care. It does not include the fact that his family was never contacted while he was in hospital (in spite of a hospital protocol to this effect), nor does it hint that the level of hospital care Alphonse received might have had something to do with his death. In the coroner's terse description, Alphonse is simply a man arrested for public drunkenness who is discovered to have had undetermined injuries and ultimately dies, whether from the undetermined injuries or alcoholism.[5]

There is a long history of medical contempt and negligence towards Indigenous people of the Cariboo Chilcotin region, but there is no comprehensive study documenting these abuses. Instead, personal accounts describe the failure to get ambulances to come to reserves, the negligence and contempt of doctors and nurses, and an institutional failure of hospitals to communicate with Indigenous communities and families.[6] This startling indifference to Indigenous life is also revealed in inquests, where it is shown to have lethal effects. In 1988, in the same hospital where Alphonse died, an Indigenous woman, Katie Ross, died of her injuries from a gunshot wound. Ross and her husband were shot near their camp in the bush, four hours from the city of Williams Lake. While her husband died instantly, Katie Ross made her way back to the camp, where her son found her a couple of hours later. He drove her to a nearby ranch, where the police were called. The RCMP testified at the inquest that although Katie Ross told them she had been shot, they checked and could find no blood or bullet wound (details the inquest disproved). Katie Ross's son then took her to an outpost nursing station, where the nurse took Ross's pulse, diagnosed emotional shock, and told the son to take her to the hospital in Williams Lake. The nurse did not assist the son to find transportation to the hospital, nor did she call an ambulance. Several hours later, when her son could find a ride to the hospital an hour away, Ross was admitted to hospital in Williams Lake. She was diagnosed with anxiety and was given sedatives. When Ross kept getting up to vomit, the dosage of sedatives was increased. She died a day later, and it was the pathologist who determined that the cause of death was an infection due to a gunshot wound in her back.

The failure of police and medical professionals to find a gunshot wound, even when told about it, and their failure to assist Ross suggest that for professionals who saw her, Ross, in Pugliese's terms, was a carcass, "that fatal animal remnant" bearing none of the "sentient categories constitutive of the unitary and affective human subject."[7] How else to explain this persistent refusal to examine her? The Ross inquest was not concerned, as we might expect, with the violent outcome of clinical negligence, and thus with the death of a human being, but rather with improving communications between Indigenous and non-Indigenous people. The focus on communications provides a euphemism for medical professionals' near complete lack of interest in Ross's injuries. As Heather Peters and Bruce Self have written, Ross's death and the subsequent inquest was a watershed moment that brought the development of a First Nations Health Liaison Program.[8] The inquest identified a serious communications issue between First Nations people and police and hospital personnel, and it recommended the development of the liaison program and cross-cultural training. The latter never got off the ground, and the liaison program took ten years before it was funded in 1999, one year before Paul Alphonse met his death in the same hospital. It was defunded two years later.

As in the Ross situation, where medical professionals did not notice a bullet wound, professionals could not recall seeing the large purple boot print on the chest of Paul Alphonse. The close parallel between the two cases, even though they are ten years apart, suggests that medical indifference to Indigenous suffering persists and continues to have lethal effects. It seems that neither bullets nor boot prints give professionals pause. Importantly, bodies that are without sufficient standing to merit attention are understood to be bodies already destroyed by alcohol. In Alphonse's case (and perhaps in Ross's, although this is not known), medical professionals focused on Alphonse's alcoholism, believing that his medical issues were primarily related to chronic drinking. The issue of separating where a victim's prior medical conditions end and police or medical abuse begins is always controversial, but no more so than when the underlying condition is chronic alcoholism or drug use. For Indigenous people, alcoholism is as racially inflected a disease as sickle cell is for people of African origin, as I show in chapter five. For instance, it is widely believed that Indigenous peoples possess an inherent inability to process alcohol, and in comparison, that whites are able to handle it better. This idea obscures the role that alcohol played in the management of Indigenous peoples and occludes the pain and violence of colonialism that have led so many Indigenous peoples to abuse alcohol. The stereotypical drunken Indian achieves its power, as all stereotypes do, precisely because alcohol abuse is a problem among Indigenous peoples, a problem that began in colonialism.[9]

In their work on the experiences of Aboriginal women in health-care settings, Jo-Anne Fiske and Annette Browne write persuasively of the "discredited Aboriginal subject," showing how a single discrediting factor, alcohol, works to mark Aboriginal women seeking health care as responsible for their own ill health, inherently sick and dysfunctional, and often beyond the pale of being helped.[10] Importantly, they comment, those viewed as unable to govern themselves are seen as undeserving citizens when it comes to health-care services and in matters of collective self-governance.[11] Factors such as alcohol abuse, whether or not they are present, "discredit" Aboriginal subjects, marking them as undeserving of services and of respect, and tying in neatly with long-standing racist ideas of Aboriginal people as polluted, child-like, and incapable of being modern subjects. Paul Alphonse confronted these ideas about alcohol addiction and Aboriginal people when he was admitted to the hospital intoxicated and in police custody. Once the fact of his alcohol addiction took over, he stood little chance of being thought of as deserving of care, and even less chance of being seen as a victim of police violence. Dehumanization, cloaked as responses to alcohol, is about understanding Aboriginal peoples' lives as being without value.

When Alphonse failed to come home to the reserve and his niece Kristy Palmantier went looking for him, she found her uncle strapped to a hospital chair. One of the first things she noticed, as she helped him go to the bathroom, was "the large purple bruise" on the right side of his chest, a bruise that had the pattern of a boot or a shoe. As the pathologist would later conclude, somebody had "stomped" on Paul Alphonse, fracturing five of his ribs. When Alphonse died shortly after his niece found him, the question of the bruise and of the kind of care he had received while in police custody and in the hospital became urgent questions for the family. During the inquest, these questions were principally taken up as "medical" issues related to Alphonse's alcohol abuse. The inquest focused on pneumonia as the official cause of death, and blunt force trauma from an undetermined source as merely an aggravating factor.

The Issue of Pneumonia

Dr Thomas Perry appeared before the inquest as an expert in clinical pharmacology, internal medicine, and pneumonia. Since people with chronic alcoholism are often admitted to hospital with pneumonia and frequently undergo alcohol withdrawal, Dr Perry was asked to shed light on the role that alcohol withdrawal played in connection with the pneumonia, and how this might have influenced the medical treatment Paul Alphonse received. Reading the hospital records and the autopsy report, Perry came to one central conclusion:

> I think what happened is at the time he was admitted to the Cariboo Hospital at around 11:30 at night on the 11th, he had something profound already going on in his lungs, and I think it's clear from the medical and the nursing records that he had identifiable new rib fractures from the X-ray, but not – not the bruise that's so obvious in the autopsy photographs that I have just seen here today. So – and he was also obviously drunk. And the initial focus of the medical and nursing staff was to categorize him as drunk and liable to alcohol withdrawal, and having substantial

> pain from fractured ribs and needing general observation. *And that there was a failure to recognize that something serious was going on in his lungs right from that time.*[12]

Perry commented that in his reading of Alphonse's chart, the nurses "don't appear to have noticed how sick he was."[13]

Although the nurses and the attending physician all heard crackles in Alphonse's lungs and noted that his oxygen intake was low, they did not conclude that pneumonia was a distinct possibility, something Perry found inexcusable. As Perry explained at the inquest, there are only three possible explanations for crackles in the lungs: pneumonia, heart failure, and, very rarely, an "interstitial lung disease."[14] Although an X-ray did not disclose pneumonia, Perry commented that this in itself was not unusual. Given the seriousness of pneumonia in an older person, let alone one with chronic alcoholism who spent time on the streets, Perry felt strongly that published guidelines would indicate that Alphonse should be automatically hospitalized for possible pneumonia. A person this sick, Perry speculated, would have had him rushing to contact family in case of cardiac arrest.[15]

The fact that alarm bells did not go off about the crackles in Alphonse's lungs may explain subsequent events. For Perry, once a patient is suspected of suffering from a serious illness, the proper course of action would be to seek to confirm the diagnosis, analyse blood cultures, and ensure adequate oxygen. In Alphonse's case, cultures were ordered for the following day, and then not again, and no effort was made to ensure that Alphonse did not pull off the oxygen mask (for instance, by contacting the family to help with care). When asked whether alcohol would have masked some of what was going on with pneumonia, Perry acknowledged that it could. Delirium and erratic behaviour such as pulling off an oxygen mask could have been due to alcohol withdrawal. It could have just as easily been due to low oxygen levels and serious infection, possibly compounded by drugs such as the Gravol and atropine given to Alphonse.[16] As these medical details reveal, the assumptions made about Indigenous people and alcohol abuse can complicate professionals' capacities to be open to other sources of suffering.

It is clear that both the emergency room physician on duty that night, Dr Wilford, and Alphonse's family doctor, Dr Neufield, concluded that Paul Alphonse was suffering from fractured ribs and alcohol abuse, but it was the latter that remained the focus. As Neufield reminded the coroner, Alphonse had had fourteen visits to the hospital for alcohol-related problems, and he bore the marks of chronic alcohol abuse, notably low body weight and malnutrition. If there were crackles in his lungs, Neufield believed that these were simply because his was the kind of chest that "will always have crackles and wheezes to it."[17] Whatever symptoms Alphonse exhibited during his stay in hospital, Neufield believed, were consistent with alcohol withdrawal and with someone who probably had chronic bronchitis.[18] Furthermore, Neufield insisted that he would have continued treating for alcohol withdrawal even if he knew that Alphonse had pneumonia, simply because fifteen per cent of people who are heavy drinkers die from alcohol withdrawal: "There is no doubt that you have to treat it aggressively."[19] He would, for instance, still have chosen to use phenobarbital, and he contested Perry's view that the drug had not been in use for twenty years. Defending himself, Neufield also maintained that no one could have seen that Alphonse had pneumonia until the day he died.[20]

The Boot Print Revisited

The boot print on Alphonse's chest is briefly explored as a contributing factor, but one about which frustratingly little is known. It is never established who delivered the blow that left a boot print, or whether the injury could have occurred while Alphonse was in police custody. When the boot print matched Alphonse's own boot, the inquest was confronted with the possibility that someone used Alphonse's own boot to stomp on him, but this line of inquiry was not pursued beyond seeking to establish (and failing) whether Alphonse's nephew could have been wearing a similar boot. If it is difficult to establish the hospital's culpability regarding failure to treat the pneumonia aggressively, the matter of the boot print complicates matters further. Dr Donna Rice, the pathologist, attributed Alphonse's death to pneumonia, but, in contrast to Perry, she believed that the broken ribs (the result of blunt force trauma) were the contributing factor. Medical professionals could not be faulted, however, for their assumption that the alcohol abuse and not the boot was the source of Alphonse's injuries. As Dr Rice opined, Alphonse's physical condition as a chronic alcoholic masked the role that blunt force trauma played in his death. The large purple bruise, which shocked Kristy Palmantier when she eventually found her uncle in the hospital on the last day of his life, presented the inquest with an intractable problem. The pathologist maintained in her autopsy report and on the stand that the bruise was seven to ten days old when

Paul Alphonse was admitted to hospital (and thus happened prior to Alphonse's arrest). She based her assessment on the fact that an injury of the kind sustained by Paul Alphonse would have led to bruising and been visible almost immediately, especially because Alphonse did not have a lot of skin tissue. However, because of his poor nutritional state and pneumonia, the healing process would have been extremely delayed and stopped altogether. As Dr Rice explained to the jury, the body chooses to fight the infection instead of healing the bruise. Because she was quite certain that the bruise would have been present at the time of his admission to the hospital or very shortly thereafter, Dr Rice's testimony posed a central difficulty: if the bruise was there, why did no one see it? For her, it was not odd that no one had noticed the bruise because it would have been covered by Alphonse's arm, a strange conclusion to reach since the arm would not have covered the chest area. Even more mysterious, if Alphonse already had his five broken ribs at the time he entered police custody and upon his first and second admissions to the hospital, why did he not present with chest pain until the second admission to the hospital? For Donna Rice, the answer lay once again in his chronic alcoholism. The alcohol dulled the pain.[21]

The first physician to see Alphonse while he was in police custody did so at 5:30 p.m. on 11 April 2000 when he was transported to the hospital. As Dr Quigg, the physician on duty, explained, apparently acknowledging his own negligence, he could have missed seeing the bruise because he was looking for a head injury (he had been told by the police that Alphonse had fallen and hit his head in the police station). He noted, however, that Alphonse did not complain of extreme pain.[22] Disagreeing with Dr Rice that a chronic alcoholic who is intoxicated feels less pain, Dr Quigg felt certain that Alphonse was not in severe pain as might be warranted by a rib injury when he saw him upon his first hospital admission that night. One can only infer, then, that for Quigg, Alphonse did not break his ribs until *after* his first admission to hospital. It is indeed contradictory that he should have had both the injury and the bruise, and yet given no indication of great pain.

When Alphonse was taken to hospital a second time on the night of the 11th complaining of pain in the chest area, there was little recorded interest in his pain and in what might have caused the rib fractures. Alphonse had been "stomped on," according to Dr Rice, but few charged with his care had pursued how he came to break his ribs. The emergency room nurse, Elaine Cawley, testified that she asked Alphonse why his chest hurt, and she had to ask him twice before she got a mumbled answer that he guessed he fell. She could not recall where the RCMP officer Irwin was when she posed this question to Alphonse.[23] The attending physician, Dr Wilford, did not ask about the source of the fractured ribs. He did not recall seeing any bruising. Dr Neufield, Alphonse's family physician who saw Alphonse in the hospital, had only the vaguest recollection of a bruise and maintained, when pressed to be more specific, that the point of care for him was not the bruising but the pain from the fractured ribs and the problem of alcohol withdrawal.[24] In sum, no medical professional displayed any enduring interest in how Alphonse came to fracture his ribs. It was as though his condition required no explanation. Alcoholism is advanced as the reason why no one saw the bruise (he did not complain of pain) and as a reason why we know the bruise was seven to ten days old (his state of nutrition and pneumonia exacerbated by his chronic alcoholism retarded his healing but also caused bruising to be very visible early on). No one saw the boot print for certain, although the pathologist declared that it must have been hyper-visible. The boot's impact likely broke five ribs and was a contributing factor to Alphonse's death, yet little attention was given to it beyond establishing that it did not belong to a police officer and did belong to Alphonse himself. No professional seems to have considered that Alphonse may have been suffering from Acute Respiratory Distress Syndrome, a condition that would have been the response to sustained rib fractures and would likely cause death unless treated with a breathing tube under monitoring in an intensive care unit.[25] For many of those testifying, alcohol abuse explained all mysteries and contradictions. Alphonse, it seems, could not simply be an old man with a serious case of pneumonia, nor could he be an old man whom someone (and possibly the police) had violently assaulted. He could only be a chronic alcoholic.

In their recommendations, the jury suggested that the hospital develop guidelines for dealing with the "troopers,"[26] the Aboriginal men and women of Alphonse's generation who are residential school survivors and suffer from alcohol addiction; that it pay attention to the medical expert, Dr Perry, who had noted the hospital's antiquated and ill-considered methods for treating alcoholics; and that it chart all bruises. Recommendations concerning the police consisted of reminding the RCMP that there should be working surveillance cameras and secure seating in booking areas, and that mattresses and blankets should be provided to elderly Aboriginal prisoners. Incidents involving prisoners needing medical attention should be documented.

Further, the RCMP should learn how to deal with First Nations populations, and in particular, populations such as the troopers. Many of these recommendations, particularly those urging respect for Aboriginal peoples and those suggesting the need to have working surveillance cameras, repeat the recommendations made by Commissioner Anthony Sarich eight years earlier in an inquiry into police brutality in the Cariboo Chilcotin (the same area where Paul Alphonse lived), and they repeat recommendations made in other inquests into the deaths of Aboriginal people in custody, as I discuss later on.[27] Ordinary care remains elusive for Aboriginal people over generations.

Part Two. The Jail: A Population beyond Help

Police perform the routines of maintaining public space free from contamination, duties that involve the arrest and detention of degenerate bodies, but that cannot also include the duty to actively care for such surplus, contaminated, and wounded populations. If the assumption of Indigenous life as wasted life is shrouded in medicine when a death has occurred in hospital, in a jail this option is less available. At the same time, since custodial care can easily be presented as a lesser kind of care than medical care, it is easier to maintain that a body has simply given out and a natural death has occurred when there has been an Indigenous death in jail. This line of argument is very much in evidence in the case of A., who died in her cell after she spent a night in custody. The inquest works diligently to construct the argument that A.'s death in the cells was merely the end of a process rather than the end of a life.

At around 9 p.m. on 9 May 2002, two police officers noticed two obviously intoxicated women walking in a ditch on a dry reserve. At the inquest, one of the officers recalled his encounter with A., one of the two women:

> Her speech was slurred and her eyes were half shut, and she was like swearing, both of them were, and so we arrested them for being intoxicated on a dry reserve, so I took her by the … the right arm to escort her to the police vehicle, and she pulled her … She pulled her arm away from me and struck me on my … my chest, and I just took her arm again. I said, "That wasn't a nice way to act," and I asked her not to do that again, which she didn't.[28]

The women were taken to the detention unit and spent the night in separate cells. At 5 a.m., A. wanted to talk to someone and called for the guard, J., a woman whom she knew. A. wanted to talk about the apprehension of her nine-year-old son by child protection authorities. They spoke for twenty minutes, and J. said she would come back later if A. wanted to talk some more. At 6 a.m., J. checked on A. and found her breathing but not waking up. By 7:30 a.m., J. told one of the police officers that she was worried about A. Together they checked on A. and found that her breathing was laboured and heavy. They called for an ambulance from the RCMP cells, only one hundred feet away. Fifteen or twenty minutes later, when the ambulance arrived, A. was dead. The arresting officer told the coroner he was totally shocked by the death since it had been such a routine arrest. It was "simply [an] intoxicated person."[29] The corporal clarified that the arrest was so routine that he took very limited notes and did not notice any signs of A. being ill.

We come to know A. only through the questions that are asked of witnesses at the inquest, questions posed by the coroner's counsel. These questions highlight A.'s own role in her demise. Unlike the Alphonse inquest, A.'s family did not have their own lawyer, resulting in few challenges to counsel for the coroner and an uncontested view of A.'s life as an alcoholic. We learn that A. had been drinking for several days, and that she most often drank hairspray. The nursing coordinator at the reserve noted that she had never seen A. sober and commented that A. had poor health generally, with high cholesterol and out-of-control diabetes which she managed poorly. If A. had taken better care of herself, the nurse opined, she might have survived her medical emergency. A.'s seventeen-year-old daughter confirmed her mother's ill health and her drinking "with lots of people." When asked about it repeatedly, A.'s daughter also confirmed that her mother did not always take her medications. We even learn about the kind of food A. was eating, and the kind of food available in the house. Counsel puts on record that A.'s household ate Kraft Dinner macaroni and chicken noodles, all nutrition-poor and extremely cheap food.

Although the bulk of the inquest was devoted to A.'s health and habits, a little time at the end of the inquest was devoted to the guard J. When asked how she felt about A.'s death, J. said simply, "I feel bad about myself that I lost her in the cells."[30] People were accusing J. of having killed A., and she said that she felt guilty. The coroner concluded that death was due to "long term consumption of alcohol."[31] As he summarized for the jury, A. was a diabetic who was not compliant in taking her medication. Reading aloud the pathologist's "one sentence" summary of the autopsy – "Severe fatty degeneration of the liver and the presence of hardly any normal liver cells on microscopic examination and diffuse strong positive for fat could cause her death any time"[32] – the coroner laid the basis for his own address to the jury: Death comes suddenly to people like A. It is no one's fault. The inquest was able to wrap up in two days. The jury recommended that guards check on prisoners every five to ten minutes and that police check with prisoners if they have specific medical needs or medications before they are taken to the cells. The inquest into A.'s death intentionally paints a picture for us of the inevitable death in custody of an alcoholic, severely diabetic, poor, Indigenous woman. It is hard to find anything in this story but confirmation that Indigenous bodies simply give out, and that the prison is a place where this is likely to happen. Not even kindly guards such as J. can stop the process. In inquests, Indigenous deaths in custody are always regarded as timely deaths. The cells are spaces of death where people die; it is simply the last stop on a road littered with failing bodies, a road that begins on the reserve. Through their emphasis on failing bodies, inquests confirm that there is no calling to account of anyone for their failure to care in such spaces.

C.T. and a Race of "Shallow Breathers"

In the two cases I discuss in this section, C.T. and S.Q., both died the same weekend, and both were arrested the same day, 4 August 2007, in the province of British Columbia. S.Q. died that same day, and C.T. died in the early morning of 5 August 2007.[33] A coincidence but an indicator nonetheless of the patterns of Indigenous deaths, two men, in two different cells, die around the same time. The inquests into their deaths reveal that they were indeed of a kind, that is, both were treated as having bodies that were merely remnants. They were not seen as humans enduring injuries and ill health.

At 6:30 p.m. as he waited for his buddy to find a ferry ride home to the reserve, C.T. was arrested for being drunk in a public place. The arresting officer knew him well as someone who frequently got drunk, and, as he explained at the inquest, he arrested C.T. for his own good. For Sergeant Lucas, drunk Aboriginal people who are booked regularly "know now they're in a warm place and they can just go to sleep and not worry about anything, and that's how I viewed it."[34] C.T. was polite and friendly, and thanked the officer when he was given a blanket and a mattress (something that is not given to everyone). Once in the cell, C.T. was checked from a distance by a civilian guard who acknowledged (in conversation with a police officer that night) that it is hard to tell if someone is breathing. The log book established that C.T. had not moved for two hours. The camera in the cell that enables guards (who are not allowed into the cells without an officer) to check prisoners was not working, something the guard knew. At 4 a.m., a guard called for officers and alerted them that C.T. had not moved. The guard called for an ambulance. A constable tried to shake C.T. awake, was unable to do so, and called for a mask and first aid kit. He attempted two breaths of CPR. The officer did not do chest compressions and, by his own admission, did not "really" attempt to do CPR because he knew C.T. was dead. He then took photos of the dead prisoner. When the ambulance arrived, no one briefed the attendants about what had happened.

At the inquest, the civilian guard testified that from past experience he knew that C.T. was "a shallow breather, as a lot of Native people are."[35] He was not therefore unduly worried about C.T. appearing not to move or to breathe. The guard had even taught C.T. in kindergarten and was confident in what he knew about him. If one does not check bodies that belong to shallow breathers, it is likely that one also expects their imminent demise. This same guard calmly accepted that C.T. was dead, and once he phoned for the ambulance (informing dispatch that the prisoner was already dead), he did not go back to the cell to find out if he could help or even to establish what was going on. As he explained to the coroner with irritation, "I tried to stay out of the way. I'm not – I mean, I don't have as much first aid ability as they do, for crying out loud."[36] It is difficult to find a word to describe the responses of the guards and the police officers in this case. They were not altogether indifferent; indeed, some understood detention as the most humane option possible. Notwithstanding protocols and procedures about checking on prisoners every thirty minutes, prison guards and police offer little evidence that they see their charges as imperiled and vulnerable and as requiring such care, even though, paradoxically, it is their prisoners' vulnerability that justified detention in the first place.

The inquest offers few clues as to the presence of an outright racial hostility that might account for the guards' and police officers' indifference and negligence. Instead we can trace a noticeable and persistent belief in the pathological vulnerability of Indigenous peoples and an equally strong conviction these were not the kinds of bodies one treated with care. The pathologist was unable to establish cause of death. Taking care to itemize C.T.'s medical history, including (as happened in A.'s case) his "large fatty liver" and large heart, the coroner concluded that the actions of the police and guards did not in any way change the outcome for C.T.[37] He would have likely died anyway. There is a steady racializing that makes wounds and injuries appear as innate and therefore unfixable. C.T.'s condition of ill health is so naturalized – they all breathe shallowly and have fatty livers – that the guards' indifference can be seen as reasonable. The coroner and the jury can believe Constable Lucas when he presents C.T.'s detention as a humanitarian gesture, as simply the kindest thing one can do to a people so beyond help, and find no contradiction in his bringing a man who is incapacitated into the warmth and yet failing to check if he is breathing. Assumptions about race dissolve such contradictions. Even as it conveys the futility of care, the inquest preserves the possibility of room for improvement. The inquest concludes with recommendations for guards to physically check cells every fifteen minutes and to have mandatory working cameras and better CPR training. Police officers are reminded to fill out and consult C13 forms that describe a prisoner's condition. The jury further recommends that the band receive funding for alcohol and drug prevention, and that the state make an effort to provide sports facilities for younger generations.[38] In the following case, abandonment is again demonstrated, as police officers and others make clear their belief that death is always imminent for their Indigenous prisoners, a situation about which they can do nothing. Instead, injured Indigenous people become "biohazards" deposited in cells and left to die, as in S.Q.'s case.

S.Q.: "I Don't Want Him to Die in the Cells"

S.Q. was drinking when he was arrested. S.Q. apparently picked a fight with L., and either a punch or a kick from L. brought S.Q. smashing down on the concrete in an unbroken fall. Sergeant Dickie received a call on his radio informing him that a man was down nearby and that an ambulance had been called. He found S.Q. conscious, not very alert, and with a good-sized bump on his head. Dickie knew S.Q. well and thought him unusually subdued in comparison to the other times he had arrested him, times in which he had sometimes also fallen and hit his head while intoxicated.[39] S.Q. was taken to a nearby clinic, where he was seen by his family physician. The doctor released S.Q. to the care of the police (since S.Q. had nowhere else to go and was very intoxicated with a head injury). Questioned as to why it did not occur to him to send S.Q. to be assessed by emergency, the doctor offered the following:

> Yeah certainly did, it was something that did cross my mind as well. As I mention, at the time he was – he was more or less stable other than the intoxication and my concern was more just monitoring, but I certainly did

> give consideration to having him go to the hospital. But I – I didn't make that move. I thought he'd been in and out of the hospital so many times in – in recent weeks and months, I just wasn't sure what the emergency department was going to say if I phoned again, and so I – but, as I say, I think the main thought was that I just wanted him monitored primarily.[40]

Apparently apprehensive about the hospital viewing S.Q. as a nuisance, his doctor preferred to take his chances with the police as monitors. Curiously, although he wanted S.Q. monitored, the doctor did not provide instructions to the police as to how to deal with prisoners with head injuries, and did not warn them that chronic alcoholics are more likely to have complications from head injuries. He was also unaware that S.Q. had had a seizure in the cells two days earlier and had been admitted to hospital then, although he indicated that he knew of S.Q.'s other multiple hospital admissions. (It is of note that a friend of S.Q., who has since died, tried to persuade the police to take S.Q. to the hospital and may have tried continually throughout the day.)[41] S.Q.'s doctor knew his patient's history and was well aware of his fragility, yet took few steps to ensure his well-being.

S.Q.'s history, head trauma, and gross intoxication did not prompt police officers to treat S.Q. as particularly vulnerable. Sergeant Dickie did not attempt to speak to S.Q. when he transported him to the jail (a twenty-minute ride), something one might consider strange if monitoring for a head wound is necessary. When they arrived at the station, S.Q. was apparently covered in drool and excrement, and Constable Slater went in search of latex gloves in order to properly deal with him. As Slater told the inquest, S.Q. "was a biohazard to pick up and carry."[42] Sergeant Dickie did not wait for Slater's return and claims that he took S.Q. out of the police truck himself and laid him on the cold concrete ground, something that seems implausible given how hard it would be for one man to carry another, especially when the latter is almost inert. When Slater returned with the gloves, the two officers dragged S.Q. to the cells. There is some dispute as to whether the guard on duty was told of the head injury, but the C13 form, which is filled out at booking and intended to record the condition of the prisoner and other important details, contains a notation that S.Q. had a head injury. The form does not indicate whether a rousability check (which is part of protocol) was done upon booking.

For six hours, S.Q. did not change position, and the guard on duty noted only that she checked him and that he was breathing. When another guard, Scott Strickland, came on duty, he recalled that S.Q. had

had a seizure two days ago, and he suggested that S.Q. should be taken to the hospital. Despite his stated concern about S.Q. needing hospital care, Strickland did not then check on S.Q. more carefully. When Corporal Falebrinza overheard the conversation about the hospital that occurred between the guards, he insisted that a doctor had already declared S.Q. fit for incarceration and pronounced that "we can't go doctor-shopping."[43] As Strickland indicated at the inquest, "[T]hat was good enough for me."[44] Corporal Falebrinza maintained that Strickland's concern was that S.Q. might die in the cells. Perhaps sharing that concern, Falebrinza (who also claims that he did not know of the head injury even though it had been recorded) testified that he called S.Q.'s name, and the latter grunted, which indicated to him that there was no need to go to the hospital.

Falebrinza's testimony provides insight into the nature of the response to S.Q. on the part of the guards and the police. S.Q. was someone to be warehoused, rather than cared for. The testimony bears repeating in full:

> And they said we're going to take – I believe it's – the guard Scotty Strickland at that point had said we're going to take Q … up to the – the hospital, I don't want him in – I don't want him in cells. He had a seizure two days previously and so I don't want him in cells, I don't want – I don't want him to die in cells. And I had asked well – well, what is – the seizure was two days previous. What has changed in his condition from when Sgt. Dickie had brought him in the afternoon, when he'd booked him in, like what had changed. And he'd booked him in, like what has changed. And at some point during that, I had approached the cell, the – it was actually – I believe it was the drunk tank number 2. I did approach the – the actual drunk tank and I – I'd called out and I said S, and he had sort of – he grunted and – and lifted his head, which with somebody brought in at the level of intoxication that he – was assumed that he was at, would have been proper – didn't cause me any real concern, and so I said we can't go doctor-shopping. We can't take him back to Penticton Hospital simply because of – we don't want him in our cells. He has to go somewhere.[45]

Over the course of several hours, other prisoners were brought to the cell, and the police maintained that they checked S.Q.'s breathing and noted that he made slight movements and grunts. When questioned about when and how such "rousability" checks were done, however, it becomes clear that checking to see if the prisoner is conscious or alive is not the priority of the police. As Sergeant Dickie explained:

> There are occasions when, you know, obviously sometimes when we bring in intoxicated people we don't want to wake them up ... because of, you know, violent situations things like that, you know, original – or initially anyway.[46]

The sentiment that waking up prisoners was more trouble than it was worth also emerges in Sergeant Tremblay's testimony about his knowledge of the thirty-minute rousability policy:

> But I – I will say this, that in most cases where drunks or people that are being brought in for – in a drunken state – if they are calm for 30 minutes, it's a – it's a blessing, and I can't see a guard going in there and rousing them every 30 minutes just to have him create a disturbance.[47]

Care, it seems, is the last thing on the minds of the guards and police officers.

At 9:30 p.m. that night, a guard asked a police officer to check S.Q., and the latter determined that he was not "rousable." The guard called for an ambulance, informing dispatch that it was a routine rather than an emergency matter. The paramedics who arrived seven minutes later considered S.Q. to be a serious case, and at the hospital it was determined that he had intracranial bleeding. He was rushed to a hospital nearby, where he could be seen by a neurologist, but he was pronounced dead upon arrival.

As with C.T., it is not immediately evident that the police and medical personnel bear any specific racial animus to S.Q. or indeed to Indigenous people specifically. Instead, believing themselves to be on familiar terrain, terrain they understand to be the warehousing of drunks who are simply sleeping off the effects of alcohol, they find nothing in S.Q.'s history or head trauma to prompt them to act otherwise. We can locate race thinking in this incapacity to think that the body before them is one to whom a duty of care is owed. The RCMP officer in charge of the investigation into S.Q.'s death found little to worry him in the files of the case. Challenged about specific moments of apparent negligence, Sergeant Tremblay offered a significant defence of the police's actions. If there was a lax enforcement, for instance, of the rousability requirements, it was only because S.Q. had been there so often and had always managed to walk out on his own steam.[48] Guards and officers could be forgiven for believing that this time was no different. The police did the best they could, he insisted, with someone who would have died anyway:

> Perhaps the question that – that begs to be asked is why is Mr. Q in our custody to begin with? Let's say, for instance – let's say, for instance, that Cst. – or Sgt. Dickie would have chosen not to bring him in to Penticton detachment cells. What would have happened then? Who would have been there to check on his rousability? No one. Perhaps he would have died in a park, perhaps on a park bench, perhaps on his couch … Would we be here today? No. So I think we have to be careful. We have to take in – a couple of things into consideration. People who enter that threshold, the threshold of our detachment cellblock, are at extremely high risk. We accept that and there's measures [*sic*] – we take whatever measures we can to prevent those people from – from dying in our custody. We don't encourage it, we don't like having to go through this process. But what I'm concerned about is that if it comes to ignoring those people, the needs of these people and our members begin turning their back – or turning their backs on because they don't want to experience this type of thing, then I'm afraid that these people are in fact going to start meeting their demise in places other than the – the cellblock. So I think the question that begs to be answered – begs to be asked and answered is – is why he was there in the first place, and – and I think the answer to that is 'cause there's nowhere else for him to go … He wasn't admitted, so he becomes arrestable because in this case he's not able to look after himself. There's perhaps a chance that he's going to re-offend by – causing a disturbance or – or getting into another altercation, so he's taken into custody.[49]

Sergeant Tremblay delivers a stark warning to the coroner and the jury: "We don't like having to go through this process." If the police decide that they will simply stop arresting Indigenous people because of the possibility of an inquest into their deaths, then Indigenous people will meet their demise in places other than the cellblock. They will also continue to cause disturbances. Sergeant Tremblay cannot imagine that police have a duty to care. Faced with such warnings, there is little new for a jury to propose. The jury enjoins the police to properly fill out C13 forms and ensure that guards are trained in how to assess prisoner responsiveness. As though expressing frustration with the scope of what can be said, the jury emphasizes that police must never assume that a prisoner is simply sleeping off the effects of alcohol. To monitor, the jury notes, means to watch or observe without interruption.[50]

Prior medical conditions, moments of acute traumas (blows to the head), communicative acts such as a friend's plea that S.Q. be taken to the hospital, and C13 forms pervasively ignored are outside the ambit of custodial care. S.Q.'s grunts in response to a question, Paul Alphonse's mumbles when asked about who might have stomped on him, and C.T.'s failure to respond when called do not unduly disturb medical and police professionals; perhaps grunts and mumbles are all they expect. It is not surprising that administrative systems fail and that there is such an entrenched failure to exercise care, given the widespread belief that to exercise care is to waste effort. In the face of this logic, coroners' recommendations that have to do with C13 forms, policies on head traumas, and better monitoring procedures will likely be ignored, as they have been so many times before. Inquests memorialize Indigenous disappearance anew.

It is difficult to believe there has been negligence on the part of police or medical personnel, because inquests ply us with descriptions of addiction and damaged livers. Death in these circumstances, they conclude, is hardly mysterious. T.M., for example, was arrested for public intoxication. He was so intoxicated he was unable to sign his name while being booked, a condition that did not overly concern the police. His autopsy revealed that he had a blood alcohol level three times the legal limit, as well as an unknown quantity of methadone in his blood. Bill Watt, the guard on duty, was warned to check T.M. closely and testified that he did so. Watt felt he could see whether or not T.M. was breathing through the cell door, even though T.M. had not moved in several hours. T.M. stopped breathing several hours after he was booked. When asked about the three deaths he had experienced in his six years as a guard, Watt responded simply: "People die."[51] Like A. discussed earlier, T.M. just became part of the statistics about severely intoxicated people who die in the cells a few hours after being arrested. The sheer amount of detail about Indigenous bodies destroyed and minds lost, a forensically staged drama, obscures the possibility that police or guards have acted violently. We do not easily see the violence of neglect when we are inundated with these details and are more easily persuaded that Indigenous people have caused their own demise. It is difficult to distinguish explicitly racist intention from indifference, but the outcome remains the same: Indigenous death.

V.A., a thirty-three-year-old Indigenous woman who was denied access to her asthma inhalers and to medicine for nausea, died in custody, malnourished and suffering from morphine withdrawal. V.A., in the throes of an asthma attack on a hot August day, was driven to hospital in a squad car. Inexplicably, the heater was on full blast in the car.[52] It is never established what responsibility the police bore for her death. Amidst the details about her malnourished and damaged body, it is only possible to believe that the police could have been a little more careful than they were with V.A. Police indifference, an indifference that borders on deliberate neglect, is also visible in the case of A.C. A.C. asked to go to the hospital and felt that he was dying; he was ignored and died in custody of pancreatitis. As the family lawyer, Don Worme, recalled, the essence of the pathologist's testimony at the inquest was that A.C. was going to die anyway; taking him to the hospital would not have changed that. Protesting that "there were more humane ways to die than the way A.C. died," Worme tried to make the case not only for Indigenous dignity but for Indigenous life. His own response, that "when a man says he is going to die, you listen," is not one that the inquest considers.[53] As with A.C. and V.A., fatty livers, diseased lungs, and cancerous cells explain it all.

Part Three. Suicides: Resisting Dehumanization

The conviction that Indigenous life is wasted life and that prisons are merely warehouses for the dying surfaces in police and health professionals' testimonies. When a chance arises to contest this story, Indigenous people insist it is their humanity that is at issue. While inquests into suicide cases demonstrate how entrenched is the conviction that little can be done for a dying race, they also show Indigenous challenge to the hegemonic story, as in the suicide of A.E. while in prison. One-third of Indigenous deaths in custody in Saskatchewan involve suicide.[54] Inquests into these deaths set out to determine what could be done to limit the opportunities an inmate has to commit suicide. They typically explore whether there can be procedures to identify at-risk inmates, counselling options, more routine checks on inmates, and the elimination of hanging points in cells. Inquests stage Indigenous suicide as something prisons can do little about beyond renewed vigilance. Institutional failings are masked by the story of a people bent on self-destruction.

A.E., a prisoner on remand from the far North, appears to have planned his suicide carefully, asking a fellow inmate to smudge him, giving away his books, and making a dummy with his blankets to fool guards into thinking he was in his bed. A.E. hanged himself with a shoelace, choosing a corner of his cell that would be partially obscured by a door. Guards performing their mandatory checks by shining a flashlight through the cell window reported that they found it difficult to tell that A.E. was not actually in his bed. The mandatory check every four hours to check for breathing, again with a flashlight shone through the cell window, failed to uncover the dummy made of sheets in the bed. The inquest into A.E.'s death was an unusual one; although the family had no legal representation, they were able to vigorously challenge the coroner and various witnesses. Their interventions accomplished what neither the guards' flashlights nor the coroner's counsel could manage, namely to shine a light on what went so terribly wrong in A.E.'s incarceration. Family members asked pointed questions about how the system dealt with prisoners on remand who had not yet been tried or sentenced. Such people, the family insisted, are likely to be deeply emotionally shocked. What was done to deal with their emotional states? When prisoners come from the North, have little education, and speak little English, they are especially isolated and emotionally distressed. How aware were correctional officers of "our people"? one family member asked.[55] Pressing the matter further, a second family member, T., asked whether professional help was available to prisoners on remand. Advised that elders were sometimes made available, T. pointed out the obvious: elders could not offer professional psychiatric help.[56] Were there other suicides at the prison? T. asked, and was incredulous when the official questioned replied there had been two, but he could not remember the details. Did the guards really care about whether or not inmates lived?

> Okay. I was just amazed that you were saying you vaguely recollected that there was [*sic*] two prior suicide attempts. I guess I mean something like that would strike me as being really of a serious nature and something that I wouldn't really vaguely recollect. I guess that's sort of the – the tone I am – I was talking about initially when I said, you know, you punched a clock and, you know, there's got to be more than that in your role of a human being, whether, you know, they're in that situation or, you know, law-abiding citizens. I mean they're still an important part of … our system.[57]

How did it happen, another family member asked, that there was so little professionalism among prison personnel? When she phoned the prison, staff would inform her that she had reached Ford Motors and not the prison. As a teacher herself, who abides by a professional code of ethics, this family member wanted to know why she had encountered such unprofessional conduct. Through their pointed questions, A.E.'s family inserted into the inquest the crux of the matter concerning a death in custody: how is an inmate's humanity respected? Officials testifying at the inquest were anxious not to be "misunderstood," as one official put it, yet most could supply no concrete answers to the questions raised by the family.

The jury's recommendations only repeat what so many other inquests have already established: proper hourly checks, well-lit cells, psychiatric checks on remand inmates, and culturally sensitive activities. The cases involving physically or mentally ill persons, prisoners who are addicts or alcoholics, and those who commit suicide all share the pernicious and systemic inhumanity of the prison that A.E.'s family tried so hard to pin down. Yet it remains difficult to call anyone to account, and inquests continue to provide the setting for replaying a story of how difficult it is to care for a people so poorly equipped for modern life. I have shown that inquests do not investigate the indifference and dehumanization that Indigenous people name, which is visible in the mundane details about how guards interact with families and with prisoners themselves.

Conclusion. Towards an Anatomy of Indifference

Indigeneity is often viewed as a disabling "condition"; indeed, the most progressive of inquests and inquiries, those that acknowledge injury to Indigenous people, insist on a direct parallel between Indigeneity and disability.[58] Not surprisingly, the "natural body" made possible by viewing disability as a flawed version of humanity is the same "natural body" that installs the settler as owner of himself and owner of land. Flawed bodies (insufficiently modern bodies frozen in a pre-modern, pre-capitalist mode)[59] are not owners, as the legal principle of *terra nullius* confirms. It is immensely useful to settler society to believe that Indigenous people are on the brink of death and are always flawed bodies. Writing about the depiction of Indians as ghosts in American national literature, Renée Bergland observes that

> the ghosting of Indians is a technique of removal. By writing about Indians as ghosts, white writers effectively remove them from American lands, and place them, instead, within the American imagination.[60]

It is as though Native Americans have vanished into the minds of those who have dispossessed them. Confining Indians to the "spectral," European Americans become original citizens. Bergland's provocative argument that ghosts are also powerful figures who haunt and her declaration that the land is haunted because it is stolen remind us that settlers cannot simply forget those whom they have confined to the spectral, particularly when we consider that the land is still being stolen and Indians remain very much alive. Settlers' feelings of dread and creeping horror remain, Bergland suggests, and considerable anxiety surrounds the way European Americans imagine themselves as the original citizens of this land and as a people innocent of conquest and violence. The very thought of Indians must be forcefully repressed, yet "the nation is compelled to return again and again to an encounter that makes it both sorry and happy, a defiled grave upon which it must continually rebuild the American subject."[61] The inquest may be usefully compared to the defiled grave of which Bergland speaks, the place where bodies (and bones) are made to give up their secrets, but only those secrets that confirm the settler as legitimate owner of the land. The inquest is undeniably a haunted place.

The inquest stages Indigeneity as dysfunction, incurable illness, disability, and a threat to the healthy social body. Both an event and a place, the inquest transforms the colonial condition into a medical one, legitimizing the violence that is performed at the police station, on the streets, and in the hospital, wherever settlers encounter Indigenous people and demarcate between the human and less than human through acts of violence described as help. Coroners often cast themselves as reminding others of their ethical requirement to remedy Indigeneity. A dutiful coroner may even instruct society in what Rod Michalko (in reference to disability) has termed the "banal courtesies": in the case of disability, the injunction to be sensitive to the misfortune of others (don't stare), and in the case of Indigeneity, the self-conscious practice of cultural sensitivity, usually limited to an Indigenous prayer or healing circle at the inquest, perhaps an eagle feather decorating the printed commissioner's report, and a plethora of recommendations reminding us to be sensitive to cultural practices and to the special vulnerabilities of a sick and dysfunctional population.[62] Amidst all this, the killing indifference that I have traced through many cases persists. What would it mean to dissect indifference, instead of its object? In this chapter, I suggested the focus must be on widespread assumptions made by state actors that Indigenous people are always on the brink of death, are authors of their own demise, and do not deserve full care. These assumptions and the practices of neglect to which they give rise amount to dehumanization, the failure to believe that Indigenous life matters.

Chapter Five

The Medico-legal Alliance: Anthany Dawson and the Diagnosis of Excited Delirium

I do not know as a fact that the police caused Anthany's death. I DO know that no person should be taken into custody by violence when they are offering no resistance. The actions of the police surrounding Anthany's death call into the question the relationship of the police force, not only with respect to First Nation's people, but with all people.

Nancy Dawson, mother of Anthany Dawson[1]

Introduction

At approximately 3:40 p.m. on the afternoon of 11 August 1999, Anthany Dawson left a message on his mother's answering machine: "Hey, Mom. On my way home."[2] The message is heartbreaking given Dawson's subsequent death, but it is also uncanny, because not more than thirty minutes later, Anthany Dawson would be seen running through the streets of Victoria, screaming and tearing off his clothes. Many witnesses who heard his screams that day, screams and moans that went on for over twenty minutes, describe them as full of anguish and desperation. For witness Noel Manual, they were screams of "sheer terror."[3] Only one witness, Constable Lawrence Hemstad, who was the first officer on the scene, refuted the idea that Dawson's screams were screams of pain, anguish, or distress. They were the result of overdosing on drugs, the former RCMP officer testified, something he had seen many times in his career and particularly when he had worked on Vancouver's Downtown East Side.[4] Dawson ran through the streets, stopping to lie down on the road and screaming loudly. When ambulance and police personnel arrived, he offered no verbal responses but instead kept screaming. Eight witnesses reported that a police officer on the scene punched him several times. One off-duty sheriff, whom one witness described as a big, muscular man who looked like a bouncer, appeared to sit on Dawson to restrain him.[5] After several efforts to subdue him, Dawson was restrained with handcuffs in a position some describe as hog-tying (where hands are bound to feet or where hands are bound and feet are bound) and transported to a gurney, face down. Once in the ambulance, a paramedic noticed that Dawson was not breathing. CPR was administered en route to the hospital. Dawson did not respond, and two days later, he was taken off life support and pronounced dead.

Dawson's screams and his behaviour that fateful day in August almost correspond to the criteria for "excited delirium syndrome," defined by its most often cited expert, pathologist Dr Vincent Di Maio, as involving "the sudden death of an individual, during or following an episode of excited delirium, in which an autopsy fails to reveal evidence of sufficient trauma or natural disease to explain the death."[6] Di Maio, a renowned expert on gunshot wounds, a former editor-in-chief of the *Journal of Forensic Medicine*, and an expert who has often testified on behalf of the police (for example, in the highly publicized 2013 shooting of a Black youth, Trayvon Martin, by George Zimmerman, a security guard at a gated community)[7] is the co-author, with Theresa Di Maio, of the widely used book *Excited Delirium Syndrome: Cause of Death and Prevention*.

From its inception as a syndrome in the 1980s (although researchers are often at pains to provide a longer history), excited delirium syndrome has been connected to police, medical, and coronial actions. It emerges only when police force is at issue, when there is evidence of drug use or mental distress, and when the physical evidence of trauma is inconclusive. Not surprisingly, excited delirium syndrome is controversial, with some researchers and judges suggesting that the syndrome too handily exonerates police, especially in cases involving racial minorities and mentally ill people. Many medical and legal researchers accept that the syndrome is real, however, and believe it is useful to prepare police and other professionals to deal with the syndrome (now increasingly shortened to ExDS) in order to prevent fatalities. In Anthany Dawson's case, drug use was minimal (only trace amounts of marijuana were found in his blood, and he had been off hard drugs for a few years), and there was no prior history of mental illness or episodes of acute mental distress. Nevertheless, a coroner's inquest concluded that Dawson died of restraint-associated cardiac arrest, an accidental death brought on by aggravated delirium, complicated by a presumed genetic abnormality called a CPT deficiency and marijuana use. Relying heavily on medical expertise, the jury concluded that the police were not to blame for Dawson's death.

In this chapter, I explore how the inquest is structured to support the idea of a medical and drug-related cause of death. This outcome is especially likely when the victim belongs to a group historically marked as threatening and irrational, and with whom the police have had previous encounters. The inquest rarely attends to such histories, and in ruling out details about the social context, the inquest limits the chances that what happened that day to Anthany Dawson could be connected to the use of excessive force by the police. Medical knowledge production is key to the end result of attributing death to Indigenous pathological frailty rather than to police brutality, an argument I make by exploring the history and application of ExDS to deaths in custody. While other groups, such as those deemed mentally ill or anyone who is racialized, can be governed through what I describe below as the ExDS apparatus, I emphasize how Indigeneity as a colonial condition is what is expressly occluded in the inquest into Anthany Dawson's death. In part one, I discuss the medico-legal alliance of colonial and racial regimes, beginning, by way of introduction, with colonial India, but moving quickly to contemporary North America and the United Kingdom. In part two, I explore the Dawson inquest, showing the operation of the same alliance and how it obscures the colonial relationship between Indigenous peoples and police. I conclude with a consideration of the relationship between policing and land.

In her first public statement following his death, Anthany Dawson's mother made clear her own view that police force was the central issue. No one should be treated the way her son was treated. While Nancy Dawson's sentiment is widely shared by non-Indigenous people who have lost loved ones in the same way, her statement that police actions shed light on police/First Nations relationships as well as on police relationships to other groups is a reminder that the specific, historical settler relationship to Indigenous peoples must be examined. The inquest's reluctance to examine what Indigeneity had to do with police actions suggests that something more than police attitudes to vulnerable people is at issue. If Indigenous peoples are to remain trespassers in the settler town, policing practices must accomplish their eviction. As part of modern practices of rule, law must approve of these evictions through the marking of the Indigenous body as inherently degenerate.

As in the inquests and inquiries discussed in preceding chapters, the Dawson inquest remains faithful to the logic of the "vanishing Indian," the construct, that is, of a pathologically fragile individual belonging to a race for whom death is always imminent. The genetic abnormality that takes on such a central role in the coronial explanation for Dawson's death comes as close to innatism (a paradigm of irredeemable human difference) as is possible, recalling colonial paradigms of genetic inferiority and human development scales.[8] It is this logic that makes it difficult to examine police actions. Inquests begin from the premise that police force is necessary, and participate in the naturalization of practices of extreme force through the production of the Indigenous body as a body that only extreme force can control. Medical knowledge is party to this production.

Part One. Colonial Legal Precedent: The Boot and the Liver

Under the British Raj in colonial India, Jordanna Bailkin writes, the law often considered the following situation: if a Briton kicked an Indian, fatally rupturing his spleen, was the Briton guilty of murder?[9] Since some Indians in Bengal and Assam had enlarged spleens due to repeated bouts of malaria, and since Bengal and Assam were also "flashpoints of interracial violence and nationalist agitation, medical evaluations of the Indian spleen were deeply relevant to criminal jurisprudence."[10] Reviewing boot and spleen cases between the 1870s and 1920s in British India, Bailkin shows that through "the investigation of the Indian spleen, the British boot was rendered something less than murderous."[11] Medical evidence was introduced to make the case that persons with enlarged spleens could be killed by even a trivial amount of violence. Enlarged spleens, although possible in both Indians and Europeans, came to be seen as an Indian characteristic, because enlarged spleens often occurred after a bout of malaria, and malaria itself was taken as a sign of racial degeneration: "Only Europeans who indulged in 'native' practices, such as opium abuse, were considered susceptible to pathologies of the spleen."[12] Indian bodies were thus seen as "pathologically fragile."[13] If enlarged spleens were seen as inevitably Indian, the boot was "an unmistakable marker of foreignness in India (the western shod foot versus the bare foot of the Hindu)."[14] Invoking the military and "an era of ceaseless drilling and parading, the boot was both a material marker of territorial conquest and part of the spectacle thereof."[15] As the Indian press of the day, *Oudh Punch*, was quick to grasp, the racial underpinnings of the boot and spleen cases were inescapable. Indian spleens were always at risk of British boots.[16]

The title of Bailkin's article, "The Boot and the Spleen: When Was Murder Possible in British India?," startled me when I first came across it, because it recalled the death of Paul Alphonse (discussed in chapters three and four), who died in hospital while in police custody in British Columbia. Alphonse had a large purple boot print on his chest, which few of the police or medical personnel with whom he came into contact apparently noticed. In one thousand pages of the inquest into Alphonse's death, it seemed to me that the boot print on Alphonse's chest (how it got there, when it first emerged, who noticed it, and who asked questions about it) faded in importance in inverse proportion to the attention given to the fact that Alphonse was a chronic alcoholic. Because the savage kick that someone delivered to an alcoholic old man was eventually relegated to a secondary rung, I thought that I might well be writing a book called "The Boot and the Liver." The focus on damaged spleens and livers can appear as a progressive move, since it leads to the conclusion that Indigenous people are ill and should be treated more humanely than the police appear to do when they respond to Indigenous people. If the problem is defined as biological, however, ultimately the only place where blame can be laid is on Indigenous peoples themselves. It then becomes enormously difficult to consider dispossession and to show the persistent inhumanity that it both requires and produces and that colonizers exhibit towards those whom they have dispossessed. Put in the terms of colonial India and contemporary Canada, the boot is never the focus of the law.

Excited Delirium: A Story of the Boot and the Heart

Today, if there is any immediate comparison to the boot and spleen cases of the British Raj, it would be British and North American cases involving the deaths of racial minority men while being restrained by police, prison, or army officials. In 1998, Richard Tilt, the director of Prison Services for the United Kingdom, explained to the media that the death of Alton Manning, a Black man who died in custody while in a neck hold (the third Black man to die in custody between October and December 1995), possibly occurred because African-Caribbean men with "sickle cell traits" were more likely to suffer positional asphyxia than whites.[17] As Simon Dyson and Gwyneth Boswell show, the linking of sickle cell traits to death while being restrained invokes several racial discourses at once. Sickle cell anemia, a serious inherited blood disorder, affects people of African and African-Caribbean, Indian, Arabic, and Mediterranean descent; one in three hundred people of African-Caribbean descent in the United Kingdom and the United States are affected.[18] As Dyson and Boswell explain, the "sickle cell trait is the carrier state where a person carries a gene associated with sickle cell, but is not ill themselves."[19] The carrier state and the full illness are often confused in the cases involving sudden death. Interestingly, while sickle cell attracts attention in cases of sudden death in custody, it has not done so when individuals require treatment or protection from discrimination that arises when their carrier status becomes known. Prisoners suffering from sickle cell have sometimes died because their treatment needs were ignored.[20] Dyson and Boswell note that hospital staff in both the United Kingdom and the United States are reluctant to provide pain-relieving drugs to Black people on the basis that Black people misuse drugs. Reviewing British and American cases where a link was made between sickle cell anemia (either traits or illness) and "positional asphyxia" (where death results from pressure on the neck), Dyson and Boswell conclude that in the sickle cell cases, the Black body is constructed as an inherently diseased body, and the reference to sickle cell deflects accusations of racism or culpability for death. The cases they review include, for example, Donald Flemming of Buffalo, New York, who died in police custody after a robbery. The medical examiner concluded that his heart attack had been brought on by cocaine abuse and sickle cell traits. However, the director of the funeral home handling Flemming's body reported that he had found a giant gash on Flemming's head, an injury that was not reported by the examiner.[21]

Sudden in-custody death syndrome (SICDS), as the phenomenon of deaths of individuals restrained by the police came to be called (in association with the mysterious sudden infant death syndrome or SIDS), was coined to describe cases where death was the result of a type of asphyxiation. Positional asphyxia or restraint asphyxia refers to "asphyxiation death while in a prone position and hog-tied restraints in whole or in part from respiratory compromise."[22] Associated with an episode of "excited delirium" preceded by psychotic breakdown as a result of drug use, sudden in-custody deaths were then explained as restraint-related deaths, where there was no single, easily identifiable cause of death. The medical literature describes victims of SICDS as exhibiting unusual strength and aggression, agitation and paranoia. As with the boot and spleen cases discussed earlier, "[m]edical examiners argue that people who die of excited delirium death syndrome while restrained are not victims of incompetence or brutality, but rather victims of their own long term drug use, which resulted in a strained heart that further exacerbated the victim's condition."[23] Some medical experts suggest that what individuals are really dying from is an overdose of adrenalin and insist that one can tell the difference medically between death as a result of police abuse (beatings, hog-tying, and so on) and death due to excited delirium. In contrast, critics point out that all such cases share "a proclivity for dying in police custody."[24] The American Civil Liberties Union has been particularly vocal in its criticism of the use of excited delirium to explain deaths in custody, and the media has also expressed scepticism of the phenomenon, uncovering stories, for example, of a Black man assaulted by police, hit forty times with a baton, who, it was concluded, died of excited delirium.[25]

The Syndrome as a Medico-legal Alliance

Medical conditions frequently have a connection to legal interests, and it is useful to reconstruct excited delirium as a medico-legal alliance, tracing the apparatus of knowledge production that regulates what we can and cannot know about who is to blame for a death in custody. Specifically, how does excited delirium operate to make undue use of force impossible (to paraphrase Bailkin's question discussed earlier)? How, in other words, does excited delirium operate as an apparatus of governance? The propensity of medical explanations to remove from the analysis any social context and their capacity to engage in what Toni Morrison describes as an economy of stereotype, "a quick and easy image without the responsibility of specificity, accuracy, or even narratively useful description,"[26] are two features of the medico-legal apparatus. It is useful to examine a recent legal article by Michael L. Storey, "Explaining the Unexplainable: Excited Delirium Syndrome and Its Impact on the Objective Reasonableness Standard for Allegations of Excessive Force," which is representative of its genre.[27] As the title indicates, the death of an agitated man (it is always a man) in police custody is cast from the beginning as a mysterious event requiring unusual explanation. Immediately, the possibility of excessive force becomes rare and almost beyond imagining.

Storey begins with a sequence of events one finds in both medical and legal literature, a narrative that starts with the individual and not with his context. A man starts yelling, flailing, and disrobing. He appears impervious to pain. Police arrive to find an agitated man who is sweating profusely and doesn't communicate or respond to verbal commands. The police cannot control the man. They use an electronic stunning device (Taser) and/or place a knee on his neck and use their weight to hold him down. The more the man thrashes, the more weight has to be applied. Somewhere in this process, the police realize that the man is no longer breathing. The sequence of events varies only slightly. Sometimes the man's hands and feet are bound, and the man is face down when it is discovered he is no longer breathing. In this latter scenario, Storey asserts that the method of restraint itself does not restrict breathing; restraint is merely the circumstance under which breathing stops.

Legal or medical analysts such as Storey often write unabashedly on the side of the police, with no pretense of objectivity. Storey frames his argument as a response to public perception that instances of ExDS are instances of police brutality, a perception he believes is fueled by a media only interested in controversy. Quoting the Di Maios, Storey writes: "The continued media attention is fueled because the average person cannot conceptualize the violence with which such individuals can struggle."[28] The contest is, from the outset, the experts versus the average person, the latter described as only interested in laying blame, punishing, or suing, and unable to grasp the exigencies of policing and, in particular, just how violent an agitated person can be. Public outrage continues when a local medical examiner releases the cause of death as due to cocaine-induced excited delirium. Often repeating the phrase "the average person," Storey is adamant that critics who suggest ExDS is merely a cover for police brutality simply do not understand medical science. If they did, they would know that force is always reasonable, given how violent and unpredictable agitated men are. In effect, murder is never possible with such unmanageable bodies. Although science is writ large here, in fact Storey relies heavily on the Di Maios, with an occasional reference to other journalistic articles and to one or two other frequently cited medical researchers. The science referred to is simple: an already stressed heart (from drug use, a pre-existing genetic condition, or a psychiatric disorder, the latter sometimes including intellectual impairment) gives out when a struggle with police makes the body demand more oxygen; a chronic condition exhibits acute symptoms, and there is a physical response (too much adrenalin) to a psychological problem.[29] Death results from a lack of oxygen, an event described by one medical practitioner as "a neuro-cardiac event."[30] The medical terms and listing of symptoms operate here to cast a shield of objectivity that avoids the obvious: what if the police use too much force?

Since the American Medical Association currently does not recognize excited delirium syndrome, Storey accounts for their position by offering the explanation that those who don't accept the existence of the syndrome are doctors who don't often work with victims who are already dead.[31] By definition, ExDS is only traceable when someone has died from restraint-associated cardiac arrest. To bolster his argument, Storey appeals to medical practitioners who have served on a Task Force formed to address the issue. Task Forces have been formed in several jurisdictions, including Canada.[32] All such Task Forces repeat the schema one finds in legal articles such as Storey's, concluding that while ExDS has an uncertain etiology, it is indeed a real syndrome. (Storey cites the "White Paper Report on Excited Delirium Syndrome" by the American College of Emergency Physicians [ACEP].)[33] Task Force reports add to the repertoire of scientific description by including statistics. For example, the ACEP white paper to which Storey refers describes the frequency of potential characteristics of ExDS cases as follows: "characteristics with 95% confidence intervals: pain tolerance 100%; tachypnea (rapid breathing) 100%; sweating 95%; tactile hyperthermia 95%; police non-compliance 90%; lack of tiring 90%; unusual strength 90%; inappropriately clothed 70%; mirror glass attraction 10%."[34]

Although the apparently technical and scientific measurement of characteristics amounts to little more than a description of any agitated person in a struggle who is removing his clothing, the accumulation of scientific-sounding data contributes to the argument that ExDS and not undue force is the cause of death. In a final circular argument, Storey advocates that we should presume in favour of the existence of ExDS, because providing a medical framework is the only way police officers might be prepared to deal with it.[35] If upon following this argument, one is tempted to ask questions about use of force, Storey notes that not all individuals who are restrained die – only those with ExDS do. Further, Tasers are not any more at fault than the weight of a police officer, because those who appear to die from Tasers do not die immediately. Pleading that we need to understand the entirety of circumstances when a case involves force, Storey rests his argument on the assertion that emotionally disturbed persons always require the use of extraordinary force. A court should therefore look at the condition of the suspect and the training of the police officer.[36] Notably, the court is not enjoined to examine the actions of the police officer, and any frame other than the medical one is ruled out from the start. If the circularity of the above arguments is easy to detect, it is also clear that the label "emotionally disturbed" conveys a condition that we might describe as *homo sacer*. Nothing committed against an emotionally disturbed person can be considered a crime, to invoke Agamben.[37]

The *Journal of Forensic and Legal Medicine* regularly publishes articles along the same narrative lines as Storey's. For example, in 2012, Gary M. Vilke, Jason Payne-James, and Steven B. Karch, three physicians who participated in a meeting organized by the National Institute of Justice that included law enforcement officers, emergency room personnel, forensic pathologists, and psychiatrists, summarized the current knowledge about ExDS. They noted that patients with the syndrome present with "altered sensorium and aggressive agitated behavior, and a combination of other symptoms including 'superhuman' strength, diaphoresis, hyperthermia, propensity to break glass, attraction to light or lack of willingness to yield to overwhelming force."[38] If ExDS remains a syndrome and not a disease, it is only because the condition lacks a clear definition and pathophysiologic etiology. Setting out to shed light on the condition, these three physicians first suggest a link between ExDS and the nineteenth century clinical condition known as Bell's mania, in which individuals labelled mentally disturbed exhibited symptoms of delirium.[39] At that time, however, the condition was associated with psychiatric illness, whereas in the contemporary period, it is most often associated with cocaine abuse. People with psychiatric illnesses who stop taking their medications may, however, also exhibit the symptoms of ExDS. In 2009, Canadian police recorded 698 encounters involving use of force and identified the presence of ten symptoms or more in over three per cent of cases.[40] Vilke, Payne-James, and Karch report that there are no clear reasons why some people exhibiting these symptoms die and others don't. It is only clear that the majority who die do so shortly after a violent struggle.[41] Rather than concluding that this pattern requires us to consider the role of force in causing death, the authors explain the pattern as revealing that severe acidosis (an abnormal increase in blood acidity) plays a prominent role in death. Given this physiological state, the authors recommend that medical and police professionals should learn to recognize the symptoms and work towards the goal of understanding the situation as a medical emergency, obtaining physical control so as to avoid prolonged struggle, and then having medical personnel administer a sedative. As they sum up: "Identify, Control, Sedate, and Transport."[42]

Legal Narratives

In those rare cases where coroners or commissioners of inquiry reject ExDS explicitly, judges and legal professionals have pointed out that the line of reasoning which begins with ExDS carries the danger that police use of force will not be sufficiently interrogated. In his report on the inquiry into the death of Robert Dziekanski, a Polish visitor to Canada who died in the Vancouver airport within minutes of police using a conducted energy weapon popularly known as a "Taser," Commissioner Thomas Braidwood is unequivocal:

> It is not helpful to blame resulting deaths on "excited delirium," since this conveniently avoids having to examine the underlying medical condition or conditions that actually caused death, let alone examining whether use of the conducted energy weapon and/or subsequent measures to physically restrain the subject contributed to those causes of death.[43]

As Braidwood makes clear, police need to learn to de-escalate situations involving emotionally disturbed persons. Noting that police training practices too often rely on the manufacturer, Taser International, which advises on the condition they call ExDS and implicitly supports the use of force, Braidwood identifies the way in which knowledge about ExDS travels from manufacturer to police to coroner and is at pains to elaborate on counter information that deals with the use of force on persons described as vulnerable. Of note, for instance, an Australian study of Taser weapons concluded that police officers should receive further guidance when Tasers are directed towards people with mental illness, children, pregnant women, elderly people, people affected by alcohol or drugs, people with a heart condition or implanted defibrillators, and Indigenous Australians.[44] Presumably, in the case of Indigenous Australians, police were likely to use Tasers inappropriately. Braidwood concludes that Tasers are the least useful strategy (they do not appear to have led to a decrease in deaths due to police use of guns, for example) and often pre-empt other, more effective approaches of de-escalation.

Relying on some of the same medical experts as did Commissioner Braidwood, Madame Justice Anne Derrick also concludes that in the case of Howard Hyde,[45] a mentally ill man who died after a struggle with police during booking, police restraint was a factor in his death. Rejecting medical experts who testified that the cause of death was

ExDS associated with paranoid schizophrenia, Derrick points out that this medical explanation omits the external factor of restraint.

> The use of excited delirium to explain sudden deaths with no anatomic findings implies that the person had something wrong with them that caused their inexplicable death. Manner of death may then be classified as "natural" rather than "accidental." I take the same view as Dr. Butt on this issue and do not accept that this would have been appropriate in Mr. Hyde's case or similar cases.[46]

An officer weighing three hundred pounds sat on Mr Hyde and may well have compromised his ability to breathe. Like Braidwood, Derrick determines that it is not wise to train police officers in identifying ExDS, given that this simply discourages the use of alternative, more effective, and less lethal strategies.

Both Braidwood and Derrick stress that a more effective approach involves recognizing the humanity of the person who is in crisis, as did the 2014 verdict of the coroner's jury in the Ontario inquest into the deaths of three mentally ill Ontarians who died at police hands.[47] In Derrick's words, "At an immediate, fundamental level, what Mr. Hyde needed was human contact, reassurance and kindness … Understanding this is to understand Mr. Hyde's humanity and recognize in him, ourselves."[48] The humanity of the Other is precisely what is at issue in police encounters with Indigenous people and with those considered to be mentally ill. At the heart of the debate over ExDS is the issue of threat. Police usually argue that the use of force was proportionate to the level of threat an individual presented. It is not uncommon to hear at inquests and inquiries arguments by police that the individual in question possessed superhuman strength. One can trace the linguistic strategies intended to convey the non-humanity of those against whom force must be deployed. The further a person is from the category of "human," the more legitimate exercising force becomes. Both mental illness and race offer well-worn discursive tracks that evict people from the category of human. As critical race and disability rights scholars have shown, it has long been believed that racialized groups and those declared mentally ill pose a particular threat to social order. Catherine Carstairs, for example, has shown how drug-taking has historically been assumed to be a racial matter; cocaine acquired its reputation as the most dangerous drug because of its association with Black men.[49] Social reform involving the control of drugs is inevitably racialized, standing in for control of racialized populations.

Importantly, when details such as race impinge on what Dorothy E. Smith described in her work on coronial findings of suicide as an insistence on endogeny, phenomena without external causes, out of time and place, the specific histories of relations between police and vulnerable groups are deemed irrelevant.[50] Howard Hyde, a man with a mental illness, for instance, had a well-founded fear of being Tasered since he had already been Tasered by police. Similarly, Anthany Dawson would have had no reason to trust the police of Victoria, having been repeatedly stopped by them on numerous occasions and having encountered racism. While such factors do not automatically indict police, they are reasons to interrogate police responses to marginalized groups. In effect, the history that lies between the racialized and those considered mentally ill and police has a bearing on how we examine who did what to whom. It is this line of argument that the medico-legal alliance successfully pre-empts, working in tandem with the historical taboo that exists in white settler societies against naming racism and ongoing colonialism.

Part Two. The Inquest

In her address to the jury at the conclusion of the inquest into Anthany Dawson's death, Coroner Dianne Olson offered a framework to jurors for use in their deliberations that clearly emphasized a medical explanation over police use of force. Stressing that inquests are about death prevention, and not about finding blame, the coroner began by observing that Anthany Dawson had used marijuana on the day he was apprehended, and on days before. Her description of Dawson's behaviour that day, very akin to the list of ExDS characteristics, included the following: "screaming loudly"; "holding his head groaning"; "removed articles of clothing and his shoes and resumed running"; "lying on the roadway"; "not verbally responding to their [police] questions or their requests"; "very agitated"; "sweating heavily." She then noted the sequence of events: "He, again, laid down on the roadway near Bank Street where a police officer attempted to detain him with the assistance of an off-duty peace officer who had been driving by and stopped to offer assistance. Additional police officers responded, and together with ambulance personnel, attempted to place Mr. Dawson on the stretcher. After some resistance he was secured, facedown, and put into the awaiting ambulance. Moments later, Mr. Dawson was noted to be unresponsive."[51]

To this description and sequence, the coroner added that all evidence failed to reveal signs of internal injuries to the head, neck, and torso, and only inconsequential "friction abrasions" were found;[52] toxicology studies revealed no drugs in Dawson's system except for marijuana. Finally, Dawson was hyperthermic when he arrived at the hospital, with a body temperature of forty degrees Celsius, a result perhaps of exertion on a warm day.[53] The jury was instructed that the pathologist, Dr Gray, concluded that death was caused by "restraint-associated cardiac arrest due to an agitated delirium state associated with cannabis use and hyperthermia."[54] Having set the stage for how the jury ought to consider Dawson's death, the coroner then stated with confidence that "positional asphyxia was not considered to have contributed materially to his death."[55] If neither force nor cocaine use were factors, and marijuana amounts were negligible (although not noted as such by the coroner in her summation), then the diagnosis of ExDS is not as easily made. Resolving the problem, the coroner explained to the jury that "a remarkable coincidence" led the inquest to Dr MacLeod, who, upon reading the details of the inquest in the newspaper, discovered that one of his patients was a cousin of Anthany Dawson, a patient who had a rare genetic mutation identified as CPT-1, normally only a pediatric problem that leads to sudden infant death syndrome (SIDS) but one that he believed could emerge in adulthood when "triggered."[56] The inquest was thus temporarily halted to enable Dawson's DNA to be tested. Although Anthany Dawson was found to possess only one of the genetic mutations, Dr MacLeod believed that cardiac arrest could have been triggered by marijuana use in someone with the genetic mutation CPT-1. He recommended the adoption of genetic testing. The coroner advised the jury to consider in their recommendations how best to identify CPT-1 patients. Taking the coroner's summation seriously, the jury concluded that death was accidental and recommended a medic alert bracelet, better medical record keeping, and cultural sensitivity training.[57]

In contrast to the thrust of the coroner's instructions to the jury, which stressed marijuana use and a genetic mutation, the family of Anthany Dawson offered a different view of events when they appeared before a police complaints forum, held after the inquest, to make a ten-minute presentation on Dawson's death. Describing her nephew as a twenty-nine-year-old in pretty good health, Yvon Gesinghaus stressed that Anthany was in "medical distress" that had to do with the head area, which his family speculated was some kind of seizure.[58] Witnesses heard a police officer say, "Roll over, roll over; when I tell you to fucking roll over, you roll over," before punching Dawson twice in the head.[59] "Keep in mind" that the punching occurred when Anthany was in the middle of a seizure, Dawson's aunt advised the panel.[60] Dawson was also restrained by having his hands tied behind his back and face placed down on a stretcher. As she told the panel, "Now, consider your nephew without blood pressure or a pulse, handcuffed behind his back, and someone is going to perform CPR. What do you think the odds of success are?"[61] Having raised doubts about the use of force and noted the possibility that Anthany Dawson was in serious medical distress when police approached him, Gesinghaus then told the review panel that friends had urged the family to hire a private investigator to find out what had happened. In the meantime, the police had released statements to the media that Dawson had had a drug overdose, even though the amount of marijuana in his system was minute.[62] Addressing police and coronial responses, Gesinghaus itemized that no police officer took notes, that a critical incident report was never filed, and that the police did not look for witnesses until the family pressed the issue. Further, police lawyers had repeatedly reassured the family that there would be a public hearing and that they could postpone their questions until then. These two competing narrative streams (the genetic mutation and force) flowed through the inquest, a contest between the boot and the liver.

The Contest between Boot and Liver

As the first witness at the inquest, Nancy Dawson insisted on materializing her son as an artist and an only child who "was killed."[63] Confronted from the start by lawyers seeking to place on record the story of an emotionally disturbed and drug-addicted youth, Nancy Dawson acknowledged that until 1996, when twenty-six-year-old Anthany checked himself into a treatment centre without telling anyone, her son had had problems with addiction. Adding that Anthany's difficulties were "like all other native families," and notably those "having to deal with racism," she resisted any emphasis on his history prior to 1996.[64] Focusing instead on the son who was into health food and went swimming at pools in Victoria whenever he got a chance, the son who had undergone a tremendous change at the treatment centre, she tried to put on record his artistic achievements and the details of a life lived between his traditional community in Kingcome Inlet and Victoria.[65] Responding to the efforts of counsel to have the police enter on record documents from her son's pre-1996 life, Nancy Dawson suggested that documents supporting her son's recovery since 1996 should also be placed on the public record.[66] She acknowledged that the family suspected police brutality from the start. They asked Dr Gleason to check Anthany's chest area for bruising, and Dr Gleason responded by saying, "I am not going to help you go after the police on this."[67] (In her own testimony, Gleason denied having said this.)[68] When asked if she realized that her son had been drinking on the day he was detained, Nancy Dawson reminded the coroner of the importance of the toxicology report, which showed no alcohol content. She felt that the scrapes on her son's arms were not "abrasions," as the medical report said, but rather "big hunks of skin missing."[69] Nancy Dawson told the coroner that in the face of police attitudes to Indigenous peoples, the family had no option but to hire a private investigator to probe the conditions of Anthany's death and to seek a second pathologist report. The sparring between police counsel and Dawson reached the point where counsel for the coroner and the coroner herself intervened to call a halt to the efforts to put Anthany's past drug and counselling history on the table.[70] Tensions between the police and Indigenous people entered at these moments, and intensified when a juror reported being confronted by someone in the parking lot and when pictures of Anthany Dawson were placed on all the vehicles in the parking lot.[71]

The Hospital Encounter

When Anthany Dawson arrived at the hospital by ambulance, the first impulse on the part of doctors was to consider drugs, specifically cocaine. Intensive care physician Dr Bonnie Gleason testified that she spoke to Dawson's aunt, Yvon Gesinghaus, by telephone the day Dawson was admitted and that the aunt indicated he used drugs. She advised Gleason that Dawson's mother did not know about Anthany's drug use.[72] Gesinghaus, who would later speak to the Police Complaints Commission about the police use of force, was never called to testify, although she was the only one who was alleged to have provided any evidence of Dawson's recent connection to drugs and alcohol. Dr Gleason also remembered that the aunt said she could not recall the last time Anthany used drugs.[73] Others testified that Dawson had been clean for five years or more. Dr Gleason did not recall who first told her of Dawson's potential drug use, but in the hospital report, the yes box was checked with respect to alcohol and drug use. Beside the checked box, a nurse had written that Anthany had been clean for three weeks but relapsed four days ago, information that had come from the aunt on the telephone.[74] Dr Gleason treated Dawson with thiamine for alcohol abuse, as she wrote in her notes that day, but at the inquest, she maintained that every patient, regardless of history, is given this drug.[75] Challenged about the extent to which she had automatically concluded Dawson was a drug addict and alcoholic, and the extent to which she had taken at face value whatever she had been told by ambulance and police personnel about Dawson's condition, Gleason simply repeated that she trusted what these professionals said about him and had no reason to doubt them.[76] Testifying that she had been told Dawson was placed on the stretcher on his back and that she did not ask paramedics and police about restraints or force applied to the chest area by someone sitting on Dawson, she nevertheless assumed excess force did not play a role in his death.[77] When Dr Gleason was recalled on 20 November 2000 to discuss the finding of a genetic abnormality, she agreed with Dr MacLeod that CPT-1 could have contributed to what happened to Anthany Dawson, but commented that in medicine it was often difficult to have one unifying diagnosis. Anthany Dawson "had a lot of things going on," she opined.[78] At the end of her testimony, Dr Gleason was asked by counsel for the family if it would have helped in her dealings with the family to have had a First Nations liaison worker.[79] We are left to speculate on what her difficulties were in dealing with the family. The question, however, would leave the path open for the jury to suggest cross-cultural sensitivity training for professionals dealing with Indigenous peoples, a standard recommendation when it is believed that cultural communication is the problem.

Restraint-related cardiac arrest and ExDS made their first appearance when Dr McFadyen, the emergency room physician on duty when Dawson was brought in, was asked by counsel for the coroner about it.[80] Testifying that he had heard of ExDS, Dr McFadyen added that he thought the issue of restraints (something Dr Gleason did not ask about) was an important factor to consider. He believed restraint-related deaths were reported for cocaine users, and he suspected cocaine because he could not explain cardiac arrest in such a young person.[81] (Until the inquest, Dr McFadyen was not aware of Dawson's cocaine and drug use recorded in hospital admissions prior to 1992.) Concerned about a possible head injury because Anthany had the lowest coma score possible, Dr McFadyen specifically asked paramedics and police about force and whether a choke-hold had been applied.[82] He was told there had been no choke-hold, but Anthany had been held face down and his arms were cuffed behind his back when he was transferred to the ambulance. Since Dr McFadyen could not definitively conclude that these circumstances had blocked Anthany's breathing passages, the matter of restraints as contributing to death was dropped until testimony from the pathologist, Dr Laurel Gray.[83]

The Remarkable Coincidence

It would have been hard to avoid the colonial connection entirely when the inquest turned to the genetic make-up of Anthany Dawson as evidence of an underlying medical condition that might have caused or contributed to his death. Indeed, Dr Patrick MacLeod, a geneticist whose fortuitous connection of Anthany Dawson to a patient of his with a genetic mutation known as CPT-1, was himself aware that the relation between scientists and the Aboriginal community was historically fraught. Drawn to a newspaper account of Anthany Dawson tearing off his clothes as he ran through the streets of Victoria, Dr MacLeod reported that he immediately felt that Anthany exhibited the signs of a metabolic disorder.[84] When he read the next day that Dr Gleason believed Anthany Dawson exhibited "gross metabolic derangement" (as indicated by hyperthermia), he made a note in his file about the case.[85] Coincidence built upon coincidence, and four days later he received a call from one of his patients whom he had been investigating for a rare inborn genetic disorder, who sought confirmation of his medical appointments on the day Anthany Dawson died. This patient, a cousin of Anthany Dawson, had been asked by the coroner to confirm his whereabouts that day. (The transcript does not make clear why this would have been the case.) Dr MacLeod then got in touch with the coroner, and upon reviewing the medical records, believed his hunch that Anthany had a genetic mutation was correct. He recommended that he test a small sample of Anthany Dawson's liver and obtained the family's consent to do so. The tests showed that Anthany had a CPT-2 deficiency (related to CPT-1).

The scientific story that unfolded was at least as remarkable as the coincidence that had brought Dr MacLeod to the inquest in the first place. To begin with, Dr MacLeod's patient, a cousin of Anthany's, was the first person in the medical literature with this particular genetic mutation who had survived to adulthood. In infants, the condition results in SIDS. Uncannily, on 4 August 1999, Dr MacLeod received a fax from a lab in Texas indicating that his patient had a CPT-1 deficiency, and on 11 August, the day Anthany Dawson died, he happened to be dictating a letter to individuals in Kingcome Inlet identifying himself as a medical doctor compiling a family history of his patient, a fact that only his patient and a nurse at the clinic would have known.[86] Second, there was new evidence that a second mutation could produce the same effect of triggering a biochemical reaction of the kind he suspected happened to Anthany on the day he died. Dr MacLeod's patient had this reaction when he fasted and when he ate fish and chips (owing to the fatty acids). The body becomes unable to break down the fatty acids and starts to burn muscle, producing severe cramps and compromising the kidneys. Exercise and sleep deprivation could also trigger episodes. While anyone who runs a few blocks could exhibit tissue breakdown, Dr MacLeod felt that Anthany exhibited an extreme amount of breakdown. Describing his research path, Dr MacLeod presented himself as someone who was reluctant to explore the cultural dietary aspects of the CPT disorder, and who was mindful of research protocols when it came to cultural issues and Aboriginal peoples. He therefore informally cleared his research on the Dawson family with Dr Taiaiake Alfred of the University of Victoria, a specialist in matters of Indigenous governance and a well-known Indigenous academic.[87]

Cross-examined by counsel for the Dawson family, Dr MacLeod acknowledged that he did not know a great deal about the CPT-2 deficiency he found in Anthany Dawson. He could only speculate if Anthany Dawson's previous hospital admissions had been due to the muscle cramping he associated with the disorder. Initially wrongly concluding that there had been research on adults other than his own patient, Dr MacLeod acknowledged his error and confirmed that research did not in fact shed light on adults with the deficiency. A great many of the connections he made amounted to conjecture. Pressed to consider that restraints could have led to blocked airways that in turn would have produced the hypoxia (a reduced amount of oxygen supply to the brain and the heart muscle) leading to arrhythmia and cardiac arrest, Dr MacLeod granted that this could certainly be the case.[88] It was hard to isolate CPT-1 or CPT-2 as the main factor contributing to death. Ending his testimony emphasizing that he tried hard to make his research a family issue and not a population issue,[89] Dr MacLeod recommended medical alert bracelets for family members with the deficiency.

Positional Asphyxia

Toxicology reports showed there were no drugs in Dawson's system other than trace amounts of marijuana, likely ingested the night before, which the toxicologist determined was unlikely to have a bearing on his death. The pathologist, Dr Laurel Gray, who performed a forensic examination on Dawson, concluded there was no evidence of head injury, no evidence that Dawson was a chronic abuser of drugs, and only superficial injuries inconsistent with the heavy blows some witnesses thought they saw. Dawson was a healthy young man. Declaring the specific cause of death to be the "anoxic brain injury" that follows cardiac arrest, Gray nevertheless offered the theory that Dawson may have died from restraint-associated cardiac arrest. Clarifying that in the literature this type of cardiac arrest has been associated with positional asphyxia, an individual in a prone or "hog-tied" position from which he or she cannot breathe properly, Dr Gray noted that while cases may have an element of this, "many of these deaths seem to occur so suddenly before an element of respiratory embarrassment seems to occur."[90] In effect, "it's not the restraint per se that causes the arrest but it's all the other physiologic effects associated with the restraint that connect together to produce such an outcome."[91]

Dr Gray's speculation here repeats the arguments found in Storey's article and others published in *The Journal of Forensic Medicine*. Relying on the idea that a restraint-related death typically has many factors, Dr Gray was able to consider restraint as a factor without laying the full blame at the feet of the police and paramedics who made the decision to keep Anthany Dawson in a prone position and "hog-tied." Since there was little or no evidence of drug use for Dawson, there had to be some other contributing factor. Pressed to find this factor, Gray speculated that there might have been an underlying metabolic situation or possibly cannabis use with hyperthermia. Both diagnoses presented empirical challenges, and a way had to be found to buttress them. The marijuana hypothesis rested on a single journal article in which it was reported that a patient developed severe hyperthermia after smoking a marijuana cigarette and jogging on a warm day. Since it was not possible to definitively establish the marijuana connection, the inquest remained with the possibility of a genetic condition as an underlying factor. Here, the testimony of Dr Patrick MacLeod provided some ballast for Dr Gray's assessment, as she indicated.

From Biology to the Social: The Taboo of Race

Colonialism had only a ghostly presence in the inquest. Other than a slight nervousness indicated by Dr MacLeod's awareness of ethical protocols regarding medical research with Aboriginal peoples and his anxiety about doing family rather than population research, Indigenous/settler relations did not explicitly enter the room. When the inquest turned to the encounter between Dawson and the police, an encounter witnessed by dozens of people, colonialism's shadow became slightly more pronounced, but it never came into the full light of day.

The world in which Anthany Dawson lived is one where a large chasm separates Indigenous peoples and settlers, economically, geographically, and socially. A world divided into two (Fanon's well-known phrase) is apparent in witness recollections of the events surrounding Anthany Dawson's death. At noon on 19 July, when Dawson's car broke down in the country, he approached a house and asked to buy gas. The owners refused, and Dawson then walked to a garage where its owner, Jason Austin, agreed to supply gas and drove with Dawson to his car. As the garage owner testified, the owners of the house where Dawson had asked for gas were "visibly upset" and openly conveyed their suspicion of Dawson.[92] Even with the gas, the car wouldn't start, and Dawson proposed to walk the twenty kilometres into town, refusing an offer to be driven by Austin to the bus stop. His offer notwithstanding, Austin then instructed his son to lock the doors and to call him if Dawson showed up again. Austin testified that he thought Dawson had "a grin fixed on his face," and he recalled that Dawson did not bother once to say thank you, something Austin felt meant "he was just only half with me."[93] Whether or not Austin's testimony about Dawson's strangeness that day occurred with the benefit of hindsight, what is salient is the perception that Dawson's behaviour was considered uncivil and strange. It is in these ways that Dawson's racial difference as a threatening foreignness finds its way into non-Indigenous recollections of what happened that day. In contrast to the testimony of the garage owner, Dawson seemed fine to the Indigenous cousins and friends with whom he relaxed later that afternoon, although they remembered that he said he was hot. They did not discover until sometime later that he did not even drink the two beers they had offered to him. He promised to meet his friends later that night, after going home for a shower.[94]

What did onlookers see when they encountered Dawson that afternoon? Gail Plant's daughter thought Dawson might be having an epileptic seizure,[95] as did Emily Robertson and Chelsea Garside, who remembered that Dawson was very coordinated and not at all exhibiting the demeanor of someone drunk or on drugs.[96] Tasha Libertore recalled that a gentleman she talked to suggested she was seeing someone in the grip of "a schizophrenic episode,"[97] and Debra Robertson thought it was a "psychotic episode," an experience her daughter had.[98] (Her testimony about Dawson's struggling and screaming was enlisted to make the case that Dawson possessed superhuman strength.)[99] Ian MacCusish recalled assuming that Dawson might be on a drug like cocaine, which would give him the energy he appeared to have.[100] Heather Price felt the same, describing Dawson as "not of sound mind."[101] Several witnesses felt the police and ambulance attendants appeared not to know what to do, talking to each other as they put on their latex gloves, and even laughing, a response the police acknowledged but explained as a normal stress-relieving practice.[102]

All witnesses described the effort it took to subdue Anthany Dawson. R. Atherton saw one police officer hitting Dawson quite hard initially in order to subdue him.[103] J.L. Angus agreed and said he saw two punches thrown at a man who appeared to be struggling hard to get away from the police.[104] His wife thought she saw four punches altogether, something she felt was uncalled for.[105] Others, such as Mark Sim, believed it was simply difficult for the police officer on the scene to subdue a naked, struggling man who continuously screamed as though in great pain.[106] Susan Mullins saw Dawson's struggle to get up and away from the police and ambulance personnel as "superhuman,"[107] and Michael Fallis believed Dawson was "more powerful than the police," which was why one officer had his knee on Dawson's back.[108] Clement Huot, who readily identified Dawson as "Native," heard the police officer say to Dawson, "When I tell you to fucking roll over, you roll over," as he smacked Dawson with a closed fist.[109] Sharon McLean felt sick about what she felt was police "aggression" when she saw a policeman repeatedly punch Dawson.[110] It is never possible to confirm whether punches were thrown, and the officer in question categorically denied using force. Such a possibility surfaced at odd moments, such as when witnesses remembered police officers chuckling after the first punches were thrown.[111] That witnesses could put what they observed into a frame about the policing of Indigenous people in the city of Victoria is hard to determine, since no questions were asked about whether or not the scene was unusual for them. It is nonetheless hard to believe that witnesses considered what was happening on the street that day without having prior views about Indigenous people in Victoria. Race and Indigeneity remain a taboo subject, around which a near-absolute silence is maintained.

Police Testimonies and the Taboo of Indigeneity

Perhaps the most salient feature of police testimonies was the shared sentiment that Dawson was not in any way familiar as someone they knew, or even as someone Indigenous. Constable Lawrence Hemstad was the first police officer on the scene. He appeared after the ambulance had arrived and found Dawson lying on the ground, yelling and pounding the ground with his fists. Convinced that Dawson was overdosing from drugs and recalling his prior experience, which he clarified was on Vancouver's Downtown East Side (where there is a concentration of Indigenous people), when asked by coroner's counsel whether he was aware that Dawson was an Aboriginal person, he replied, "It didn't cross my mind."[112] Describing Dawson as extremely violent and unresponsive to his commands, Constable Hemstad said he then tried to coordinate with other police. Constable Sheldan arrived on his motorcycle and was able to pursue Dawson, who in the meantime had taken off his pants and started running away. When Constable Sheldan caught up with Dawson and (in several witness accounts) placed his knee on a still-struggling Dawson, a large man (in all witness and police accounts) approached and offered his help to subdue Dawson. Constable Sheldan reportedly told Constable Hemstad that he took a punch to his mouth from Dawson, but most witnesses describe seeing Constable Sheldan throwing the punches. Although he maintained that he did not recognize Dawson, Constable Hemstad had had contact with him a number of times over ten years in what he described as incidents involving drug-related behaviour, and he claimed he had heard a lot of stories about Dawson over the years.[113] Hemstad had even used a lot more force in other encounters than the force applied on the day Dawson died in an effort to subdue him. For his part, Constable Sheldan did not think Dawson was on drugs. He believed it was a mental health issue. He did not try to talk to Dawson, although he declared Dawson unresponsive. He too had had a previous encounter with Dawson, but said that he did not know Dawson that day.[114] Admitting that he was the smallest officer on the police force, Constable Sheldan found Dawson hard to control and was saved by the appearance of a large man whom he recognized as a trained peace officer. Adamant that he used the appropriate amount of force in his punches, Sheldan was not aware that Dawson had suffered cardiac arrest soon after he left the scene. He did not think the incident warranted extensive notes, and he never approached others to ask them if they had any questions of him.[115]

The large man in question, George Moldovanos, a 280 pound off-duty court officer, testified that Dawson was extremely powerful and that it took a great deal of effort to get him in a prone position in order to handcuff him.[116] He didn't recall sitting on Dawson, but remembered seeing blood and worrying that he didn't have gloves on. Anxious to get into his car to return home to wash up, he asked Constable Sheldan if he could simply write in his report that a passer-by had assisted him.[117] By the time other police arrived on the scene, they saw a handcuffed Dawson, whom Constable Sheldan referred to as a Section 28 (a mental health case).[118] Corporal Trudeau, one of these officers, did not recognize Dawson, although he had given him a ticket the night before for squealing his tires as he left the McDonald's parking lot.[119] He too had had many dealings with Anthany Dawson. Constable Dale Saunderson helped restrain Dawson on the stretcher; he testified he was not surprised when he went into the ambulance to help turn Dawson over that Dawson was not moving.[120] Nevertheless, Saunderson did not take notes and did not answer questions when the RCMP investigated the case. Constable Mark Knoop stopped to put his gloves on as he approached the scene. He felt that they had placed Dawson face down on the stretcher to avoid being spit at. There was a lot of saliva from all the yelling and screaming, he testified, and he was worried about being hit by saliva.[121] Police testimonies are rife with hints that the encounter between Dawson and the police was one that was typical for Victoria. Although no one claimed to have recognized Dawson, many had had previous contact with him. Many, too, indicated their sense of contact with something diseased or dirty. In spite of all the screams coming from Dawson, the incident had a quality of the ordinary about it for these officers. They chuckled and laughed, and didn't take extensive notes about the incident. It is the event's very ordinariness that stands out.

Conclusion. Policing the Colonial City

What is the relationship between the police and Indigenous people? Is this relationship similar to police relationships with other groups? Should anyone be treated the way that Anthany Dawson was treated? These questions, raised by Dawson's mother at the very start of the inquest, never received the inquest's attention. Instead, whenever the use of force was discussed, such as when witnesses recounted that police punches seemed excessive, the focus did not remain long on the actions of the police officers and quickly returned to Dawson. Possible drug use, excited delirium, CPT genes, and other medical issues effectively dislodge inquiries into police conduct, an outcome Commissioner Thomas Braidwood warned about in the inquiry into the death of Robert Dziekanski.

If the lines of inquiry in the Dawson inquest seldom strayed into the domain of police use of force, it is also true that anyone wishing to challenge police on the use of force quickly runs into the standard defence that police are in the business of using force. Indeed, Victoria's police Complaint articulated just such a position in 2010 when a YouTube video of an arrest resulted in the finding by the Office of the Police Complaint Commissioner that a police officer had used excessive force. The video is not shocking to police officers, Commissioner Jamie Graham explained to the media. As he put it, "This is use of force. This is what we're trained to do."[122] It is worth noting that Graham was the same police chief who declared (as chapter three discusses) that Frank Paul, an Indigenous man who was unable to walk and was left by police to die in an alley in Vancouver, was simply the kind of man who crawled. The police, he noted then, often have to deal with people who have to be dragged; dragging Frank Paul into an alley in a cold, wet night was not something unusual.[123]

We can also locate police impunity in a broader context in which police accountability is hard to pursue in the province of British Columbia. As a 2012 report of the British Columbia Civil Liberties Association (BCCLA) detailed, the province of British Columbia had the greatest number of in-custody deaths in Canada (267 in the fifteen years between 1992 and 2007, with more than twice as many deaths in custody per year than any other province studied, including Ontario, which had 113 deaths between 1993 and 2007).[124] Police accountability has been one of the BCCLA's most significant concerns, specifically issues around police investigating themselves. The BCCLA and the inquiry into Frank Paul's death noted that the Crown seldom prosecutes police for the intentional application of force causing death. As Cameron Ward, a lawyer who has worked on cases of deaths in custody and police misconduct in British Columbia since the 1980s, notes, when police are prosecuted, it is extremely rare to get convictions.[125] Further, as the Frank Paul inquiry revealed, there is a stark contrast between the investigation of a civilian and a police officer. In the case of a police officer suspected of contributing to a death in custody, the investigation often fails to proceed in a timely manner, police officers' notes frequently go missing (as happened in the Dawson inquest), and by the time of an inquest or inquiry, "the story doesn't evolve. It is already prepared and is a carefully crafted explanation."[126]

The broader issue of police accountability must be contextualized in contemporary settler colonial relations. Criminal lawyers describe the sheer impossibility of charging a police officer for an Indigenous death in custody and suggest that not much has changed in the province of British Columbia since the early 1970s, when Fred Quilt's death in custody was simply regarded as the death of another drunken Indian.[127] In a province where Indigenous people represent five per cent of the provincial population, and forty-four per cent of the Indigenous population is under twenty-five as opposed to twenty-seven per cent of the non-Indigenous population, Indigenous people are the most impoverished segment of the population. They have higher unemployment rates, live in substandard housing, and more than half of them have been diagnosed with at least one chronic condition.[128] Given these statistics and the perniciousness of Indigenous deaths in custody, we need to consider what settler colonialism has to do with both elevated rates of deaths in custody and the recurring response in inquests that Indigenous people are responsible for their own demise.

Dispossession

If the settler town of Victoria now imagines itself as a piece of old England, Penelope Edmonds observes in her book *Urbanizing Frontiers*,[129] it is only because the expropriation of Indigenous land and the ongoing eviction of Indigenous peoples from city space continues apace. Edmonds emphasizes that racial segregation is enacted at the municipal level. The police, as agents of the state charged with the control of bodies deemed to threaten the social order, are central actors in marking the racial lines of the settler city (an insight Fanon offered), and police use of force against Indigenous bodies comes to be seen as intrinsic to policing. Edmonds urges us to rethink our notions of how dispossession is accomplished. While we often focus on the acquisition of lands outside the settler society, she reminds us that dispossession also requires "the regulation, segregation, and harassment of Indigenous peoples *within* settler-colonial towns."[130]

In Victoria, Indigenous peoples were the majority for much of the late nineteenth century, and their presence in the city provoked settler fears that precipitated increasing control of Indigenous bodies on city streets. It is for this reason that Edmonds stresses we should study the "formative racializations [that] were brokered spatially in the streetscape."[131] Control of First Nations peoples on city streets only increased as settlers sought to wrest control of land from urban Indigenous peoples, a dynamic we should keep in mind when considering policing in contemporary Victoria. During the 1850s and 1860s, for instance, the Lekwammen reserve on the inner harbour was a site of great contestation; wresting control of this land required the production of Indigenous bodies as out of place in the settler city. The city had to become known as white space, Edmonds shows, a fictive racial purity that had to be inscribed on the ground through control of First Nations bodies. Policing was key to the making of the settler city as white. Clearing the city streets of Indigenous people at night (later bolstered by a pass system) became a regular part of police activities, and other spatial measures of regulation proliferated, including designing the city according to a grid and managing First Nations presence through separating Tribes (each with its own Native constable) along the lines of the grid. Edmonds notes that this use of disciplinary power existed alongside the violence of sovereign power. That is, the grid and overt physical force worked in tandem.[132]

If the construction of Indigenous peoples as "criminal, drunken, displaced and anomalous in the streetscape," a designation that persisted in the twentieth century, required specific policing and legal strategies, the twenty-first century requires no less.[133] Edmonds reports on the land claims negotiations of 2006, in which the Lekwammen and Esquimalt First Nations settled a land claim for Victoria's inner city. While the settlement may be a cause for celebration, we should not view it as an indicator that dispossession has ended. Instead, the settlement owes its existence to a claim from the past, "a reserve set out for First Nations over which the legislative buildings of an entire province were built."[134] It is useful to recall colonialism as a process, as this fine scholarship on the city of Victoria urges. If we understand dispossession as ongoing and as requiring the same policing strategies outlined in *Urbanizing Frontiers*, we must consider the inquest as a place where some of these same colonial processes are revealed and endorsed. Police enjoy considerable opportunity to exercise force when the inquest regularly establishes that Indigenous bodies are too damaged to easily survive modern life. If we consider medicalization as a biopolitical tactic, designating some bodies as pathologically fragile, or, paradoxically, as physically threatening, and consider what is enabled by the entrenchment of this view in law, we come to understand the taboo about race and coloniality, so evident in the inquest into Anthany Dawson's death, as reflecting not only settler anxieties about Indigenous presence, but, more fundamentally, a willful division of populations into the respectable and the degenerate.

Early on in the inquest, when no satisfactory explanation for Anthany Dawson's behaviour was forthcoming, a juror asked whether it might have had anything to do with his initiation as a *hamatsa* dancer, the highest ranking dance in the Potlatch system. Ironically, the *hamatsa* dance, as Nancy Dawson explained to the juror, is about a man lost in the bushes who returns and is much respected because he has survived. Anthany Dawson was considered to have survived drugs and anger at racism, and had been reportedly clean for about five years. Could Anthany's behaviour be a "flashback to initiation," the juror wondered, given that the dance is about a wild man who has been brought back.[135] Affirming that her son had never lived in the woods, Nancy Dawson tried to put to rest the idea that what happened to Anthany Dawson was a culturally specific descent into madness and recovery. Inquests leave few options besides ones invoking madness, ceremony, and myth. Either one believes in a little-known genetic mutation that causes "gross metabolic derangement," or one is left with mythology. The last thing that could have caused death is the overuse of force on an emotionally and physically distressed man. To consider this option more fully would have necessitated a conversation about relations between settlers, the police, and Indigenous peoples, and this, more than anything else, remains taboo. Witnesses found it hard to describe Anthany Dawson as Indigenous, as though saying the word would take them too far down the road to a place where race and history matter. A willful racelessness, a history without settlers, remain the two hallmarks of the law. In this way, inquests prove receptive to stories that the dead caused their own demise, and Indigenous people as well as those considered emotionally disturbed continue to die in custody. To disrupt this pattern, at the very least there must be a naming of the colonial and the racial and an interrogation of the patterns they produce and require.

Chapter Six

"It Happened More than Once": Freezing Deaths in Saskatchewan

For Patricia Monture-Angus, Mohawk Scholar

The kid went out, got drunk, went for a walk and froze to death.[1]

Alleged comment, Sergeant Jarvis, investigating officer, Stonechild case

We had indicated, as I understand, that we didn't have any other incidents of this nature. In fact, we have. And that's come to my attention, and I think we have to take ownership of things that have transpired. It happened more than once and we fully admit that and, in fact, on behalf of the police department I want to apologize to those people who we had said it was a one-of-a-kind incident.

Russell Sabo, police chief[2]

It's a very old practice to get rid of the Indian who was inebriated or mad.

Sakej Henderson, legal scholar[3]

Introduction

No death invokes Canada more than a freezing death. A country that makes icons of its fields of ice and snow, and whose citizens are daily reminded in the national anthem that they are the "True North strong and free," should not be able to take lightly such deaths, that is, to regard them as inevitable. Seventeen-year-old Neil Stonechild, whose body was found in a field in the northwestern section of the city of Saskatoon on 29 November 1990, died with strange marks on his wrists and face. Viewing his body before burial, his family wondered if someone had broken his nose, and his older brother, who had been arrested himself, thought the marks on his brother's wrists looked like handcuff marks.[4] His death was not seriously investigated until a decade later in 2000, when the RCMP, investigating the deaths of two Indigenous men, Rodney Naistus and Lawrence Wegner, found in similar circumstances, and the case of a third man, Darryl Night, who survived after being dropped off by police in the same area of Saskatoon, added Stonechild to their list of suspicious deaths.

This chapter examines inquests and an inquiry into freezing deaths in the Canadian province of Saskatchewan. It outlines the racial-spatial economies of which these deaths are a part, and it proposes that the structural relations of settler colonialism produce and sustain ongoing, daily evictions of Indigenous people from settler life, evictions that are inevitably violent. The colonial city belongs to the settler, and Indigenous presence in the city inevitably contests settler occupation. Indigeneity unsettles, challenging the settler's claim to legitimacy by calling into question the colonial state's most enduring fiction that Indigenous people are a dying race. White settler colonies such as Canada, Australia, and the United States all have similar histories of evicting Indigenous peoples from cities, and policing evolved to maintain these colonial arrangements.[5] The dumping of Indigenous people to the outskirts of the city is a practice born of the settler's need to maintain the colonial city's lines of force. Today, when dumping comes under legal scrutiny, as it did in the inquiry into the death of Neil Stonechild and in inquests into freezing deaths, it is either transformed into a practice of a few bad cops or denied outright. What remains on legal record, however, are the racial-spatial economies of the settler city and its persistent devaluation of Indigenous life, a devaluation that law both produces and sustains. The colonial project is a lethal project, repeatedly inviting settlers into the business of disposing of Indigenous life. Few are able to resist the invitation, understanding their own lives as premised on Indigenous disappearance.

In part one, I present ideas about the racial-spatial economies of the colonial city. In part two, I examine the death of Neil Stonechild and law's response to this death in the form of the Wright inquiry. In the making of public memory, Stonechild's death is attributed to policing gone awry. Police "anger" is acknowledged but only as exceptional. The inquiry concludes that there exists cultural misunderstanding between the police and Aboriginal peoples. And yet, the inquiry reveals a pervasive and active dehumanization of Aboriginal people, a dehumanization so bureaucratized that, with rare exceptions, hardly an officer could be found who was troubled by Neil Stonechild's death, and almost no one devoted their full professional energies to its investigation. With a profound indifference to Indigenous death as their key feature, spaces of the policing of Indigenous populations bear a close resemblance to spaces of exception where law authorizes its own suspension. There can be no failure to care, and thus no responsibility for it, in such a zone. In part three, I examine inquests into the freezing deaths of Rodney Naistus and Lawrence Wegner, two young Indigenous men who died a decade after Stonechild, exploring what these deaths tell us about policing and law's response to it. I explore two movements in space and time: Naistus and Wegner as they moved through the city towards their death in the frozen fields of the northwestern section of the city and the journey we are invited on by the inquest, a journey through which we come to understand the deaths of Naistus and Wegner as no one's fault but their own. Across the landscape of Indigenous deaths in custody in Saskatchewan, including deaths in prison, deaths due to suicide, and deaths that occur in violent confrontation with the police, the Indigenous body is a body that cannot be murdered. As M. NourbeSe Philip has written, in law the slave is considered an object of property and thus "not capable of being murdered."[6] Relatedly, I argue that the Indigenous body, as always outside of the human, is also not capable of being murdered. Exploring the conventional contours and devices of the legal narrative that turns Indigenous death into a story of a dysfunctional or "troublesome" population meeting a predictable end, freezing deaths are only ever considered the final instalment in wasted lives.

Part One. The Racial-Spatiality of the Colonial City

> For modernity, inside has tended to connote subjectivity, the realm of deep feelings, of Truth; outside suggests physicality, human difference, strangeness.[7]

In the most elemental way possible, a freezing death is the outcome of movement: from the space of the living to the space of the dead, from a space of warmth and shelter from the elements to a space of extreme cold and danger. It is useful to think about freezing deaths in terms of space and movement. The inquest reveals, in the first instance, that young Indigenous men and women are in the city but not of it, moving through city space as shadowy figures in periphractic space, banished within.[8] Who is and is not of the city? Goldberg's careful and now iconic consideration of race and urban location begins to answer this question by charting how "[r]acisms become institutionally normalized in and through spatial configuration."[9] The racialized, at once a condition marked on the body (skin, wounds) and an invisibility (non-persons), cannot occupy the same space as Europeans and the Europeanized. The city belongs to rational men and women, individuals who are owners of themselves. In liberalism, to become an individual, Radhika Mohanram reminds us, is to progress out of body and into mind.[10] How else to mark the line between owner and owned, person and non-person, belonging and non-belonging, if not spatially? Importantly, fences or borders are enactments rather than permanent lines; settlers lay constant siege to the city, inscribing their claims on the ground and on bodies in the language of rationality and order, thereby marking the lines of force of the colonial project.[11] It is not only that Indigenous peoples must be confined to reserves, but their own necessary incursions into settler spaces (incursions due to the impoverished conditions of reserves)[12] must also be policed and constrained if the line is to hold. There cannot be much work for Indigenous people to do in the colonial city, and Indigenous presence in the city must be continuously policed. As Laura Hudson writes, drawing on Achille Mbembe:

> Colonial sovereignty winds up overwriting racial difference with narratives of "wars without end" and with bunkers and checkpoints that monitor and control a resistant, dominated population that cannot be fully absorbed into the institutions of the state. Taken by force, colonial lands are built upon the blood and bones of the colonized, both those killed in the struggle for sovereignty, and those consigned to die in impoverished and invisible excluded spaces of native towns. In colonial occupation, two maps cover the same ground; two nations occupy the same space and vie for power, an example of the unstable boundaries of modernity's inside/outside.[13]

There is a gendered component to the colonial arrangements Hudson describes. The policing of Indigenous women often occurs within a context of prostitution, both actual and presumed.[14] However, for both Indigenous men and women, evictions from the city take place in the context of police patrol in areas of the city where Indigenous peoples are the majority. As the Aboriginal Justice Implementation Commission[15] (created in 1999 to develop an action plan based on the recommendations of the 1991 Manitoba Public Inquiry into the Administration of Justice and First Nations People)[16] described for the province of Manitoba, a historic tension exists between Indigenous peoples and the RCMP, originating in the fear of Indigenous insurrection but continuing today as a solidified mistrust of the police by Indigenous peoples and a documented over-policing (arrests, charges, and so on) as well as under-policing (failure to provide services when needed).[17] As several research reports have confirmed, regardless of gender, Indigenous people on city streets are widely assumed by both the public and the police to be out of place as alcoholics, drug users, gang members, prostitutes, and criminals.[18] This finding, of course, is not to deny such problems; it is merely to emphasize that all Indigenous bodies are regulated by the presumption that they are not respectable citizens.

How does the inquest arrange its own and our knowledge of the movements of Indigenous people in the city? Here too we might return to Goldberg who put it starkly, drawing on Herbert Spencer's notion of degeneration. In the colonial imaginary, races have their proper places; when removed (dispossessed), they generate pathologies, pathologies that the body politic must guard against.[19] Alcohol and drug abuse become the evidence of this pathology and not evidence of dispossession; if we find frozen bodies on a field outside of town, it can only be the outcome of these pathologies and not the result of drawing lines of force. Alcohol or drugs, mental incapacity, and mental illness, whether present or not, become both cause and effect, the explanation for why otherwise healthy young men's bodies lie frozen in places just outside the city. We need not dwell, then, on journeys that begin in the back of a police cruiser. We need not ask what the policing is for and where it leads. Indeed, it is imperative to head off at the pass any such intrusions into the story of the pollution of the body politic and the evictions that are required to maintain its purity.[20] You lay waste to yourself; we have not laid waste to you. This will become the mantra of inquests and inquiries into freezing deaths. It is what we might also term a pedagogy as well as a racial-spatial economy, that is to say, instruction on who and where we are, a lesson made true on the ground.

Waste and Its Spaces

Scholars have identified the condition of being surplus under colonialism and capitalism as one of being marked for death through an increasing animalization. Hudson comments on the reduction of surplus populations to animals, a banishment to the constitutive outside:

> One key quality of surplus populations is that their numbers and proportions expand beyond the ability of capital to incorporate them, leaving them in circumstances little beyond bare life of the animal. As the commodity form becomes unstable with the devaluation of labor power, humanness is no longer regarded as sufficient to determine moral value, leading to instabilities in the constitution of the human-animal divide.[21]

Both humans who are less than human and animals find themselves penned in (prisons, zoos) under regimes where they are surplus.[22] Without moral standing, surplus beings are also outside the law. Prisons, for example, are increasingly spaces where people's suffering is seen as "non-criminal" and prisoners "are seen as more beast than human."[23] As Hudson importantly reminds us, the state of nature is both "the undifferentiated world prior to human law" and the place where law has authorized its own absence.[24] It is useful to remember Michael Taussig's space of death, the place "where the Indian, African, and white gave birth to a New World."[25] As Sylvia Wynter,[26] Achille Mbembe,[27] and Denise Ferreira da Silva[28] each show, the condition of modern life is Black/Indigenous death, the "necropolitics" of bare life. In these spaces of death (or spaces of exception for Agamben),[29] where law operates through its suspension, those marked for death are simultaneously inside and outside the law and the body politic.

Analysing "the brutality of the urban present,"[30] Vinay Gidwani and Rajyashree N. Reddy suggest that we return to the meaning of waste for Enlightenment thinkers such as John Locke.[31] If for Locke waste is the political Other of value, things cast out as excess or detritus, Gidwani and Reddy note that what jeopardizes urban life is waste within: that which refuses to be improved.[32] They emphasize that waste is "*material excess that is unruly and improper*: disordered matter, or matter out of place."[33] If under colonialism those who did not make rational use of their lands (for Locke, Indians of India, but also Indigenous peoples) had to be evicted from the modern, in the urban present similar evictions occur. Giving examples from the contemporary Indian context, Gidwani and Reddy provide a framework for how I propose that we consider freezing deaths and the racial-spatial economies of which they are a part:

> The casual evictions of street vendors and slum dwellers in Bangalore; the killings of vulnerable migrant children on the outskirts of Delhi; the stories of street children eliminated by police in Mumbai; or the mysterious disappearances of ragpickers in police lock-ups in Delhi are, we suggest,

> not anomalies. They are rather applications of the supplementary, violent, order of "police" that has *always* coexisted with the ethical order of "police" as *salus publica* – the wellbeing of the public – that we encounter in different guises in the writings of Thomas Hobbes, John Locke, Adam Smith and Jeremy Bentham, the order of "police" that Michel Foucault identified as the wellspring of governmental power.
>
> In this supplementary order of "police" excess matter – "waste" – is either expelled or else violently absorbed through primitive accumulation when it becomes a threat to the liberal social order of "property" and "economy." Often the excess matter is "surplus humanity" that is *superfluous* to a regime of capitalist value.[34]

We will see in the inquiry into Neil Stonechild's death, and in inquests into the freezing deaths of Rodney Naistus and Lawrence Wegner, that the contemporary colonial city is constituted through a series of expulsions and evictions, the excretion of waste in modern society. Marked as surplus humanity, Indigenous peoples endure intense policing in the city. When these evictions and expulsions end in death, law is the "biopolitical tactic"[35] that will teach us what has happened is simply waste disposal. At inquests and inquiries, we will learn it is impossible to chart harm, negligence, or indifference towards a group to whom so little is owed and who are marked above all by their own superfluity.

The argument I propose, that freezing deaths are the outcome of what is understood as waste disposal both in law and society, stands in contradistinction to how such evictions are typically understood. The sparse research literature on what has been called "dumping," for instance, considers the practice to originate in police who are attempting a more informal approach to keeping order and taking a hard line approach to law and order.[36] Frustrated police transport troublesome people out of the city, removing a problem from one domain to another and avoiding in the process the administrative work that comes with formally detaining someone. When dumping exposes the vulnerable to danger, scholars have tended to consider this an unintentional consequence of an admittedly irregular police practice. That police are able to take the risk that a person who has been dumped might die is not something many scholars closely examine. Those critical scholars who consider the role that racism plays in police decisions to dump racialized individuals do not connect dumping to the annihilative impulse at the heart of establishing settler sovereignty.[37] That is, they do not consider the threat that Indigeneity poses to the settler's position as legitimate owner, a profound challenge to the settler state and to individual settlers who must believe in their own entitlement. One consequence of failing to connect dumping to sovereignty is that we cannot make sense of police responses to freezing deaths – the casual, apparently incompetent investigations of them, for instance, and the widespread police indifference to the loss of Indigenous life. Importantly, the law's response, to consider the deaths to be the result of a strange cultural incompatibility between police and Indigenous peoples (the conclusion of the inquiry into Neil Stonechild's death, as I discuss in part two) or, more often, to consider freezing deaths as the natural demise of a dying people (as in the Wegner and Naistus inquests, discussed in part three), becomes comprehensible only when we take sovereignty into account. Dumping inscribes settlers' claims on the ground and upholds the racial order on which colonialism depends. We can expect, then, that dumping will have widespread social and legal approval.

Part Two. "A Chasm Separates Us": The Wright Inquiry and Neil Stonechild

Through the surveillance, arrest, detention, and brutalizing of Indigenous peoples, to say nothing of outright murder, colonial power is made tangible. It is the Indigenous body on which colonial power must first be inscribed. Taussig reminds us that colonizers "mimic the savagery they have imputed" to others, understanding their acts of violence as necessary in the face of the threat posed by the colonized.[38] Yet terror, like the torture on which it so often depends, defies a standard rational explanation. How to make sense of the decision to brutalize and then leave a man to die, and to remain apparently impervious to the consequences of one's actions? How to understand the collective indifference to his death, evident even when the law appears to be calling the police to account? Taussig suggests we consider "intricately construed, long standing, unconscious cultural formations of meaning," abandoning facticity. In the space of death, "reality is up for grabs."[39] In the inquiry into the death of Neil Stonechild, what becomes visible, even as it defies rational explanation, is a widespread collective indifference to Indigenous death. The frozen fields of the prairie become a place where reality is up for grabs, a space where law has authorized its own suspension.

When the province of Saskatchewan established a judicial inquiry into Stonechild's death, and the commission began its hearings in September 2003, the handcuff marks on Neil Stonechild's wrists became one of the commission's preoccupations. Experts deliberated if the marks on Stonechild's wrists were the result of the youth falling on the frozen grasses and twigs of the prairie or on its crusted snow. Might they have come from the wrist cuffs of his own soft cotton lumberjack coat tightening on flesh after he had fallen? Alternatively, could the marks have come from handcuffs, specifically, police-issued handcuffs, possibly used first to hit Stonechild in the face and later to bind his wrists? Frozen prairie grasses or police-issued handcuffs – in the inquiry, each item belongs to a world view, and the extent that one is favoured over the other stakes out the "sides" of the debate. Handcuffs offer evidence of Stonechild's death as a death in custody; prairie grasses, on the other hand, can help us to accept the investigating officer's quick assessment of the body in the snow: "The kid went out, got drunk, went for a walk and froze to death."

The inquiry into Neil Stonechild's death chose the handcuffs side of the debate. The details implicating police were hard to ignore. The Honourable David Wright, commissioner of the inquiry, believed the testimony of Jason Roy, Neil Stonechild's friend, that he saw Neil, bloodied and bruised, in the back of a police cruiser on the night of 24 November 1990. Commissioner Wright came to the conclusion that Stonechild had been in the custody of Constables Larry Hartwig and Brad Senger around midnight of 24 November and that Stonechild died of exposure in the early morning hours of 25 November. While the commissioner concluded that the 1990 investigation into Stonechild's death was superficial and totally inadequate, and that higher-ups ignored reports that Stonechild's death was a suspicious one, he did not connect these actions outright to murder or even to racism. Damning as the details were, they did not, in the commissioner's mind, indicate an entrenched and systemic devaluing of Indigenous life among police. They only indicated, as Joyce Green has written, "a tense relationship" between two communities (Aboriginal and police) who are culturally different. As Green shows, cultural difference entirely replaced anti-Aboriginal violence in Wright's report of the inquiry into Neil Stonechild's death.[40] Writing of the "chasm" that separates Aboriginal and non-Aboriginal people, and noting that the two communities "do not know each other and do not seem to want to," Commissioner Wright ends his report with a ringing endorsement of the 1991 *Justice on Trial: Report of the Task Force on the Criminal Justice System and Its Impact on the Indian and Metis People of Alberta*,[41] in which Aboriginal problems in the justice system are attributed to Aboriginal people's cultural practices (such as failing to make eye contact with authority figures, or telling police what they want to hear).[42] If Aboriginal cultural practices complicate relations with the police, the commissioner nevertheless found it difficult to ignore entirely that the Saskatoon Police Service did not once indicate a desire to improve relations with Aboriginal people. He recommended that police be trained in race relations and anger management, and suggested ways in which the two communities might better get along, principally through improved liaison and better complaints and investigation procedures. The commissioner did not make clear who was angry, and one can only presume he believed that Constables Hartwig and Senger were frustrated with Stonechild for his drunken and disorderly conduct and wanted to teach him a lesson, a lesson that ended in his death. If indeed the Constables engaged in what researchers identify as a "shadow system" of police punishment[43] (intended to teach drunks a lesson without engaging the justice system), what does it mean that a young man's life is risked in the interest of discipline? What might be the sources of a rage that goes so far? These are questions the inquiry does not pursue.

An observer at the Stonechild inquiry would have had to engage in mental gymnastics, if not a complex round of psychic denials, to avoid the issue of race and colonialism as white witness after white witness, with rare and notable exceptions, stonily denied wrongdoing, doggedly insisted that they could not remember, suggested that prairie grasses could lacerate and leave grooves on an inert face. Police officers who simply could not fathom what was wrong with a drop-off in sub-zero temperatures on the edge of town, and those who appeared to have easily maintained a ten-year silence about the body discovered there, give a face to the idea of authorized violence. Where there might have been shame, grief, or outrage, there was only coldness, calculation, and indifference on the part of many white officers.

A Granite Structure of Indifference to Indigenous Death

In Saskatchewan, "starlight tours" is the term used to describe the police practice of dropping off Indigenous men in an isolated area outside the city. That there is a popular term is testimony to the fact that it happened more than once. The practice of drop-offs is a lethal one when the temperature is minus twenty-eight degrees Celsius and if the long walk back to town is undertaken without proper clothing and shoes. Sakej Henderson, an Indigenous legal scholar, notes that in

Saskatoon, Indigenous activists have long viewed freezing deaths suspiciously, but until Darryl Night came forward, it was hard to verify the connection between police and the deaths.[44] For their part, police explain drop-offs as part of policing the prairie city. Officers Ken Munson and Dan Hatchen, for instance, explained that they dropped Darryl Night near the power plant, the area where all three men's bodies were found, because Night wanted to be dropped there to "walk off his anger" before returning to what he said was his home, a half-hour's walk away.[45] Bruce Bolton, a retired police officer and the supervisor who had approved the quick closing of the Stonechild file, testified that he himself had dropped someone off in an isolated area thirty-five years earlier. When asked by the commissioner why he did it, Bolton explained: "What I can recall of the incident, the person was dealt with several times during my shift in which he was making a nuisance of himself at a hospital, as a matter of fact, and he was requesting a ride home. The hospital, of course, would not pursue any charges for his actions and it was a case of him requesting a ride home every night."[46] Apparently tired of being called for, Bolton taught this nuisance a lesson. We do not learn if the person in question was Indigenous, but the inquiry learned that Bolton was disciplined for his actions and that the incident was well known in the police department at the time. Other drop-offs were also well known. For example, an officer was disciplined in 1976 for dropping three Indigenous people, including a pregnant woman, outside city limits and leaving them to walk back to the city.[47] A second police officer who participated in the inquiry revealed that he would sometimes transport a person causing a disturbance to another location several blocks away, a process he described as "unarresting" a person.[48] Behind these actions, explained as borne of frustration or even acquiescence to Indigenous requests, lies an ominous incapacity to imagine Indigenous peoples as within the circle of humanity and a deep drive to ensure that they remain literally and figuratively outside of it. Who, after all, would willingly walk in sub-zero temperatures, inebriated and without proper clothing, and who would consider this activity safe?

By all accounts, Neil Stonechild was a handsome, joyful seventeen-year-old, but also an alcoholic whose addiction often brought him into trouble with the law. Amidst the scant details about the youth, who painted murals, won a wrestling championship, attended Alcoholics Anonymous, and had close relationships with his mother and siblings, there are stories of his alcoholic belligerence, break-ins, and causing disturbances. Stonechild was serving a six-month sentence at the Yarrow Youth Farm, an open custody facility for young offenders.[49] On the night of 24 November, Stonechild and his friend Jason Roy set off drinking and partying. Recalling he had learned on the bus earlier in the evening that his former girlfriend, Lucille Horse, and her companion were going to be babysitting at her sister's apartment in Snowberry Downs, Stonechild and Roy set off from an apartment where they had been drinking at 11 p.m. to try to find the apartment where Lucille Horse was babysitting. They stopped at a 7-Eleven convenience store to warm up (an indicator of how few public spaces of shelter were available to them), and it is likely that Stonechild caused a disturbance. A witness testified that officers Hartwig and Senger stopped him and asked for identification; the officers said they were looking for Neil Stonechild because there had been a disturbance at the 7-Eleven. Commissioner Wright noted that the evidence establishes that officers Hartwig and Senger stopped Stonechild there.[50]

Police records confirm that two officers received a call, "Drunk to be removed, Neil Stonechild, seventeen years old," from dispatch on the night of 24 November and that constables Larry Hartwig (whose regular partner was Ken Munson, implicated in the drop-off of Darryl Night) and Bradley Senger, a new police officer, were on their way to find Stonechild at 11:51 p.m.[51] Constable Hartwig used the computer in the cruiser a few minutes later to search the name "Tracy Horse," the false name Stonechild's friend Jason Roy gave to the officers when they stopped him. Roy testified he gave a false name that night because he was afraid he too would be put in the back of the police cruiser along with his friend. Roy was let go and watched his terrified friend being driven off. Haunted and plagued with nightmares, he told several people, including the police investigator and a counsellor, that he saw Stonechild in the back of the cruiser, bloodied and screaming that the cops were going to kill him. Both Hartwig and Senger maintained they did not remember whether Stonechild was in their vehicle on the night of 24 November, and both claimed not to recognize Stonechild's name (a name they had nonetheless entered into the computer that night, and a person whom Hartwig had arrested or ticketed several times prior, as confirmed in the testimony of Sergeant Wylie). Through the simple device of "I don't remember," both avoid being directly connected to the drop-off, although a polygraph test administered to Constable Senger suggested that he was lying about Stonechild not being in the cruiser that night.

Incongruously, on the witness stand, Constable Hartwig boasted of his excellent memory. He could recall both a minor and a major incident of that night's shift, but declared he had no memory of Neil Stonechild in the cruiser. When he was interviewed in 2000 by the RCMP, Hartwig stated that Stonechild had not been in his custody, but added that he had heard two officers had arrested Stonechild and detained Roy, who had given the false name Tracy Horse to them. When asked how he came to know the name Tracy Horse, Hartwig replied that he had learned of the name through newspaper articles. The inquiry confirmed that this detail did not appear in any media reports; it is likely that Hartwig could only have known the name and its connection to Jason Roy because he himself had entered it on the police computer on the night of 24 November. Faced with such a chilling possibility, Commissioner Wright concluded that Hartwig "recalled what happened, and his assertions are a deliberate deception designed to conceal his involvement."[52] Hartwig's duplicity was matched by other police officers. The paper file of the investigation into Stonechild's death was destroyed in 1998, and when the investigation was re-opened in 2000, investigators had no written reports to go on until an Indigenous officer, Ernie Louttit, came forward with a copy he had made in 1990 when he had tried to get the investigator to probe the file more thoroughly. Officer Louttit was told in no uncertain terms to back off when he complained in 1990, and he made a copy of the file to pursue his own investigation, but gave up after a few years. The paper file indicates that Sergeant Keith Jarvis closed the file on Neil Stonechild on 5 December 1990 and that he spent a mere twenty hours on the investigation. Jarvis told the inquiry that he thought Stonechild was heading for a nearby adult correctional centre and got lost, an implausible theory, given that Stonechild would have known he would not be admitted there. Only ever understood as passing through the colonial city, en route to prison or reserve, the young Stonechild cannot be imagined as of the city. If he ended up frozen to death in a field outside of town, it could only be of his own volition.

Jarvis's appearance at the inquiry began a long line of appearances by white police officers, most of whom revealed an indifference to Stonechild's death and a subsequent cover-up during the investigation of their participation. The officers at the scene, and those charged with processing the reports afterwards, all failed to consider the death as warranting extensive investigation. Stonechild's clothing was destroyed, and there was little or no follow-up with Jason Roy's testimony. Senior officers approved closure of the file, and, most damning of all, police misled the media about how much of an investigation had actually been carried out on the Stonechild file and whether or not Hartwig and Senger were suspects. The very highest ranks continued through the years to suppress details, up to and including the moment that a public inquiry was called. In sum, few police officers behaved ethically with respect to Neil Stonechild. Some lied, others could not remember, and all but two (tellingly, an Indigenous officer and a white officer who had an adopted Indigenous son who knew Stonechild) could not find it in their hearts to pursue the story of what happened to Neil Stonechild.

From where does the collective indifference to the loss of Indigenous life come? It is tempting to consider the role of gender here, given that all the police officers involved were men who were performing what scholars have referred to as hegemonic masculinity, which I have elsewhere argued is organized around masculinity and whiteness.[53] Of deep interest to me is the way that a focus on the performance of hegemonic masculinity can obscure a widespread and entrenched devaluing of Indigenous life on the part of individual white persons of both genders, particularly those who wield power. What are we to make of legal actors such as Commissioner Wright, who accumulates the evidence of a collective devaluing of Indigenous life but is unable to pursue accountability (at least insofar as findings of guilt) and unwilling to interpret the evidence as anything other than an incompatibility between two different cultures? One obvious explanation is that legal processes, such as inquiries, largely function as performances of the law's, and thus colonial society's, essential goodness, a staging, that is, of its commitment to the rule of law. Freezing deaths are highly controversial when the circumstances surrounding them include evidence of a stunning level of police indifference, incompetence, and duplicity. The commissioner deals with the controversy by turning our attention to a framework guaranteed to cleanse public memory of the violence and dehumanization: cultural difference. If the problem is one of culture, then we need not consider racial hierarchy, and there need not be a consideration of the relationship between police and Indigenous peoples as a colonial one. To reconcile the duplicity and unethical behaviour of the police, behaviour that appears to be institutionalized, with the staging of the essential goodness of the state requires a parallel staging of Indigenous difference, a difference understood as a resistance to modern life, as a descent into alcoholism and criminality. When he concludes that both "sides" are to blame for the police failures uncovered at the inquiry, Commissioner Wright transforms a drop-off and the

mark of police handcuffs on the face and wrists of the dead into a story of "a hard to police population" and "a police force that didn't try hard enough." In the inquests discussed in part three, we see the same fidelity to the story of Indigenous difference, a difference that prompts us to understand Indigenous people as the authors of their own demise. Equally on record, however, are the racial-spatial economies of the city and the evictions that law must disavow if it is to preserve settler sovereignty.

Part Three. Mapping Freezing Deaths: Rodney Naistus and Lawrence Wegner

"I watch myself when I am in the city."[54]

To gather when one is dislocated, Goldberg reminds us, is to resist.[55] Gathering is emplacement and survival, a refusal to budge. Goldberg asks: where can the racially marginalized go in the settler city? Rodney Naistus came from Onion Lake First Nations, a Cree reserve that straddles the border between Alberta and Saskatchewan in Treaty Six territory. Naistus also came from the prison to the city. The week before he was found frozen to death in a field just over one kilometre from the power plant where Darryl Night was dropped by the Saskatoon police, twenty-three-year-old Rodney Naistus was released from a Saskatchewan correctional centre. Invited for a night out by his brother Darryl, with whom he spent time in several group homes while they were children[56] (an early eviction from family life), Naistus headed for Saskatoon on the bus. He had arranged to meet his close relative Charlene Baptiste in a mall, along with his half-brother Sheldon Lee Bear. Baptiste gave Naistus her address and directions to her apartment, and thought that he might stay either with her or her brother Dale. Naistus and his brother Darryl stayed at Charlene Baptiste's apartment on the night of 27 January 2000. Baptiste, who did not come home that night, returned on Friday, 28 January with Rodney Harper, and after playing Nintendo, all four young people went to the Redrock Grill. Naistus and his brother stopped off en route briefly at Dale Baptiste's house, and he too came to the bar, where they met a bricklayer, Pat Cooper, for the first time. Apart from Cooper, they had limited money and did not drink more than three or four beers while at this bar.[57] After playing pool and gambling slots, the group left the bar at around 6 p.m. to continue drinking in the apartment of Charlene Baptiste. They piled into a cab (with the exception of Dale, who couldn't fit into the cab) and stopped to buy more beer. Charlene recalled that they then spent the hour "remembering old times and laughing." They were all "half cut," by which she meant partially intoxicated, when Naistus and Cooper left her apartment and set out for a club to "find some girls." The two men took a bus downtown.

With maybe ten dollars in his pocket to cover the bus fare back to Onion Lake Reserve, Naistus arrived at the JAX nightclub with Cooper, his new friend, but was refused entry because of his attire (he was wearing a sleeveless shirt) and likely because both men were drunk. The men continued to Winston's bar, where Naistus played the gambling machines. When they left the bar, as Pat Cooper testified, a woman pushed Naistus and told him to "fuck off." She left with Cooper to continue to another bar. Naistus went off in another direction and was not seen again. When his body was found, a witness, Charity Dawn Nighttraveller, called police to report that she had seen Naistus in a 7-Eleven convenience store, one of the few places to get warm (as the Stonechild inquiry revealed). The store's cameras did not confirm this. Others thought they had seen Naistus at the club C-Weeds, but Calvin Chocan from Onion Lake, who knew Naistus well, was certain that he was neither there nor at a party at a Weldon Avenue house, near where Darryl Night was picked up by police officers Munson and Hatchen the day before. The next day, Naistus's frozen body was found by a passing jogger, Pat Lorje, a woman who was also a member of the provincial parliament. Lorje described to the inquest the body frozen blue, the thin clothing and a jacket pulled up to the neck, revealing the bare chest of a young man with tears in his eyes. She noticed his brush cut and tattoos, and, as she commented to a journalist later, knew immediately that he was Native.[58]

Periphractic Marginalization

Rodney Naistus's exclusion from the city was a continuous one, enacted over time (generations). In their study of homeless urban Aboriginal peoples, Evelyn Peters and Vince Robillard note that until the 1940s, most Aboriginal people lived on reserves, but by 2006, forty-five per cent lived in cities.[59] Inferior levels of economic development and the poor condition of reserve housing pushed many Aboriginal people off reserve. The majority of them were fleeing poverty but also the family conflict that poverty, lack of educational and employment opportunities, and the dysfunction created by alcoholism and violence produces. Some male respondents of the study left the reserve to spend time in correctional institutions. Once they were in the city, racism, poverty, dysfunction, and low levels of education (obtained either in residential schools or nonresidential schools) combined to limit employment and housing options.

The geographic layout of the city of Saskatoon confirms urban Indigenous marginalization. In a study of race relations in Saskatoon, Cara Spence explores the housing sector and shows that Saskatoon has the highest rate of economic segregation compared to any other Canadian urban centre. Aboriginal people, the fastest growing segment of the population in Saskatoon, are younger than their non-Aboriginal counterparts (forty per cent are under fifteen as compared to twenty-two per cent of the non-Aboriginal community), and two-thirds live in poverty, earning less than $20,000 annually. Geographically concentrated on the west side of the city, this young, poor population largely lives in substandard housing. Educators have linked housing options to the population's rate of academic failure; for example, "school children living on the West side switch schools three times a year owing to inadequate housing."[60] Describing policing in Saskatoon and other prairie cities with a high Aboriginal population as "racialized," Elizabeth Comack suggests that police, confronted with "the daunting task of responding to the 'disorder' that results from these social conditions," draw upon the colonial and racist social order of which they are a part, using strategies such as dumping "to reproduce order when dealing with troubled and troublesome people."[61] The explanation that police are driven to the strategy of starlight tours by the difficulties of their jobs, harnessing their racism to the unenviable task of cleaning up city streets, mystifies policing and sustains the police story that when violence occurs, it originates in the difficulties and stressors of policing. More fundamentally, such explanations leave out the willingness to risk Indigenous life that lies at the heart of dumping. We will need to go beyond the difficulties of policing a poor and socially excluded population and to transcend facticity, as Taussig advises, to grasp that waste disposal is in fact the disposal of a human being. Police-initiated transjurisdictional transport of troublesome persons (PITT)[62] is not simply, then, a police strategy gone wrong, but an annihilative impulse around which the settler city is organized.

From the moment he got off the bus and sought out family and friends, whose own disjunctive inclusion reveals itself in apartments and bars in the city's West End and in the highly policed streets surrounding them, Rodney Naistus was in the city but not of it. In Saskatoon, we see the spatial-racial economy enacted, in the first instance, when poverty produces a concentration of Indigenous people in poor housing, a periphractic marginalization, to return to Goldberg, where spaces that are in the city but not of it are fenced off invisibly, its residents deprived of services, private space (crowded apartments), and public space, the latter accomplished by policing that makes the streets a militarized zone for Indigenous bodies. There is informally restricted access to clubs and restaurants, leaving the marginalized to gather where the monetary and emotional costs (less racism) are likely to be lower than elsewhere. If we follow Rodney Naistus, we see the movements of the dispossessed from one space of confinement and surveillance to another, in the city but not of the city, a place where young Indigenous people nonetheless reach out to each other in community, refusing eviction. Naistus comes to the city apparently still wearing the clothes he wore when he entered the "work camp,"[63] clothing woefully inadequate for the Saskatchewan winter.[64] Here, in apartments and bars, he meets his family and friends. They drink together, and write their names on his cap, as he sets off with a pal to find women. When money and friendship run out, only the street is left. To be forced onto the streets is to become prey. It can only end badly. There is no other space to be but the prison, the police station, the drunk tank, and the lethal sub-zero temperatures of outside, all destinations that begin in the back of a police cruiser.

As if it could operate a satellite to track the past, the inquest begins by asking an RCMP officer to trace Naistus's last movements on a map. Even a simple exploration via Google Maps of these movements generates an embodied sense/knowledge of how space and subjectivity are intertwined in a colonial settler context. Mapping establishes that all activities take place over a very small geographical area, no more than a few kilometres from the edge of the city and geographically distant from middle-class areas. The testimonies of Indigenous witnesses reveal a social world of economically marginalized young people, some of whom attend college or university, but none of whom will be understood simply as college students or young people partying on a Friday night. Related to each other either by blood or through membership in the same reserve communities, these young people look after each other. Drinking is part of what the group has in common, although financial limitations and perhaps race limit where the drinking is done. As with other young people, there are specific nightclubs (JAX, near the bus station, C-Weeds, and Red Rock Grill) and specific apartment buildings and houses, all on the west side of Saskatoon. Calvin Chocan, for instance, attended a party at 725 Weldon (the apartment building where Darryl Night had attended a party), at which there were several people from the Onion Lake Band. He did not recall seeing Naistus there that night. Far from understanding these movements as revealing a world of youthful partying, kinship, and care, the inquest forms a picture of Indigenous people leading a dissolute life that is bound to end badly. Alcohol and its connection to Indigenous bodies cancel out other possibilities. Questions posed to Indigenous witnesses make this world appear as a shadow world, a world that is the antithesis of respectability, where young people drink for long hours in less than reputable places. We learn what Indigenous people drink, where, when, and for how long, and the details easily eclipse any others, such as the love and support that Naistus appears to have received when he left the penitentiary and arrived in Saskatoon, and the evidence of lives lived in community.

A Coronial Narrative of Freezing Deaths

Police establish that there was only one set of footprints at the scene and acknowledge under questioning by counsel for the family, Darren Winegarden, that it is possible Naistus was dropped off and had started walking, although they did not investigate this possibility at the time.[65] On his own initiative, Constable Yuzdepski followed the footprints, but he was not directed to do so by the Major Crimes Unit when they were called to investigate. In 2001, when the RCMP took over the investigation, a videotape of a constable walking the route Naistus might have taken was made in response to the coroner's request for one.[66] Freezing deaths are discussed at the inquest, but a codified story takes shape early on about how they come about. Stories that might run counter to this codified narrative are actively discouraged. For example, Pat Lorje, the MPP who found Naistus and who paid careful attention to footprints at the scene, returning several times during the day she found Naistus, actively considered why there seemed to be only one set of footprints. In an article based on an interview with Lorje, the magazine *Saturday Night* reported that she suspected Naistus might have been dumped.[67] Requesting that the coroner recall Lorje to explain her comment to the magazine, Winegarden alluded delicately to the need to consider "the totality of circumstances, the holistic experience" from the "First Nations' perspective," presumably an experience in which, during the winter of 2000, three Indigenous men were found frozen to death in the same area of the city.[68] The coroner rejects this idea and does not permit Lorje's recall.

The story of freezing deaths that breaks through the surface of detail about excessive drinking and inadequate clothing is a different one than Lorje's. Questioning an RCMP officer, the coroner establishes that the police investigated and rejected the theory that Naistus could have been dumped by a taxi driver deprived of his fare. Sergeant Bob Peters (then of the Major Crimes Unit) informs the coroner that there had been "a rash" of freezing deaths that winter, something he felt occurred when people were "partying, and ventured out to get sick, and that is where they ended up."[69] Dr Terrance Moyana, a pathologist, acknowledged his awareness of freezing deaths and maintained that they happened once or twice a year and that it was possible to freeze fairly quickly in Saskatchewan's weather. His story was a rural one:

> And I guess the typical story that we got of some of the cases I did before, there would be a person, maybe there was a get-together, it is usually out in the country, there was a get-together or maybe drinking at one residence, and the houses being fairly spread apart in the country, one person would see the lights to his house in the distance and then they try to walk home. Really maybe told not to do because it is really cold and then they sometimes insist and then they die of cold exposure somewhere between the two houses. That is a fairly typical story.[70]

Established as more typical of the country than the city, freezing deaths are uncoupled from any possibility that they could be the result of murder. Dr Graeme Dowling, chief medical examiner for the province, confirmed that cold exposure is not normally treated as a suspicious death.[71] People go out into a sparsely populated area, and they freeze to death: a banal occurrence.

The codified story is given further credence when the inquest tests the theory that Naistus was simply someone who got lost, either because he was unfamiliar with Saskatoon or was illiterate and could not determine the street sequence, since they were marked by letters of the alphabet. Charlene Baptiste was interviewed on 19 February at 8 or 10 p.m. at the RCMP office. An Indigenous officer, Constable Cory Lerat, tried to establish what Naistus might have been doing in the industrial area of the city where he was found. The Constable asked Baptiste whether Naistus had enough education to know his alphabet (the streets were marked by letters). Baptiste recalled that she thought the question was "stupid," because it made Naistus look dumb. It is difficult to tell from a transcript what Baptiste could have meant when she answered one of Constable Lerat's questions by saying that Naitsus was slow, like her brother Dale. Pressed by counsel for the family to explain, she could only say that it was hard to explain what she meant, but she didn't mean that Naistus was dumb.[72] When she was asked if Naistus might possibly have been going to pick up bottles at the nearby landfill, Baptiste noted that she thought this question too was a stupid one, since it was 2 a.m. on a cold morning, and she could not imagine who would go to collect bottles at that time. In any case, she commented to Constable Lerat that Naistus was "a home kind of person" who wouldn't be collecting bottles. Marked as surplus in these questions, a member of a population without employment who survives on the remains of garbage dumps and landfills, Naistus himself acquires the patina of what Michelle Yates (writing on "the labor theory of value and disposability in contemporary capitalism") notes is "a kind of disposability and throwing away within capitalism … little more than the human-as-waste, excreted from the capitalist system."[73]

Policing

It proves difficult to substantiate the story of an allegedly drunk, illiterate man, a possible collector of waste, who did not know his way around town and may simply have gotten lost. Forensics could only establish that Naistus could have been at the lower end rather than the upper level of intoxication.[74] The police appear not to have thoroughly investigated either tire tracks or footprints, but this is in dispute, often by the coroner himself. The Naistus inquest took place one year after Darryl Night's story led to constables Munson and Hatchen being charged with dropping him off near the power plant on an extremely cold night, the day before Naistus was found. It was inevitable, then, that the shadow of this event would fall on the Naistus inquest. Police Officer Dean Hoover testified that some districts are policed more often than others. His own district 6 bordered on district 7 (the area of Saskatoon that included the Stroll), where Naistus was found. It is established that on the night of 28 January, most officers were working elsewhere, but Munson and Hatchen were working in district 8. Further, between the hours of 1:18 a.m. and 2:24 a.m., they were recorded as being on a break, after which they were called to a domestic dispute and were in the vicinity (one hundred yards) from Dale Baptiste's house, where Naistus might have been headed.

Winegarden, counsel for the family, laid out for the coroner the family's theory as to what happened that night. Naistus could have been picked up by the two officers and then dropped in the area where he was found, perhaps because the officers were headed to the domestic dispute. DNA in the squad car proved inconclusive, but Naistus's clothes were never tested for the DNA of the two officers. Arguing that Munson and Hatchen should be called to testify, Winegarden is criticized for his speculations about their involvement and his insistence that their movements be "mapped." He counters that other assumptions were "mapped," namely the party on Weldon Avenue, for which there is no evidence that Naistus attended. Unproven and damaging evidence had already been entered on record, for example, that a constable had asked Charlene Baptiste if Naistus knew his alphabet, a question that suggested Naistus was illiterate and got lost of his own accord. On this latter point, Winegarden wins the day (the coroner declaring that he found the question about Naistus's illiteracy inappropriate), and the inquest hears from Munson and Hatchen, although the coroner reminds counsel that the two officers are about to be sentenced for dropping off Darryl Night and that he does not want their testimony at the inquest to influence their sentencing hearing. Munson and Hatchen insist they did not have Naistus in their cruiser at any time on the night of 28 January or the early morning of 29 January 2000. They maintain they would have noted this, even though they had not noted that Darryl Night was in their cruiser the night before.

Coronial care for police witnesses stands in stark contrast to the treatment of Indigenous witnesses. As in other inquests, the coroner and the police routinely mix up Indigenous names: Night stands in for Naistus,[75] a Freudian slip that betrays not only the unconscious possibility that both are cases of dumping by officers Munson and Hatchen, but also more generally, the interchangeability of the Native body and its status as less than human. Two Indigenous sisters who testify, the Nighttraveler sisters, are more than once referred to as the Nightcrawler sisters, and when Charlene Baptiste is confused with Charity Nighttraveler, counsel for the family is obliged to point out that Nighttraveler is "kind of a well-known name in First Nations country."[76] As if this were not enough, Indigenous people themselves refer to each other differently from the official record; Rodney was Steve to his family and friends.[77] The coroner reminds several Native witnesses to speak up, even instructing Dale Baptiste to spit out his gum.[78] The instructions have the effect of infantilizing Indigenous participants and emphasizing their difference. The coroner remarks that witnesses are transient and hard to contact (although it is not clear that he is referring only to Indigenous witnesses).[79] If the inquest has difficulty pinning down Indigenous life, it succeeds in leaving us with a record of its strangeness, its difference, its physicality, its habitat. We are left only with the possibility that Naistus caused his own demise through his habits and his own nature. The police are in consequence seen as saddled with a difficult job, which the inquest will help them improve. The recommendations advise police to keep records of who is in their cruisers and to patrol isolated areas during the winter months. In such a story, the possibility that Naistus was driven to his death is next to impossible.

When asked how much he had had to drink on the night of 28 January, an Indigenous witness, Calvin Chocan, told the coroner that he had had maybe six beers. He explained, "I watch myself when I am in the city. I don't like indulging myself when I am not at home sort of."[80] What is there to be watchful of? The cold? The police? The inquest does not pursue these questions. In their submission to the Wright inquiry, the Federation of Saskatchewan Indian Nations (FSIN) noted that the FSIN had to create a Special Investigations Unit to receive complaints about police in order to accommodate the flood of calls they received from callers about their experience with police. Indigenous people had to be watchful of the police; the back of a police cruiser was indeed something to be feared, as the eight hundred or so calls to the office of the Assembly of First Nations made clear when the RCMP began its investigations into the deaths of Stonechild, Naistus, and Wegner.[81]

Lawrence Wegner: "It Reads like a Murder Mystery"

> There is a possibility that there might be a cover up. It reads like a murder mystery, I know that. It seems unfathomable in a lot of ways and maybe we should make a movie out of it some day, but the fact is, it is a possibility.[82]

Lawrence Wegner came not from a prison or a reserve but from a university in the city, where he was studying to be a social worker. His landlady described him as an honest young man who very much wanted to serve his community by becoming a social worker.[83] Like Rodney Naistus, however, he too would be marked as someone who could only have caused his own death, a marking accomplished by references to his mental illness and drug use. Amidst these details, it is hard to consider the possibility that Wegner might not have been the author of his own demise. If the inquest leaves us with any clue that it might be otherwise, it is only in the everyday details of life in Saskatoon, details that confirm a racially divided world, a world "cut in two," in Fanon's words.

Wegner went missing on 31 January 2000, when the temperature in Saskatoon fell to minus twenty-two degrees. He was found frozen solid on 3 February. There were superficial abrasions on his wrist. Dressed far too lightly for the weather, Wegner was found in a T-shirt and without shoes; ominously, his coat and shoes were never found. Several police witnesses recalled that his socks were clean and without holes, indicating that he could not have walked far without shoes. There was only one set of tracks, but the first police officers on the scene contaminated it, and Wegner's movements could not be traced for certain. The tracks seemed to indicate that Wegner had gotten up and fallen over. They ended near a "prairie road." The socks, a key piece of evidence, were washed by Wegner's family when his clothes were returned, and it was never established whether they had in fact been clean and without holes. A police officer who walked the route Wegner was assumed to have taken found his own socks to be very worn, dirty, and with holes.

In the documentary film *Two Worlds Colliding* about freezing deaths in Saskatoon, Indigenous lawyer Don Worme stands at the site where Lawrence Wegner was found. Our imaginations run wild as the camera pans over the frozen field. The sheer emptiness of the landscape, its frozen beauty, seems to spell danger and death because there is so little shelter from the elements and because of its isolation. It is impossible to believe that anyone would come here of their own volition on an extremely cold night. There is something utterly terrorizing about the prospect of being left here on an intensely cold night. The camera captures Wegner's mother on the same landscape, touching the frozen prairie grasses and wondering why the police couldn't see her son as human. The grasses are the same kind that experts (rejecting the theory that the marks were caused by police-issued handcuffs) speculated caused the marks on Neil Stonechild's wrists. As inquests typically do, the Wegner inquest worked with the hypothesis that Wegner simply wandered off in a drug-induced psychosis and came to the area near the dump where he froze to death, the same story that the Naistus inquest pursued, with drugs taking the place of alcohol. As with these other freezing deaths, spatiality lends coherence to the narrative about dysfunction and wasted lives that end near the dump.

"The Worst Place That Wegner Could Have Lived"

Through a focus on place, the inquest maps Wegner's movements and geographically organizes our understanding of what happened to him. From the coroner's point of view, Lawrence Wegner's problems began and ended with where he lived. Until shortly before his death, Wegner lived in a group home and saw a psychiatric nurse once a month for medication. This medication could be taken all at once (which would increase its effect), or it could be taken in multiple doses.[84] Caught stealing his own medicine from the landlady, Jocelyn Schandler, at the group home, Wegner was kicked out and went to live with friends, twenty-one-year-old Brent Ahenakew and nineteen-year-old Jennifer Heidle. The coroner characterized this couple's apartment as "the worst place where Lawrence Wegner could have gone to live," the environment providing him with the opportunity to take drugs and exposing him to conflict of the kind that added substantially to his stress.[85] Working with the hypothesis that the mental health system had failed Wegner in allowing him to leave the group home and to live with friends, the coroner explored the idea that community treatment orders should have mandated where Wegner could live.

Throughout the inquest, Wegner's condition as a drug addict provided the dominant frame through which to understand what happened on the night of his death. Friends and one expert sought to make the story more complex to no avail. For example, although it was established that Wegner took drugs, especially when in the company of friends, no one close to Wegner had ever seen him in a psychotic state. Wegner was initially diagnosed with drug-induced psychosis. The psychiatrist whom he saw two days before he disappeared found no evidence of psychosis and altered this earlier diagnosis to mood disorders. The details that would support the story of Wegner's wandering off in a drug-induced psychosis, notably Wegner's state of undress at the time of his death, puzzled many who knew him. Jocelyn Schandler recalled that he was a "meticulous dresser" who was unlikely to be dressed as he was found.[86] Friends remembered that he hated the cold, dressed warmly, and usually asked for rides because he hated to walk in the winter. Toxicology reports confirmed that Wegner had smoked marijuana, but no other drugs were found in his system.

While there were parts in Wegner's story to indicate that drugs may have played a part in what happened, there were also details that suggested police involvement. The police enter Wegner's story when he called 911 at 9 a.m. on the morning of Sunday, 30 January from the apartment of Jennifer Heidle and Brent Ahenakew. Worried that Heidle was in an abusive situation, Wegner assisted police in trying to get her to leave for a crisis centre. Reportedly unable to handle conflict, Wegner left the apartment at 8 p.m. that night when the couple started fighting again. Ahenakew lent Wegner his boots and coat in the hope that Wegner would come back. Neither Heidle nor Ahenakew remembered much of what happened later that night, but all those who were in the apartment maintained that Wegner was not as stoned as the others when he left. Around 10 p.m., Bev Urchenko heard a knock on her door and heard something about a delivery. An hour later, she heard a man screaming and saw two policemen in a car parked in front of the Whitecap's house. Jennifer Whitecap had called police around 10:30 p.m. to report a man who had knocked on their door too, yelling "pizza, pizza." Jennifer and her mother, both Indigenous, were concerned that the man was wearing white socks, no shoes, and only a T-shirt. Sergeant Marsland, who took the 911 call, informed her that a car was in the area and would be advised to look for someone matching this description. Marsland could not confirm that he did indeed alert the officer in the area. Marsland, whose work performance had been criticized, struck the coroner who listened to a tape recording of 911 calls as "cold and uncaring."[87]

Darlene Katcheech and Benita Moccassin, who both knew Wegner (whom they called "Wagonburner"), testified that somewhere between 11 p.m. and 12 a.m. on the same night they saw Wegner being pushed into a police car in front of the hospital. These women did not come forward for eighteen months after they were initially interviewed by the police, and after Benita called the FSIN in November 2001.[88] Both changed small details of their story, and the coroner advised the jury that their testimonies were unreliable owing to the time lag.[89] One of the women gave details about one of the arresting officers they saw that night to a police artist, who was able to provide a sketch to police. There does not appear to have been any follow-up with the sketch.[90] The coroner advised the jury to "spend no time trying to figure out if the sketch represents a particular officer."[91] A third witness, Chastis, who was also Indigenous, claimed that he saw the police arresting an Indigenous man in front of the hospital, but his testimony was also discredited. Chastis claimed that he continued driving past the hospital, and when he got to the area near the power station, went up on a rail bridge because he thought there was a fire. He saw a police car in the distance. Although he offers a detailed story, Chastis earned the coroner's censure when he explained that he saved the information about the police car at the power plant for the inquest in order to surprise the jury, initially reporting to the police only the arrest in front of the hospital.

A disturbing pattern of indifference to Indigenous life emerges during the testimonies of some white witnesses, an indifference tinged with anxiety perhaps, but shaped nonetheless by the sense that an Indigenous man walking without shoes and wearing only a T-shirt on an extremely cold night was not something to be overly worried about.

For instance, an employee of Co-Op Fuels saw a man, whom he believed was Indigenous, walking on the train tracks without shoes and wearing only a T-shirt. He called out to him but took no further action. Graham Anderson explained that he felt compelled to testify at the inquest when he heard that the event had "turned racial" and that people were considering the police's role in Wegner's death. Two truck drivers also saw someone walking with inadequate clothing for the weather, and one also saw a police car and flashed his lights to warn the police. Neither man attempted to call the police. It is difficult at the inquest to establish why, despite knowing the dangers of the cold that night, these witnesses were not worried enough to call the police. Most disturbing of all was the sentiment, as the family lawyer, Curtis, summed up, that these witnesses simply believed "there is always weird stuff that happens down there ... That it was just another incident."[92]

Treatment of Witnesses versus Responses to Police

Indigenous witnesses described their fear and suspicion of the police. Jocelyn Schandler told the coroner that she had received strange phone calls from someone claiming to be police; others said that they had been under surveillance. None of this information was deemed relevant for the jury to hear. Darlene Katcheech and Benita Moccassin explained their eighteen-month delay in coming forward by describing themselves as "plain old scared" (in Benita's words).[93] Darlene Katcheech described herself as feeling very "nervous" at the inquest. She recalled her late father had warned her that the "police can be dirty."[94] Living with the memory of what happened to Wegner was difficult, she told the coroner, and she had spent a long time worrying about what she should tell the Wegner family. Eliza Whitecap, whose daughter called the police, believed that the police never come when they are called. Eliza, who described herself as not speaking English well, extended her distrust to the coroner himself, suspecting that he mixed up her name several times in a deliberate attempt to confuse her.[95]

In this racially divided legal world of fearful Indigenous witnesses whose testimonies are easily discredited and white witnesses who are anxious to defend the police but communicate their familiarity of the world where drop-offs occur, the possibility that police removed Lawrence Wegner's shoes and left him on the edge of town on a freezing cold night is ruled out of hand. The coroner instructs the jury accordingly: "It is my advice to you that there is no evidence at this inquest of a practice by Saskatoon police of dumping people off."[96] The story that ultimately won the day was the one about Lawrence Wegner spending his last few days in the apartment of Brent Ahenakew and Jennifer Heidle. The coroner's recommendations focused on housing for those with mental health and drug problems. He also recommended that the police should keep better records of their 911 calls and that everyone should attend an obligatory cross-cultural awareness session, since the legal system had to consider Indigenous culture. As would be the case in the Stonechild inquiry years later, cultural difference stands in for the marking of Indigenous bodies as challenges to be overcome, chaos to be contained, waste to be expelled.

Conclusion. Rituals of Purification

> When it [waste] cannot be easily expelled it is simply abandoned, thrust into a zone of indistinction where it is regulated but not considered worth redeeming.[97]

It is easy to see why settler society must engage in a constant purification of itself, an eviction of Indigenous bodies from settler spaces and their confinement to the zone of indistinction. The settler's emplacement depends on this eviction, both materially and symbolically. Inquests and inquiries into Indigenous deaths in custody provide a means of tracking the evictions that end in death, the racial-spatial economy of the settler city, and the periphractic spaces (in the city but not of the city) where Indigenous bodies are "regulated but not considered worth redeeming."[98] The inquest arranges our understanding of these geographies of violence so that we come to see freezing deaths as the destiny of a people, the end point for those who refuse to be improved. But the inquest and the inquiry also reveal features of the zone of indistinction. We see its rituals of purification: arrest, detain, evict. In law these become performances: measure (bruises on wrists), classify (their alcohol consumption and mental illness), conclude (with their difference, not ours, no matter how many deceptions). The full measure of the law does not apply to those in a state of nature, since the state of nature is the place where law has authorized its own absence. Because Indigenous people are considered as waste, as people no one can help or harm, Indigenous death in custody is banal. Inquests and inquiries ensure that we know this.

Conclusion

Tombstone Data

Recognizing colonialism as a central explanation – if not the central explanation for Aboriginal overrepresentation in the justice system is essential.

Patricia Monture-Angus[1]

"Surely there can't be that many Aboriginal people dying in police custody!" In the seven years during which I undertook research for this book, this comment was the most common response from non-Indigenous people to my attempt to explain what I was working on. (Indigenous people, on the other hand, know intimately about deaths in custody, a common occurrence for many communities.) The word "surely" suggests that the speaker has taken offence or, at best, is merely incredulous about the claim that too many Indigenous people are dying in police custody. All this death can't be true of Canadian police and medical personnel. In a country where colonialism is rarely acknowledged, even as something of the past, let alone of the present (the Prime Minister is on record as saying it never happened, and prominent people, among them a previous leader of the Opposition in his scholarly days, insist that settlement was peaceful), the "surely" remonstrates with anyone who insists that Indigenous lives matter and that all this death is unacceptable.

Anticipating the "surely" yet again, I ought to have begun the book with statistics. I am pessimistic, however, that numbers can deal with the utterances of "surely." How many deaths would be enough to provoke concern? If, as I have argued in the preceding chapters, settlers believe that Indigenous people are a dying race, then it would be impossible to determine when death is the outcome of deliberate injury and when it is not. Indeed, the numbers by themselves can even be used to bolster the case that Indigenous people really are a dying race. "People die," one prison guard told a coroner, implying that there was not much he could do when a prisoner died in the cells. It's better that they die in the cells rather than on the streets, a police officer opined, unconcerned about the sick prisoner he didn't bother checking on, who had died on his watch. Colonialism has wreaked, and continues to wreak, havoc on Indigenous communities. It leaves in its wake a trail of alcohol and drug abuse, mental illness, and above all deep poverty, conditions that lead to untimely death. Under these circumstances, many refuse to believe that a deeply dehumanizing impulse towards Indigenous people runs through settler society. It is easier to see Indigenous death as inevitable, the outcome of addiction and disease. Accustomed in their own minds to dealing with Indigenous people as the living dead, police betray themselves when they label the personal data they collect on prisoners (such as name and age) as "tombstone data."[2] Instead of reconciling ourselves to Indigenous death, what would it mean to remember that colonialism is ongoing and that the historic devaluing of Indigenous life continues in institutions and in the hearts and minds of state actors and other settlers alike?

As I have maintained throughout this book, settler societies have a profound investment in "disappearing Indians." The process of making a people disappear is not simply one of elimination. Rather, it is a process that involves marking (materially and symbolically) the Indigenous body as one that is not up to the challenge of modern life, a condition that leaves the settler as legitimate heir to the land. Settlers stand to gain in two significant ways from Indigenous disappearance. First, if "Indians" are disappearing, the settler can legitimately become the original owner of the land. Second, the settler assists "Indians" into modernity, a thankless and futile task in the settler's eyes, but one that confers upon the settler legitimacy as a modern subject. The settler as humanitarian is understood as committed to civilization and to the rule of law, and is not associated with the barbarism of dispossession and genocide. Within such a context, counting the numbers of dead bodies in custody and explaining how and why people die is a complicated business. The numbers offer the opportunity to confirm an old colonial belief (they are dying due to an inherent incapacity to survive modern life) as much as they do the opposite (we are killing them). Evidently, it is necessary to go beyond the numbers if we are to distinguish one story from the other. The overemphasis on the numbers can indicate a reluctance to confront what lies beneath them.

Deaths in custody run the gamut from deaths resulting from being struck by a police cruiser, being pepper sprayed, and being restrained to shooting and freezing deaths, and deaths due to suicides, overdoses, falls, and ill health. Unless we believe that Indigenous people are always on the brink of death, dying from their own pathologies, we are obliged to consider what the numbers and the circumstances of death tell us about the overall response of settler society towards Indigenous peoples. Although we can survey the panoply of death, the dehumanization that this book names does not become visible until we focus on the behaviour of state actors. The failure of professionals to help a sick person, the frequency with which guns or Tasers are used, the numbers of suicides that take place in prisons (indicating how many Indigenous prisoners are driven to suicide and how easy it is for prisoners to kill themselves), and the willingness to risk Indigenous life, as in police drop-offs in sub-zero temperatures, all suggest an abiding disregard for Indigenous life. The same is true of the consistent reluctance in inquests and inquiries to explore the responses of state actors to Indigenous people. Only ever implicit in the numbers, moments of inhumanity, moments when a person's life is deemed to be worthless are often papered over in inquests and inquiries with recommendations proposing that state actors develop greater cultural sensitivity, remember to check cameras in police stations and hanging points in cells, create protocols for dealing with alcoholics, and learn to take better care of Indigenous prisoners in hospitals and jail cells. Oft-repeated, the recommendations indirectly confirm that settler society finds it difficult to provide the barest minimum of care and respect to a population it over-polices and incarcerates at rates that are among the highest in the Western world. There is a "failure to respond," concludes the correctional investigator for Canada, Howard Sapers.[3] When I examine the numbers, it is this failure to respond that I attempt to track, asking where it comes from, what it sustains, and how it might change.

The Phenomenon of Indigenous Deaths in Custody

The Canadian public likely learned about Indigenous deaths in custody as a phenomenon for the first time when freezing deaths in Saskatchewan brought Canada international censure. In 2001, Amnesty International's annual report named freezing deaths associated with police drop-offs of Indigenous men outside the city of Saskatoon as a cause for concern.[4] In 2004, both the US Department of State in its annual

Country Reports on Human Rights Practices and Rodolfo Stavenhagen, UN Special Rapporteur on the Situation of Human Rights and Fundamental Freedoms of Indigenous People, indicted Canada for its treatment of First Nations peoples, notably in the area of police practices.[5] Despite international notoriety, public interest in Indigenous deaths in custody has never been high. Native organizations strive to keep the issue alive. For instance, the First Nations Summit Chiefs in the British Columbia Assembly of First Nations passed a resolution in summer 2003 regarding "too many shootings of Aboriginal people by police and too many deaths of Aboriginal people while in police custody."[6] The Native Court Workers and Counselling Association of British Columbia then prepared a report[7] on Aboriginal people in British Columbia and other parts of Canada who have been shot by police, died in custody, or died as a result of police action or inaction. The Association found that between 1971 and 2003, at least nineteen Aboriginal people died in police custody or were shot by the police in British Columbia. It is noteworthy that sixty per cent of these deaths occurred in police custody, as opposed to prison, indicating that police/Aboriginal relations are extremely fraught.

As the Native Court Workers emphasized, its preliminary survey of sources and incidents was necessary because there was no systematic compilation of information about Aboriginal deaths in custody and no in-depth exploration of the nature of these deaths or of the law's response to them. This in itself is significant, betraying the state's deep reluctance to examine too closely what happens to Indigenous people in the criminal justice system. In British Columbia, the Coroners Service does not identify Indigenous deaths, but has a record of 267 police-involved deaths for the period 1992 to 2007, an average of eighteen deaths per year.[8] The inquiry into Frank Paul's death in 2007 included testimony that ten per cent or twenty-eight of the people on this list were Aboriginal in a province of over four million, where Aboriginal people make up only 4.4 per cent of the population.[9] From media reports and from the data generated by the inquiry into Frank Paul's death, a portrait emerges of Indigenous deaths in custody in British Columbia that includes death in the cells, death from police Tasers and guns, death from asphyxiation, and death arising from being breached (police transport of individuals from one area to another), for example, Frank Paul, who was left by the police in an alley where he died. Police cruisers, vans, lock-up cells, and prisons are violent places for Indigenous people.

Incarceration

It is often argued that more Indigenous people die in custody than any other group simply because they are overrepresented in the arrest, detention, and imprisonment statistics. The rising rates of incarceration for Indigenous peoples in Canada certainly deserve particular attention in any analysis of deaths in custody, because they indicate a structural problem that flies in the face of a theory of individual pathology. In his 2008–2009 annual report, Howard Sapers, the correctional investigator for Canada, noted the following:

> It is distressing to note that despite many well-intentioned efforts and reforms to address the plight of Aboriginal people in the criminal justice system, the incarceration rate for Aboriginal people has increased from 815 per 100,000 in 2001/02 to 983 per 100,000 in 2005/06. Aboriginal rates of incarceration are now almost nine times the national average. One in five federally incarcerated offenders is a person of Aboriginal ancestry. Among women offenders, the overrepresentation is even more dramatic – an astounding 32% of women in federal penitentiaries are Aboriginal.[10]

In his 2009–2010 annual report, Sapers continued to recite the grim statistics. While Aboriginal people comprise less than four per cent of the Canadian population, they account for twenty per cent of the total federal prison population.[11] Aboriginal women offenders in particular grew by ninety-seven per cent between 2002 and 2012 and constitute the fastest growing segment of the offender population.[12] When examined provincially (ninety-seven per cent of admissions to custody are to provincial institutions),[13] the statistics are equally disturbing. For instance, in Saskatchewan, Aboriginal peoples represent eighty-one per cent of all adults sentenced to custody, and Aboriginal representation in prison is seven times greater than their representation in the population. Importantly, the incarceration rates for Aboriginal people in Saskatchewan are still three to five times greater than for non-Aboriginal peoples, even when controlling for education and employment.[14] Analysing the trends of high incarceration rates for Aboriginal offenders in all provinces for the years 1978 to 2001, Julian Roberts and Ronald Melchers conclude that, taking into account demographics, crime rates, and criminal justice policy changes such as the implementation of Section 718.2 (e) of the *Criminal Code* requiring judges to consider alternatives to imprisonment and to pay particular attention to Aboriginal offenders, the number of Aboriginal offenders sent to prison was higher in 2001 than it was in 1978. While custodial admissions declined for all groups during this period, the decline was much less for Aboriginal than for non-Aboriginal groups.[15] As Roberts and Melchers point out, specific policy changes designed to address the problem of Aboriginal overrepresentation in prisons have not resulted in progress.

Patricia Monture-Angus comments that if we view this landscape of persistent overrepresentation and disregard the role that colonialism plays in producing this pattern, we assume that historical relations between colonizer and colonized have simply ended.[16] The few state-generated statistics of deaths in custody by race suggest that colonialism, and the dehumanization on which it is based, is alive and well. For  instance, federally, there has been one research study on deaths in custody conducted on behalf of the correctional investigator for Canada. The study, authored by Thomas Gabor, examined eighty-two reported suicides, homicides, and accidental deaths in prison from 2001 to 2005. Over sixty per cent of these deaths were suicides (nearly all by hanging), with the remainder split between homicides and accidents. All but one of the prisoners who died were male, and three of every ten were under thirty years of age.[17] Aboriginal people accounted for more than one fifth of the deaths in custody examined by Gabor. Seemingly recognizing that Aboriginal deaths in custody are a specific phenomenon requiring immediate solutions, Howard Sapers, the correctional investigator for Canada, complained in his 2009–2010 annual report that the Canadian government has paid little attention to his recommendations, refusing, for example, to appoint a deputy commissioner of Aboriginal Corrections and failing to allow for greater Aboriginal community involvement in Correctional Services.[18] The political response clearly shows a refusal to consider the situation of Aboriginal people in the justice system as unique and urgent.

Within such an institutional context, the behaviour of individual prison guards mimics the political indifference and leads to death. In his report *A Failure to Respond*,[19] Sapers describes what indifference looks like in the case of one man's death. The dead person was a fifty-two-year-old Indigenous man who self-inflicted a life-threatening wound but subsequently called for help. Help, when it did come, fell far short. Prison employees, Sapers concluded, "failed to respond in a manner that might have preserved life, and, subsequently, inconsistently reported critical information related to the death."[20] Sapers's report offers important details about the man who died. Incarcerated at the age of twenty with a sentence of twenty-eight months, he soon received an additional ten-year sentence for incidents that occurred while in prison. Released and reoffending some years later, the man was then convicted of manslaughter and sentenced to seventeen years in federal custody. He had a well-known history of alcoholism and depression, and had made three prior suicide attempts. In the course of his life in prison, the man received very little help, although he had some contact with an elder with whom he had begun to explore his residential school experiences. If the deceased man's profile is a typical one for Indigenous offenders, the prison's response is even more typical. The failure to respond began long before the moment when the prisoner tried to take his life, and the last, fatal incident reveals the outline of a deep inhumanity. As Sapers establishes, when prison guards responded to the call for help, they did not try to "enter into any dialogue" with the injured man. They did not follow up when he showed them his bleeding arms and failed to check his wounds until he passed out. Aware of his blood loss and later lying about it, guards wrote in their report that they believed the man was drunk, something later shown to be false in the toxicology reports. Guards also lied about the fact that they had left the dying man in his cell unattended. Once the ambulance arrived, however, they applied leg irons to the prisoner's legs in preparation for his transport (apparently more concerned about security than providing help), lying about the timing of this action in their final report. When a National Board of Investigation took up the matter, it heard allegations from staff and other offenders that "discrimination" played a role in staff responses. Neither these allegations nor the employees' failure to respond overly concerned the National Board, although their final report recommended establishing an Aboriginal awareness/sensitivity program, a recommendation that has never been implemented.

While the above case may seem shocking or unusual, as the chapters of this book have shown, the details of an Indigenous person's death in custody and the state and individuals' responses seldom vary from this particular case discussed by the correctional investigator. Although one can appreciate the correctional investigator's condemnation of the staff and the system that resulted in a man being left to die, his recommendations that prisons develop better emergency responses and that employees undergo anti-discrimination training (destined, in any event, to be ignored) cannot address the depth of inhumanity that guards and administrators, and their political bosses, display. These attitudes are clearly widespread and systemic. It would seem imperative, then, that when considering the rates of Indigenous deaths in custody and the patterns revealed in the interactions, we should begin with this casual, systematized inhumanity which Sapers uncovered in his investigation of one man's death. In and of themselves, the numbers do not enable us to track dehumanization, although they point the way.

Saskatchewan: A Case in Point

Saskatchewan ranks as the jurisdiction with the highest rate of incarceration in Canada. In this small Canadian province of just over a million people, Cree, Dakota, Dene (Chipewyan), Nakota (Assiniboine), and Saulteaux constitute approximately twelve per cent of the general population.[21] As the chart in the appendix shows, there were approximately 116 known deaths in custody for the period from 1995 to 2013, an average of six deaths per year. As there is no central site for collecting statistics and no formal records are kept of prisoners by race, it is hard to determine how many deaths in custody there actually were and how many of the 116 people who died were Indigenous. Cross referencing media reports with inquest summaries from the government of Saskatchewan and information gained from legal practitioners indicates that at least forty to fifty per cent of the 116 deaths were Indigenous, a number likely to be much higher, given that Indigenous people make up more than three-quarters of the prison population. The majority of deaths happen in the jails of Prince Albert and Saskatoon, but deaths also occur on highways, in hospitals and healing lodges, on streets, and in fields. Almost a third of Saskatchewan's deaths in custody are classified as suicides, and almost fifteen per cent involve police use of force, including shootings, Taser-related or pepper spray–related deaths, freezing deaths, and deaths resulting from restraints. The remaining deaths (approximately fifty per cent), whether classified as accidental, natural, or homicide, involve falls or other medical crises.

My interest in the numbers has been to trace patterns of indifference and overt violence on the part of state actors towards a prisoner population that is produced, historically and in the present, through colonial forces. The chart can only hint at these historical and contemporary complexities. For instance, in the largest category of deaths in custody for Saskatchewan, suicides, one can just glimpse the effects of an ongoing colonial violence. Seemingly an individual choice, there is hardly a suicide that does not reveal state-sponsored violence in Indigenous people's lives. When a police shooting results in death, and the police, the coroner, and the media consider the death as a "suicide by cop," that is, a death which occurs because the person wanted to die at the hands of the police, it is impossible to separate suicide from police violence. In 1999, a nineteen-year-old man was found hanging in his cell. His aunt noted at the inquest that he had begun to drift away from his family and culture after attending residential school.[22] Another young man, described as "periodically suicidal" and diagnosed with a form of schizophrenia, killed himself in a facility described as having staff shortages.[23] A twenty-eight-year-old mother of five took her life while in solitary confinement in 2000.[24] The acting warden commented to the press that the young woman fit the profile of inmates who are transferred to this prison because they are deemed too hard to manage elsewhere. A study released one week earlier confirmed that solitary confinement is particularly hard for Aboriginal women.[25] As Colin Tatz has argued, "Aboriginal suicide is different." A continuum of violence in Aboriginal people's lives, including being deprived of land rights and sustainable communities as well as ongoing settler violence from state and non-state actors, produces a collective for whom suicide makes sense.[26] Critically reviewing Tatz's book on Aboriginal suicide, Leonie Cox adds that "in some senses death brings them [Aboriginal people] into being from a state of non-being, a final gestalt that speaks to governments, the general public, and their families and networks."[27] She suggests that even scholars such as Tatz, who wish to escape a framework that views Aboriginal suicide as individual pathology, can end up reinscribing it by representing Aboriginal people as simply unable to cope and as only being in need of healing, individualist strategies that do not address "the structures and patterned inequalities" of colonialism.[28] Cox's critique resonates for the Canadian context: one can trace proposals for healing lodges made decades ago, some of which have been implemented, but with negligible impact on the suicide rates among Aboriginal prisoners.[29]

The colonial violence obscured in suicides is also masked in those deaths in custody often labelled accidental, which involve the provision of medical care to a people who are assumed to be alcoholic and ill. The role that alcohol plays in untimely death is hard to ascertain. Of the 116 deaths, thirty-five occurred in a context in which alcohol was deemed to have played a part. For instance, seventeen individuals were arrested for public intoxication, and thirteen were intoxicated when shot by police. In several cases, the circumstances of death indict police and medical practitioners for a remarkable indifference and cruelty. For example, an intoxicated V.A., who was asthmatic, was denied access to her inhalers by the police during transport. The heat was turned on in the police cruiser despite the extreme heat of the August day. V.A.

died while being admitted to prison.[30] Similarly, a man who suffered a seizure while obtaining a meal at a soup kitchen was pepper sprayed to death by a police officer in the ambulance while he was being transported to hospital. The coroner's jury concluded that excited delirium and not pepper spray was the cause of death.[31] A forty-eight-year-old woman died in hospital after sustaining a head injury while getting out of a police cruiser. Blood work confirmed that she was not intoxicated at the time of death, as the police had suggested.[32] A man arrested for public intoxication who had fallen a number of times was taken to hospital after he was found unresponsive in his cell. He was not given medical treatment and was released. An inquest determined that draining blood from his brain would have saved his life. In all of these deaths, alcohol is presumed to be a major factor. The belief that a victim has caused his or her own demise cancels out any possibility that police and health-care professionals have been brutal, neglectful, or uncaring. As is evident in all the cases discussed in this book, a legal focus on Indigenous dysfunction and ill health obscures how colonial power is imprinted on Indigenous bodies in a myriad of everyday ways.

Deaths involving police use of force, ranging from guns to pepper spray, confirm that the police relationship to Indigenous peoples in Saskatchewan is a violent one. In 2008, Saskatchewan recorded its worst year for fatal and non-fatal shootings, as the *Leader Post* reported.[33] In this category of death, it is also difficult to ascertain what story is revealed in the numbers, especially because no statistics are kept about police use of force. The circumstances of death reveal that the police use force in diverse situations, including cases involving domestic disputes and those where individuals are considered armed and threatening. "You can play with the numbers any way you want," Michael Tochor, chair of the Saskatchewan Police Commission, opined, suggesting that the high number of police shootings could be seen as evidence of the police encountering more violent criminals who are less respectful of authority.[34] But as then chief of the Saskatchewan Indian Nations, Chief Lawrence Joseph, countered, given who died in police shootings, one could also wonder why some incidents end peacefully and others end in death. Indeed, of the deaths by police shooting, only two are not confirmed as Indigenous. Amidst the debate about what the numbers mean, it is only clear that a high number of Indigenous people die in encounters with police and that factors such as alcohol abuse and crime rates require consideration, as do police skills and their responses to Indigenous people. Beyond a doubt, taken as a composite, the number of Indigenous deaths in custody due to suicide, ill health, and police use of force reveal that something is terribly amiss between Indigenous people and the settler colonial state, something that for the most part the state prefers to ignore.

Scholarship on Indigenous Deaths in Custody

Complicated by the inadequacy of data, the casual inhumanity that is a feature of so many settler interactions with Indigenous peoples has been hard to theorize. Traditional theories of racism, for instance, are hardly able to capture the depth and persistence of this inhumanity. Critical scholars have tended to focus on racism without understanding its connection to the maintenance of a settler colonial social order, thus missing the deeply entrenched nature of societal views of Indigenous people as sub-human and the material consequences of such views for settlers and Indigenous people alike. A wide range of contemporary sociological and statistical data in both Canada and the United States focus on the racial dimensions of police violence and show that the deadly use of force by police officers is disproportionately directed at racialized populations. As Scot Wortley and Terry Roswell summarize, explanations for racialized police violence have ranged from a racial animus model (the violence is due to a few racist "bad apples"), a devaluation or stereotype model (the violence emerges out of general societal attitudes to First Nations peoples), crime models (the violence is due to the overrepresentation of racial minorities in certain types of crime), and finally the police subculture model (norms of masculinity prevail in police subcultures that encourage violence). These scholars suggest that all these factors are likely to be operating in the violence directed at Indigenous and Black populations.[35] While studies of racialized police brutality contribute to an understanding of both the racial basis of the violence as well as the racism inherent within the criminal justice system, such analyses often do not show the particular ways in which violence against Indigenous peoples is historically and structurally constituted, nor do they explain why the violence is so persistent and excessive against this group and what the violence secures.

When exploring excessive police violence against Indigenous people, scholars sometimes see colonialism but few colonizers. In 2012, Elizabeth Comack, a criminologist, published *Racialized Policing: Aboriginal People's Encounters with the Police*.[36] Concerned to show how race and racism operate in the practice of policing, Comack offers the concept of racialized policing in order to call attention to how the police reproduce the social order of which they are a part. Comack shows that policing entails the policing of individuals as well as the policing of spaces. The police, she recalls, were originally colonial police, and then, as now, they play a central role in the containment and management of Aboriginal people as a subject population. Today, given Aboriginal poverty and social exclusion, the police are responsible for what Comack describes as "the daunting task of responding to the 'disorder' that results from these social conditions."[37] Analysing police drop-offs of Aboriginal men outside the city where they freeze to death, Comack describes the lethal practice as "a strategy that police use to reproduce order when dealing with troubled and troublesome people."[38] Although she recognizes the colonial basis in the patterns of policing Aboriginal peoples, Comack stops short of interrogating what the practice of drop-offs reveals about settler and police subjectivities, particularly the disregard for Aboriginal life that such incidents reveal. As Mrs Wegner, the mother of one of the Indigenous men found frozen to death, asked, "Who would do such a thing?"[39] Canadian scholars have not fully grappled with this most basic question in a way that recognizes the deep disregard for Indigenous life so many state actors display. Scholars in other parts of the settler colonial world are sometimes more forthright, naming the disregard for Indigenous life as colonial violence and theorizing its persistence in settler colonial societies as a central aspect of how settler states are organized. Here, too, however, the emphasis has not been on the "who," that is, on state actors in a settler colonial state.

Other Jurisdictions: Australian Deaths in Custody

As a white settler society that emerged from British colonial rule, Australia shares with Canada a common history of the dispossession of Indigenous peoples and an ongoing colonial relationship visible in high Indigenous incarceration and death-in-custody rates. Australia's response to elevated rates of Indigenous deaths in custody came earlier and was more vigorous than Canada's, but ultimately, Australian strategies have done little to address the persistence of violence against Indigenous peoples, in large part because the underlying coloniality of the state's relationship with Indigenous peoples has not been addressed. In response to strenuous protests by Aboriginal peoples, Australia established a Royal Commission into Aboriginal Deaths in Custody (RCIADIC) in October 1987. The commission investigated the deaths of ninety-nine Aboriginal and Torres Strait Islander people who died in police, prison, or juvenile custody during the decade of the 1980s, among them eighty-eight males and eleven females. The vast majority of these deaths were associated with police custody (and not with prison or juvenile detention). The causes of death were established as hanging, trauma, deaths associated with substance abuse, and deaths from natural causes. As these categories already indicate, it was hard to pin down the culpability of state actors, and the commission concluded that there was no indication of foul play "in the sense of unlawful, deliberate killing of Aboriginal prisoners by police officers."[40] Its failure to indict state actors notwithstanding, the commission uncovered the patterns and conditions under which death occurred, patterns that persist for the Australian and the Canadian contexts. For instance, the data collected confirmed that in all cases those who died in custody had multiple encounters with the justice system and lives dramatically regulated by intense state involvement. As the commission stated, "For each individual there are files maintained by agents of the State: schools, community welfare, adoption, medical, police, prison, probation and parole and, finally, coroners' files document each life to a degree that few non-Aboriginal peoples lives would be recorded."[41] If the commission acknowledged the heavy hand of the state in Aboriginal peoples' lives and their extreme overrepresentation in custody, it also emphasized the role of alcohol, disease, and dysfunction, and the difficulties these factors posed for the state.

The detailed descriptions of the ninety-nine cases examined by the Australian royal commission left scholars and activists with a record that, although it remained under-examined and under-theorized by the commission itself, has had a significant impact on how Australians have come to understand the phenomenon that is Aboriginal death in custody. The commission noticed, for example, that for Aboriginal peoples, hangings occurred in police cells rather than in prisons, a pattern that did not apply for non-Aboriginal custodial deaths.[42] If the majority of hangings occurred within two hours of being entered into custody, then their connection to the conditions of lock-up, including failure to check on prisoners and to examine and acknowledge injuries sustained prior to custody, had to be significant. Prisoners with head injuries, pre-existing medical conditions, mental illness, and symptoms related to extreme alcohol consumption were often neglected to the point of death. The commission noted that the men and women who died in custody had journeyed through the carceral and health-care systems in an "unending rotation" that had little to do with care. Commenting that as a community Australians seemed incapable of responding to the problem posed by Aboriginality, the commissioners speculated that "the sensitivities of those involved in the process are dulled by sheer repetition."[43] This observation has been made in the Canadian context, for example, in the inquiry into the death of Frank Paul. In sum, the ninety-nine cases shed light on something far more damning than the sensitivities of those caught in a bad system. Documenting an absence of thorough investigations of deaths, the routine failure to follow protocols or a persistent inattention to previous recommendations, a stunning indifference to suffering, a punitive and malevolent policing, and circumstances of suspicious deaths, RCIADIC had before it the evidence of a full-blown and violent colonial encounter. Having opened the door on the phenomenon called "Aboriginal death in custody," the commission concluded that high rates of Aboriginal deaths in custody were related to disproportionately high rates of incarceration and to the severely disadvantaged social, economic, and cultural position of Indigenous people in Australia. The RCIADIC stopped short of confronting the other factors contributing to deaths, namely the violence of state actors and an entrenched, systemic devaluing of Indigenous life.

A plethora of recommendations notwithstanding, RCIADIC, in the view of several Australian scholars, changed little. In a national overview of deaths in custody between 1980 and 1998, Vicki Dalton, drawing on the data gathered by the Australian Institute of Criminology (mandated since RCIADIC to monitor deaths in custody nationally), showed that deaths in police custody had declined significantly since 1987, perhaps attributable to police implementing some of the recommendations for dealing with those in police custody. However, deaths in prison custody since that time have risen steadily. Whereas during the 1980s prison deaths averaged thirty-one per year and accounted for sixty-one per cent of all custodial deaths, in 1998 the number of deaths had increased to seventy-six and accounted for eighty-eight per cent of all custodial deaths that year.[44] Dalton cites one example of RCIADIC's lack of impact. Despite RCIADIC's recommendation to remove hanging points in prison cells (a major cause of all custodial deaths), prisons are still being built with them, and hanging deaths continue to occur. Although Indigenous adults represent only two per cent of the Australian population, they represented eighteen per cent of the prison population, and over fifteen per cent of inmate deaths in prison were of Indigenous prisoners.[45] Paul Wildman notes that for Western Australia alone, with a population of over two million, there were six Aboriginal deaths in custody in 1999.[46] For Wildman, RCIADIC failed conspicuously to have an impact on deaths in custody for the simple reason that it devoted less than two per cent of its recommendations to the deeper issues of causation, land, and self-determination, and viewed deaths in custody through the eyes of the existing bureaucracy and not through the eyes of Indigenous Australia. Notably, since incarceration rates have increased, Wildman emphasizes that only an exploration of the wider context in which Aboriginal deaths in custody occur will have an impact on death rates. Incarceration rates, Wildman suggests, amount to "a form of sanctioned disappearances." Scholars who explore the wider context generally neglect to consider who settlers become in these arrangements, that is, how we become able to sanction and implement disappearances at all.

Australian scholars emphasize the link between a colonial structure and violence. Chris Cunneen, for instance, locates the "violence of incarceration" to the colonial dispossession of Aboriginal peoples, not only in the sense that colonialism destroys communities and produces the profound economic, social, and political marginalization of which many scholars speak, but also because it requires and sustains extreme violence against Aboriginal peoples.[47] Arguing that police violence against Aboriginal peoples is excessive because the relationship is an intensely colonial one, Cunneen proposes that the term "terror" is a more useful one than, for example, "discrimination." Detailing police practices of terror in Aboriginal communities (police assaults, for example) and in prisons (practices including torture), Cunneen relies on the data gathered from surveys and inquiries in which Aboriginal testimony consistently identifies the extreme practices of police violence directed towards their communities and the indifference of the law towards settler and police violence. In its report to the UN Committee Against Torture, the Deaths in Custody Committee for Western Australia consider several cases of the torture of Aboriginal people in custody.[48] Clearly, state-sponsored violence against Aboriginal people continues apace.

Scholars and activists who emphasize terror and state-sponsored violence identify carceral spaces for Indigenous Australians as spaces of death and note the historical continuities between such spaces. Dinesh Wadiwel, for instance, writing of Palm Island, where in 2004, an Aboriginal man named Mulrunji (Cameron Doomadgee) died in a police cell with broken ribs, a ruptured spleen, and a liver split in two, considers the island in terms of its history as a penal colony for Aboriginal peoples and concludes that such spaces are zones of exception or concentration camps where, as Agamben defined them, nothing committed against the inmates can be considered a crime.[49] Drawing on Achille Mbembe's ideas about necropolitics and death-worlds, Wadiwel argues that Palm Island functioned as a zone without regular law, where racialized practices of colonization instituted a bureaucratized, sovereign violence. Police culpability for Mulrunji's death was hard to pursue in such a space of historical and contemporary violence, as Keenan, Watson, and Tedmanson show respectively in their analyses of colonial violence on Palm Island.[50] Other scholars emphasize the carceral and necropolitical line that runs through multiple practices of the settler colonial state. For example, Suvendrini Perera and Joseph Pugliese connect the practices that produce Aboriginal deaths in custody to the ones that produce the ever-increasing deaths of migrants held in detention centres across Australia.[51]

Towards an Anti-Colonial Approach

This book has emphasized colonial terror and considered the state's relationship to Indigenous bodies (and other racialized bodies)[52] as one characterized by intense violence. Whether deaths in custody are marked as suicides, due to natural causes, ill health, or suspicious circumstances, an approach that stresses the colonial requires that deaths in custody be contextualized. To focus on the colonial is to place emphasis on the history of the relationship between Indigenous peoples and the state, a history of forced removals, camps, reserves, residential schools, and punishment. To historicize in this fashion also means that we connect what goes on inside the police cells or the prison to what goes on outside, mapping the regular imprinting of colonial power on Indigenous bodies across space and time, and recognizing the stunning inhumanity of these interactions. Finally, this approach emphasizes a consideration of colonial subjectivities, the production of state actors who understand Indigenous bodies as sub-human, those who routinely fail to care for Indigenous bodies or who actively brutalize them as well as those judicial and legal actors who refuse to call such individuals to account. "Who would do such a thing?" should remain a central question. Put differently, how does it come to be that the condition of modern life is Indigenous annihilation, an annihilation that so many participate in or endorse?

Anti-Colonial Education

The pernicious idea that it has all been simply a cultural misunderstanding persists in education. We have yet to develop anti-colonial pedagogies that would invite students to examine their complicity in an ongoing colonialism, one in which Indigenous peoples are disproportionately incarcerated and overrepresented in deaths in custody. While universities are happy to promote courses on Indigenous knowledge, and individual students enthusiastically participate in smudging ceremonies, there is less willingness to consider issues of Indigenous sovereignty and colonial violence. As in education, inquests and inquiries follow the line that if there is a problem in the criminal justice system, the problem is a cultural one. There is hardly an inquest or inquiry that does not include a recommendation for cultural sensitivity training for white and non-Indigenous police officers, for instance. The emphasis on cultural sensitivity notwithstanding, the routine invocations to remember to have working cameras in police cruisers and police stations and to fill out the appropriate forms that list prisoners' illnesses begs the question of why such recommendations have had to be endlessly repeated to little avail. The question, Why don't things change?, is a question that requires us to reconsider whether the problem really is simply one of cultural misunderstanding. If constables Larry Hartwig and Brad Senger, the two police officers who drove Neil Stonechild to the outskirts of town where he froze to death, had a better understanding of Indigenous cultures, would they have done what they did? It is useful to recall that Constable Hartwig boasted of his own understanding of Aboriginal culture and described his participation in sweat lodges in his interview for the film *Two Worlds Colliding*. Would an understanding of Mi'kmaq traditions have enabled police officers to believe that Frank Paul deserved more than to be left in an alley on a cold night? It is here that the issue of colonialism comes to the fore. Colonialism, as an ongoing material project entailing the dispossession of Indigenous peoples, produces, even as it relies upon, the notion of humanity and sub-humanity that circulates throughout the cases discussed in this book. Quick fixes, Monture-Angus reminds us, don't work if they divert attention away from "the larger structural problems within the system."[53] The larger problem is a systematized inhumanity.

One can hardly deny the connection between high rates of deaths in custody and high detention and incarceration rates, the latter an outcome of the policing of a deeply marginalized and dispossessed population. Historicizing these rates and patterns reveals a continuum of violence imprinted on Indigenous bodies, not only over time but across spaces. The violence directed at Indigenous peoples a century ago, the violence of residential schools, and now the rate of Indigenous children in foster care who are dying together represent an unbroken line of violence over time. These examples must be connected to the violence Indigenous women encounter on the streets of contemporary Canada,[54] the number of reserves without safe drinking water, the HIV infection rate on Vancouver's Downtown East Side, the fact that a young Indigenous man has four times the chance of going to prison than finishing high school, and the extremely high suicide rates for young Indigenous people. Contemporary Canada is a place where it is possible for Brian Sinclair, an Indigenous man in a wheelchair, to wait thirty-six hours in the emergency room of the city of Winnipeg and finally to die in the waiting room. It is also a place where an inquest into Sinclair's death balks at the idea of examining systemic racism.[55] Seldom does a week go by without a report of untimely Indigenous death under suspicious circumstances, deaths that reveal that something is terribly wrong between Indigenous and non-Indigenous Canada. What sense can be made of twelve hundred missing and murdered Indigenous women[56] or the media report of a twenty-three-year-old Indigenous woman who apparently committed suicide in a police cruiser, where she had been left alone because the jail in a remote northern community did not have adequate heating?[57] In January 2014, three guards in riot gear held a naked Michael Nehass, a Tahltan man, to the floor of a prison cell in Whitehorse, Yukon. Videotaped naked for his court hearing, even as he pleaded for a towel to cover up, Nehass, an intergenerational survivor of residential schools and a man allegedly with several mental disorders, faced a judge and several lawyers, none of whom objected to the naked state of the prisoner. In lodging a human rights complaint, the father of Michael Nehass revealed that his son had only been outside four times in two years, that he was held in a segregation cell where the light was never fully turned off, and that he had attempted suicide, a fact that was never communicated to the family. Nehass's father also said that he was often prevented from seeing his son for periods of up to a year.[58] Dehumanization hardly captures the torture and humiliation of Michael Nehass. The Indigenous world of contemporary Canada, while rife with such events, is notably a place of intense Indigenous resistance to colonialism. Indigenous people have the highest birthrate in Canada, a testimony to their refusal to be "disappearing Indians."[59] They continue to vigorously protest their dispossession in the streets and in the courts. Is their refusal to disappear the reason for ongoing settler violence?

In failing to confront the material basis to colonial logic head on, settlers reveal their investment in the fiction that colonialism is a thing of the past. If we start with the reality of an ongoing colonialism, we can better reflect on the inhumanity that such a project requires. Then and only then will we be able to reject the fantasy of settler civility and refuse the game of improvement. Instead, we can work for Indigenous sovereignty and towards the relations of respect it necessarily installs. To develop relationships of genuine reciprocity with Indigenous peoples, we non-Indigenous peoples must embark on this anti-colonial journey. The epitaph on Paul Alphonse's gravestone reads: "One Tough Cowboy." It is a phrase full of truth, irony, and love. If colonialism and Hollywood gave us John Wayne and the white fantasy of cowboys roaming the frontier subduing Indians, it also gave us Indians who repurpose the term "cowboy," reminding us that in Canada men like Alphonse were the real cowboys, the ones who built the ranches, rode in the rodeos, and played a mean fiddle. Indigenous resistance marks the pages of the inquests and inquiries I have studied here and is a powerful reminder of why Indigenous sovereignty remains necessary and urgent, not only for the salvation of Indigenous peoples but also for non-Indigenous peoples if, that is, we do not want to be a part of a "cruel modernity."[60]

Appendix

Deaths in Custody: Saskatchewan 1995–2013

	Race	Type of death	Initials	Age	Sex	Date of death
1	Native	Freezing/Saskatoon	N.S.[1]	17	M	1990-11-25
2	Native	Shooting/RCMP. No inquest record found.	D.M.[2]	23	M	1994-05-11
3	Native	Shooting/Prince Albert Police	F.P.[3]	28	M	1995-03-31
4	Native	Shooting/Regina Police Service	D.D.C.[4]	20	F	1996-01-28
5	Native	Suicide (Hanging)/Regina Provincial Correctional Centre	H.M.[5]	19	M	1999-11-05
6	Native	Suicide (Hanging)/Regional Psychiatric Centre	S.F.[6]	23	M	2000-01-01
7	Native	Freezing/Saskatoon. Unable to stand upon release due to alcohol intoxication. Died hours after being released from SPS custody.	L.J.D.[7]	53	M	2000-01-19
8	Native	Freezing/Saskatoon	R.H.N.[8]	25	M	2000-01-29
9	Native	Freezing/Saskatoon	L.K.W.[9]	30	M	2000-02-03 (Date Found)
10	Native	Suicide (Hanging)/SK Penitentiary	E.S.B.[10]	28	F	2000-02-05
11	Native	Overdose/Died hours after being released from SPS custody. Arrested for public intoxication.	D.D.I.[11]	33	M	2000-02-19

(Continued)

	Race	Type of death	Initials	Age	Sex	Date of death
12	Native	Suicide (Hanging)/Prince Albert Grand Council Spiritual Healing Lodge	G.J.O.[12]	38	M	2000-03-24
13	Native	Suicide (Hanging)/Remand in Regina Provincial Correctional Centre	K.B.S.[13]	33	M	2000-05-14
14	Native	Shooting/RCMP. "The shooting occurred in a field … 8 kilometres west of Saskatoon."[14] Pepper spray used. Was drinking.	M.B.[15]	33	M	2001-04-27
15	Native	Shooting/SPS (RCMP Present). Shot in a field along the same highway as M.B. outside Saskatoon. (Almost twice legal limit.)	K.G.M.[16]	33	M	2001-05-19
16	Native	Excited Delirium (Cardiac Arrhythmia)/Regina Police Service. Pepper sprayed in ambulance.	V.C.[17]	32	M	2001-07-10
17	Native	Undetermined/Pine Grove Correctional Centre, Prince Albert. Denied use of asthma inhalers while being transported to prison. Autopsy was unable to determine the exact cause of death but ruled that evidence long-term IV drug use. The jury made seven (7) recommendations, mostly suggesting that consideration should be given to building a medical/detention facility to accommodate detainees who are intoxicated, that all transport vehicles have suitable operational climate controls, and that at least one person in each shift should be trained in "suicide intervention."	V.A.[18]	33	F	2001-08-21
18	Native	Suicide (Hanging)/Saskatoon Provincial Correctional Centre	R.B.[19]	27	M	2002-02-03

	Race	Type of death	Initials	Age	Sex	Date of death
19	Native	Overdose/Pine Grove Correction Centre, Prince Albert	S.F.K.[20]	37	F	2002-02-19
20	Native	Sudden Death (Fatty Liver)/ Pelican Narrows RCMP Detachment Cells. Drinking on dry reserve.	A.M.S.[21]	43	F	2002-05-10
21	Native	Natural (Acute Necrotizing Pancreatitis) or Accidental (high levels of oxazepam)/Yorkton RCMP Holding Cells. Picked up for public intoxication, asked to be taken to hospital, but died in cells.	A.R.C.[22]	40	M	2002-08-28
22	Native	Hit by Wakaw RCMP Vehicle riding his bike	D.R.C.[23]	17	M	2002-09-15
23	Native	Suicide (Hanging)/SK Penitentiary	A.B.J.M.[24]	23	M	2003-01-03
24	Native	Excited Delirium (Cocaine Induced – Ruled Accidental)/ Regina Police Service	M.J.A.[25]	34	M	2003-06-19
25	Native	Hit by Kamsack RCMP vehicle. No inquest record found.	Unknown[26]	19	M	2003-09-11
26	Native	Head Injury (Intracranial Bleeding and Skull Fracture)/ Prince Albert Police Station. Picked up for public intoxication outside hospital, had severely low blood sugar. Hit head in police station.	L.L.S.[27]	48	F	2004-08-03
27	Native	Suicide (Hanging)/Remand in Prince Albert Correctional Centre	A.E.[28]	50	M	2004-08-28
28	Native	Shooting/La Ronge RCMPStandoff.	S.M.[29]	38	M	2004-08-30
29	Native	Overdose/SPS Custody Cells. Internally hidden package ruptured.	D.S.[30]	42	F	2005-06-26
30	Native	Suicide (Hanging)/Prince Albert Correctional Centre	F.P.[31]	27	M	2005-08-15

(Continued)

	Race	Type of death	Initials	Age	Sex	Date of death
31	Native	Undetermined (potentially drank cleaning fluid)/Prince Albert Correctional Centre	J.B.[32]	43	M	2005-10-21
32	Native	Overdose (Methadone/Alcohol)/ SPS Custody Cells. Arrested for breach – consuming alcohol.	T.D.M.[33]	38	M	2006-05-28
33	Native	Shooting/RCMP Sniper (Muskowekwan First Nation)	D.K.P.[34]	44	M	2006-11-13
34	Native	Stroke/RCMP Holding Cells. Arrested in Pinehouse, died in Saskatoon Hospital.	V.L.[35]	40	M	2007-01-02
35	Native	Suicide (Hanging)/in Saskatchewan Hospital, North Battleford Garage. Was in custody at the time – unclear in what manner.	I.D.B.[36]	35	M	2007-07-30
36	Native	Suicide (Hanging)/Regina Provincial Correctional Centre	M.R.T.[37]	52	M	2007-12-4
37	Native	Shooting/ SPS. Jury ruled it "Suicide by Cop." Had been drinking.	D.C.D.[38]	38	M	2007-12-22
38	Native	Shooting/Prince Albert Police. Blood alcohol level 30 mg away from lethal level.	J.M.M.[39]	44	F	2008-03-18
39	Native	Died from infection (likely due to IV drug use) while at large; fled from hospital when he saw police there for another matter.	E.W.D.[40]	43	M	2008-04-02
40	Native	Shooting /RCMP (White Bear First Nation). Jury ruled it was "Suicide by Cop." FSIN demanded inquiry. Alcohol was a factor.	K.C.W.S-M.[41]	21	M	2008-06-14
41	Native	Shooting/La Loche RCMP (Clearwater River Dene First Nation). Blood alcohol more than 3 times the legal limit.	H.H.[42]	38	M	2008-09-02
42	Native	Unknown/House Arrest – electronic monitoring (died in Regina General Hospital)	B.H.[43]	31	M	2008-12-08

	Race	Type of death	Initials	Age	Sex	Date of death
43	Native	Freezing/Beauval RCMP Detachment. Escaped custody after being arrested for alcohol on dry reserve. Police failed to report him missing to family for 13 hours.	K.L.[44]	19	M	2009-01-11 (Date Found)
44	Native	Suicide/Regional Psychiatric Centre. Self-injury with razor; died from complications related to injuries.	L.R.B.[45]	51	M	2009-02-22
45	Native	Multiple Organ Failure (possibly from Tylenol OD)/North Battleford RCMP Cells (died in hospital). "Disorderly conduct due to what police thought was intoxication."[46]	I.P.[47]	34	F	2009-06-10
46	Native	Overdose (Tylenol)/SPS Custody Cells. Picked up for public intoxication (no alcohol found in system).	B.T.D.[48]	19	M	2010-07-03
47	Native	Head Injury/SPS Custody Cells (died in hospital). Arrested for public intoxication; head injury sustained prior to arrest.	S.R.[49]	46	M	2010-07-15
48	Possible	Suicide (Hanging)/Saskatoon Provincial Correctional Centre. Transferred to North Battleford hospital from SPCC after a suicide attempt.	E.W.T.[50]	19	M	1995 Inquest
49	Possible	Unknown/Pine Grove Correctional Centre. Found in her cell in "medical distress" and transferred to hospital.	P.T.[51]	20	F	1997-02-13
50	Possible	Unknown/Regina Provincial Correction Centre (died in hospital)	Q.D.K.[52]	22	M	1997-12-20
51	Possible	Unknown/SK Penitentiary. Pronounced dead shortly after arrival at hospital.	L.S.[53]	26	M	1998-03-11
52	Possible	Unknown/Prince Albert Correctional Centre	I.L.[54]	19	M	1998-06-05

(Continued)

	Race	Type of death	Initials	Age	Sex	Date of death
53	Possible	Shooting/Regina Police Service	J.J.E.[55]	16	M	1998-09-10
54	Possible	Suicide (Hanging)/RCMP Cells (Wollaston Lake)	E.J.H.[56]	52	M	1999-04-12
55	Possible	Suicide (Hanging)	F.T.G.[57]		M	2000 Inquest
56	Possible	Suicide (Hanging)/Moose Jaw Police Service Cells	(Unnamed)[58]	16	F	2002-08-14
57	Possible	Unknown/Cumberland RCMP Custody	C.R.D.[59]	26	M	2003-07-20
58	Possible	Suicide (Hanging)/SPS Custody Cells. Arrested for warrants/ breach, appeared drunk.	J.E.A.[60]	34	F	2004-02-17
59	Unknown	Unknown/RCMP (Estevan); "detained … under the provisions of the Mental Health Act."[61]	B.A.M.[62]	22	M	1994-10-17
60	Unknown	Unknown/Inmate at the St. Louis Rehabilitation Centre (south of Prince Albert)	R.S.T.[63]	44	M	1994-10-27
61	Unknown	Unknown/Regina Provincial Correctional Centre	R.K.[64]	22	M	1994-11-12
62	Unknown	Unknown/Regional Psychiatric Centre	J.E.[65]	37	M	1995-09-04
63	Unknown	Unknown/Regional Psychiatric Centre	R.A.G.[66]	36	M	1995-10-16
64	Unknown	Unknown/SK Penitentiary	R.T.M.[67]	53	M	1996-04-09
65	Unknown	Unknown/Prince Albert Provincial Correctional Centre	J.L.[68]	26	M	1996-08-03
66	Unknown	Unknown/Regina Provincial Correctional Centre	M.J.L.[69]	34	M	1996-11-14
67	Unknown	Unknown/Regina Provincial Correctional Centre	W.K.S.[70]	26	M	1997-01-06
68	Unknown	Suicide (Hanging)/SK Penitentiary	C.M.R.[71]	44	M	1997-05-11
69	Unknown	Suicide/Saskatoon Provincial Correctional Centre.	M.G.[72]	20	M	1997-06-13
70	Unknown	Unknown/Prince Albert Police Service Custody (died in Victoria Hospital)	T.H.F.[73]	27	M	1997-07-13

	Race	Type of death	Initials	Age	Sex	Date of death
71	Unknown	Unknown/Prince Albert Provincial Correctional Centre	E.E.B.[74]	36	M	1997-08-10
72	Unknown	Suicide (Hanging)/Regina Provincial Correctional Centre	D.S.C.[75]	33	M	1997-10-01
73	Unknown	Suicide (Hanging)/Saskatoon Provincial Correctional Centre	R.W.D.[76]	49	M	1997-12-20
74	Unknown	Unknown/Moosomin RCMP Cells	A.J.P.[77]	73	M	1998 Inquest
75	Unknown	Unknown/SK Penitentiary	A.G.[78]	66	M	1998 Inquest
76	Unknown	Unknown/SK Penitentiary	S.V.B.[79]	21	M	1998-05-28
77	Unknown	Unknown/SPS Custody (died in hospital)	M.O.[80]	45	M	1998-10-01
78	Unknown	Suicide (Hanging)/Regina Provincial Correctional Centre	K.B.E.[81]	21	M	1999 inquest
79	Unknown	Natural Causes (Bile Peritonitis)/Regional Psychiatric Centre	R.L.H.[82]	49	M	1999-07-15
80	Unknown	Unknown/Régina Provincial Correctional Centre (died in hospital)	C.M.[83]	18	M	1999-11-12
81	Unknown	Unknown/Regina Provincial Correctional Centre. "He collapsed at a work site."[84]	R.P.[85]	49	M	1999-12-08
82	Unknown	Cardiac Failure (likely drug overdose)/Corrections Canada Community Residential Facility in Regina.	N.T.S.[86]	48	M	2000-01-05
83	Unknown	Acute Pneumonia/SK Penitentiary (died at hospital)	G.R.C.[87]	44	M	2000-02-02
84	Unknown	Unknown/ Regional Psychiatric Centre	D.M.[88]	44	M	2000-11-01
85	Unknown	Accidental (Hanging)/SK Penitentiary	M.E.M.[89]	20	M	2001-03-11
86	Unknown	Suicide (Hanging)/SK Penitentiary	C.J.[90]	29	M	2001-08-31
87	Unknown	Excited Delirium/Regina Police Service. Pepper spray.	M.J.S.[91]	35	M	2001-09-01

(Continued)

	Race	Type of death	Initials	Age	Sex	Date of death
88	Unknown	Accidental Overdose/SPS Custody Cells. Picked up for public intoxication.	D.E.B.[92]	57	M	2001-09-26
89	Unknown	Unknown/Regional Psychiatric Centre (died in hospital)	E.L.[93]	63	M	2001-11-17
90	Unknown	Natural (Kidney Cancer)/ Regional Psychiatric Centre; "died … while under palliative care."	W.A.[94]	49	M	2001-12-24
91	Unknown	Overdose (Morphine)/Regional Psychiatric Centre	D.T.[95]	34	M	2002-01-01
92	Unknown	Suicide (Hanging)/ Forensic Unit of the Saskatchewan Hospital in North Battleford	G.P.V.[96]	38	M	2002-01-01
93	Unknown	Unknown (reported heart attack)/Riverbend Institution	P.P.[97]	72	M	2002-02-03
94	Unknown	Unknown/in Police Custody; died in Swift Current Regional Hospital	B.L.[98]	45	M	2002-10-27
95	Unknown	Suicide (Hanging)/Saskatoon Provincial Correctional Centre.	D.F.C.[99]	23	M	2002-11-05
96	Unknown	Suicide (poisoning – Antifreeze)/SPS Custody Cells. SPS assumed was intoxicated.	B.D.[100]	43	M	2002-11-20
97	Unknown	Natural (Kidney and Liver Failure – Hep C)/Regional Psychiatric Centre; "… under palliative care at St. Paul's Hospital."	J.W.[101]	58	M	2003-04-10
98	Unknown	Suicide (Hanging)/Oskana Community Correctional Centre (on conditional release)	A.G.M.[102]	46	M	2003-08-16
99	Unknown	Suicide (Hanging)/Saskatoon Provincial Correctional Centre	P.D.[103]	31	M	2003-09-14
100	Unknown	Suicide (Hanging)/Saskatoon Provincial Correctional Centre	L.S.[104]	41	M	2003-09-30
101	Unknown	Shooting/SPS. Crystal Meth was considered a factor.	A.W.M.[105]	35	M	2004-04-30

	Race	Type of death	Initials	Age	Sex	Date of death
102	Unknown	Suicide (Hanging)/Regina Provincial Correctional Centre	A.V.[106]	48	M	2005-04-23
103	Unknown	Suicide (Hanging)/Regina Provincial Correctional Centre	R.T.[107]	31	M	2005-07-16
104	Unknown	Suicide (Hanging)/SK Penitentiary	M.M.[108]	52	M	2005-12-13
105	Unknown	Overdose (after being released from hospital)/SPS Custody Cells. Pepper spray.	W.A.S.[109]	46	M	2006-01-02
106	Unknown	Suicide (Hanging)/SK Penitentiary	T.C.A.[110]	31	M	2006-09-22
107	Unknown	Overdose (Methadone)/ Regional Psychiatric Centre	A.C.[111]	33	M	2007-03-26
108	Unknown	Overdose (Fentanyl)/Released from Regina Provincial Correctional Centre – electronic monitor on bail	G.R.[112]	31	M	2007-08-16
109	Unknown	Alcohol Poisoning/Regina Police Service Cells. Arrested for public intoxication.	S.N.S.[113]	47	M	2008-04-12
110	Unknown	Unknown/Federal Inmate died in Royal University Hospital in Saskatoon. Multiple chronic and serious health issues.	N.G.L.[114]	34	M	2008-08-18
111	Unknown	Suicide (Hanging)/Regina Provincial Correctional Centre	D.P.[115]	39	M	2008-09-26
112	Unknown	Accidental (Prone Restraint Asphyxia)/Regina Police Service. Pepper spray.	C.M.[116]	38	M	2008-10-09
113	Unknown	Suicide (Hanging)/Swift Current RCMP Cells. Arrested for being drunk and confrontational.	C.J.C.[117]	36	M	2009-04-17
114	Unknown	Suicide (Overdose)/SPS Custody Cells	J.H.[118]	34	M	2009-09-09
115	Unknown	Suicide (Hanging)/Remand in Saskatoon Provincial Correctional Centre	T.A.P.[119]	27	M	2010-06-24
116	Unknown	Suicide (Overdose)/Swift Current RCMP detachment	D.G.[120]	54	M	2010-07-16

Notes

Introduction

1 Farlex, *TheFreeDictionary.com*, s.v. "disappear," http://www.thefreedictionary.com/disappear.
2 Audra Simpson, *Mohawk Interruptus: Political Life Across the Borders of Settler States* (Raleigh, NC: Duke University Press, 2014), 7–8.
3 I use the term Indigenous except when others use Aboriginal, First Nations, Native, or (typically for the American context) Indian. Wherever possible, I refer to the specific nation/tribe/community.
4 Alphonse family, in discussion with the author, Williams Lake, British Columbia, 24 October 2008.
5 Delgamuukw v. British Columbia [1991] BCSC, 79 DLR (4th) 185 at 342.
6 A. Dirk Moses, "Genocide and Settler Society in Australian History," in *Genocide and Settler Society: Frontier Violence and Stolen Indigenous Children in Australian History*, ed. A. Dirk Moses (New York: Berghahn Books), 29.
7 Lorenzo Veracini, "The Other Shift: Settler Colonialism, Israel, and the Occupation," *Journal of Palestine Studies* 42, no. 2 (Winter 2013): 5.
8 Phillip Scraton and Kathryn Chadwick, "Speaking Ill of the Dead: Institutional Responses to Deaths in Custody," *Journal of Law and Society* 13, no.1 (Spring 1986): 93–115.
9 Simon Pemberton, "Demystifying Deaths in Police Custody: Challenging State Talk," *Social and Legal Studies* 17, no. 2 (2008): 237–62.
10 Simpson, *Mohawk Interruptus*, 2.
11 Ibid., 11.
12 Ibid., 3.
13 Leanne Simpson, "Elsipogtog Protest: We're Only Seeing Half the Story," *Huffington Post*, 22 October 2013, accessed 29 September 2014, http://www.huffingtonpost.ca/leanne-simpson/elsipogtog-racism_b_4139367.

html. I am grateful to Kate Milley for directing my attention to Simpson's words.

14 Patricia Monture-Angus, "Standing against Canadian Law: Naming Omissions of Race, Culture, Gender," in *Locating Law: Race/Class/Gender Connections*, ed. Elizabeth Comack with Sedef Arat-Koç et al. (Halifax: Fernwood Publishing), 93.

15 For a chronology of *Delgamuukw v. British Columbia*, see the summary review prepared by Mary C. Hurley, Law and Government Division of the Parliamentary Research Branch, Library of Parliament, titled "Aboriginal Title: The Supreme Court of Canada Decision in *Delgamuukw v. British Columbia*" (January 1998, revised February 2000), available at http://www.parl.gc.ca/content/lop/researchpublications/bp459-e.pdf.

16 John Borrows, "Sovereignty's Alchemy: An Analysis of *Delgamuukw v. British Columbia*," *Osgoode Hall Law Journal* 37, no. 3 (1999): 537–96.

17 Leslie Thielen-Wilson, "White Terror, Canada's Indian Residential Schools, and the Colonial Present: From Law towards a Pedagogy of Recognition" (PhD diss., University of Toronto, 2012).

18 Borrows, "Sovereignty's Alchemy," 569.

19 Phillip Joseph Deloria, *Playing Indian* (New Haven, CT: Yale University Press, 1998), 91.

20 Scott Richard Lyons, *X-Marks, Native Signatures of Assent* (Minneapolis: University of Minnesota Press, 2010.), 59.

21 Borrows, "Sovereignty's Alchemy," 592.

22 Peter Fitzpatrick, "Doctrine of Discovery," in *A Companion to Racial and Ethnic Studies*, ed. David Theo Goldberg and John Solomos (Malden, MA: Blackwell Publishers, 2002), 25–30.

23 Mabo v. The State of Queensland (No.2) [1992] 175 CLR 1. For a critical analysis, see Peter Fitzpatrick, "'No Higher Duty': *Mabo* and the Failure of Legal Foundation," *Law & Critique* 13, no. 3 (October 2002): 233–52.

24 Peter Fitzpatrick, "'Enacted in the Destiny of Sedentary Peoples': Racism, Discovery and the Grounds of Law," *Balayi: Culture, Law and Colonialism* 1, no. 1 (2000): 11–29.

25 Tsilhqot'in Nation v. British Columbia [2007] BCSC 1700 (CanLII), available at http://www.can.lii.org/en/bc/bcsc/doc/2007/2007bcsc1700/2007bcsc1700.htmlQ3. See especially paragraphs 1012, 1048, 1066, 1067, 1075, 1077, 1081, and 1294.

26 Ibid.

27 William v. British Columbia [2012] BCCA 285, available at http://www.canlii.org/en/bc/bcca/doc/2012/2012bcca285/2012bcca285.html.

28 William v. British Columbia [2013] SCC 34986.

29 Tsilhquot'in Nation v. British Columbia [2014] SCC 44, Docket 34986, 26 June 2014, accessed 25 September 2014, https://scc-csc.lexum.com/scc-csc/scc-csc/en/item/14246/index.do.
30 Songhees Nation v. British Columbia. [2014] BCJ 2376. BCSC. J.K. Bracken J. 23 September 2014. For a case summary, see http://www.lawyersweekly.ca/index.php?section=lawnetarticle&docno=552.
31 Canadian Press, "BC Supreme Court Set Limits on Recent First Nations Victory," *CBC.ca*, 25 September 2014, accessed 25 September 2014, http://www.cbc.ca/news/canada/british-columbia/b-c-supreme-court-set-limits-on-recent-first-nations-victory-1.2777846.
32 Tsilhquot'in National Government, *Tsilhqot'in National Government: Final Submission*, Federal Review Panel, New Prosperity Gold-Copper Mine Project, 23 August 2013 (Williams Lake, BC: Canadian Environmental Assessment Agency, 2013), doc. # 1146, accessed 14 November 2013, http://www.ceaa-acee.gc.ca/050/documents/p63928/93669E.pdf.
33 Cole Harris, *Making Native Space: Colonialism, Resistance, and Reserves in British Columbia* (Vancouver: UBC Press, 2002), xvii.
34 Ibid., xxi.
35 Ibid., 269–70.
36 Indian Claims Commission, *Williams Lake Indian Band: Village Site Inquiry* (Ottawa: Indian Claims Commission, March 2006), accessed 30 March 2014, http://iportal.usask.ca/docs/ICC/WilliamsLake_eng.pdf.
37 Ibid., 125.
38 Mary-Ellen Kelm, *Colonizing Bodies: Aboriginal Health and Healing in British Columbia, 1900–1950* (Vancouver: UBC Press, 1998).
39 Ibid., 39.
40 Ibid., 57.
41 Ibid., 71.
42 Elizabeth Furniss, *Victims of Benevolence: The Dark Legacy of the Williams Lake Residential School* (Vancouver: Arsenal Pulp Press, 1995), 11.
43 R v. O'Connor [1995] 4 SCR 411.
44 Beverly Sellars, *They Called Me Number One: Secrets and Survival at an Indian Residential School* (Vancouver: Talonbooks, 2013).
45 James Daschuk, *Clearing the Plains: Disease, Politics of Starvation, and the Loss of Aboriginal Life* (Regina: University of Regina Press, 2013).
46 Paul Q. Thistle, *Trade Relations in the Lower Saskatchewan River Region to 1840* (Winnipeg: University of Manitoba Press, 1986).
47 I am grateful to Bonita Lawrence for reminding me to complicate the story of the impact of European diseases on Indigenous health.
48 Thistle, *Trade Relations*, 182.

49 Ibid.,100.
50 See, for example, Sarah Carter, *Capturing Women: The Manipulation of Cultural Imagery in Canada's Prairie West* (Montreal: McGill-Queen's University Press, 1997).
51 Ibid., 153–62.
52 Ibid., 182.
53 Ibid., 163.
54 Ibid., 171.
55 Ibid., 177.
56 Ibid., 180.
57 Ibid., 186.
58 Sherene Razack, "Gendered Racial Violence and Spatialized Justice: The Murder of Pamela George," *Canadian Journal of Law and Society* 15, no. 2 (2000): 91–130.
59 Native Women's Association of Canada (NWAC), "Fact Sheet: Missing and Murdered Aboriginal Women and Girls," Ottawa: NAWC, accessed 20 March 2014, http://www.nwac.ca/files/download/NWAC_3D_Toolkit_e_0.pdf; Daniel Leblanc, "List of Missing, Killed Aboriginal Women Involves 1,200 Cases," *Globe and Mail,* 1 May 2014, http://www.theglobeandmail.com/news/national/rcmp-dont-deny-report-of-more-than-1000-murdered-missing-native-women/article18363451/.
60 Samira Kawash, "The Homeless Body," *Public Culture* 10, no. 2 (1998): 329.
61 Moses, "Genocide and Settler Society."
62 Ibid., 28.
63 Patrick Wolfe, "Settler Colonialism and the Elimination of the Native," *Journal of Genocide Research* 8, no. 4 (2006): 387–409.
64 Andrea Smith, "Heteropatriarchy and the Three Pillars of White Supremacy: Rethinking Women of Color Organizing," in *The Color of Violence: The Incite! Anthology*, ed. INCITE! Women of Color Against Violence (Cambridge, MA: South End Press, 2006), 68.
65 Moses, "Genocide and Settler Society," 32.
66 Barbara Perry, *Silent Victims: Hate Crimes against Native Americans* (Tucson: University of Arizona Press, 2008), 85.
67 Kristy Palmantier, in discussion with author, Williams Lake, BC, 28 October 2008.
68 Andrea Smith, "Indigeneity, Settler Colonialism, White Supremacy." In *Racial Formation in the Twenty-First Century*, ed. Daniel Martinez HoSang, Oneka LaBennett, and Laura Pulido (Berkeley and Los Angeles: University of California Press, 2012), 66–90.

69 Brenna Bhandar, "The First Nations of Canada Are Still Waiting for the Colonial Era to End: The Government Continues to Ignore the Sovereignty of Indigenous Inhabitants, Even Though It Was Granted in 1763," *TheGuardian.com*, 21 October 2013, accessed 22 October 2013, http://www.theguardian.com/commentisfree/2013/oct/21/canada-colonial-mentality-first-nations.

70 Reuel Amdur, "Omnibus Crime Bill Bad for Natives," *First Nations Drum*, 3 September 2011, accessed 9 May 2014, http://www.firstnationsdrum.com/2011/09/omnibus-crime-bill-bad-for-natives/.

71 Jean Franco, *Cruel Modernity* (Durham, NC: Duke University Press, 2013), 48.

72 Leslie Thielen-Wilson, "White Terror."

73 See Denise Ferreira da Silva, *Toward a Global Idea of Race* (Minneapolis: University of Minnesota Press, 2007).

Chapter One

1 Achille Mbembe, "Necropolitics," trans. Libby Meintjes, *Public Culture* 15, no. 1 (2003): 12.

2 Nicholas Blomley, *Unsettling the City: Urban Land and the Politics of Property* (New York: Routledge, 2004), 106.

3 Suzanne Fournier, "267 Cop-related Deaths in B.C. Over Past 15 Years: Statistics at the Frank Paul Inquiry Reveal What One Lawyer Calls a 'Staggering' Number of Deaths at the Hands of Police," *The Vancouver Province*, 15 January 2008, http://www.canada.com/theprovince/news/story.html?id=707223ef-cf82-4c1e-832c-90e547cd4dd0.

4 Alvin C. Hamilton and C. Murray Sinclair, *Report of the Aboriginal Justice Inquiry of Manitoba*, vol. 1: *The Justice System and Aboriginal People*, Manitoba Public Inquiry into the Administration of Justice and First Nations People (Winnipeg: Province of Manitoba, 1991).

5 Royal Commission on Aboriginal Peoples (Canada), Highlights from *People to People, Nation to Nation: Report of the Royal Commission on Aboriginal Peoples* (Ottawa: Minister of Supply and Services Canada, 1996), accessed 13 June 2003, http://www.aadnc-aandc.gc.ca/eng/1100100014597/1100100014637.

6 Patricia Monture-Angus, "Lessons in Decolonization: Aboriginal Overrepresentation in Canadian Criminal Justice," In *Visions of the Heart: Canadian Aboriginal Issues*, eds. David Long and Olive Patricia Dickason, 335–54 (Toronto: Harcourt Canada, 2000), 365.

7 Zygmunt Bauman, *Wasted Lives: Modernity and Its Outcasts* (Malden, MA: Polity Press, 2004), 5.
8 Samantha Ashenden, *Governing Child Sexual Abuse: Negotiating the Boundaries of Public and Private, Law and Science* (London and New York: Routledge, 2004).
9 Adam Ashforth, "Reckoning Schemes of Legitimation: On Commissions of Inquiry as Power/Knowledge Forms," *Journal of Historical* 3, no. 1 (1990): 4.
10 Ibid., 17.
11 Ann Laura Stoler, *Along the Archival Grain: Epistemic Anxieties and Colonial Common Sense* (Princeton: Princeton University Press, 2009), 143.
12 Ashforth, "Reckoning Schemes of Legitimation," 17.
13 Dara Culhane, "Their Spirits Live within Us: Aboriginal Women in Downtown Eastside Vancouver Emerging into Visibility," *The American Indian Quarterly* 27, no. 3 (2003): 595.
14 Bauman, *Wasted Lives*, 77.
15 Achille Mbembe, "Life, Sovereignty, and Terror in the Fiction of Amos Tutuola," *Research in African Literatures* 34, no. 4 (2003): 1.
16 William H. Davies, Commissioner, *Alone and Cold: Interim Report of the Davies Commission Inquiry into the Death of Frank Paul* (Vancouver: The Davies Commission, 2009), http://frankpaulinquiryca.nationprotect.net/report/Interim/. Hearings occurred between November 2007 and May 2008. The hearing excerpts are referenced as *Frank Paul Inquiry Transcripts, 2007–2008, 2010.* For witness transcripts, see http://frankpaulinquiryca.nationprotect.net/hearings.php. Commissioner Davies issued his Interim Report, *Alone and Cold*, on February 12, 2009. Hearings resumed in November and December of 2010 in order to address the Criminal Justice Branch's response to the death of Frank Paul, specifically the decision on the part of Crown Prosecutors not to proceed with criminal charges against Sgt. Sanderson and Cst. Instant in the death of Frank Paul. Commissioner Davies released his final report, *Alone and Cold: Criminal Justice Branch Response*, on May 19, 2011. See http://frankpaulinquiryca.nationprotect.net/report/Final/.
17 Davies, *Alone and Cold* (Interim Report).
18 Ibid., 396.
19 Ibid., 16.
20 Ibid., 187–8.
21 Ibid., 17.
22 Ibid., 405.
23 Ibid., 421.
24 Ibid., 429.

25 Ibid.
26 Ibid., 439.
27 Ibid., 431.
28 This is "culturalization," where problems are attributed to culture and not to domination. See Sherene H. Razack, *Looking White People in the Eye: Gender, Race, and Culture in Courtrooms and Classrooms* (Toronto: University of Toronto Press, 1998).
29 Davies, *Alone and Cold* (Interim Report), 44.
30 Ibid., 178.
31 Ibid., 177–8.
32 David Theo Goldberg, *Racist Culture: Philosophy and the Politics of Meaning* (Malden, MA: Blackwell Publishers, 1993), 186.
33 Aimé Fernand David Césaire, *Discourse on Colonialism*, trans. Joan Pinkham (New York: Monthly Review Press, 1972, 2000).
34 Andrea Smith, *Conquest: Sexual Violence and American Indian Genocide* (Cambridge, MA: South End Press, 2005), 9.
35 Ibid., 10.
36 Hortense J. Spillers, "Mama's Baby, Papa's Maybe: An American Grammar Book," *Diacritics* 17, no. 2 (1987): 67. I am grateful to Rashne Limki for bringing this article to my attention.
37 Ibid., 67.
38 Ibid., 68.
39 Ibid.
40 Davies, *Alone and Cold* (Interim Report), iv–v.
41 Ibid., iv–v.
42 James Douglas, "James Douglas, BC Ambulance Service," *Frank Paul Inquiry Transcripts 2007–2008, 2010* (Vancouver: The Davies Commission, 16 November 2007), 110, accessed 20 January 2012, http://frankpaulinquiryca.nationprotect.net/transcripts/2007-11-16.pdf#JamesDouglas.
43 Ibid., 74.
44 Ibid., 134.
45 Ibid., 15.
46 Ibid., 15–16.
47 Ibid., 16–18.
48 Douglas Eastwood, BC Ambulance Service, in "Peggy Clement, Frank Paul Family Member," *Frank Paul Inquiry Transcripts 2007–2008, 2010* (Vancouver: The Davies Commission, 13 November 2007), 43–4, accessed 20 January 2012, http://frankpaulinquiryca.nationprotect.net/transcripts/2007-11-13.pdf#PeggyClement.
49 Douglas, "James Douglas, BC Ambulance Service," 76.

50 Russell Sanderson, "Russell Sanderson, VPD," *Frank Paul Inquiry Transcripts 2007–2008, 2010* (Vancouver: The Davies Commission, 7 January 2008), 50–1, accessed 20 January 20, 012, http://frankpaulinquiryca.nationprotect.net/transcripts/2008-01-07.pdf#RussellSanderson.

51 Currie Low, "Currie Low, Nurse, Vancouver Detox Centre," *Frank Paul Inquiry Transcripts 2007–2008, 2010* (Vancouver: The Davies Commission, 26 November 2007), 83, accessed 20 January 2012, http://frankpaulinquiryca.nationprotect.net/transcripts/2007-11-26.pdf#CurrieLow.

52 Robert George Rothwell, "Robert George Rothwell, Inspector, Vancouver Police Department (resumed)," *Frank Paul Inquiry Transcripts 2007–2008, 2010* (Vancouver: The Davies Commission, 1 February 2008), 93, accessed 20 January 2012, http://frankpaulinquiryca.nationprotect.net/transcripts/2008-02-01.pdf#RobertRothwell.

53 Ken Low, "Ken Low, Correctional Officer," *Frank Paul Inquiry Transcripts 2007–2008, 2010* (Vancouver: The Davies Commission, 26 November 2007), 62, accessed 20 January 2012, http://frankpaulinquiryca.nationprotect.net/transcripts/2007-11-26.pdf#KenLow.

54 Kelliher, in "Richard A. Mulder, VPD (Sgt. 683)," *Frank Paul Inquiry Transcripts 2007–2008, 2010* (Vancouver: The Davies Commission, 20 November 2007), 5, accessed 20 January 2012, http://frankpaulinquiryca.nationprotect.net/transcripts/2007-11-20.pdf#RichardMulder.

55 Achille Mbembe, "Aesthetics of Superfluity," *Public Culture* 16, no. 3 (2004): 381.

56 Ibid.

57 Ibid., 392.

58 Samira Kawash, "The Homeless Body," *Public Culture* 15, no. 1 (1998): 319–39.

59 Ibid., 325.

60 Mbembe, "Necropolitics."

61 Kawash, "The Homeless Body," 327.

62 Ibid., 329.

63 Ibid., 330.

64 Ibid., 334.

65 Ibid., 337.

66 Russell Sanderson, "Russell Sanderson, VPD (resumed)," *Frank Paul Inquiry Transcripts 2007–2008, 2010* (Vancouver: The Davies Commission, 9 January 2008), 11–12, accessed 20 January 2012, http://frankpaulinquiryca.nationprotect.net/transcripts/2008-01-09.pdf#RussellSanderson.

67 Davies, *Alone and Cold* (Interim Report), 91.

68 Ibid., 92.

69 Ibid., 6.
70 Ibid., 93.
71 See exchange in "David Instant, VPD (resumed)," *Frank Paul Inquiry Transcripts 2007–2008, 2010* (Vancouver: The Davies Commission, 11 January 2008), 69–72, accessed 20 January 2012, http://frankpaulinquiryca.nationprotect.net/transcripts/2008-01-11.pdf#DavidInstant.
72 Ibid., 73.
73 Davies, *Alone and Cold* (Interim Report), 94.
74 Ibid., 95–6.
75 Ibid., 6.
76 Ibid., 100.
77 Ibid., 101.
78 Ibid., 389.
79 Ibid., 107.
80 Peggy Clement, "Peggy Clement, Frank Paul Family Member," *Frank Paul Inquiry Transcripts 2007–2008, 2010* (Vancouver: The Davies Commission, 13 November 2007), 88, http://frankpaulinquiryca.nationprotect.net/transcripts/2007-11-13.pdf#PeggyClement.
81 Mr Martland, in "Matthew Jarvie Adie," *Frank Paul Inquiry Transcripts 2007-2008, 2010* (Vancouver: The Davies Commission, 4 April 2008), 83, 88–9, accessed 20 January 2012, http://frankpaulinquiryca.nationprotect.net/transcripts/2008-04-04.pdf#MatthewAdie.
82 Jamie H. Graham, Chief Constable of the Vancouver Police Department, "Death of Frank Paul," Memo to the City Manager, City of Vancouver, on 28 April, 2004, Media Release, 5 May 2005, http://mediareleases.vpd.ca/2004/05/05/death-of-frank-paul/.
83 Ibid.
84 It is important to note here that even when the VPD attempted to mend things in 2006 through initiating a process with the Aboriginal community, it continued to portray, through photographs of the entrance to the Detox Centre, that Paul was left in a protected, well-lit, and well-travelled laneway, an inaccuracy that Commissioner Davies notes in order to point out that the Department's efforts have not been well received by the community. Davies, *Alone and Cold* (Interim Report), 132.
85 Stewart Philip in "Peggy Clement, Frank Paul Family Member," *Frank Paul Inquiry Transcripts 2007–2008, 2010* (Vancouver: The Davies Commission, 13 November 2007), 16, accessed 20 January 2012, http://frankpaulinquiryca.nationprotect.net/transcripts/2007-11-13.pdf#PeggyClement.
86 Ibid., 52–4.
87 Ibid., 17.

88 Mbembe, "Life, Sovereignty, and Terror."
89 Mbembe, "Necropolitics."
90 Mbembe, "Life, Sovereignty, and Terror," 1.
91 Mbembe, "Necropolitics," 40.
92 Ibid., 38.
93 Culhane, "Their Spirits Live within Us."
94 Ibid., 598.
95 Amnesty International (Canada). *Stolen Sisters: A Human Rights Response to Discrimination and Violence against Indigenous Women in Canada* (Ottawa: Amnesty International Canada, 2004), http://www.amnesty.org/en/library/info/AMR20/003/2004.
96 Native Women's Association of Canada (NWAC), *Voices of Our Sisters in Spirit: A Report to Families and Communities*, 2nd ed. (Ottawa: Status of Women Canada, March 2009), 88, accessed 21 January 2011 http://www.nwac.ca/sites/default/files/reports/NWAC_Voices%20of%20Our%20Sisters%20In%20Spirit_2nd%20Edition_March%202009.pdf.
97 Kendra Nixon et al., "The Everyday Occurrence: Violence in the Lives of Girls Exploited through Prostitution," *Violence Against Women* 8, no. 9 (2002): 1016–43; Culhane, "Their Spirits Live within Us"; Melissa Farley, Jacqueline Lynne, and Ann J. Cotton, "Prostitution in Vancouver: Violence and the Colonization of First Nations Women," *Transcultural Psychiatry* 42, no. 2 (2005): 242–71; Leslie Robertson and Dara Culhane, *In Plain Sight: Reflections on Life in Downtown Eastside Vancouver* (Vancouver: Talonbooks, 2005); Audrey Huntley *"Go Home Baby Girl": A Documentary*, directed by Audrey Huntley (Canada: Canadian Broadcasting Corporation, 2006), DVD; Leslie Robertson, "Taming Space: Drug Use, HIV, and Homemaking in Downtown Eastside Vancouver," *Gender, Place and Culture* 14, no. 5 (2007): 527–49.
98 Sherene H. Razack, "Gendered Racial Violence and Spatialized Justice: The Murder of Pamela George," *Canadian Journal of Law and Society* 15, no. 2 (2000): 91–130.
99 Daniel Leblanc, "List of Missing, Killed Aboriginal Women Involves 1,200 Cases," *Globe and Mail*, 1 May 2014, http://www.theglobeandmail.com/news/national/rcmp-dont-deny-report-of-more-than-1000-murdered-missing-native-women/article18363451/.
100 See, for example, Susan Boyd, Donald Macpherson, and Bud Osborn, *Raise Shit! Social Action Saving Lives* (Black Point, NS: Fernwood Publishing, 2009); Larry Campbell, Neil Boyd, and Lori Culbert, *A Thousand Dreams: Vancouver's Downtown Eastside and the Fight for Its Future* (Vancouver: Greystone Books, 2009).

101 See, for example, Phillip Stenning and Carole LaPrairie, "'Politics by Other Means': The Role of Commissions of Inquiry in Establishing the 'Truth' About 'Aboriginal Justice' in Canada," in *Crime, Truth and Justice*, ed. John Pratt and George Gilligan (Devon, UK: Willan Publishing, 2004), 139–60.
102 Blomley, *Unsettling the City*, 143.
103 Ibid., 109.
104 Ibid.
105 Ibid., 114.
106 Ibid., 109.
107 Mbembe, "Necropolitics," 35.
108 Ibid., 39.
109 Davies, *Alone and Cold* (Interim Report), 196.

Chapter Two

1 Steven Kelliher, Counsel for First Nations Leadership Council and Paul Family, "Mr. Kelliher, (Submission)," *Frank Paul Inquiry Transcripts, 2007–2008, 2010* (Vancouver: The Davies Commission, 14 December 2010), 37, accessed 20 January 2012, http://frankpaulinquiryca.nationprotect.net/transcripts/2010-12-14.pdf#Kelliher.
2 Breaching originated as a legal term to describe a person disturbing (breaching) the peace who could consequently be removed by the police and taken to another part of the city. In the city of Vancouver, breaching became controversial when three people breached to Stanley Park were beaten up by police. A new police recruit was a whistle blower. See "Vancouver Police Officers in Court over Alleged Beatings," *CBC News*, 22 March 2003, http://www.cbc.ca/news/canada/vancouver-police-officers-in-court-over-alleged-beatings-1.412029.
3 William H. Davies, Commissioner, *Alone and Cold: Interim Report of the Davies Commission Inquiry into the Death of Frank Paul* (Vancouver: The Davies Commission, 12 February 2009), accessed November 7, 2010, http://frankpaulinquiryca.nationprotect.net/report/Interim/.
4 Denise Ferreira da Silva, *Toward a Global Idea of Race* (Minneapolis: University of Minnesota Press, 2007), xiv.
5 Kay Anderson, *Race and the Crisis of Humanism* (London and New York: Routledge, 2007), 17.
6 Patrick Brantlinger, *Dark Vanishings: Discourse on the Extinction of Primitive Races, 1800–1930* (Ithaca, NY: Cornell University Press, 2003).
7 Anderson describes Europe's encounter with Australia's Aborigines. I am suggesting that a similar ontological crisis unfolded wherever Europeans encountered Indigenous peoples, although there are likely to be small

differences in how the crisis emerged and how it continues to emerge. For a discussion of the challenge that Indigeneity posed for European self-knowledge, see Robert Stam and Ella Shohat, "Whence and Whither Post-colonial Theory?" *New Literary History* 43, no. 2 (2012): 371–90.

8 Ferreira da Silva, *Toward a Global Idea of Race*, xiii.

9 Ibid., xiv.

10 Ibid., 206.

11 Ibid., xxxi.

12 Audra Simpson, "Settlement's Secret," *Cultural Anthropology* 26, no. 2 (2011): 205. Simpson references Patrick Wolfe, "Settler Colonialism and the Elimination of the Native," *Journal of Genocide Research* 8, no. 4 (2006): 387–409.

13 Peter Fitzpatrick, "Enacted in the Destiny of Sedentary Peoples: Racism, Discovery and the Grounds of Law," *Balayi: Culture, Law and Colonialism* 1, no. 1 (2000): 11–29.

14 Gillian Cowlishaw, "Disappointing Indigenous People: Violence and the Refusal of Help," *Public Culture* 15, no. 1 (2003): 108.

15 Ibid., 104; Dian Million, *Therapeutic Nations: Healing in an Age of Indigenous Human Rights* (Tucson: University of Arizona Press, 2013).

16 Simpson, "Settlement's Secret," 206.

17 Ibid., 207.

18 Humanitarianism has a long-standing connection to colonial and neocolonial violence, as I discuss in Sherene H. Razack, "Stealing the Pain of Others: Reflections on Canadian Humanitarian Responses," *The Review of Education, Pedagogy, and Cultural Studies* 29, no. 3 (2007): 375–94.

19 Jamie H. Graham, Chief Constable of the Vancouver Police Department, "Death of Frank Paul," Memo to the City Manager, City of Vancouver, on 28 April, 2004, Media Release, 5 May 2005, http://mediareleases.vpd.ca/2004/05/05/death-of-frank-paul/.

20 Pamela Dawes, Constable, "Pam Dawes, VPD (PC1652)," *Frank Paul Inquiry Transcripts 2007–2008, 2010* (Vancouver: The Davies Commission, 19 November 2007), 106, accessed 20 January 2012, http://frankpaulinquiryca.nationprotect.net/transcripts/2007-11-19.pdf#PamDawes.

21 Janet Ross, Correctional Officer, "Janet Ross, Correctional Officer," *Frank Paul Inquiry Transcripts 2007–2008, 2010* (Vancouver: The Davies Commission, 19 November 2007), 165, accessed 20 January 2012, http://frankpaulinquiryca.nationprotect.net/transcripts/2007-11-19.pdf#JanetRoss.

22 Elizabeth Jean Prince, Constable, "Jean Prince, VPD (PC1676)," *Frank Paul Inquiry Transcripts 2007–2008, 2010* (Vancouver: The Davies Commission, 19 November 2007), 187–8, 196–9, accessed 20 January 2012, http://frankpaulinquiryca.nationprotect.net/transcripts/2007-11-19.pdf#JeanPrince.

23 In this respect, Frank Paul provoked the responses we are familiar with in connection with disability. I have elsewhere drawn on Rod Michalko's brilliant analysis of Robert Ladimer's killing of his twelve-year-old daughter, Tracy, who was born with cerebral palsy. Ladimer's defense was that his act of murder was actually a mercy killing. Michalko points out that this logic can only work if we understand Tracy as having a life not worth living. As a brain-damaged infant, Tracy was considered barely human and barely alive; personhood was impossible for her. She was, Michalko argued, not merely the reminder of death, but death itself. To kill her was to kill someone who was already dead. Her murder could not be a crime. See Rod Michalko, *The Difference That Disability Makes* (Philadelphia, PA: Temple University Press, 2002), 103–11.

24 Jacky Talmet, Charlotte de Crespigny, Lynette Cusack, and Peter Athanasos, "'Turning a Blind Eye': Denying People Their Right to Treatment for Acute Alcohol, Drug and Mental Health Conditions – An Act of Discrimination," *Mental Health and Substance Use: Dual Diagnosis* 2, no. 3 (October 2009): 249. See also Jo-Anne Fiske and Annette Browne, "Aboriginal Citizen, Discredited Medical Subject: Paradoxical Constructions of Subjectivity in Health Care Policies," *Policy Sciences* 39, no. 1 (2006): 91–111.

25 Dr John Butt, "Dr. John Butt, Private Consultant in Forensic Medicine," *Frank Paul Inquiry Transcripts 2007–2008, 2010* (Vancouver: The Davies Commission, 19 March 2008), 16–19, accessed 20 January 2012, http://frankpaulinquiryca.nationprotect.net/transcripts/2008-03-19.pdf#JohnButt.

26 Ibid., 21.

27 Prince, "Jean Prince, VPD (PC1676)," 196.

28 Peggy Clement, as quoted by Steven Kelliher in his final submission to the Davies Commission during the final phase regarding the Criminal Justice Branch's response to the death of Frank Paul. See Kelliher, "Mr. Kelliher, (Submission)," 5.

29 Giorgio Agamben, *Homo Sacer: Sovereign Power and Bare Life*, trans. Daniel Heller-Roazen (Stanford, CA: Stanford University Press, 1998), 3.

30 See Kelliher, "Mr. Kelliher, (Submission)," 15–37.

31 It is of note that there are differences between Australian and Canadian settler colonialism. As Peter Russell comments, however, "despite major differences in their early colonial relations with native peoples – the treaty relations and recognition of native land rights in British North America versus the *terra nullius* practices in Australia – by mid-century these burgeoning settler democracies were adopting much the same policies for dealing with the 'native problem.'" Peter Russell, *Recognizing Aboriginal*

Title: The Mabo Case and Indigenous Resistance to English-Settler Colonialism (Toronto: University of Toronto Press, 2005), 100.

32 Kelliher, "Mr. Kelliher, (Submission)," 32.

33 Ibid., 27.

34 Ibid., 32.

35 Ibid., 18. Kelliher comments that "Mr. Ewert simply concludes that the actions of the police officers involved were not a marked departure from those of a reasonable person who could, nor could either of the officers, reasonably have foreseen the harm."

36 Ward, "Mr. Ward (Submission)," *Frank Paul Inquiry Transcripts 2007–2008, 2010* (Vancouver: The Davies Commission, 15 December 2010), 8, http://frankpaulinquiryca.nationprotect.net/transcripts/2010-12-15.pdf#Ward.

37 Ibid., 8.

38 Ibid., 7.

39 Ibid., 18–22.

40 Steven Kelliher questioning Larry Campbell. See Larry William Campbell, "Larry Campbell, BC Coroners Service," *Frank Paul Inquiry Transcripts 2007–2008, 2010* (Vancouver: The Davies Commission, 25 January 2008), 29–36, http://frankpaulinquiryca.nationprotect.net/transcripts/2008-01-25.pdf#LarryCampbell.

41 Steven Kelliher questioning Jeannine Robinson. See Jeannine Robinson, "Jeannine Robinson, BC Coroners Service," *Frank Paul Inquiry Transcripts 2007–2008, 2010* (Vancouver: The Davies Commission, 23 January 2008), 143–5, http://frankpaulinquiryca.nationprotect.net/transcripts/2008-01-23.pdf#JeannineRobinson.

42 Ibid., 22–6, 62–5.

43 Cameron Ward questioning Terry Smith. See Terry P. Smith, "Terry Smith, BC Coroners Service," *Frank Paul Inquiry Transcripts 2007–2008, 2010* (Vancouver: The Davies Commission, 28 January 2008), 59–107, http://frankpaulinquiryca.nationprotect.net/transcripts/2008-01-28.pdf#TerrySmith.

44 Cameron Ward, in discussion with the author, Vancouver, British Columbia, 27 November 2008.

45 Adam Ashforth, "Reckoning Schemes of Legitimation: On Commissions of Inquiry as Power/Knowledge Forms," *Journal of Historical Sociology* 3, no. 1 (1990): 17.

46 Radhika V. Mongia, "Impartial Regimes of Truth: Indentured Indian Labour and the Status of the Inquiry," *Cultural Studies* 18, no. 5 (September 2004): 763.

47 Ann Laura Stoler, *Along the Archival Grain: Epistemic Anxieties and Colonial Common Sense* (Princeton: Princeton University Press, 2009), 22.

48 Ibid., 141–3.

49 Ibid., 256.
50 For how a hegemonic story of misery triumphs over Indigenous resistance, see Cowlishaw, "Disappointing Indigenous People," 107.
51 Dian Million, *Therapeutic Nations*, 6.
52 Ibid., 106.
53 Refer to submissions offered on 28 April 2008, *Frank Paul Inquiry Transcripts 2007–2008, 2010* (Vancouver: The Davies Commission, 28 April 2008), http://frankpaulinquiryca.nationprotect.net/hearings.php.
54 Ibid., 5–7.
55 Ibid., 6–7.
56 Ibid.
57 Ibid., 9–11.
58 Susan Zieger, *Inventing the Addict: Drugs, Race, and Sexuality in Nineteenth-Century British and American Literature* (Amherst: University of Massachusetts Press, 2008), 4.
59 Peter Ferentzy, "Foucault and Addiction," *Telos* 125 (Fall 2002): 168.
60 Mariana Valverde, *Diseases of the Will: Alcohol and the Dilemma of Freedom* (Cambridge: Cambridge University Press, 1998).
61 Zieger, *Inventing the Addict*, 10.
62 Ibid., 21.
63 Ibid., 11.
64 Ferentzy, "Foucault and Addiction," 185n68.
65 Zieger, *Inventing the Addict*, 22.
66 Ibid., 26.
67 Paul Wells, "Harper Swings and Misses on Insite: The PM Came Close to Shutting Down Insite, Only to Be Reminded There Are Still Some Limits to his Reach," *Macleans.ca*, 10 October 2011, accessed 1 August 2012, http://www.macleans.ca/authors/paul-wells/swing-and-a-miss/.
68 Dr Tomislav Svoboda, "Dr. Tomislav Svoboda," *Frank Paul Inquiry Transcripts 2007–2008, 2010* (Vancouver: The Davies Commission, 28 April 2008), 60, http://frankpaulinquiryca.nationprotect.net/transcripts/2008-04-28.pdf#TomislavSvoboda.
69 Ibid., 64.
70 Ibid., 88.
71 Ibid., 102.
72 Ibid., 101.
73 Ibid., 112.
74 Andrew Yellowback, in "Art Manuel, Manager of the Annex Harm Reduction Programme and Co-director of the Infirmary Programme," *Frank Paul Inquiry Transcripts 2007–2008, 2010* (Vancouver: The Davies Commission,

28 April 2008), 112–44, http://frankpaulinquiryca.nationprotect.net/transcripts/2008-04-28.pdf#ArtManuel.

75 Andrew Yellowback, in "Neil Boyd, Professor," *Frank Paul Inquiry Transcripts 2007–2008, 2010* (Vancouver: The Davies Commission, 28 April 2008), 112–13, http://frankpaulinquiryca.nationprotect.net/transcripts/2008-04-28.pdf#SarahGoforth.

76 Ibid., Commissioner Davies, 118.

77 John de Haas, Inspector, Vancouver Police Department, in "Art Manuel, Manager of the Annex Harm Reduction Programme and Co-director of the Infirmary Programme," 188, 184–5.

78 Ibid., Jim Hauck, Manager, Addiction Services, Vancouver Coastal Health, 188.

79 Ibid., Chris Livingstone, Western Aboriginal Harm Reduction Society, 238.

80 Ibid., 234

81 Ibid., Jim Hauck, 241.

82 William H. Davies, Commissioner, *Alone and Cold: Criminal Justice Branch Response; Final Report of the Davies Commission Inquiry into the Response of the Criminal Justice Branch* (Vancouver: The Davies Commission, 19 May 2011), accessed 2 September 2011, http://frankpaulinquiryca.nationprotect.net/report/Final/.

83 Ibid., 167–98.

84 Ibid., 241–2.

85 Steven Kelliher, interview by author, Victoria, British Columbia, 28 October 2008.

86 Ferreira da Silva, *Toward a Global Idea of Race*, xxxvi.

87 Kelliher, "Mr. Kelliher, (Submission)," 88.

88 Stoler, *Along the Archival Grain*, 66.

89 Elizabeth A. Povinelli, *The Cunning of Recognition: Indigenous Alterities and the Making of Australian Multiculturalism* (Durham, NC: Duke University Press, 2002). See also Glen S. Coulthard, "Subjects of Empire: Indigenous Peoples and the 'Politics of Recognition' in Canada," *Contemporary Political Theory* 6, no. 4 (2007): 437–60.

90 Simpson, "Settlement's Secret," 209.

91 Ibid., 212.

92 Ibid., 213.

Chapter Three

1 Chief Nancy Sandy, in S.A. Cloverdale, Coroner, *Coroner's Report into the Death of Paul Alphonse* (Coroners Service of British Columbia, Ministry of Justice, 29 October – 1 November 2001; 4–8 March 2002), 910.

2 Richard Slotkin, *Gunfighter Nation: The Myth of the Frontier in Twentieth-Century America* (Norman, OK: University of Oklahoma Press, 1998), 14.
3 Band is the term used by many Indigenous nations in Canada, for example, The Williams Lake Indian Band.
4 Slotkin, *Gunfighter Nation*, 10.
5 Ibid.
6 Ibid.
7 Sherene H. Razack, "When Place Becomes Race," in *Race, Space and the Law: Unmapping a White Settler Society*, ed. Sherene H. Razack (Toronto: Between the Lines, 2004), 1–20.
8 Taiaiake Alfred, "Deconstructing the British Columbia Treaty Process," in *Dispatches from the Cold Seas: Indigenous Views on Self-Governance, Ecology and Identity*, ed. Curtis Rattray and Tero Mustonen (Tampere, FI: Tampere Polytechnic, 2001), 31; Adam J. Barker, "The Contemporary Reality of Canadian Imperialism: Settler Colonialism and the Hybrid Colonial State," *American Indian Quarterly* 33, no. 3 (Summer 2009): 325–51; Carole Blackburn, "Searching for Guarantees in the Midst of Uncertainty: Negotiating Aboriginal Rights and Title in British Columbia," *American Anthropologist* 107, no. 4 (2005): 586–96; John Borrows, "'Because It Does Not Make Sense': Sovereignty's Power in the Case of *Delgamuukw v. The Queen 1997*," in *Law, History, Colonialism: The Reach of Empire*, ed. Diane Kirby and Catharine Coleborne (Manchester, UK: Manchester University Press, 2001), 190–206; Peter R. Grant, "Recognition and Reconciliation: The British Columbia Experience," *Gestion des Revendications et Litiges Autochtones* (23–4, February 2010), accessed 23 May 2010, http://www.grantnativelaw.com/pdf/RecognitionandReconciliationTheBCExperience.pdf; Matt James, "Scaling Memory: Reparation Displacement and the Case of BC," *Canadian Journal of Political Science/Revue canadienne de science politique* 42, no. 2 (June 2009): 363–86; Fae L. Korsmo, "Claiming Memory in British Columbia: Aboriginal Rights and the State," *American Indian Culture and Research Journal* 20, no. 4 (1996): 71; Bradford W. Morse, "Indigenous Peoples of Canada and Their Efforts to Achieve True Reparations," in *Reparations for Indigenous Peoples: International Comparative Perspectives*, ed. Federico Lenzerini (New York: Oxford University Press, 2008), 271–316; Brian Slattery, "The Metamorphosis of Aboriginal Title," *The Canadian Bar Review* 85 (2006): 255–86; Brian Slattery, "Aboriginal Rights and the Honour of the Crown," *Supreme Court Law Review* 29 (2005): 433–45; Andrew John Woolford, *Between Justice and Certainty: The British Columbia Treaty Process* (Vancouver: UBC Press, 2005); Andrew John Woolford, "Negotiating Affirmative Repair: Symbolic Violence in the British Columbia Treaty Process," *Canadian Journal of Sociology* 29, no. 1 (2004): 111–44.

9 Kristy Palmantier, in *Coroner's Report into the Death of Paul Alphonse*, 732.
10 Ibid., Dr Jennifer Rice, 866.
11 Ibid., Coroner Cloverdale, 1005.
12 Frantz Fanon, *The Wretched of the Earth*, trans. Constance Farrington (New York: Grove Press, [1963] 1968).
13 Ibid., 39–40.
14 Ibid., 40.
15 Ministry of Interior Health, RCMP Williams Lake Detachment, and the Williams Lake Indian Band, "Media Release," 1 April 2005.
16 Bob Irwin, Cst., Reg. #37029, interview by Cpl J. Holmes, Kamloops Major Crime Unit, Williams Lake Detachment, "Statement re the Sudden Death of Paul Alphonse, Williams Lake Detachment File #2000-2915," at 13:38 hrs, 28 April 2000.
17 Ibid., 5.
18 *Coroner's Report into the Death of Paul Alphonse*, 937.
19 Ibid., 14.
20 Ibid., 981.
21 Irwin, "Statement re the Sudden Death of Paul Alphonse," 6.
22 This notion of baiting Indigenous people into complying with the police can also be found in the death in custody of Frank Paul. Police would offer Paul candy bars in order to get him to enter the paddy wagon. See Davies, *Alone and Cold: Criminal Justice Branch Response; Final Report of the Davies Commission Inquiry into the Response of the Criminal Justice Branch* (Vancouver: The Davies Commission, 19 May 2011), 43–4.
23 Irwin, "Statement re the Sudden Death of Paul Alphonse," 2.
24 Ibid., 3.
25 *Coroner's Report into the Death of Paul Alphonse*, 100, 565.
26 Ibid., Corporal Sullivan, 608.
27 Ibid., 969.
28 Victoria Freeman, *Distant Relations: How My Ancestors Colonized North America* (Toronto: McLelland & Stewart, 2000).
29 Anna Haebich, "Marked Bodies: A Corporeal History of Colonial Australia," *Borderlands* 7, no. 2 (2008): 10.
30 Interview with Nancy Sandy (Chief of the Williams Lake Band), British Columbia, Williams Lake, 6 February, 2009.
31 *Coroner's Report into the Death of Paul Alphonse*, 944.
32 Ibid., 11.
33 Ibid., 945–46. In response to a question from Cynthia Callison, counsel for the family, a civilian guard on duty at the same time, James Abe, acknowledged that Irwin was probably alone with Alphonse for a few seconds while Alphonse was lying on the ground. See also Ibid., 681.

34 Clifford Lewis, statement in *Investigation Report no. 2000–2915, re Sudden Death of Paul Alphonse*, Royal Canadian Mounted Police, Williams Lake, British Columbia, 18 April 2000.
35 Radhika Mohanram, *Black Body: Women, Colonialism and Space* (Minneapolis: University of Minnesota Press, 1999), 26–7.
36 Ibid., 27.
37 *RCMP Investigation Report no. 2000–2915, re the Sudden Death of Paul Alphonse*, Royal Canadian Mounted Police, Williams Lake Detachment File #2000-–2915, Major Crime Unit File # 2000–975, at 18:23 hrs, 19 April 2000.
38 Ibid., 4.
39 Nora Tenale, interview by Cst. G. Krebs, Kamloops Major Crime Unit, *RCMP Investigation Report no. 2000–2915*.
40 Ibid., 5.
41 Ibid., 11.
42 *RCMP Investigation Report no. 2000–2915*.
43 Ibid., 32.
44 Interview with Nancy Sandy (Chief of the Williams Lake Band), Williams Lake, British Columbia, 6 February 2009.
45 Ibid.
46 Corporal Krebs, in *Coroner's Report into the Death of Paul Alphonse*, 38–63.
47 *RCMP Investigation Report no. 2000–2915*, 31.
48 Ibid., 33.
49 Ibid., 29.
50 Only the encounter between a white man and an Indigenous woman in prostitution has a similar history. See Sherene H. Razack, "Gendered Racial Violence and Spatialized Justice: The Murder of Pamela George," *Canadian Journal of Law and Society* 15, no. 2 (2000): 91–130.
51 Mary Edmunds, *They Get Heaps: A Study of Attitudes in Roebourne, Western Australia* (Canberra: Aboriginal Studies Press, 1989).
52 Ibid., 155.
53 Ibid., 106.
54 Ibid.
55 Anna J. Secor, "An Unrecognizable Condition Has Arrived: Law, Violence, and the State of Exception in Turkey," in *Violent Geographies: Fear, Terror, and Political Violence*, ed. Derek Gregory and Allan Pred (New York: Routledge, 2007), 47.
56 Ibid., 47–8.
57 *Coroner's Report into the Death of Paul Alphonse*, 18. It is noteworthy that the Cariboo-Chilcotin Justice Inquiry criticized the RCMP for refusing to reveal any discipline it imposes on its officers. See Cariboo-Chilcotin

Justice Inquiry (BC), *Report on the Cariboo-Chilcotin Justice Inquiry*, Anthony Sarich, Commissioner (Victoria: Cariboo-Justice Inquiry, 1993).

58 *Coroner's Report into the Death of Paul Alphonse*, 965.

59 Ibid., 767, 763.

60 Denise Ferreira da Silva, "Towards a Critique of the Socio-Logos of Justice: The Analytics of Raciality and the Production of Universality," *Social Identities* 7, no. 3 (2001), 421.

61 Nancy Sandy noted that the troopers stayed sober for the day when they testified, a tribute, she felt, to Paul Alphonse and the importance they attached to the inquest proceedings. Interview with Nancy Sandy, 6 February 2009.

62 Lily Michel, in *Coroner's Report into the Death of Paul Alphonse*, 116.

63 Ibid., 119.

64 Interview with Nancy Sandy, 6 February 2009.

65 *Coroner's Report into the Death of Paul Alphonse*, 253.

66 Ibid., 852.

67 Not all of the forty-seven complaints dealt with excessive force. They included individuals getting roughed up against a police car, harassment if the police were doing an investigation, and complaints of excessive force.

68 Amy Sandy, in *Coroner's Report into the Death of Paul Alphonse*, 839–64.

69 Ibid., Sharon Taylor, 827.

70 *Coroner's Report into the Death of Paul Alphonse*, 868.

71 Ibid., 77–89.

72 Ibid., 988–99.

73 Ibid., 889.

74 *Report on the Cariboo-Chilcotin Justice Inquiry*.

75 *Coroner's Report into the Death of Paul Alphonse*, 912.

76 Ibid., 899.

77 Interview with Kristy Palmantier (niece of Paul Alphonse), Williams Lake, British Columbia, 24 October 2008.

78 See Deborah Coles and Helen Shaw, "Comment: Deaths in Custody – Truth, Justice, and Accountability? The Work of INQUEST," *Social Justice* 33, no. 4 (2006): 136–41.

79 Chris Cunneen," Indigenous Incarceration: The Violence of Colonial Law and Justice," in *The Violence of Incarceration*, ed. Phil Scraton and Jude McCulloch (New York: Routledge), 1–18.

80 Ibid., 211.

81 *Report on the Cariboo-Chilcotin Justice Inquiry*, 10.

82 Ibid., 10.

83 Ibid., 13.

84 Ibid., 18.

85 Ibid.
86 Ibid., 8.
87 Ibid.
88 Ibid., 14.
89 Ibid., 28.
90 Ibid., 26, 28.
91 Ibid., 27.
92 Elizabeth Furniss, "Indians, Odysseys and Vast, Empty Lands: The Myth of the Frontier in the Canadian Justice System,"*Anthropologica* 41, no. 2 (1999): 195–208.
93 Ibid., 202.
94 Interview with Kristy Palmantier, 24 October 2008.
95 Interview with Alphonse family, Williams Lake, British Columbia, 24 October 2008.
96 Interview with Nancy Sandy, 6 February 2009.
97 Ministry of Interior Health, RCMP Williams Lake Detachment, and the Williams Lake Indian Band, "Media Release," 1 April 2005.

Chapter Four

1 Martin Heidegger, quoted in Joseph Pugliese, *State Violence and the Execution of Law: Biopolitical Caesurae of Torture, Black Sites, Drones* (New York: Routledge, 2013), 169.
2 Ibid., 168.
3 Ibid.
4 Ibid., 169.
5 S.A. Cloverdale, Coroner, *Coroner's Report into the Death of Paul Alphonse* (Vancouver: Coroners Service of British Columbia, Ministry of Justice, 29 October – 1 November 2001; 4–8 March, 2002), 6.
6 See, for example, the memoir of Beverly Sellars, former Xat'sull Chief. Beverly Sellars, *They Called Me Number One: Secrets and Survival at an Indian Residential School* (Vancouver: Talonbooks, 2013).
7 Pugliese, *State Violence*, 169.
8 Heather I. Peters and Bruce Self, "Colonialism, Resistance and the First Nations Health Liaison Program," *Currents: New Scholarship in the Human Services* 4, no. 1 (2005): 1–21.
9 Renisa Mawani shows, for instance, that alcohol provisions concerning Aboriginal people were integral to maintaining spatial boundaries between white settlers and racial Others. Laws were also vigorously enforced because they generated large revenues. Renisa Mawani, "In Between and Out of Place: Mixed-Race Identity, Liquor, and the Law in

British Columbia, 1850–1913," in *Race, Space and the Law: Unmapping a White Settler Society*, ed. Sherene H. Razack (Toronto, Between the Lines, 2004), 51.

10 Jo-Anne Fiske and Annette Browne, "Aboriginal Citizen, Discredited Medical Subject: Paradoxical Constructions of Subjectivity in Health Care Policies," *Policy Sciences* 39, no. 1 (2006): 91–111.

11 Ibid., 94.

12 *Coroner's Report into the Death of Paul Alphonse*, 150, emphasis added.

13 Ibid., 152.

14 Ibid., 153.

15 Ibid., 155.

16 Ibid., 161.

17 Ibid., 489.

18 Ibid., 498.

19 Ibid., 502.

20 Ibid., 503.

21 *Coroner's Report into the Death of Paul Alphonse*, 356.

22 Ibid., 382–3.

23 Ibid., 443.

24 Ibid., 519

25 This interpretation was suggested by Dr Barry Lavallee of the University of Manitoba. Personal email communication, 25 January 2014.

26 Ministry of Interior Health, RCMP Williams Lake Detachment, and the Williams Lake Indian Band, "Media Release," 1 April 2005.

27 Anthony Sarich, Commissioner, *Report on the Cariboo-Chilcotin Justice Inquiry* (Victoria, BC: Cariboo-Chilcotin Justice Inquiry, 1993).

28 John Nyssen, Coroner, *Coroner's Inquest into the Death of A.M.S.* (Regina: Coroners Service of Saskatchewan, Ministry of Justice for the Government of Saskatchewan, 3–4 June 2003), 44–5.

29 Ibid., 59.

30 Ibid., 104.

31 Ibid., 112.

32 Ibid., 109.

33 Beth Larcombe, Coroner, *Coroner's Report into the Death of C.T.* (Port Alberni: Coroners Service of British Columbia, Ministry of Justice, 19–21, February 2008); Tonia Grace, Coroner, *Coroner's Report into the Death of S.Q.* (Penticton: Coroners Service of British Columbia, Ministry of Justice, 27–29 May, 3 June 2008).

34 *Coroner's Report into the Death of C.T.* (19 February 2008), 8.

35 *Coroner's Report into the Death of C.T.* (20 February 2008), 50.

36 Ibid., 55.
37 *Coroner's Report into the Death of C.T.* (21 February 2008), 65–8.
38 Ibid., 73–5.
39 *Coroner's Report into the Death of S.Q.* (27 May 2008), 44.
40 Ibid., 126.
41 Ibid., 15–24.
42 Coroner's *Report into the Death of S.Q.* (28 May 2008), 5.
43 Ibid. (29 May 2008), 9.
44 Ibid. (28 May 2008), 70.
45 Ibid. (29 May 2008), 9.
46 Ibid. (27 May 2008), 85.
47 Ibid. (3 June 2008), 78.
48 Ibid., 80.
49 Ibid., 80–1.
50 Ibid., 71–2.
51 Lori Coolican, "Methadone, Alcohol Bad Mix, Inquest Hears; Mountney Breathing in Cell According to Commissionaire," *Star-Phoenix*, 24 January 2008: A7.
52 Betty Ann Adam, "Expert Unable to Pinpoint Exact Cause of Inmate's Death," *Star-Phoenix*, 22 October 2002: A6; Darren Bernhardt, "Detox Centre to Be Built in Saskatoon," *Star-Phoenix*, 8 May 2003: A1; "Asthma Victim Died after Police Withheld Inhalers," *Calgary Herald*, 16 October 2002.
53 Donald Worme, interview with author, Saskatoon, Saskatchewan, 25 February 2009.
54 See the appendix.
55 Alma Wiebe, Coroner, *Coroner's Report into the Death of A.E.* (Prince Albert: Coroners Service of Saskatchewan, Ministry of Justice for the Government of Saskatchewan, 21–23 March 2005), 28.
56 Ibid., 70–2.
57 Ibid., 204
58 See, for example, the inquiry into the death of Frank Paul. William H. Davies, Commissioner, *Alone and Cold: Criminal Justice Branch Response. Final Report of the Davies Commission Inquiry into the Response of the Criminal Justice Branch* (Vancouver: The Davies Commission, 2011).
59 Radhika Mohanram, *Black Body: Women, Colonialism and Space* (Minneapolic: University of Minnesota Press, 1999), 22.
60 Renée L. Bergland, *The National Uncanny: Indian Ghosts and American Subjects* (Hanover, NH: University Press of New England, 2000), 1.
61 Ibid., 22.

62 Rod Michalko, *The Difference That Disability Makes* (Philadelphia, PA: Temple University Press, 2002), 101. The inquiry into the death of Frank Paul is decorated this way (see Davies, *Alone and Cold*). The Coroner permitted healing circles and prayers at the inquest into the death of Paul Alphonse (see *Coroner's Report into the Death of Paul Alphonse*). Notably, these "banal courtesies" sometimes provide Indigenous people with small openings through which a colonial account might be pushed through.

Chapter Five

1 Nancy Dawson, "Press Release of Nancy Dawson, 15 September, 1999," in "Mysterious Death of Native Artist: Family, Lawyer, Aboriginal Community Await Answers," *Turtle Island Native Network News*, July 2000, http://www.turtleisland.org/news/anthanynews.htm.

2 Nancy Dawson, in Diane Olson, Coroner, *Coroner's Inquest into the Death of Anthany James Dawson*, vol. 1 (Victoria: Coroner's Court of British Columbia, 17 July 2000), 37.

3 Noel Jason Manual, in *Coroner's Inquest into the Death of Anthany James Dawson*, 63.

4 Constable Lawrence Hemstad, in *Coroner's Inquest into the Death of Anthany James Dawson*, 23–4 November 2000, 9.

5 Mark Sim, in *Coroner's Inquest into the Death of Anthany James Dawson*, 21 November 2000, 46.

6 Theresa G. Di Maio and Vincent J.M. Di Maio, *Excited Delirium Syndrome: Cause of Death and Prevention* (Boca Raton, FL: Taylor & Francis Group, 2006), 1.

7 Lizette Alvarez, "Martin Was Shot as He Leaned Over Zimmerman, Court is Told," *The New York Times*, 9 July 2013, http://www.nytimes.com/2013/07/10/us/teenager-was-over-zimmerman-as-he-was-shot-expert-says.html.

8 Kay Anderson, *Race and the Crisis of Humanism* (London and New York: Routledge, 2007).

9 Jordanna Bailkin, "The Boot and the Spleen: When Was Murder Possible in British India?" *Comparative Studies in Society and History* 48, no. 2 (2006): 462–93.

10 Ibid., 463.

11 Ibid.

12 Ibid., 478.

13 Ibid., 480.

14 Ibid., 481.
15 Ibid., 483.
16 Ibid., 481, note omitted. "Spleen complains that it has a very deadly foe in the fist of rampant Anglo-Saxons, and no system of medicine, English or native, can prescribe anything which may make it strong enough to stand the blows of its adversary … Under these circumstances, Spleen earnestly prays that it not be placed in the bodies of natives, where its fate is sealed, but may be sent to some other region, where it may be beyond the reach of its enemy." Quote drawn from *Oudh Punch* 1884, where a figurative "Indian Spleen" addresses "Colonial India" in the matter of British boots causing the deaths of Indians.
17 Simon M. Dyson and Gwyneth Boswell, "Sickle Cell Anaemia and Deaths in Custody in the UK and the USA," *The Howard Journal* 45, no. 1 (2006): 16.
18 Ibid., 22.
19 Ibid., 15.
20 Ibid., 19.
21 Ibid., 18.
22 Debra Robinson and Shelby Hunt, "Sudden In-Custody Death Syndrome," *Topics in Emergency Medicine* 27, no. 1 (2005): 36.
23 Ibid., 42.
24 Tom Zeller, "Deaths in Custody: Excited Delirium or Excessive Force?" *The New York Times*, 27 February 2007, http://thelede.blogs.nytimes.com/2007/02/27/deaths-in-custody-excited-delirium-or-excessive-force/?_r=0.
25 Laura Sullivan, "Tasers Implicated in Excited Delirium Deaths," *NPR*, 27 February 2007, http://www.npr.org/templates/story/story.php?storyId=7622314.
26 Toni Morrison, *Playing in the Dark: Whiteness and the Literary Imagination* (New York: Vintage Books, 1992), 67.
27 Michael L. Storey, "Explaining the Unexplainable: Excited Delirium Syndrome and Its Impact on the Objective Reasonableness Standard for Allegations of Excessive Force," *St. Louis University Law Journal* 56, no.2 (Winter 2012): 633–64.
28 Ibid., 634, with reference to Di Maio and Di Maio, supra note 12.
29 Ibid., 637.
30 Ibid., 644.
31 Ibid., 644–5.
32 Dr Stan Kutcher, Dr Matt Bowes, Fred Stanford et al. *Report of the Panel of Mental Health and Medical Experts Review of Excited Delirium* (Nova Scotia:

Minister of Justice and Attorney General, 30 June 2009), accessed 13 April 2014, http://www.novascotia.ca/just/public_safety/_docs/Excited%20Delirium%20Report.pdf.

33 American College of Emergency Physicians, "White Paper Report on Excited Delirium Syndrome," September 2009, https://www.ncjrs.gov/App/Publications/abstract.aspx?ID=260278.

34 DeBard et al., quoted in Storey, "Explaining the Unexplainable," 646. See note 114.

35 Ibid., 647.

36 Ibid., 661.

37 Giorgio Agamben, *Homo Sacer: Sovereign Power and Bare Life*, trans. Daniel Heller-Roazen (Stanford, CA: Stanford University Press, 1998), 3.

38 Gary M. Vilke, Jason Payne-James, and Steven B. Karch, "Excited Delirium Syndrome (ExDS): Redefining an Old Diagnosis," *Journal of Forensic and Legal Medicine* 19, no. 1 (2012): 7–11.

39 Ibid., 8.

40 Ibid., Hall et al., 11n31.

41 Ibid., 9.

42 Ibid., 10.

43 Thomas R. Braidwood, Commissioner, *Restoring Public Confidence: Restricting the Use of Conducted Energy Weapons in British Columbia*, Braidwood Commission on Conducted Energy Weapon Use (Vancouver: The Braidwood Commission, 18 June 2009), 15.

44 Ibid., 209–210.

45 Anne S. Derrick, Provincial Court Judge, *Report of the Fatality Inquiry into the Death of Howard Hyde*, Report Pursuant to the *Fatality Investigations Act* (Halifax, NS: Provincial Court, Province of Nova Scotia, 30 November 2010), http://www.courts.ns.ca/Provincial_Court/NSPC_documents/NSPC_Hyde_Inquiry_Report.pdf.

46 Ibid., 212, notes omitted.

47 David Eden, Coroner, "Verdict of Coroner's Jury, Office of the Chief Coroner, Province of Ontario, Regarding Reyal Jardin Douglas, Sylvia Klibingaitis, Michael Eligon." Coroner's Court, Toronto, 15 October 2013–12 February 2014, http://www.mcscs.jus.gov.on.ca/stellent/groups/public/@mcscs/@www/@com/documents/webasset/ec167854.pdf.

48 Derrick, *Report of the Fatality Inquiry into the Death of Howard Hyde*, 386.

49 Catherine Carstairs, "'The Most Dangerous Drug': Images of African-Americans and Cocaine Use in the Progressive Era," *Left History: An Interdisciplinary Journal of Historical Inquiry and Debate* 7, no. 1 (2000): 46–61.

50 Dorothy E. Smith, "No One Commits Suicide: Textual Analysis of Ideological Practices," *Human Studies* 6, no.1 (1983): 309–59.

51 *Coroner's Inquest into the Death of Anthany James Dawson* (1 December 2000), 4–5.
52 Ibid., 5.
53 Ibid., 5–6.
54 Ibid., 6.
55 Ibid., 6.
56 Ibid., 6–7.
57 Ibid., 13–17.
58 Yvon Gesinghaus (Presentation), in *Report of Proceedings (Minutes and Hansard): Special Committee to Review the Police Complaint Process*, 37th Parl., 3rd Sess., No. 16 (Victoria: Legislative Assembly, 11 April 2002, http://www.leg.bc.ca/cmt/37thparl/session-3/pcp/hansard/l20020411p.htm.
59 Ibid.
60 Ibid.
61 Ibid.
62 Ibid.
63 Nancy Dawson, in *Coroner's Inquest into the Death of Anthany James Dawson*, vol. 1, 17 July 2000, 8.
64 Ibid., 11.
65 Ibid., 13.
66 Ibid., 44.
67 Ibid., 19.
68 Ibid., Dr Bonnie Gleason, 75–6.
69 Ibid., Nancy Dawson, 28.
70 Ibid., 45.
71 *Coroner's Inquest into the Death of Anthany James Dawson*, vol. 3, 19 July 2000, 27.
72 Dr Bonnie Gleason, in *Coroner's Inquest into the Death of Anthany James Dawson*, vol. 2, 18 July 2000, 25.
73 Dr Bonnie Gleason, in *Coroner's Inquest into the Death of Anthany James Dawson*, vol. 1, 17 July 2000, 73.
74 Dr Bonnie Gleason, in *Coroner's Inquest into the Death of Anthany James Dawson*, vol. 2, 18 July 2000, 30.
75 Ibid., 16–18.
76 Ibid., 18.
77 Ibid., 25–6.
78 Dr Bonnie Gleason, in *Coroner's Inquest into the Death of Anthany James Dawson*, 20 November 2000, 9.
79 Ibid., 30.
80 Dr Roderick McFadyen, in *Coroner's Inquest into the Death of Anthany James Dawson*, vol. 2, 18 July 2000, 55.

81 Dr Roderick McFadyen, in *Coroner's Inquest into the Death of Anthany James Dawson*, vol. 3, 19 July 2000, 9.

82 Ibid., 2.

83 Dr Laurel H. Gray, in *Coroner's Inquest into the Death of Anthany James Dawson*, 14 November 2000, 68. Dr Gray, when asked by John Orr, the counsel to the Coroner, as to a possible cause of Dawson going into a cardiac arrest, stated it as "restraint-associated cardiac arrest."

84 Ibid., 3.

85 Ibid.

86 Ibid., 41–2.

87 Ibid., 19.

88 Ibid., 39.

89 Ibid., 45.

90 Ibid., Dr Laurel H. Gray, 68–9.

91 Ibid., 69.

92 Jason Austin, in *Coroner's Inquest into the Death of Anthany James Dawson*, vol. 3, 19 July 2000, 54.

93 Ibid., 61.

94 Troy Lagis, in *Coroner's Inquest into the Death of Anthany James Dawson*, 15 November 2000, 39–49.

95 Gail Plant, in *Coroner's Inquest into the Death of Anthany James Dawson*, 16 November 2000, 2–17.

96 Emily Robertson, in *Coroner's Inquest into the Death of Anthany James Dawson*, 17 November 2000, 54–71; Chelsea Garside, in *Coroner's Inquest into the Death of Anthany James Dawson*, 16 November 2000, 18–33.

97 Tasha Libertore, in *Coroner's Inquest into the Death of Anthany James Dawson*, 17 November 2000, 14.

98 Ibid., Debra Robertson, 33.

99 Ibid., 50–4.

100 Ian MacCuish, in *Coroner's Inquest into the Death of Anthany James Dawson*, 16 November 2000, 40.

101 Heather Price, in *Coroner's Inquest into the Death of Anthany James Dawson*, 22 November 2000, 87.

102 Rebecca Steele, in *Coroner's Inquest into the Death of Anthany James Dawson*, 17 November 2000, 5; Corrie Atherton, in *Coroner's Inquest into the Death of Anthany James Dawson*, 20 November 2000, 78.

103 R. Atherton, in *Coroner's Inquest into the Death of Anthany James Dawson*, 20 November 2000, 68–9.

104 J.W. Angus, in *Coroner's Inquest into the Death of Anthany James Dawson*, 20 November 2000, 88–98.

105 Ibid., K.A. Angus, 118.

106 M. Sim, in *Coroner's Inquest into the Death of Anthany James Dawson*, 21 November 2000, 46–71.

107 Susan Mullins, in *Coroner's Inquest into the Death of Anthany James Dawson*, 22 November 2000, 9.

108 Ibid., Michael Fallis, 20.

109 Ibid., Clement Huot, 28.

110 Sharon McLean, in *Coroner's Inquest into the Death of Anthany James Dawson*, 23–24 November 2000, 5.

111 Colin Dales, in *Coroner's Inquest into the Death of Anthany James Dawson*, 21 November 2000, 21.

112 Constable Lawrence Hemstad, in *Coroner's Inquest into the Death of Anthany James Dawson*, 23–24 November 2000, 10.

113 Ibid., 68.

114 Ibid., Constable J.P.R. Sheldan, 82.

115 Ibid., 96–8.

116 George Moldovanos, in *Coroner's Inquest into the Death of Anthany James Dawson*, 28 November 2000, 7–8.

117 Ibid., 11.

118 Ibid.

119 Ibid., Corporal W.J. Trudeau, 53.

120 Ibid., Constable D.G. Saunderson, 80.

121 Ibid., Constable M. Knoop, 96.

122 Jamie H. Graham, quoted in Louise Dickson, "Man Kicked by Cop Was Seeking Police Help When Arrested," *Vancouver Province*, 26 March 2010, http://www.bcpolicecomplaints.org/victoria_police_brutality2.html.

123 Jamie H. Graham, Chief Constable of the Vancouver Police Department, "Death of Frank Paul," Memo to the City Manager, City of Vancouver, on 28 April 2004, Media Release, 5 May 2005, http://mediareleases.vpd.ca/2004/05/05/death-of-frank-paul/.

124 David MacAlister, *Police Involved Deaths: The Need for Reform* (Vancouver: BC Civil Liberties Association, 2012), https://bccla.org/wp-content/uploads/2012/03/2012-BCCLA-Report-Police-Involved-Deaths4.pdf. Over the timeframe studied, one person died every 3 weeks in British Columbia, one every 6.5 weeks in Ontario, one every 19.5 weeks in Saskatchewan, one every 31 weeks in New Brunswick, one every 45.5 weeks in the Northwest Territories, and one every 71 weeks in the Yukon. British Columbia had the greatest number of deaths per year per capita of the provinces, with one death for every 254,550 people per year, compared with one death for every 1.63 million people per year in Ontario; one death for every 457,000 people per year in New Brunswick; and one death for every 392,100 people per year in Saskatchewan. For provinces where

race was noted for those who died in custody, fifty-five per cent (Yukon) and thirty-eight per cent (Saskatchewan) were Aboriginal.

125 Ibid., Cameron Ward, 186.

126 Author interview with Cameron Ward, Vancouver, British Columbia, 27 November 2008.

127 Author interview with Steven Kelliher, Victoria, British Columbia, 28 October 2008; Author interview with Cameron Ward.

128 Shelly Milligan, "2006 Aboriginal Population Profile for Victoria," in *2006 Aboriginal Population Profiles for Selected Cities and Communities: British Columbia*, Online Catalogue 89-638-X, no. 4 (Ottawa: Statistics Canada, 2010), http://www.statcan.gc.ca/pub/89-638-x/2010004/article/11086-eng.pdf.

129 Penelope Edmonds, *Urbanizing Frontiers: Indigenous Peoples and Settlers in 19th-Century Pacific Rim Cities* (Vancouver: UBC Press, 2010).

130 Ibid., 202.

131 Ibid., 204.

132 Ibid., 209.

133 Ibid., 211.

134 Ibid., 238.

135 Nancy Dawson, in *Coroner's Inquest into the Death of Anthany James Dawson*, vol. 1, 17 July 2000, 55.

Chapter Six

1 Alleged response of Sgt. Jarvis, the investigating officer in 1990 into Neil Stonechild's death, when asked by a fellow police officer what he thought of the Stonechild file. See David H. Wright, Commissioner, *Report of the Commission of Inquiry into Matters Relating to the Death of Neil Stonechild* (Regina: Coroners Service of Saskatchewan, Ministry of Justice for the Government of Saskatchewan, October 2004), accessed 5 November 2004 http://www.justice.gov.sk.ca/stonechild/finalreport/, 124.

2 Police Chief Russell Sabo, quoted in "Indepth: Neil Stonechild; Who was Neil Stonechild?" *CBC News Online*, 3 November 2005, accessed 25 July 2013, http://www.cbc.ca/news2/background/stonechild/#top.

3 Sakej Henderson, Director of the Native Law Centre, quoted in DeNeen L. Brown, "Left for Dead in a Saskatchewan Winter: A Survivor's Story Exposes Police Abuse of Indigenous Canadians," *The Washington Post*, 22 November 2003, final edition: A01, http://injusticebusters.org/2003/Night.htm.

4 Susanne Reber and Rob Renaud, *Starlight Tour: The Last, Lonely Night of Neil Stonechild* (Toronto: Random House Canada, 2005), 71.

5 See, for example, Penelope Edmonds, *Urbanizing Frontiers: Indigenous Peoples and Settlers in 19th-Century Pacific Rim Cities* (Vancouver: UBC Press, 2010); Amanda Nettlebeck and Russell Smandych, "Policing Indigenous Peoples on Two Colonial Frontiers: Australia's Mounted Police and Canada's North-West Mounted Police," *The Australian and New Zealand Journal of Criminology* 43, no.2 (2010): 356–75.

6 M. NourbeSe Philip, *Zong!* (Middletown, CT: Wesleyan University Press, 2008), 191.

7 David Theo Goldberg, *Racist Culture: Philosophy and the Politics of Meaning* (Malden, MA: Blackwell, 1993), 186.

8 Anna Secor makes this argument about Kurdish refugees in Turkey. See Anna J. Secor, "An Unrecognizable Condition Has Arrived: Law, Violence, and the State of Exception in Turkey," in *Violent Geographies: Fear, Terror, and Political Violence*, ed. Derek Gregory and Allan Pred (New York: Routledge, 2007), 37.

9 Goldberg, *Racist Culture*, 185.

10 Radhika Mohanram, *Black Body: Woman, Colonialism, and Space* (Minneapolis: University of Minnesota Press, 1999), 16.

11 Goldberg, recalling Fanon, *Racist Culture*, 191.

12 Evelyn J. Peters and Vince Robillard, '"Everything You Want Is There': The Place of the Reserve in First Nations' Homeless Mobility," *Urban Geography* 30, no. 6 (2009): 652–80.

13 Laura Hudson, "A Species of Thought: Bare Life and Animal Being," *Antipode* 43, no. 5 (2011): 1665.

14 See Sherene H. Razack, "Gendered Racial Violence and Spatialized Justice: The Murder of Pamela George," *Canadian Journal of Law and Society* 15, no. 2 (2000): 91–130.

15 Paul L.A.H. Chartrand and Wendy J. Whitecloud, *Aboriginal Justice Implementation Commission Final Report* (Winnipeg, MB: Government of Manitoba, 2001), http://www.ajic.mb.ca/reports/final_toc.html.

16 Alvin C. Hamilton and C. Murray Sinclair, *Report of the Aboriginal Justice Inquiry of Manitoba*, 3 vols. (Winnipeg: Province of Manitoba, 1999), http://www.ajic.mb.ca/volume.html.

17 Ibid., vol 1, *The Justice System and Aboriginal People*, chapter 16, "Policing."

18 See Christine A. Walsh et al., "Homelessness and Incarceration among Aboriginal Women: An Integrative Literature Review," *Pímatisíwin: A Journal of Aboriginal and Indigenous Community Health* 9, no. 2 (2011): 363–86; Saskatchewan Indian Institute of Technologies, *Urban First Nations People without Homes in Saskatchewan* (Saskatoon: Saskatchewan Indian Institute of Technologies, Asimakaniseekan Askiy Reserve, 2000), accessed 5

November 2000, http://www.ywcaregina.com/Programs/Homelessness-Poverty/Homeless%20Urban%20First%20Nations.pdf; Insightrix Research Inc., *The Saskatoon Housing and Homelessness Plan, 2011–2014* (Saskatoon: Saskatoon Homeless Advisory Committee, March 2011), accessed 1 October 2013, http://www.saskatoon.ca/DEPARTMENTS/Community%20Services/PlanningDevelopment/Documents/Neighbourhood%20Planning/Housing/Housing%20and%20Homelessness%20Report%202011%20final.pdf. On case studies from British Columbia, Alberta, Saskatchewan, and Manitoba, see Katie McCallum and David Isaac, *Feeling Home: Culturally Responsive Approaches to Aboriginal Homelessness; Research Report* (Vancouver: The Social Planning and Research Council of British Columbia and the Centre for Native Policy and Research, July 2011); Stephen Gaetz et al., *The State of Homelessness in Canada, 2013* (Toronto: Canadian Homelessness Research Network Press, 2013); Native Women's Association of Canada (NWAC), "Aboriginal Women and Homelessness: An Issue Paper," (paper prepared for the National Aboriginal Women's Summit, Corner Brook, NL, 20–22 June 2007), accessed 21 January 2011, http://ywcacanada.ca/data/research_docs/00000281.pdf; and Aboriginal Standing Committee on Housing and Homelessness (ASCHH), *Plan to End Aboriginal Homelessness in Calgary* (Calgary: ASCHH, November 2012), accessed 4 December 2012, http://www.aschh.ca/Plan%20to%20End%20Aboriginal%20Homelessness%20in%20Calgary%202012.pdf.

19 Goldberg, *Racist Culture*, 200.

20 Ibid., 187.

21 Hudson, "A Species of Thought," 1660.

22 Ibid.

23 Ibid., 1671.

24 Ibid., 1676n5.

25 Michael Taussig, *Shamanism, Colonialism, and the Wild Man: A Study in Terror and Healing* (Chicago: University of Chicago Press, 1987), 5.

26 Sylvia Wynter, "Unsettling the Coloniality of Being/Power/Truth/Freedom: Towards the Human, After Man, Its Overrepresentation – An Argument," *CR: The New Centennial Review* 3, no. 3 (2003): 257–337.

27 Achille Mbembe, "Necropolitics," trans. Libby Meintjes, *Public Culture* 15, no. 1 (2003): 11–40.

28 Denise Ferreira da Silva, *Toward a Global Idea of Race* (Minneapolis: University of Minnesota Press, 2007).

29 Giorgio Agamben, *State of Exception*, trans. Kevin Attell (Chicago: University of Chicago Press, 2005).

30 Vinay Gidwani and Rajyashree N. Reddy, "The Afterlives of 'Waste': Notes from India for a Minor History of Capitalist Surplus," *Antipode* 43, no.5 (November 2011): 1653.

31 Ibid., 1649.

32 Ibid., 1626.

33 Ibid., 1627 (emphasis in the original).

34 Ibid., 1653 (emphasis in the original).

35 Ibid., 1649.

36 William King and Thomas Dunn, "Dumping: Police-Initiated Transjurisdictional Transport of Troublesome Persons," *Police Quarterly* 7, no.3 (2004): 339–58.

37 Elizabeth Comack writes: "In many respects, the stories of Neil Stonechild, Rodney Niastus, Lawrence Wegner, and Darryl Night epitomize the troubled lives endured by many Aboriginal people in this racialized space. All of them, for instance, had in common problems with drug and alcohol abuse. Given their regular contact with the Saskatoon Police Service, they were cast as 'troublesome.' Regardless of the name used to describe the practice – starlight tours, drop-offs, dumping, breaching, or unarresting – the act constitutes one of the racialized policing strategies that officers utilize in their efforts to contain and control this troubled and troublesome population. Whether emanating from frustration in dealing with repeat troublemakers, disillusionment with other sectors of the criminal justice system for being 'too soft on crime,' a sense of entitlement in imposing their own brand of 'street justice,' or simply being tasked with the insurmountable assignment of managing the effects of a systemic problem, police officers may well turn to this racialized practice as a way of fulfilling their role as reproducers of order." Elizabeth Comack, *Racialized Policing: Aboriginal People's Encounter with the Police* (Halifax and Winnipeg: Fernwood Publishing, 2012), 151.

38 Taussig, *Shamanism, Colonialism, and the Wild Man*, 9.

39 Ibid.

40 Joyce Green, "From Stonechild to Social Cohesion: Anti-Racist Challenges for Saskatchewan," *Canadian Journal of Political Science/Revue canadienne de science politique* 39, no. 3 (2006): 507–27.

41 R.A. Cawsey, Chairman, *Justice on Trial: Report of the Task Force on the Criminal Justice System and Its Impact on the Indian and Metis People of Alberta* (Edmonton: Government of Alberta, 1991).

42 Wright, *Report of the Commission of Inquiry into Matters Relating to the Death of Neil Stonechild*, 208–9.

43 Simon Pemberton, "Demystifying Deaths in Police Custody: Challenging State Talk," *Social and Legal Studies* 17, no.2 (2008): 242.
44 Sakej Henderson, quoted in Brown, "Left for Dead."
45 Candis McLean and Stuart McLean, *When Police Become Prey*, directed by Candis McLean and Stuart McLean, written by Candis McLean (Calgary: Silver Harvest Productions, 2007), documentary, 90 minutes.
46 Bruce Bolton, quoted in Wright, *Report of the Commission of Inquiry into Matters Relating to the Death of Neil Stonechild*, 196.
47 Donald E. Worme, "Submissions on Behalf of Stella Bignell and the Family of Neil Stonechild to the Commission of Inquiry into the Matters Relating to the Death of Neil Stonechild," (Saskatoon: Semaganis Worme & Missens, Barristers & Attorneys-At-Law, 2004), accessed 30 March 2014, http://www.justice.gov.sk.ca/stonechild/finalsubs/Bignell%20-%20Final%20Written%20Submissions.pdf, 4–6.
48 Wright, *Report of the Commission of Inquiry into Matters Relating to the Death of Neil Stonechild*, 131.
49 Ibid., 59.
50 Ibid., 192.
51 Ibid., 73.
52 Ibid., 82.
53 Sherene H. Razack, *Dark Threats and White Knights: Peacekeeping and the New Imperialism* (Toronto: University of Toronto Press, 2004), 57–63.
54 Calvin Chocan, council member, Onion Lake Band, testifying at the Naistus inquest. See H.M. Harradence, *Coroner's Inquest into the Death of Rodney Hank Naistus* (Saskatoon: Coroners Service of Saskatchewan, 30–1 October, 1–3 November 2001), 914.
55 Goldberg, *Racist Culture*, 189.
56 *Coroner's Inquest into the Death of Rodney Hank Naistus*, 654.
57 Ibid., Rodney Harper, 493.
58 Pat Lorje, quoted in Brian Hutchinson, "Frozen Ghosts," *Saturday Night Magazine*, 19 August 2000, 30.
59 Peters and Robillard, "Everything You Want Is There," 653.
60 Cara J.A. Spence, "An Analysis of Race Relations in Saskatoon, Saskatchewan: The Contributions of the Housing Sector," Bridges and Foundations Project on Urban Aboriginal Housing (Saskatoon: Bridges and Foundations, 2004), http://www.bridgesandfoundations.usask.ca/reports/analysis_racerelations.pdf, 18.
61 Comack, *Racialized Policing*, 25–8.
62 King and Dunn, "Dumping."
63 Hutchinson, "Frozen Ghosts," 55.

64 *Coroner's Inquest into the Death of Rodney Hank Naistus*, 1116.
65 Ibid., 265.
66 Ibid., 283.
67 Pat Lorje, quoted in Hutchinson, "Frozen Ghosts," 55.
68 *Coroner's Inquest into the Death of Rodney Hank Naistus*, 102.
69 Ibid., 566.
70 Ibid., 155–6.
71 Ibid., 309–10.
72 Ibid., 479.
73 Michelle Yates, "The Human-As-Waste, the Labor Theory of Value and Disposability in Contemporary Capitalism," *Antipode* 43, no. 5 (November 2011): 1680.
74 *Coroner's Inquest into the Death of Rodney Hank Naistus*, 214–15.
75 Ibid., 1032.
76 Ibid., 551, 574, 575, and 1116.
77 Ibid., 545.
78 Ibid., 613.
79 Ibid., 743–4.
80 Ibid., 914–15.
81 Silas E. Halyk, "Submission of the Federation of Saskatchewan Indian Nations to the Commission of Inquiry into the Matters Relating to the Death of Neil Stonechild (Saskatoon: Halyk Kennedy Koskie Knox, Barristers and Solicitors, 2004), accessed 30 March 2014, http://www.justice.gov.sk.ca/stonechild/finalsubs/FSIN-finalsub.pdf, 34–5.
82 G.J. Curtis, lawyer for the Wegner family, in H.M. Harradence, Coroner, *Coroner's Inquest into the Death of Lawrence Kim Wegner* (Saskatoon: Coroners Service of Saskatchewan, Ministry of Justice for the Government of Saskatchewan, 2002), 2385.
83 Ibid., 464.
84 Ibid., Dr Remillard, 2836–7.
85 Ibid., 2837.
86 Ibid., 492.
87 Ibid., 2869.
88 Ibid., 2295.
89 Ibid., 2856.
90 Ibid., 2747–55.
91 Ibid., 2857.
92 Ibid., 873.
93 Ibid., 2146.
94 Ibid., 2354.

95 Ibid., 764.
96 Ibid., 2868.
97 Gidwani and Reddy, "The Afterlives of 'Waste,'" 1653.
98 Ibid.

Conclusion

1 Patricia Monture-Angus, "Lessons in Decolonization: Aboriginal Overrepresentation in Canadian Criminal Justice," in *Visions of the Heart: Canadian Aboriginal Issues*, ed. David Long and Olive Patricia Dickason (Toronto: Harcourt Canada, 2000), 363.
2 Tonia Grace, *Coroner's Report into the Death of S.Q.* (Penticton: Coroners Service of British Columbia, Ministry of Justice, 27 May 2008), 56.
3 Howard Sapers, *A Failure to Respond: Report on the Circumstances Surrounding the Death of a Federal Inmate* (Ottawa: Office of the Correctional Investigator, Government of Canada, 2008), last modified 16 September 2013, http://www.oci-bec.gc.ca/cnt/rpt/oth-aut/oth-aut20080521-eng.aspx.
4 Amnesty International, "Canada: Covering Events from January to December 2000," in *Amnesty International Report 2001*, accessed 30 March 2014, http://www.refworld.org/pdfid/3b1de371c.pdf.
5 U.S. Department of State, Bureau of Democracy, Human Rights, and Labor, "Canada," in *2004 Country Reports on Human Rights Practices* (Washington: Bureau of Public Affairs, 28 February 2005), accessed 8 November 2013, http://www.state.gov/j/drl/rls/hrrpt/2004/41752.htm; Rodolfo Stavenhagen, UN Special Rapporteur on the Situation of Human Rights and Fundamental Freedoms of Indigenous People, "Mission to Canada," addendum to *Indigenous Issues: Human Rights and Indigenous Issues*, Report to the Sixty-First Session of the Commission on Human Rights (New York: UN Economic and Social Council, 2004), accessed 8 November 2013, http://www.gcc.ca/pdf/INT000000012.pdf.
6 Quoted in Nancy Hannum, *Aboriginal Deaths and Injuries in Custody and/or with Police Involvement: An Initial Survey of Information and Incidents in British Columbia, Saskatchewan, Manitoba and Ontario; Preliminary Report* (Vancouver: Native Court Worker and Counselling Association of British Columbia, 23 September 2003), accessed 1 October 2013, http://nccabc.pmhclients.com/images/uploads/nccabc_aboriginaldeathsincustody.pdf.
7 Hannum, *Aboriginal Deaths and Injuries in Custody*.
8 Coroners Service of British Columbia, "Statistics 1992 to 2007: BC Custody/Police-involved Deaths" (Burnaby: Emergency Management BC,

Ministry of Public Safety and Solicitor General, Office of the Chief Coroner, 16 October 2007).

9 See "Peggy Clement, Frank Paul Family Member," *Frank Paul Inquiry Transcripts 2007–2008, 2010* (Vancouver: The Davies Commission, 13 November 2007), accessed 2 May 2014, http://frankpaulinquiryca.nationprotect.net/transcripts/2007-11-13.pdf#PeggyClement, 53–4. BC Grand Chief Stewart Philip provided the inquiry with a long list of names of Aboriginal people who died in custody in British Columbia. See also Cameron Ward, quoted by S. Fournier in "267 Cop-related Deaths in B.C. Over Past 15 Years," *The Vancouver Province*, 25 January 2008, accessed 2 May 2014, http://www.canada.com/theprovince/news/story.html?id=707223ef-cf82-4c1e-832c-90e547cd4dd0.

10 Howard Sapers, Correctional Investigator of Canada, *Annual Report of the Office of the Correctional Investigator, 2008–2009* (Ottawa: Office of the Correctional Investigator, 2009), accessed 2 May 2014, http://www.oci-bec.gc.ca/cnt/rpt/pdf/annrpt/annrpt20082009-eng.pdf.

11 Howard Sapers, Correctional Investigator of Canada, *Annual Report of the Office of the Correctional Investigator, 2009–2010* (Ottawa: Office of the Correctional Investigator, 2010), accessed 2 May 2014, http://www.oci-bec.gc.ca/cnt/rpt/pdf/annrpt/annrpt20092010-eng.pdf.

12 Steve Rennie, The Canadian Press, "Huge Increase in Number of Aboriginal Women in Canadian Prison," *Toronto Star*, 2 December 2014, http://www.thestar.com/news/canada/2014/12/02/huge_increase_in_number_of_aboriginal_women_in_canadian_prisons.html.

13 Julian V. Roberts and Ronald Melchers, "The Incarceration of Aboriginal Offenders: Trends from 1978 to 2001," *Canadian Journal of Criminology and Criminal Justice* 45, no. 2 (April 2003): 217.

14 Samuel Perreault, "The Incarceration of Aboriginal People in Adult Correctional Services," Statistics Canada, *Juristat* 29, no. 3 (July 2009), last modified 28 October 2009, http://www.statcan.gc.ca/pub/85-002-x/2009003/article/10903-eng.pdf. Perreault states: "Education and employment characteristics help to explain some of the representation of Aboriginal adults in custody. However, the incarceration rates for Aboriginal adults aged 20 to 34 still remain higher than for their non-Aboriginal counterparts even when high school graduation and employment are considered. For instance, for every 1,000 Aboriginal adults in Alberta aged 20 to 34 with a high school diploma and employed as of Census Day, there were 2.4 with the equivalent characteristics in prison. Among their non-Aboriginal counterparts, the rate was 0.6. In addition, the incarceration rates for Aboriginal populations differ across the provinces (for which data exist).

Other factors beyond education and employment, therefore, may also contribute to the representation of Aboriginal adults in custody. However, other indicators of socio-economic status, such as income, are not collected by the ICSS."

15 Roberts and Melchers, "The Incarceration of Aboriginal Offenders."

16 Monture-Angus, "Lessons in Decolonization."

17 Thomas Gabor, *Deaths in Custody: Final Report Submitted to the Office of the Correctional Investigator* (Ottawa: Office of the Correctional Investigator, Government of Canada, 28 February 2007), accessed 9 September 2012, http://www.oci-bec.gc.ca/cnt/rpt/oth-aut/oth-aut20070228-eng.aspx.

18 Sapers, *Annual Report of the Office of the Correctional Investigator, 2009–2010*, 43–5.

19 Sapers, *A Failure to Respond*.

20 Ibid.

21 The total population of Saskatchewan in 2009 was 1,053,960. The Saskatchewan Indigenous population was 129,138. "First Nations in Saskatchewan," Aboriginal Affairs and Northern Development Canada – Saskatchewan Region, accessed 15 August 2012, http://www.aadnc-aandc.gc.ca/eng/1100100020616/1100100020653.

22 Mike O'Brien, "Inquest Urges Changes," *Leader Post*, 18 March 2000: A3.

23 Lori Coolican, "Staff Shortage Factor in Suicide: Coroner's Jury Recommends Increasing Staff at Regional Psychiatric Centre to Combat Suicide Attempts," *Star-Phoenix*, 15 April 2000: A3.

24 "Female Inmate Commits Suicide: Mother of Five Took Life while in Solitary Confinement," *Sudbury Star*, 7 February 2000: A4.

25 Dan Zakreski, "Suicide Points to Study's Concern," *Star-Phoenix*, 7 February 2000: A1.

26 Colin Tatz, *Aboriginal Suicide Is Different: A Portrait of Life and Self-Destruction* (Canberra: Aboriginal Studies Press, 2001).

27 Leonie Cox, "Review of *Aboriginal Suicide Is Different: A Portrait of Life and Self-Destruction* by Colin Tatz," *The Australian Journal of Anthropology* 13, no. 3 (2002): 373.

28 Ibid.

29 See, for example, Paulette Peirol, "Why So Few Suicides in P4W?" *The Whig Standard*, 11 December 1991: 3.

30 Betty Ann Adam, "Expert Unable to Pinpoint Exact Cause of Inmate's Death," *Star-Phoenix*, 22 October 2002: A6; Darren Bernhardt, "Detox Centre to Be Built in Saskatoon," *Star-Phoenix*, 8 May 2003: A1; "Asthma Victim Died after Police Withheld Inhalers," *Calgary Herald*, 16 October 2002.

31 Mark O'Brien, "Native Man Who Fought with Regina Police Dies: Officer Uses Pepper-Spray on Man in Ambulance," *Star-Phoenix*, 12 July 2001: A3;

Barb Pacholik, "Inquest Opens into Pepper Spray Case," *Leader Post*, 18 February 2003: B1; Barb Pacholik, "'Excited Delirium' Blamed," *Leader Post*, 27 February 2003: B1.

32 "Sask.: Inquest Told Woman Who Died in Police Custody Wasn't Drunk," *Canadian Press Newswire*, 8 November 2005.

33 Barb Pacholik, "Reasons Behind Shootings a Mystery," *Leader Post*, 7 November 2008: A1.

34 Ibid.

35 Scot Wortley, with research support from Terry Roswell, *Police Use of Force in Ontario: An Examination of Data from the Special Investigations Unit; Final Report* (Toronto: African Canadian Legal Clinic), accessed 2 May 2014, http://www.attorneygeneral.jus.gov.on.ca/inquiries/ipperwash/policy_part/projects/pdf/AfricanCanadianClinicIpperwashProject_SIUStudy-byScotWortley.pdf.

36 Elizabeth Comack, *Racialized Policing: Aboriginal People's Encounters with the Police* (Halifax and Winnipeg: Fernwood Publishing, 2012).

37 Comack, *Racialized Policing*, 28.

38 Ibid., 25.

39 "Mrs. Wegner," in *Two Worlds Colliding*, directed by Tasha Hubbard (Canada: National Film Board of Canada, 2005), VHS.

40 Elliott Johnston, Commissioner. *Report of the Royal Commission into Aboriginal Deaths in Custody (RCIADIC): National Report, Volume 1* (Canberra: Australian Government Publishing Service, 1991), chapter 3.

41 Ibid., Section 1.2.11.

42 Ibid., Section 3.2.22.

43 Ibid., Section 3.3.80.

44 Vicki Dalton, "Death and Dying in Prison in Australia: National Overview, 1980–1998," *The Journal of Law, Medicine and Ethics* 27, no. 3 (1999): 270.

45 Ibid., 271.

46 Paul Wildman, "The Litany of Death: A Deep Futures Critique of the Australian Royal Commission into Aboriginal Deaths in Custody," *Futures* 34, no. 6 (2002): 572.

47 Chris Cunneen, "Indigenous Incarceration: The Violence of Colonial Law and Justice," in *The Violence of Incarceration*, ed. Phil Scraton and Jude McCulloch (New York: Routledge, 2009), 209, 221.

48 Deaths in Custody Watch Committee (WA) Inc., *Report to the Committee Against Torture for Consideration Together with Australia's Reports to the Committee: Pursuant to Article 19 of the Convention Against Torture/Deaths in Custody Watch Committee (WA) Inc.* (Ascot, WA: The Committee, 2000), http://websearch.aic.gov.au/firstaicPublic/fullRecord.jsp?recnoListAttr=recnoList&recno=252047.

49 Dinesh Wadiwel, "'A Particularly Governmental Form of Warfare': Palm Island and Australian Sovereignty," in *Our Patch: Enacting Australian Sovereignty*, ed. Suvendrini Perera (Perth, WA: Network Books, 2007), 149–66.
50 Sarah Keenan, "Australian Legal Geography and the Search for Postcolonial Space in Chloe Hooper's *The Tall Man: Death and Life on Palm Island*," *Australian Feminist Law Journal* 30 (2009): 173–99; Joanne Watson, *Palm Island through a Long Lens* (Canberra: Aboriginal Studies Press, 2010); Deidre Tedmanson, "Isle of Exception: Sovereign Power and Palm Island." *Critical Perspectives on International Business* 4, no. 2/3 (2008): 142–65.
51 Suvendrini Perera and Joseph Pugliese, "White Law of the Biopolitical," *Journal of the European Association of Studies on Australia* 3, no.1 (2012): 87–100.
52 Sherene Razack, "Racial Terror: Torture and Three Teenagers in Prison," *Borderlands* 13, no. 1 (2014), http://www.borderlands.net.au/Vol13No1_2014/razack_torture.pdf.
53 Monture-Angus, "Lessons in Decolonization," 367.
54 Maryanne Pearce, "An Awkward Silence: Missing and Murdered Vulnerable Women and the Canadian Justice System" (LD diss., University of Ottawa, 2013).
55 "Sinclair's family, Aboriginal Organizations Pull Out of Inquest," *Winnipeg Free Press*, 18 February, 2014, online edition, accessed 30 March 2014, http://www.winnipegfreepress.com/local/Brian-Sinclair-inquest-resumes-today-with-Phase-2-245978601.html.
56 Daniel Leblanc, "List of Missing, Killed Aboriginal Women Involves 1,200 Cases." *Globe and Mail*, 1 May 2014, last updated 2 May 2014, http://www.theglobeandmail.com/news/national/rcmp-dont-deny-report-of-more-than-1000-murdered-missing-native-women/article18363451/.
57 Patty Winsa, "Police Cleared after Woman Dies in Back of Cruiser on Ontario First Nation," *Toronto Star*, 22 February 2013, accessed 30 March 2014, http://www.thestar.com/news/canada/2013/02/22/police_cleared_after_woman_dies_in_back_of_cruiser_on_ontario_first_nation.html.
58 CBC News, "Michael Nehass Naked, Shackled in Yukon Video Court Appearance," accessed 27 September 2014, http://www.cbc.ca/news/canada/north/michael-nehass-naked-shackled-in-yukon-video-court-appearance-1.2641421.
59 Statistics Canada, *Aboriginal Peoples in Canada: First Nations People, Métis and Inuit*, National Household Survey 2011, Catalogue no. 99-011-X2011001

(Ottawa: Minister of Industry, 2013), http://www12.statcan.gc.ca/nhs-enm/2011/as-sa/99-011-x/99-011-x2011001-eng.pdf.

60 Jean Franco, *Cruel Modernity* (Durham, NC: Duke University Press, 2013).

Appendix

1 David H. Wright, Commissioner, *Report of the Commission of Inquiry into Matters Relating to the Death of Neil Stonechild* (Regina: Coroners Service of Saskatchewan, Ministry of Justice for the Government of Saskatchewan, October 2004), accessed 5 November 2004, http://www.justice.gov.sk.ca/stonechild/finalreport/.

2 "8 Killed by Sask. Police in Decade: Recent Saskatoon Deaths a Rarity," *Edmonton Journal*, 23 May 2001, final edition: A3; Dianne Rinehart, "Mountie behind APEC-Chairman Allegations Himself under Probe," *National Post*, 4 December 1998: A4.

3 "Police Call Inquest into Shooting Death (Floyd Piche Killed by Saskatchewan Police)," *Canadian Press NewsWire*, 4 April 1995; Ki Belhumeur, "Piches Drop Suit against P.A.," *Star-Phoenix*, 30 September 1997: A2; Government of Saskatchewan, "Inquest Called into Piche Death," news release, 4 April 1995, accessed 14 April 2014, http://www.gov.sk.ca/news?newsId=3998d45f-f3a9-4c65-8168-9b808b094cdf.

4 Sandra Cordon, "Few Care about Violence Suffered by Aboriginal Women, Group Says: Community Groups in Regina Have Called for an Independent Probe into the Fatal Police Shooting of a Woman," *The Vancouver Sun*, 8 February 1996: A4; Government of Saskatchewan, "Cyr Inquest Set for June 24," news release, 10 June 1996, accessed 14 April 2014, http://www.gov.sk.ca/news?newsId=4058f372-2c7b-43b3-8270-4c859da81916.

5 Mike O'Brien, "Inquest Urges Changes," *Leader Post*, 18 March 2000: A3; Government of Saskatchewan, "Machiskinic Inquest," news release, 13 March 2000, accessed 14 April 2014, http://www.gov.sk.ca/news?newsId=e9df14c6-54a0-491c-99e5-7d5ba30d27b9.

6 Lori Coolican, "Staff Shortage Factor in Suicide: Coroner's Jury Recommends Increasing Staff at Regional Psychiatric Centre to Combat Suicide Attempts," *Star-Phoenix*, 15 April 2000: A3; Government of Saskatchewan, "Favel Inquest," news release, 5 April 2000, accessed 14 April 2014, http://www.gov.sk.ca/news?newsId=5ec7cf15-ee0b-4657-ad1f-0ada9dbff1ae.

7 Lori Coolican, "Officer Unaware Man Needed Care, Jury Told: Startling Details of Freezing Death Emerge at Inquest," *Star-Phoenix*, 10

May 2001, final edition: A1; Lori Coolican, "Jury Wants Changes to Detention Procedures," *Star-Phoenix*, 11 May 2001, final edition: A1; Government of Saskatchewan, "Date Set for Dustyhorn Inquest," news release, 7 March 2001, accessed 14 April 2014, http://www.gov.sk.ca/news?newsId=40beebdd-456a-4169-b1aa-7c31db358705.

8 H.M. Harradence, Coroner, *Coroner's Inquest into the Death of Rodney Hank Naistus* (Saskatoon: Coroners Service of Saskatchewan, Ministry of Justice for the Government of Saskatchewan, 30–1 October 2001; 1–3 November 2001); Government of Saskatchewan, "Date Set for Naistus Inquest," news release, 25 July 2001, accessed 14 April 2014, http://gov.sk.ca/news?newsId=72667c44-3683-446e-8684-2ca65005ba2f.

9 H.M. Harradence, Coroner, *Coroner's Inquest into the Death of Lawrence Kim Wegner* (Saskatoon: Coroners Service of Saskatchewan, Ministry of Justice for the Government of Saskatchewan, 14–18, 21–3 January 2002; 4–8, 11–14 February 2002); Government of Saskatchewan, "Date Set for Wegner Inquest," news release, 5 October 2001, accessed 14 April 2014, http://gov.sk.ca/news?newsId=6dfacea8-9416-4fb7-9ee8-a4bf5249b871.

10 Dan Zakreski, "Inmates under Watch after Suicide Attempts," *Leader Post*, 11 February 2000: A6; Government of Saskatchewan, "Brass Inquest," news release, 2 June 2000, accessed 14 April 2014, http://gov.sk.ca/news?newsId=287f825b-e3b0-4e05-a920-5b3ccb34cdaf.

11 Leslie Perreaux, "Extensive Drug Scam Netted 307 Prescriptions: Inquest Hears Ironchild Frequented Multiple Doctors," *Star-Phoenix*, 15 December 2000: A1; Leslie Perreaux," Cops Failed Ironchild: Brother; Inquest Debates Extent to which Police Should Help Intoxicated People," *Star-Phoenix*, 13 December 2000: A1; Government of Saskatchewan, "Date Set for Ironchild Inquest," news release, 10 October 2000, accessed 14 April 2014, http://gov.sk.ca/news?newsId=075518b4-a944-472a-82a0-1bc8a9fcd08a.

12 "Inquest Ordered in Inmate's Death," *Star-Phoenix*, 15 September 2000: A4; Government of Saskatchewan, "Oochoo Inquest," news release, 14 September 2000, accessed 14 April 2014, http://gov.sk.ca/news?newsId=c73fd30e-2c99-46dc-aa65-aea7ee5ccf1c.

13 Mike O'Brien, "Suicide Has Inmates Questioning Jail Policies," *Star-Phoenix*, 16 May 2000: A4; Government of Saskatchewan, "Stonechild Inquest," news release, 17 January 2001, accessed 14 April 2014, http://www.gov.sk.ca/news?newsId=9ce9febf-fc6e-4677-9f5a-4c6563cc2584.

14 Government of Saskatchewan, "Date Set for Bigsky Inquest," news release, 30 May 2002, accessed 14 April 2014, http://www.gov.sk.ca/news?newsId=04f78796-a0d5-4c3b-92c9-916582473a7b.

15 Ibid.; Lori Coolican, "Inquest Recommendations No Solace to Bigsky's Mother," *Star-Phoenix*, 8 October 2002, final edition: A1; Lori Coolican, "Wife Says Victim Called Officer Racist," *Leader Post*, 3 October 2002: B2.

16 Jason Warick, "Grieving Family Question Tactics: Police Shooting Unnecessary: Mother," *Star-Phoenix*, 23 May 2001: A1; "8 Killed by Sask. Police in Decade," *Edmonton Journal*: A3; Lori Coolican, "Man Given Chance to Surrender: Cop; Backing Off Was Not an Option, Inquest Hears," *Star-Phoenix*, 27 November 2002: A3; Government of Saskatchewan, "McMillan Inquest," news release, 22 July 2002, accessed 14 April 2014, http://www.gov.sk.ca/news?newsId=f58fe6e6-6924-40d7-889e-3025ab9f8db2.

17 "Aboriginal Man Dies after Police Fire Pepper Spray," *Sudbury Star*, 12 July 2001: A10; "Inquest Set," *Leader Post*, 8 July 2003, final edition: A5; "Vernon Crowe Entered a Regina Ambulance Calmly and Exited a Dead Man after Being Pepper Sprayed by a Police Officer, a Coroner's Jury Heard Tuesday," *Canadian Press NewsWire*, 19 February 2003; Government of Saskatchewan, "Crowe Inquest," news release, 22 November 2002, accessed 14 April 2014, http://www.gov.sk.ca/news?newsId=9996be06-72ec-4d08-a378-f1530f7aa751.

18 Government of Saskatchewan, "Anaquod Inquest," news release, 3 July 2002, accessed 14 April 2014, http://www.gov.sk.ca/news?newsId=755a5244-67c0-4dd8-a484-c50133142c23; Betty Ann Adam, "Expert Unable to Pinpoint Exact Cause of Inmate's Death," *Star-Phoenix*, 22 October 2002: A6; Darren Bernhardt, "Detox Centre to Be Built in Saskatoon," *Star-Phoenix*, 8 May 2003: A1; "Asthma Victim Died after Police Withheld Inhalers," *Calgary Herald*, 16 October 2002.

19 "Saskatoon Inmate Found Hanging in Cell," *Star-Phoenix*, 8 February 2002: A4; Lori Coolican, "Inmate's Death Ruled Suicide: Family's Suspicions of Foul Play Linger," *Star-Phoenix*, 1 March 2003: A3; Government of Saskatchewan, "Bird Inquest," news release, 10 February 2003, accessed 14 April 2014, http://www.gov.sk.ca/news?newsId=d771d232-9970-45b5-a849-7ddb72a45e3d.

20 R. v. S.F.K. [2000] SKCA 28 (CanLII), http://www.canlii.org/en/sk/skca/doc/2000/2000skca28/2000skca28.html; Barb Pacholik, "Conditional Sentences Endorsed," *Leader Post*, 3 March 2000, final edition: A5; Stephen Tipper, "Jury Recommends Methadone Review," *Leader Post*, 8 March 2003, final edition, Native Issues Section: B2; Government of Saskatchewan, "Keepness Inquest," news release, 9 December 2002, accessed 14 April 2014, http://www.gov.sk.ca/news?newsId=32038692-74d0-4196-8607-3a588667f735.

21 John Nyssen, Coroner, *Inquest into the Death of A.M.S.* (Regina: Coroners Service of Saskatchewan, Ministry of Justice for the Government of Saskatchewan, 3–4 June 2003); Government of Saskatchewan, "Sewap Inquest," news release, 16 May 2003, accessed 14 April 2014, http://www.gov.sk.ca/news?newsId=6b954857-15a0-433b-adec-c2d0f09086e9.

22 Interview with Don Worme by author, Saskatoon, Saskatchewan, 25 February 2009; Jeff Grubb, Coroner, *Coroner's Inquest into the Death of A.R.C.* (Yorkton, SK: Coroners Service of Saskatchewan, Ministry of Justice for the Government of Saskatchewan, 9–13 February 2004); Government of Saskatchewan, "Cadotte Inquest," news release, 27 January 2004, accessed 14 April 2014, http://www.gov.sk.ca/news?newsId=9d52729d-7d0c-43cc-a203-23bead767b82.

23 "SGI Compensates Family of Accident Victim," *MBC Radio Online*, 28 October 2004, accessed 14 April 2014, http://www.mbcradio.com/index.php/news-archives/78-2004/1345-sgi-compensates-family-of-accident-victim-; Government of Saskatchewan, "Date Set for Campbell Inquest," news release, 26 September 2003, accessed 14 April 2014, http://www.gov.sk.ca/news?newsId=c036f235-2745-473e-a6e5-0822a7f67b83.

24 "Allan Maytwayashing," Passages, *Winnipeg Free Press*, accessed 14 April 2014, http://passages.winnipegfreepress.com/passage-details/id-74781/name-Allan_Maytwayashing/; Government of Saskatchewan, "Maytwayashing Inquest," news release, 5 January 2004, accessed 14 April 2014, http://www.gov.sk.ca/news?newsId=1719d857-a22d-4108-ac9e-982214b672ab.

25 "Martin Joseph Aubichon," *Fédération québécoise des sociétés de généalogie*, accessed 14 April 2014, http://www.federationgenealogie.qc.ca/avisdeces/avis/pdf?id=215152; Anne Kyle, "Aubichon Death Declared Accidental: Coroner's Jury," *Leader Post*, 4 September 2004, final edition: B2; Government of Saskatchewan, "Aubichon Inquest," news release, 10 August 2004, accessed 14 April 2014, http://www.gov.sk.ca/news?newsId=ab6c73a9-a49c-4ef6-a016-0da68be625b9.

26 "RCMP Vehicle Kills 19-Year-Old," *Nanaimo Daily News*, 12 September 2003: A12.

27 "Police Questioned at Sahpassum Inquest," *MBC Radio Online*, 8 November 2005, accessed April 2014, http://www.mbcradio.com/index.php/news-archives/79-2005/2649-police-questioned-at-sahpassum-inquest-; "Sask. Inquest Told Woman Who Died in Police Custody Wasn't Drunk," *Canadian Press NewsWire*, 8 November 2005; Government of Saskatchewan, "Sahpassum Inquest," news release, 24 October 2005, accessed 14 April 2014, http://www.gov.sk.ca/news?newsId=fef8e7d0-fe70-484f-a6a1-ae1f999775c0.

28 Alma Wiebe, Coroner, *Coroner's Report into the Death of A.E.* (Prince Albert: Coroners Service of Saskatchewan, Ministry of Justice for the Government of Saskatchewan, 21–2 March 2005); Government of Saskatchewan, "Eaglechild Inquest," news release, 7 March 2005, accessed 14 April 2014, http://www.gov.sk.ca/news?newsId=ecebf857-4fe6-404e-a743-55f406a6d237.

29 Interview with Don Worme; "Man Carrying Rifle Shot, Killed after Standoff in La Ronge, Sask," *Canadian Press NewsWire*, 30 August 2004; Government of Saskatchewan, "Martinot Inquest," news release, 16 May 2006, accessed 14 April 2014, http://www.gov.sk.ca/news?newsId=c9dbd89a-9ac3-4920-adec-f230704eca92.

30 "Addicts Need More Resources," *Star-Phoenix*, 21 June 2006, accessed 20 August 2009, http://www.canada.com/saskatoonstarphoenix/story.html?id=6c172406-ad62-4440-bb48-9995d1d26b82&k=15854; Janet French, "Woman's Family Suing Police," *Leader Post*, 2 August 2007: A10; Government of Saskatchewan, "Sanderson Inquest," news release, 30 May 2006, accessed 14 April 2014, http://www.gov.sk.ca/news?newsId=862474bb-0ba1-4f82-89f2-7382d05bab70.

31 "Inquest into Sask. Inmate's Death Says Nurses Need Psychological Training," *Canadian Press NewsWire*, 29 August 2006; Government of Saskatchewan, "Petit Inquest," news release, 21 August 2006, accessed 14 April 2014, http://www.gov.sk.ca/news?newsId=4fade93f-b882-4439-9582-5d626878c8cf&newsPN=Shared.

32 "Cause of Inmate's Death to Remain a Mystery," *MBC Radio Online*, 28 March 2007, accessed 14 April 2014, http://www.mbcradio.com/index.php/news-archives/81-2007/4496-cause-of-inmates-death-to-remain-a-mystery-; Government of Saskatchewan, "Burns Inquest," news release, 13 March 2007, accessed 14 April 2014, http://www.gov.sk.ca/news?newsId=8652f914-f1a9-4786-b76a-770ee397ab83.

33 Interview with Don Worme; Lori Coolican, "Methadone, Alcohol Bad Mix, Inquest Hears: Mountney Breathing in Cell, According to Commissionaire," *Star-Phoenix*, 24 January 2008: A7; Government of Saskatchewan, "Mountney Inquest," news release, 7 January 2008, accessed 14 April 2014, http://www.gov.sk.ca/news?newsId=a6720d58-8930-4fe5-a76c-32e571b132e0.

34 "Shooting on Reserve Leaves Natives Worried," *Prince George Citizen*, 18 Nov 2006, 7; Government of Saskatchewan, "Pelletier Inquest to Be Held Next Week," news release, 14 October 2008, accessed 14 April 2014, http://www.gov.sk.ca/news?newsId=b52b2292-63d6-4b3a-bc97-2fac5ca66806.

35 "Inquest Set into Custody Death," *Star-Phoenix*, 15 January 2009: A5; Pinehouse Lake: The Aboriginal Community of Pinehouse website, accessed 14

April 2014, http://www.pinehouselake.ca/; Government of Saskatchewan, "Lariviere Inquest," news release, 14 January 2009, accessed 14 April 2014, http://gov.sk.ca/news?newsId=2ffef5f8-1332-4e56-aeb4-1790b2e9734a.

36 "Brass Inquest Jury Delivers Nine Recommendations," *MBC Radio Online*, 29 January 2009, accessed 14 April 2014, http://mbcradio.com/index.php/news-archives/83-2009/6770-brass-inquest-jury-delivers-nine-recommendations; Government of Saskatchewan, "Brass Inquest," news release, 20 January 2009, accessed 14 April 2014, http://gov.sk.ca/news?newsId=dff5d56a-c046-4394-92cb-94279915d312.

37 Barb Pacholik, "Inquest into Inmate Hanging Begins," *Leader Post*, 4 March 2009: A3; Government of Saskatchewan, "Toulejour Inquest," news release, 26 February 2009, accessed 14 April 2014, http://www.gov.sk.ca/news?newsId=faf56cbc-6076-45b4-9c0f-2e8ca3a4ed97.

38 "Saskatoon Police Shootings of 2 Native People Raise Race Relations Questions," *The Canadian Press*, 28 December 2007; Jeanette Stewart, with files from David Hutton, "Inquest Jury Rules Man's Death Suicide: Police Officers Shot Dwayne Dustyhorn during 2007 Incident," *Star-Phoenix*, 5 June 2009: A1; Government of Saskatchewan, "Dustyhorn Inquest," news release 25 May 2009, accessed 14 April 2014, http://gov.sk.ca/news?newsId=85d305ef-0022-4d21-9c71-9f015cc2feb9.

39 "Family Wonders Why Police Killed Native Woman with Knife," *Canada.com*, 24 March 2008, accessed 14 April 2014, http://www.canada.com/ch/cheknews/news/story.html?id=18f7171d-334c-4101-8d5d-dcd5b4179550&k=67094; Chris Phalen, "Drug, Alcohol Mix Could Have Made Victim 'Aggressive': Police Bullet Killed Prince Albert Woman, Inquiry Hears," *Star-Phoenix*, 15 April 2010: A9; Government of Saskatchewan, "Montgrand Inquest," news release, 8 April 2010, accessed 14 April 2014, http://gov.sk.ca/news?newsId=2ca75109-4881-4730-bd59-10706e050a46.

40 "Inmate's Death to Be Examined," *Leader Post*, 18 March 2009: A6; H. Polischuk, "Infection Caused Death, Pathologist Testifies," *Leader Post*, 26 March 2009: A6 ; H. Polischuk, "Man Needed Treatment When He Fled Hospital," *Leader Post*, 25 March 2009: B5; Government of Saskatchewan, "Dubois Inquest," news release, 17 March 2009, accessed 14 April 2014, http://gov.sk.ca/news?newsId=cf7d8000-c344-4f40-bb0f-0dfbfc62be12.

41 "Saskatchewan Inquest Rules RCMP Shooting of Young Man Was a Suicide," *The Canadian Press*, 6 November 2009; Lisa Arrowsmith, "Fatal Shooting Called 'Rambo-style Policing,'" *Winnipeg Free Press*, 16 June 2008: A10; Government of Saskatchewan, "Standingready-Mckay Inquest,"

news release, 23 October 2009, accessed 14 April 2014, http://gov.sk.ca/news?newsId=42af56a2-ea67-4bc1-b06a-e51155444685.

42 "First Nations Leader Questions Use of Lethal Force," *CBC News*, 4 September 2008, accessed 14 April 2014, http://www.cbc.ca/news/canada/saskatchewan/story/2008/09/04/fsin-shooting.htmlQ12; "Jury Recommends Better Risk Analysis to Prevent RCMP Shooting Deaths," *The Canadian Press*, 6 December 2012; Government of Saskatchewan, "Haineault Inquest," news release, 14 October 2010, accessed 14 April 2014, http://www.gov.sk.ca/news?newsId=31dcb60a-7822-4e4e-864f-da56ad391d1a.

43 "Brett Henry," *Legacy.Com: Leader Post*, accessed 14 April 2014, http://www.legacy.com/obituaries/leaderpost/obituary.aspx?n=brett-henry&pid=121201676; Government of Saskatchewan, "Henry Inquest," news release, 23 October 2009, accessed 14 April 2014, http://gov.sk.ca/news?newsId=0c12f898-e098-4c19-b929-4c1918442f69.

44 "Freezing Death of Sask. Man Ruled Accidental," *CBC News*, 25 November 2010, accessed April 2014, http://www.cbc.ca/news/canada/saskatchewan/freezing-death-of-sask-man-ruled-accidental-1.927626; Government of Saskatchewan, "Lariviere Inquest," news release, 17 November 2010, accessed 14 April 2014, http://www.gov.sk.ca/news?newsId=e2a9725f-44e2-4e4c-a058-a8e55a6fb3bd.

45 Lori Coolican, "Inmate's Death Was Suicide, Jury Panel Finds: Infection Caused by Self-inflicted Razor Blade Wounds," *Star-Phoenix*, 19 November 2010: A8; Government of Saskatchewan, "Black Inquest," news release, 10 November 2010, accessed 14 April 2014, http://www.gov.sk.ca/news?newsId=5a149cb5-e274-4a4b-bc94-f2359c3f8a72.

46 "Jury Concludes Saskatchewan Woman Arrested by Police Died Accidentally," *The Canadian Press*, 9 December 2010.

47 "Video of Ida Paul's Final Hours Shown at Inquest," *MBC Radio Online*, 7 December 2010, accessed 14 April 2014, http://www.mbcradio.com/index.php/news-archives/84-2010/9322-video-of-ida-pauls-final-hours-shown-at-inquest; Government of Saskatchewan, "Paul Inquest," news release, 24 November 2010, accessed 14 April 2014, http://gov.sk.ca/news?newsId=0b25631d-f1a1-49c4-bc10-2573bdbeb4d5.

48 "Mom Queries Son's Death in Saskatoon Lockup," *CBC News*, 6 July 2010, accessed 14 April 2014, http://www.cbc.ca/news/canada/saskatchewan/mom-queries-son-s-death-in-saskatoon-lockup-1.882901; "Inquiry to Look for Cause of Death of Man in Saskatoon Jail Cell," *The Spec.Com*, 12 October 2013, accessed 14 April 2014, http://www.thespec.com/news-story/4154884-inquiry-to-look-for-cause-of-death-of-man-in-saskatoon-jail-cell/; "Police Broke Own Policy in Brandon Daniels Cell

Death: Decided against Calling Ambulance," *CBC News*, 30 October 2013, accessed 14 April 2014, http://www.cbc.ca/news/canada/saskatoon/police-broke-own-policy-in-brandon-daniels-cell-death-1.2287132; Government of Saskatchewan, "Inquest into the Death of Brandon Daniels," news release, 11 October 2013, accessed 14 April 2014, http://www.gov.sk.ca/news?newsId=7eb69747-fada-479f-a424-12b517c835e2.

49 Betty Ann Adam, "Paramedic Left Patient Unattended by Staff," *Star-Phoenix*, 12 December 2013: A3; "Inquest in Saskatoon Cell Death Recommends Better Communication with ER Workers," *The Canadian Press*, 13 December 2013; Betty Ann Adam, "Head Injury Not Assessed at Hospital: Inebriated Man Signed Waiver," *Star-Phoenix*, 10 December 2013: A3; Government of Saskatchewan, "Inquest into the Death of Stanley Robillard," news release, 25 November 2013, accessed 21 April 2014, http://www.gov.sk.ca/news?newsId=4940bf8f-f8eb-4776-8b5c-3de498dd9aef.

50 "Jury Recommends Better Monitoring," *Kingston Whig-Standard*, 10 April 1995: 3; Government of Saskatchewan, "Taniskishayinew Inquest Set for April 7," news release, 14 March 1995, accessed 14 April 2014, http://www.gov.sk.ca/news?newsId=5701afe9-8c8c-4e68-b6f1-c5615e8dfb5e.

51 Government of Saskatchewan, "Taniskishayinew Inquest April 2," news release, 16 March 1998, accessed 14 April 2014, http://www.gov.sk.ca/news?newsId=5d0fdaff-cb86-47a4-a2bb-156cc602b250.

52 Government of Saskatchewan, "Kinequon Inquest April 21," news release, 9 April 1998, accessed 14 April 2014, http://www.gov.sk.ca/news?newsId=4fa3bdf5-bce2-4115-a799-7078a51435d9.

53 Government of Saskatchewan, "Starblanket Inquest May 4," news release, 30 April 1998, accessed 14 April 2014, http://www.gov.sk.ca/news?newsId=9c6caf97-c3ac-41b7-9d33-2be0613e940d.

54 Government of Saskatchewan, "Inmate Inquest September 25, 1998," news release 11 September 1998, accessed 14 April 2014, http://www.gov.sk.ca/news?newsId=6accea44-fe49-414b-8273-6411ee2dce1f.

55 Government of Saskatchewan, "Engdahl Inquest Begins March 8, 1999," news release, 18 February 1999, accessed 14 April 2014, http://gov.sk.ca/news?newsId=daf741b3-b2e9-4cfa-b26b-722b375f0d0e.

56 "Calls for Safer Cells after Man Kills Himself," *CBC News*, 8 December 1999, accessed 14 April 2014, http://www.cbc.ca/news/canada/calls-for-safer-cells-after-man-kills-himself-1.190006; Government of Saskatchewan, "Hansen Inquest December 7, 1999," news release, 30 November 1999, accessed 14 April 2014, http://gov.sk.ca/news?newsId=43a508fc-b926-4053-a0e3-06b669a925f1.

57 Government of Saskatchewan, Department of Justice, "Jury Report," Frank Thomas Greatrix, 24 November 2000, Jerry Bell, Coroner.

58 Government of Saskatchewan, "Inquest to Be Held in Death of 16-Year-Old Female," news release, 26 February 2003, accessed 14 April 2014, http://www.gov.sk.ca/news?newsId=e7ca9e57-b1f9-4dac-b29d-40715c9f4500.

59 Government of Saskatchewan, "Dussion Inquest," news release, 19 October 2004, accessed 14 April 2014, http://www.gov.sk.ca/news?newsId=09747435-eb3c-487d-bd99-08b14b154b36.

60 Betty Ann Adam, "More Jail Safeguards Needed: Jury; Recommendations Stem from Hanging in Police Cell," *Star-Phoenix*, 7 January 2005: A5; Betty Ann Adam, "Officer Ignored Parts of Police Suicide Policy, Inquiry Hears," *Star-Phoenix*, 5 January 2005: A4; Government of Saskatchewan, "Arcand Inquest," news release, 21 December 2004, accessed 14 April 2014, http://www.gov.sk.ca/news?newsId=125a1954-490e-4ab0-bbc9-4031f150a942.

61 Government of Saskatchewan, "Massett Inquest Set for Jan. 30," news release, 6 January 1995, accessed 14 April 2014, http://www.gov.sk.ca/news?newsId=cdfa1f2d-5496-4372-8f8f-4961d5909359.

62 Ibid.

63 Government of Saskatchewan, "Robert Trudeau Inquest Set for Jan. 23," news release, 10 January 1995, accessed 14 April 2014, http://www.gov.sk.ca/news?newsId=722e0ddc-3582-4648-9c25-62ddd036fada.

64 Government of Saskatchewan, "Kehler Inquest Set for Feb. 24," news release, 14 February 1995, accessed 14 April 2014, http://www.gov.sk.ca/news?newsId=da8a2c2b-0266-4432-b9c0-e33f70b103f8.

65 Government of Saskatchewan, "Edwards Inquest Nov. 24," news release, 14 November 1995, accessed 14 April 2014, http://www.gov.sk.ca/news?newsId=5b513e4a-5ed0-4ee9-920b-b2ef8197cc3f.

66 Government of Saskatchewan, "Green Inquest February 9th," news release, 26 January 1996, accessed 14 April 2014, http://www.gov.sk.ca/news?newsId=1411fb7b-8e6b-41b1-9637-88a959f51037.

67 Government of Saskatchewan, "Morrison Inquest May 28," news release, 8 May 1996, accessed 14 April 2014, http://www.gov.sk.ca/news?newsId=a5da712a-eace-4fd7-be96-22667a3982ef.

68 Government of Saskatchewan, "Lidguerre Inquest December 17th," news release, 28 November 1996, accessed 21 April 2014, http://www.gov.sk.ca/news?newsId=7fae9eb3-2a6f-46b5-8547-bbac76d6db62.

69 Government of Saskatchewan, "Lemieux Inquest April 29th," news release, 18 April 1997, accessed 21 April 2014, http://www.gov.sk.ca/news?newsId=4624c9ad-cf58-41fe-b408-cd3de3746365.

70 Government of Saskatchewan, "Sugar Inquest June 11th," news release, 30 May 1997, accessed 21 April 2014, http://www.gov.sk.ca/news?newsId=faefd558-6c60-4028-83a5-1db714fa8966.

71 Andrea Wiebe, "Inmate Died from Asphyxiation, Inquest Rules," *Star-Phoenix*, 18 October 1997: A6; Government of Saskatchewan, "Rosiak Inquest October 17," news release, 7 October 1997, accessed 14 April 2014, http://www.gov.sk.ca/news?newsId=a8de4646-ae3a-42b6-bbdb-f522343308a7.

72 Betty Ann Adam, "Inquest Scheduled into Prison Suicide," *Star-Phoenix*, 15 November 1997: A8; Government of Saskatchewan, "Genaille Inquest November 28," news release, 14 November 1997, accessed 14 April 2014, http://www.gov.sk.ca/news?newsId=89997112-f8de-4c0a-b7e8-c13cc1721563.

73 Government of Saskatchewan, "Falloon Inquest November 6," news release, 21 October 1997, accessed 14 April 2014, http://www.gov.sk.ca/news?newsId=c4ef7355-80e0-4252-b573-8af6c3479496.

74 Government of Saskatchewan, "Bonaise Inquest December 4," news release, 20 November 1997, accessed 21 April 2014, http://www.gov.sk.ca/news?newsId=0ca23218-e943-436a-80ec-6f75f65b7e84.

75 Vicki Hall, "Inmate Threatened Suicide, Inquest Told," *Star-Phoenix*, 28 February 1998: A9; Government of Saskatchewan, "Carey Inquest February 27," news release, 10 February 1998, accessed 14 April 2014, http://www.gov.sk.ca/news?newsId=17b30eeb-0c7d-47f4-8990-edf85623ba7f.

76 Mike O'Brien, "Jury Advises Changes after Inmate's Suicide," *Star-Phoenix*, 25 April 1998: A10; Government of Saskatchewan, "Dennis Inquest April 24," news release, 9 April 1998, accessed 14 April 2014, http://www.gov.sk.ca/news?newsId=76303122-5855-4b09-913c-6edd64646734.

77 Government of Saskatchewan, "Palin Inquest February 24," news release, 5 February 1998, accessed 14 April 2014, http://www.gov.sk.ca/news?newsId=63a85bca-cddb-42bc-b4e3-b0e60d1436e9.

78 Government of Saskatchewan, "Genereaux Inquest March 9," news release, 23 February 1998, accessed 14 April 2014, http://www.gov.sk.ca/news?newsId=6eafbe1e-9a3b-44aa-817c-bc4a5b21d44f.

79 Government of Saskatchewan, "Bird Inquest to Be Held November 4, 1998," news release, 19 October 1998, accessed 14 April 2014, http://www.gov.sk.ca/news?newsId=62119c32-9819-4d49-b825-55161c991989.

80 Government of Saskatchewan, "Ohochinsky Inquest to Be Held January 20, 1999," news release, 6 January 1999, accessed 14 April 2014, http://gov.sk.ca/news?newsId=e8e448bb-d223-406e-b23a-7f8019d1887a.

81 Saskatchewan Sterling Network, "Suspect Hangs Himself in Regina Prison," *Star-Phoenix* , 26 May 1999: A5; Government of Saskatchewan, "Erickson Inquest October 7, 1999," news

release, 4 October 1999, accessed 21 April 2014, http://gov.sk.ca/news?newsId=82b18add-1fe9-44bc-a66b-e68a36576f9a.

82 Darren Steinke, "Inquest Finds Inmateed of Natural Causes [*sic*]," *Star-Phoenix*, 6 November 1999: A8; Government of Saskatchewan, "Hall Inquest November 5, 1999," news release, 25 October 1999, accessed 14 April 2014, http://gov.sk.ca/news?newsId=daefca34-2bf8-4255-ba94-57bddfe0f5fa.

83 Government of Saskatchewan, "McGilvery Inquest," news release, 3 May 2000, accessed 14 April 2014, http://gov.sk.ca/news?newsId=f0f83e2e-cebc-44a3-aaeb-9df2aa87aee4.

84 Government of Saskatchewan, "Pickford Inquest," news release, 30 March 2000, accessed 14 April 2014, http://gov.sk.ca/news?newsId=c5ed3a32-fada-495d-b9d1-8fccc1a99f1c.

85 Ibid.

86 Mike O'Brien, "Drug Overdose Likely Cause of Death: Ex-convict Only Had Six Days of Freedom before He Was Found Dead," *Leader Post*, 13 January 2001: A5; "Inquest Determines Ex-con Died of Cardiac Failure," *Prince Albert Daily Herald*, 13 January 2001: 3; Government of Saskatchewan, "Somerton Inquest," news release, 11 January 2001, accessed 14 April 2014, http://gov.sk.ca/news?newsId=f041e202-1d42-4bdf-b8cb-785b649811b2.

87 Heather Polishchuk, "P.A. Prison Requires Regular Physicians, Inquest Concludes: Inmate's Death Reveals Problems in Present System," *Star-Phoenix*, 19 September 2000: A8; Government of Saskatchewan, "Carriere Inquest," news release, 15 September 2000, accessed 14 April 2014, http://gov.sk.ca/news?newsId=e3bffe15-dcd1-4990-9b80-d2754fb9e609.

88 Government of Saskatchewan, "Date Set for Macdonald Inquest," news release, 4 May 2001, accessed 14 April 2014, http://gov.sk.ca/news?newsId=1295893e-9fb1-4e1c-920b-dccb424dc021.

89 "Inmate's Death Ruled Accidental," *Calgary Herald*, 29 September 2001: A22; Government of Saskatchewan, "Date Set for McLeod Inquest," news release, 13 September 2001, accessed 14 April 2014, http://gov.sk.ca/news?newsId=beb41ce0-1fb0-49a1-b540-2ad957fee9ce.

90 "P.A. Prison Officials Rule Inmate's Death Suicide," *Star-Phoenix*, 5 September 2001: A5; Government of Saskatchewan, "Date Set for Johnson Inquest," news release, 23 January 2002, accessed 14 April 2014, http://www.gov.sk.ca/news?newsId=4e6a55ca-2dcc-41cb-b7b2-825d0a22e88b.

91 Pamela Cowan, "Family Wanted More from Jury," *Leader Post*, 10 October 2003: B1; Government of Saskatchewan, "Stochmal Inquest," news release, 22 November 2002, accessed 14 April 2014, http://www.gov.sk.ca/news?newsId=a97660c4-45d1-4ffd-838b-2f8f3d3f1f96.

92 Betty Ann Adam, "Inquest Jury Wants Changes to 'Drunk Tank,'" *Star-Phoenix*, 13 December 2002: A15; Government of Saskatchewan, "Duane Bauman Inquest," news release, 13 November 2002, accessed 14 April 2014, http://www.gov.sk.ca/news?newsId=c373c0b0-a54e-42f6-bf04-f7817a3693ce.

93 Government of Saskatchewan, "Laderoute Inquest," news release, 22 October 2002, accessed 14 April 2014, http://www.gov.sk.ca/news?newsId=f619de09-aace-4940-86bb-448812db33e8.

94 "Inmate's Death Reviewed by Jury," *Star-Phoenix*, 11 January 2003: A10; quotation from Government of Saskatchewan, "Aikens Inquest," news release, 31 December 2002, accessed 14 April 2014, http://www.gov.sk.ca/news?newsId=7c5ad2a6-2f2c-4f6a-8a7b-b0737f29d4ad.

95 Silas Polkinghorne, "Inmate's Death an Accident, Inquest Jury Rules," *Star-Phoenix*, 14 February 2003: A5; Government of Saskatchewan, "Turchenek Inquest," news release, 19 November 2002, accessed 14 April 2014, http://www.gov.sk.ca/news?newsId=e647b7c9-c293-455f-ba14-ce830647a14a.

96 Government of Saskatchewan, "Vandall Inquest," news release, 22 October 2002, accessed 14 April 2014, http://www.gov.sk.ca/news?newsId=2ffdbac8-878b-4726-aa5a-e56d6b4af0ca.

97 "P.A. Inmate Found Dead in Residence," *Star-Phoenix*, 5 February 2002: A8; Government of Saskatchewan, "Pokjowy Inquest," news release, 22 October 2002, accessed 14 April 2014, http://www.gov.sk.ca/news?newsId=8e5a512e-f9be-4b1e-8a74-c56f34279ba9.

98 Government of Saskatchewan, "Leifson Inquest," news release, 19 September 2003, accessed 14 April 2014, http://www.gov.sk.ca/news?newsId=647418bf-0e04-451a-988e-8b6550e4bdd0.

99 Shauna Rempel, "Accused Had No Signs of Being Suicidal," *Star-Phoenix*, 7 October 2003: A7; Government of Saskatchewan, "Cunningham Inquest," news release, 17 September 2003, accessed 14 April 2014, http://www.gov.sk.ca/news?newsId=bd06c2a5-cdcd-41cb-8bee-1c27377b4dc4.

100 "Coroner's Jury Concerned Inmates Assessed by Unsupervised Paramedic Students," *Canadian Press NewsWire*, 29 April 2004; Dan Kinvig, "Antifreeze Substance Killed Man in Custody, Inquiry Hears," *Star-Phoenix*, 28 April 2004: A7; Government of Saskatchewan, "Diduck Inquest," news release, 12 April 2004, accessed 14 April 2014, http://www.gov.sk.ca/news?newsId=33895f21-c399-4059-9d9a-c34d95fb229f.

101 Quote from Government of Saskatchewan, "Woodworth Inquest," news release, 29 August 2003, accessed 14 April 2014, http://www.gov.sk.ca/news?newsId=66082982-ffda-4636-9d4d-50d3316d0dd4; "RPC Inmate Died of Natural Causes: Jury," *Star-Phoenix*, 13 September 2003: A4.

102 "Resident Found Dead in His Room," *Leader Post*, 20 August 2003: A8; Government of Saskatchewan, "McFall Inquest," news release, 8 November 2004, accessed 14 April 2014, http://www.gov.sk.ca/news?newsId=c71be895-ff2c-4d98-b76a-6e1ec3d2f19c.

103 Darren Bernhardt, "Inquest Hears of Inmate's Struggle with Depression," *Star-Phoenix*, 11 May 2004: A4; Government of Saskatchewan, "Dunn Inquest," news release, 26 April 2004, accessed 14 April 2014, http://www.gov.sk.ca/news?newsId=8ead42ba-c63b-40f0-82f9-2145c28f7e75.

104 Betty Ann Adam, "Inquest Hears Prisoner Talked about Suicide," *Star-Phoenix*, 2 June 2004: A8; Government of Saskatchewan, "Senko Inquest," news release, 18 May 2004, accessed 14 April 2014, http://www.gov.sk.ca/news?newsId=48ae27b3-d13d-4caa-9799-22029576c139.

105 Randy Burton, "Meth Addiction Strategy Inadequate," *Star-Phoenix*, 2 June 2005: A2; Government of Saskatchewan, "Moore Inquest," news release, 10 May 2005, accessed 14 April 2014, http://www.gov.sk.ca/news?newsId=9f663dd9-c424-41dc-83fe-59cf4e4bfcb0.

106 Government of Saskatchewan, "Vadasz Inquest," news release, 7 December 2005, accessed 14 April 2014, http://www.gov.sk.ca/news?newsId=c71616a7-adcd-462e-abd2-c189f49b1f5c.

107 Government of Saskatchewan, "Timms Inquest," news release, 8 February 2006, accessed 14 April 2014, http://www.gov.sk.ca/news?newsId=5d65ee47-39b6-461a-961d-61d8ee40c7e8&newsPN=Shared.

108 "Inmate Hung Himself, Guards Tell Inquest," *Star-Phoenix*, 28 November 2007: A8; Government of Saskatchewan, "Merrill Inquest," news release, 14 November 2007, accessed 14 April 2014, http://www.gov.sk.ca/news?newsId=c0ef4865-f8ab-4d00-85ae-21141b2f738f.

109 Betty Ann Adam, "Widow Sues Health Authority, Doctor," *Leader Post*, 26 February 2008: A6; Government of Saskatchewan, "Strandquist Inquest," news release, 14 May 2007, accessed 14 April 2014, http://www.gov.sk.ca/news?newsId=a189e1af-9252-4516-b7f7-2a6fca367770.

110 Matthew Gauk, "Prison Officials Stay Silent on Inquest Recommendations," *The Telegram*, 9 August 2008, accessed 14 April 2014, http://www.thetelegram.com/Living/Well-being/2008-08-09/article-169383/Prison-officials-stay-silent-on-inquest-recommendations/1; Government of Saskatchewan, "Adams Inquest," news release, 17 July 2007, accessed 14 April 2014, http://www.gov.sk.ca/news?newsId=25f7d524-96a0-4d2b-9362-2a1fc5a5f5b7.

111 David Hutton, "Family Hopes Inmate's Death Will Improve Corrections System," *Star-Phoenix*, 29 November 2008: A10; Government of Saskatchewan, "Crawford Inquest," news release,

18 November 2008, accessed 14 April 2014, http://gov.sk.ca/news?newsId=bdf29eab-3f44-47d9-8de1-0d782fa8b4b4.

112 Anne Kyle, "MD Says Painkiller Overdose Was Cause of Death," *Leader Post*, 19 November 2008: A6; Anne Kyle, "Jury Recommends Health Services Review Protocol," *Leader Post*, 20 November 2008: B8; Government of Saskatchewan, "Resler Inquest," news release, 12 November 2008, accessed 14 April 2014, http://gov.sk.ca/news?newsId=2d60a3ec-a1f4-4e21-839b-841717102d9c.

113 "Daughter Sues Over Father's Death in Custody," *Star-Phoenix*, 10 April 2010: A7; Barb Pacholik, "Procedures Revised after Prisoner's Death: Police," *Leader Post*, 11 March 2010: A5; Government of Saskatchewan, "Schwager Inquest," news release, 4 March 2010, accessed 14 April 2014, http://gov.sk.ca/news?newsId=a4a6b033-e757-4c36-8ec4-114d37bc4f64.

114 Lori Coolican, "Coroner's Inquest Hears Inmate 'Very Sick' at Time of Death," *Star-Phoenix*, 25 August 2010: A5; Government of Saskatchewan, "Little Inquest," news release, 18 August 2010, accessed 14 April 2014, http://gov.sk.ca/news?newsId=2e4e186d-f8c0-48de-bc72-e8c24c374c20.

115 Government of Saskatchewan, "Philpott Inquest," news release, 25 May 2009, accessed 14 April 2014, http://gov.sk.ca/news?newsId=46a16b17-ac3e-4bdb-be3e-bf3715c3ff0d.

116 Barb Pacholik, "Death Ruled Accidental," *Leader Post*, 22 January 2011: A3; Veronica Rhodes, "Family Wants Answers," *Leader Post*, 16 October 2008: A1; Government of Saskatchewan, "McLean Inquest to Reconvene," news release, 4 January 2011, accessed 14 April 2014, http://gov.sk.ca/news?newsId=53217745-d664-4c4b-a78a-6b2936438cfb.

117 "Inquest into Prisoners' Suicide in Saskatchewan RCMP Cells Concludes," *The Canadian Press*, 1 August 2012; Government of Saskatchewan, "Inquest into the Death of Corey John Cross," news release, 24 July 2012, accessed 14 April 2014, http://gov.sk.ca/news?newsId=5e4d97c3-5b3d-40d5-9257-2cdf0cc49044.

118 Hannah Spray, "Inquest Hears Man Died of Overdose in Custody: Paramedics Now On Duty at Facility," *Star-Phoenix*, 25 June 2013: A3; Government of Saskatchewan, "Inquest into the Death of Christopher Hiebert," news release, 20 June 2013, accessed 14 April 2014, http://www.gov.sk.ca/news?newsId=d03aca1a-aec5-491f-a262-1c6f7c6dd597.

119 Government of Saskatchewan, "Inquest into the Death of Travis Arthur Paranteau," news release, 25 April 2012, accessed 14 April 2014, http://www.gov.sk.ca/news?newsId=bb4bc33d-b9a6-4f9d-bf51-3ab83af13f84.

120 "EMS Should Be on Standby if Suspect Appears Unstable: Inquest Jury," *The Canadian Press*, 5 December 2013; Government of

Saskatchewan, "Inquest into the Death of David Gruno," news release, 18 November 2013, accessed 14 April 2014, http://www.gov.sk.ca/news?newsId=4ef81bc4-7bd7-4802-96f3-495e915a63bb.

Works Cited

Aboriginal Standing Committee on Housing and Homelessness (ASCHH). *Plan to End Aboriginal Homelessness in Calgary*. Calgary: ASCHH, November 2012. Accessed 4 December 2012. http://www.aschh.ca/Plan%20to%20End%20Aboriginal%20Homelessness%20in%20Calgary%202012.pdf.

Agamben, Giorgio. *Homo Sacer: Sovereign Power and Bare Life*. Translated by Daniel Heller-Roazen. Stanford, CA: Stanford University Press, 1998.

– *State of Exception*. Translated by Kevin Attell. Chicago: University of Chicago Press, 2005.

Alfred, Taiaiake. "Deconstructing the British Columbia Treaty Process." In *Dispatches from the Cold Seas: Indigenous Views on Self-Governance, Ecology and Identity*, edited by Curtis Rattray and Tero Mustonen, 31. Tampere, FI: Tampere Polytechnic, 2001. Available at http://web.uvic.ca/igov/uploads/pdf/GTA.bctreatyprocess.pdf.

Amnesty International. "Canada: Covering Events from January to December 2000." In *Amnesty International Report 2001*, accessed 30 March 2014, http://www.refworld.org/pdfid/3b1de371c.pdf.

Amnesty International (Canada). *Stolen Sisters: A Human Rights Response to Discrimination and Violence against Indigenous Women in Canada*. Ottawa: Amnesty International Canada, 2004. Accessed 11 November 2012. http://www.amnesty.org/en/library/info/AMR20/003/2004.

Anderson, Kay. *Race and the Crisis of Humanism*. London and New York: Routledge, 2007.

Ashenden, Samantha. *Governing Child Sexual Abuse: Negotiating the Boundaries of Public and Private, Law and Science*. London and New York: Routledge, 2004.

Ashforth, Adam. "Reckoning Schemes of Legitimation: On Commissions of Inquiry as Power/Knowledge Forms." *Journal of Historical* 3, no. 1 (1990): 1–22.

Bailkin, Jordanna. "The Boot and the Spleen: When Was Murder Possible in British India?" *Comparative Studies in Society and History* 48, no. 2 (2006): 462–93.

Barker, Adam J. "The Contemporary Reality of Canadian Imperialism: Settler Colonialism and the Hybrid Colonial State." *American Indian Quarterly* 33, no. 3 (Summer 2009): 325–51.

Bauman, Zygmunt. *Wasted Lives: Modernity and Its Outcasts*. Malden, MA: Polity Press, 2004.

Beckett, Clare. "Deaths in Custody and the Inquest System." *Critical Social Policy* 19, no. 2 (1999): 271–80.

Bergland, Renée L. *The National Uncanny: Indian Ghosts and American Subjects*. Hanover, NH: University Press of New England, 2000.

Blackburn, Carole. "Searching for Guarantees in the Midst of Uncertainty: Negotiating Aboriginal Rights and Title in British Columbia." *American Anthropologist* 107, no. 4 (2005): 586–96.

Blomley, Nicholas. *Unsettling the City: Urban Land and the Politics of Property*. New York: Routledge, 2004.

Borrows, John. "'Because It Does Not Make Sense': Sovereignty's Power in the Case of *Delgamuukw v. The Queen 1997*." In *Law, History, Colonialism: The Reach of Empire*, edited by Diane Kirby and Catharine Coleborne, 190–206. Manchester, UK: Manchester University Press, 2001.

– "Sovereignty's Alchemy: An Analysis of *Delgamuukw v. British Columbia*." *Osgoode Hall Law Journal* 37, no. 3 (1999): 537–96.

Boyd, Susan, Donald MacPherson, and Bud Osborn. *Raise Shit! Social Action Saving Lives*. Black Point, NS: Fernwood Publishing, 2009.

Brantlinger, Patrick. *Dark Vanishings: Discourse on the Extinction of Primitive Races, 1800–1930*. Ithaca, NY: Cornell University Press, 2003.

Campbell, Larry, Neil Boyd, and Lori Culbert. *A Thousand Dreams: Vancouver's Downtown Eastside and the Fight for Its Future*. Vancouver: Greystone Books, 2009.

Carstairs, Catherine. "'The Most Dangerous Drug': Images of African-Americans and Cocaine Use in the Progressive Era." *Left History: An Interdisciplinary Journal of Historical Inquiry and Debate* 7, no. 1 (2000): 46–61.

Carter, Sarah. *Capturing Women: The Manipulation of Cultural Imagery in Canada's Prairie West*. Montreal: McGill-Queen's University Press, 1997.

Cheema, Mandy. "Missing Subjects: Aboriginal Deaths in Custody, Data Problems, and Racialized Policing." *Appeal: Review of Current Law & Law Reform* 14, no. 84 (2009): 84–100.

Coles, Deborah, and Helen Shaw. "Comment: Deaths in Custody – Truth, Justice, and Accountability? The Work of INQUEST." *Social Justice* 33, no. 4 (2006): 136–41.

Comack, Elizabeth. *Racialized Policing: Aboriginal People's Encounters with the Police*. Halifax and Winnipeg: Fernwood Publishing, 2012.

Coulthard, Glen S. "Subjects of Empire: Indigenous Peoples and the 'Politics of Recognition' in Canada." *Contemporary Political Theory* 6, no. 4 (2007): 437–60.

Cowlishaw, Gillian. "Disappointing Indigenous People: Violence and the Refusal of Help." *Public Culture* 15, no. 1 (2003): 103–25.

Cox, Leonie. "Review of *Aboriginal Suicide Is Different: A Portrait of Life and Self-Destruction* by Colin Tatz." *The Australian Journal of Anthropology* 13, no. 3 (2002): 371–3.

Culhane, Dara. "Their Spirits Live within Us: Aboriginal Women in Downtown Eastside Vancouver Emerging into Visibility." *The American Indian Quarterly* 27, no. 3 (2004): 593–606.

Cunneen, Chris. "Aboriginal Deaths in Custody: A Continuing Systematic Abuse." *Social Justice* 33, no. 4 (2006): 37–51.

– "Indigenous Incarceration: The Violence of Colonial Law and Justice." In *The Violence of Incarceration*, edited by Phil Scraton and Jude McCulloch, 209–24. New York: Routledge, 2009.

– "Reflections on Criminal Justice Policy Since the Royal Commission into Aboriginal Deaths in Custody." University of New South Wales Faculty of Law Research Series, Working Paper 7, March 2008. Accessed 5 April 2014. http://law.bepress.com/cgi/viewcontent.cgi?article=1082&context=unswwps-flrps08.

Dalton, Vicki. "Death and Dying in Prison in Australia: National Overview, 1980–1998." *The Journal of Law, Medicine and Ethics* 27, no. 3 (1999): 269–74.

Daschuk, James. *Clearing the Plains: Disease, Politics of Starvation, and the Loss of Aboriginal Life*. Regina: University of Regina Press, 2013.

Deaths in Custody Watch Committee (WA) Inc. *Report to the Committee Against Torture for Consideration Together with Australia's Reports to the Committee: Pursuant to Article 19 of the Convention Against Torture/Deaths in Custody Watch Committee (WA) Inc.* Ascot, WA: The Committee, 2000. http://web-search.aic.gov.au/firstaicPublic/fullRecord.jsp?recnoListAttr=recnoList&recno=252047.

Deloria, Phillip Joseph. *Playing Indian*. New Haven, CT: Yale University Press, 1998.

Di Maio, Theresa G., and Vincent J.M. Di Maio. *Excited Delirium Syndrome: Cause of Death and Prevention*. Boca Raton, FL: Taylor & Francis Group, 2006.

Dyson, Simon M., and Gwyneth Boswell. "Sickle Cell Anaemia and Deaths in Custody in the UK and the USA." *The Howard Journal* 45, no. 1 (2006): 14–28.

Edmonds, Penelope. "Unpacking Settler Colonialism's Urban Strategies: Indigenous Peoples in Victoria, British Columbia, and the Transition to a

Settler-Colonial City." *Urban History Revue/Revue d'histoire urbaine* 38, no. 2 (Spring 2010): 4–20.

– *Urbanizing Frontiers: Indigenous Peoples and Settlers in 19th-Century Pacific Rim Cities*. Vancouver: UBC Press, 2010.

Edmunds, Mary. *They Get Heaps: A Study of Attitudes in Roebourne, Western Australia*. Canberra: Aboriginal Studies Press, 1989.

Fanon, Frantz. *The Wretched of the Earth*. Translated by Constance Farrington. New York: Grove Press, [1963] 1968.

Farley, Melissa, Jacqueline Lynne, and Ann J. Cotton. "Prostitution in Vancouver: Violence and the Colonization of First Nations Women." *Transcultural Psychiatry* 42, no. 2 (2005): 242–71.

Ferentzy, Peter. "Foucault and Addiction." *Telos* 125 (Fall 2002): 167–91.

Ferreira da Silva, Denise. "Radical Praxis or Knowing (at) the Limits of Justice." In *At the Limits of Justice: Women of Colour on Terror*, edited by Suvendrini Perera and Sherene Razack, 527–37. Toronto: University of Toronto Press, 2014.

– *Toward a Global Idea of Race*. Minneapolis: University of Minnesota Press, 2007.

– "Towards a Critique of the Socio-Logos of Justice: The Analytics of Raciality and the Production of Universality." *Social Identities* 7, no. 3 (2001): 421–44.

Fiske, Jo-Anne, and Annette Browne. "Aboriginal Citizen, Discredited Medical Subject: Paradoxical Constructions of Subjectivity in Health Care Policies." *Policy Sciences* 39, no. 1 (2006): 91–111.

Fitzpatrick, Peter. "Doctrine of Discovery." In *A Companion to Racial and Ethnic Studies*, edited by David Theo Goldberg and John Solomos, 25–30. Malden, MA: Blackwell Publishers, 2002.

– "'Enacted in the Destiny of Sedentary Peoples': Racism, Discovery and the Grounds of Law." *Balayi: Culture, Law and Colonialism* 1, no. 1 (2000): 11–29.

– "'No Higher Duty': *Mabo* and the Failure of Legal Foundation." *Law & Critique* 13, no. 3 (October 2002): 233–52.

Franco, Jean. *Cruel Modernity*. Durham, NC: Duke University Press, 2013.

Freeman, Victoria. *Distant Relations: How My Ancestors Colonized North America*. Toronto: McLelland & Stewart, 2000.

Furniss, Elizabeth. "Indians, Odysseys and Vast, Empty Lands: The Myth of the Frontier in the Canadian Justice System."*Anthropologica* 41, no. 2 (1999): 195–208.

– *Victims of Benevolence: The Dark Legacy of the Williams Lake Residential School*. Vancouver: Arsenal Pulp Press, 1995.

Gabor, Thomas. *Deaths in Custody: Final Report Submitted to the Office of the Correctional Investigator*. Ottawa: Office of the Correctional Investigator,

Government of Canada, 28 February 2007. Accessed 9 September 2012. http://www.oci-bec.gc.ca/cnt/rpt/oth-aut/oth-aut20070228-eng.aspx.

Gaetz, Stephen, Jesse Donaldson, Tim Richter, and Tanya Gulliver. *The State of Homelessness in Canada, 2013*. Toronto: Canadian Homelessness Research Network Press, 2013.

Gidwani, Vinay, and Rajyashree N. Reddy. "The Afterlives of 'Waste': Notes from India for a Minor History of Capitalist Surplus." *Antipode* 43, no.5 (November 2011): 1625–58.

Goldberg, David Theo. *Racist Culture: Philosophy and the Politics of Meaning*. Malden, MA: Blackwell, 1993.

Grant, Peter R. "Recognition and Reconciliation: The British Columbia Experience." *Gestion des Revendications et Litiges Autochtones*, 23–4 February 2010. Accessed 23 May 2010. http://www.grantnativelaw.com/pdf/RecognitionandReconciliationTheBCExperience.pdf.

Green, Joyce. "From Stonechild to Social Cohesion: Anti-Racist Challenges for Saskatchewan." *Canadian Journal of Political Science/Revue canadienne de science politique* 39, no. 3 (2006): 507–27.

Haebich, Anna. "Marked Bodies: A Corporeal History of Colonial Australia." *Borderlands* 7, no. 2 (2008): 1–18.

Halyk, Silas E. "Submission of the Federation of Saskatchewan Indian Nations to the Commission of Inquiry into the Matters Relating to the Death of Neil Stonechild." Saskatoon: Halyk Kennedy Koskie Knox, Barristers and Solicitors, 2004. Accessed 30 March 2014. http://www.justice.gov.sk.ca/stonechild/finalsubs/FSIN-finalsub.pdf.

Hannum, Nancy. *Aboriginal Deaths and Injuries in Custody and/or with Police Involvement: An Initial Survey of Information and Incidents in British Columbia, Saskatchewan, Manitoba and Ontario; Preliminary Report*. Vancouver: Native Courtworker and Counselling Association of British Columbia, 23 September 2003. Accessed 1 October 2013. http://nccabc.pmhclients.com/images/uploads/nccabc_aboriginaldeathsincustody.pdf.

Harris, Cole. *Making Native Space: Colonialism, Resistance, and Reserves in British Columbia*. Vancouver: UBC Press, 2002.

Helps, Lisa. "Body, Power, Desire: Mapping Canadian Body History." *Journal of Canadian Studies/Revue d'études canadiennes* 41, no. 1 (Winter 2007): 126–50.

Hubbard, Tasha. *Two Worlds Colliding*. VHS. Directed by Tasha Hubbard. Canada: National Film Board of Canada, 2005.

Hudson, Laura. "A Species of Thought: Bare Life and Animal Being." *Antipode* 43, no. 5 (2011): 1659–78.

Huntley, Audrey. *"Go Home Baby Girl": A Documentary*. DVD. Directed by Audrey Huntley. Canada: Canadian Broadcasting Corporation, 2006.

Insightrix Research Inc. *The Saskatoon Housing and Homelessness Plan, 2011–2014*. Saskatoon: Saskatoon Homeless Advisory Committee, March 2011. Accessed 1 October 2013. http://www.saskatoon.ca/DEPARTMENTS/Community%20Services/PlanningDevelopment/Documents/Neighbourhood%20Planning/Housing/Housing%20and%20Homelessness%20Report%202011%20final.pdf.

James, Matt. "Scaling Memory: Reparation Displacement and the Case of BC." *Canadian Journal of Political Science/Revue canadienne de science politique* 42, no. 2 (June 2009): 363–86.

Kawash, Samira. "The Homeless Body." *Public Culture* 10, no. 2 (1998): 319–39.

Keenan, Sarah. "Australian Legal Geography and the Search for Postcolonial Space in Chloe Hooper's *The Tall Man: Death and Life on Palm Island*." *Australian Feminist Law Journal* 30 (2009): 173–99.

Kelm, Mary-Ellen. *Colonizing Bodies: Aboriginal Health and Healing in British Columbia, 1900–1950*. Vancouver: UBC Press, 1998.

King, William, and Thomas Dunn. "Dumping: Police-Initiated Transjurisdictional Transport of Troublesome Persons." *Police Quarterly* 7, no. 3 (2004): 339–58.

Korsmo, Fae L. "Claiming Memory in British Columbia: Aboriginal Rights and the State." *American Indian Culture and Research Journal* 20, no. 4 (1996): 71–90.

Levinas, Emmanuel. "Useless Suffering." Translated by Richard Cohen. In *The Provocation of Levinas: Rethinking the Other*, edited by Robert Bernasconi and David Wood, 156–67. New York: Routledge, 1988.

Lyons, Scott Richard. *X-Marks: Native Signatures of Assent*. Minneapolis: University of Minnesota Press, 2010.

MacAlister, David, with Robert Holmes, Gareth Jones, Farzana Kara, André Marin, Hanna Slarks et al. *Police Involved Deaths: The Need for Reform*. Vancouver: BC Civil Liberties Association, 2012. https://bccla.org/wp-content/uploads/2012/03/2012-BCCLA-Report-Police-Involved-Deaths4.pdf.

Mawani, Renisa. "In Between and Out of Place: Mixed-Race Identity, Liquor, and the Law in British Columbia, 1850–1913." In *Race, Space and the Law: Unmapping a White Settler Society*, edited by Sherene H. Razack, 47–69. Toronto: Between the Lines, 2004.

Mbembe, Achille. "Aesthetics of Superfluity." *Public Culture* 16, no. 3 (2004): 373–405.

– "Life, Sovereignty, and Terror in the Fiction of Amos Tutuola." *Research in African Literatures* 34, no. 4 (2003): 1–26.

– "Necropolitics." Translated by Libby Meintjes. *Public Culture* 15, no. 1 (2003): 11–40.

McCallum, Katie, and David Isaac. *Feeling Home: Culturally Responsive Approaches to Aboriginal Homelessness; Research Report*. Vancouver: The Social Planning and Research Council of British Columbia and the Centre for Native Policy and Research, July 2011.

McLean, Candis, and Stuart McLean. *When Police Become Prey*. DVD. Directed by Candis McLean and Stuart McLean. Written by Candis McLean. Calgary: Silver Harvest Productions, 2007.

Mendieta, Eduardo. "Plantations, Ghettoes, Prisons: US Racial Geographies." *Philosophy and Geography* 7, no.1 (2004): 43–59.

– "Prisons, Torture, Race: On Angela Davis's Abolitionism." *Philosophy Today* 50 (2006):176–81.

Michalko, Rod. *The Difference That Disability Makes*. Philadelphia, PA: Temple University Press, 2002.

Milligan, Shelly. "2006 Aboriginal Population Profile for Victoria." In *2006 Aboriginal Population Profiles for Selected Cities and Communities: British Columbia*, Online Catalogue 89-648-X, no. 4. Ottawa: Statistics Canada, 2010. http://www.statcan.gc.ca/pub/89-638-x/2010004/article/11086-eng.htm.

Million, Dian. *Therapeutic Nations: Healing in an Age of Indigenous Human Rights*. Tucson: University of Arizona Press, 2013.

Mohanram, Radhika. *Black Body: Women, Colonialism and Space*. Minneapolis: University of Minnesota Press, 1999.

Mongia, Radhika V. "Impartial Regimes of Truth: Indentured Indian Labour and the Status of the Inquiry." *Cultural Studies* 18, no. 5 (September 2004): 749–68.

Monture-Angus, Patricia. "Lessons in Decolonization: Aboriginal Overrepresentation in Canadian Criminal Justice." In *Visions of the Heart: Canadian Aboriginal Issues*, edited by David Long and Olive Patricia Dickason, 361–86. Toronto: Harcourt Canada, 2000.

– "Standing against Canadian Law: Naming Omissions of Race, Culture, Gender." In *Locating Law: Race/Class/Gender Connections*, edited by Elizabeth Comack with Sedef Arat-Koç et al., 76–97. Halifax: Fernwood Publishing, 1999.

Morrison, Toni. *Playing in the Dark: Whiteness and the Literary Imagination*. New York: Vintage Books, 1992.

Morse, Bradford W. "Indigenous Peoples of Canada and Their Efforts to Achieve True Reparations." In *Reparations for Indigenous Peoples: International Comparative Perspectives*, edited by Federico Lenzerini, 271–316. New York: Oxford University Press, 2008.

Moses, A. Dirk. "Genocide and Settler Society in Australian History." In *Genocide and Settler Society: Frontier Violence and Stolen Indigenous Children in Australian History*, edited by A. Dirk Moses, 3–48. New York: Berghahn Books, 2004.

Native Women's Association of Canada (NWAC). "Aboriginal Women and Homelessness: An Issue Paper." Paper prepared for the National Aboriginal Women's Summit, Corner Brook, NL, 20–2 June 2007. Accessed 21 January 2011. http://ywcacanada.ca/data/research_docs/00000281.pdf.

– *Voices of Our Sisters in Spirit: A Report to Families and Communities*, 2nd ed. Ottawa: Status of Women Canada, March 2009. Accessed 21 January 2011. http://www.nwac.ca/sites/default/files/reports/NWAC_Voices%20of%20Our%20Sisters%20In%20Spirit_2nd%20Edition_March%202009.pdf.

Nettlebeck, Amanda, and Russell Smandych. "Policing Indigenous Peoples on Two Colonial Frontiers: Australia's Mounted Police and Canada's North-West Mounted Police." *The Australian and New Zealand Journal of Criminology* 43, no.2 (2010): 356–75.

Nixon, Kendra, Leslie Tutty, Pamela Downe, Kelly Gorkoff, and Jane Ursel. "The Everyday Occurrence of Violence in the Lives of Girls Exploited through Prostitution." *Violence Against Women* 8, no. 9 (2002): 1016–43.

Pearce, Maryanne. "An Awkward Silence: Missing and Murdered Vulnerable Women and the Canadian Justice System." LD diss., University of Ottawa, 2013.

Pemberton, Simon. "Demystifying Deaths in Police Custody: Challenging State Talk." *Social and Legal Studies* 17, no. 2 (2008): 237–62.

Perera, Suvendrini, and Joseph Pugliese. "White Law of the Biopolitical." *Journal of the European Association of Studies on Australia* 3, no.1 (2012): 87–100.

Perreault, Samuel. "The Incarceration of Aboriginal People in Adult Correctional Services." Statistics Canada. *Juristat* 29, no. 3 (July 2009). Last modified 28 October 2009. http://www.statcan.gc.ca/pub/85-002-x/2009003/article/10903-eng.htm.

Perry, Barbara. *Silent Victims: Hate Crimes against Native Americans*. Tucson: University of Arizona Press, 2008.

Peters, Evelyn J., and Vince Robillard. "'Everything You Want Is There': The Place of the Reserve in First Nations' Homeless Mobility." *Urban Geography* 30, no. 6 (2009): 652–80.

Peters, Heather I., and Bruce Self. "Colonialism, Resistance and the First Nations Health Liaison Program." *Currents: New Scholarship in the Human Services* 4, no.1 (2005): 1–21.

Philip, M. NourbeSe. *Zong!* Middletown, CT: Wesleyan University Press, 2008.

Povinelli, Elizabeth A. *The Cunning of Recognition: Indigenous Alterities and the Making of Australian Multiculturalism*. Durham, NC: Duke University Press, 2002.

Pugliese, Joseph. *State Violence and the Execution of Law: Biopolitical Caesurae of Torture, Black Sites, Drones*. New York: Routledge, 2013.

Razack, Sherene H. *Dark Threats and White Knights: Peacekeeping and the New Imperialism*. Toronto: University of Toronto Press, 2004.

– "Gendered Racial Violence and Spatialized Justice: The Murder of Pamela George." *Canadian Journal of Law and Society* 15, no. 2 (2000): 91–130.

– "'It Happened More than Once': Freezing Deaths in Saskatchewan." *Canadian Journal of Women and the Law* 26, no. 1 (2014): 51–80.

– *Looking White People in the Eye: Gender, Race, and Culture in Courtrooms and Classrooms*. Toronto: University of Toronto Press, 1998.

– "Memorializing Colonial Power: The Death of Frank Paul." *Law & Social Inquiry* 37, no. 4 (2012): 908–32.

– "Racial Terror: Torture and Three Teenagers in Prison." *Borderlands* 13, no.1 (2014): 1–27. http://www.borderlands.net.au/Vol13No1_2014/razack_torture.htm.

– "The Space of Difference in Law: Inquests into Aboriginal Deaths in Custody." *Somatechnics* 1, no. 1 (2011): 87–123.

– "Stealing the Pain of Others: Reflections on Canadian Humanitarian Responses." *The Review of Education, Pedagogy, and Cultural Studies* 29, no. 3 (2007): 375–94.

– "Timely Deaths: Medicalizing the Deaths of Aboriginal People in Police Custody." *Law, Culture and the Humanities* 9, no. 2 (2013): 352–74. Published electronically before print 30 June 2011. doi:10.1177/1743872111407022.

– "When Place Becomes Race." In *Race, Space and the Law: Unmapping a White Settler Society*, edited by Sherene H. Razack, 1–20. Toronto: Between the Lines, 2004.

Reber, Susanne, and Rob Renaud. *Starlight Tour: The Last, Lonely Night of Neil Stonechild*. Toronto: Random House Canada, 2005.

Rifkin, Mark. "Indigenizing Agamben: Rethinking Sovereignty in Light of the 'Peculiar' Status of Native Peoples." *Cultural Critique* 73 (Fall 2009): 88–124.

Roberts, Julian V., and Ronald Melchers. "The Incarceration of Aboriginal Offenders: Trends from 1978 to 2001." *Canadian Journal of Criminology and Criminal Justice* 45, no. 2 (April 2003): 211–42.

Robertson, Leslie. "Taming Space: Drug Use, HIV, and Homemaking in Downtown Eastside Vancouver." *Gender, Place and Culture* 14, no. 5 (2007): 527–49.

Robertson, Leslie, and Dara Culhane. *In Plain Sight: Reflections on Life in Downtown Eastside Vancouver.* Vancouver: Talonbooks, 2005.

Robinson, Debra, and Shelby Hunt. "Sudden In-Custody Death Syndrome." *Topics in Emergency Medicine* 27, no. 1 (2005): 36–43.

Russell, Peter. *Recognizing Aboriginal Title: The Mabo Case and Indigenous Resistance to English-Settler Colonialism*. Toronto: University of Toronto Press, 2005.

Rutherford, Jennifer. *Gauche Intruder*. Melbourne, AU: Melbourne University Press, 2000.

Said, Edward W. *Culture and Imperialism*. New York: Alfred A. Knopf, 1994.

Saskatchewan Indian Institute of Technologies. *Urban First Nations People without Homes in Saskatchewan*. Saskatoon: Saskatchewan Indian Institute of Technologies, Asimakaniseekan Askiy Reserve, 2000. Accessed 5 November 2012. http://www.ywcaregina.com/Programs/HomelessnessPoverty/Homeless%20Urban%20First%20Nations.pdf.

Scraton, Phil. "Lost Lives, Hidden Voices: 'Truth' and Controversial Deaths." *Race & Class* 44, no. 1 (2002): 107–18.

Scraton, Phil, and Kathryn Chadwick. "Speaking Ill of the Dead: Institutionalised Responses to Deaths in Custody." *Journal of Law and Society* 13, no.1 (Spring 1986): 93–115.

Secor, Anna J. "An Unrecognizable Condition Has Arrived: Law, Violence, and the State of Exception in Turkey." In *Violent Geographies: Fear, Terror, and Political Violence*, edited by Derek Gregory and Allan Pred, 37–53. New York: Routledge, 2007.

Sellars, Beverly. *They Called Me Number One: Secrets and Survival at an Indian Residential School*. Vancouver: Talonbooks, 2013.

Simpson, Audra. *Mohawk Interruptus: Political Life Across the Borders of Settler States*. Raleigh, NC: Duke University Press, 2014.

– "Settlement's Secret." *Cultural Anthropology* 26, no. 2 (2011): 205–17.

Slattery, Brian. "Aboriginal Rights and the Honour of the Crown." *Supreme Court Law Review* 29 (2005): 433–45.

– "The Metamorphosis of Aboriginal Title." *The Canadian Bar Review* 85, no. 2 (2007): 255–86.

Slotkin, Richard. *Gunfighter Nation: The Myth of the Frontier in Twentieth-Century America*. Norman, OK: University of Oklahoma Press, 1998.

Smith, Andrea. *Conquest: Sexual Violence and American Indian Genocide*. Cambridge, MA: South End Press, 2005.

– "Heteropatriarchy and the Three Pillars of White Supremacy: Rethinking Women of Color Organizing." In *The Color of Violence: The Incite! Anthology*, edited by INCITE! Women of Color Against Violence, 66–73. Cambridge, MA: South End Press, 2006.

– "Indigeneity, Settler Colonialism, White Supremacy." In *Racial Formation in the Twenty-First Century*, edited by Daniel Martinez HoSang, Oneka LaBennett, and Laura Pulido, 66–90. Berkeley: University of California Press, 2012.

Smith, Dorothy E. "No One Commits Suicide: Textual Analysis of Ideological Practices." *Human Studies* 6, no.1 (1983): 309–59.

Sontag, Susan. *Regarding the Pain of Others*. New York: Farrar, Straus and Giroux, 2003.

Spence, Cara J.A. "An Analysis of Race Relations in Saskatoon Saskatchewan: The Contributions of the Housing Sector." Bridges and Foundations Project on Urban Aboriginal Housing. Saskatoon: Bridges and Foundations, 2004. Accessed 7 November 2010. http://www.bridgesandfoundations.usask.ca/reports/analysis_racerelations.pdf.

Spillers, Hortense J. "Mama's Baby, Papa's Maybe: An American Grammar Book." *Diacritics* 17, no. 2 (1987): 65–81.

Stam, Robert, and Ella Shohat. "Whence and Whither Postcolonial Theory?" *New Literary History* 43, no.2 (2012): 371–90.

Statistics Canada. *Aboriginal Peoples in Canada: First Nations Peoples, Métis and Inuit*. National Household Survey 2011. Catalogue no. 99-011-X2011001. Ottawa: Ministry of Industry, 2013. Accessed 30 March 2014. http://www12.statcan.gc.ca/nhs-enm/2011/as-sa/99-011-x/99-011-x2011001-eng.pdf.

Stavenhagen, Rodolfo, UN Special Rapporteur on the Situation of Human Rights and Fundamental Freedoms of Indigenous People. "Mission to Canada."Addendum to *Indigenous Issues: Human Rights and Indigenous Issues*. Report to the Sixty-First Session of the Commission on Human Rights. UN Doc E/CN.4/2005/88/Add.3. New York: UN Economic and Social Council, 2004. Accessed 8 November 2013. http://www.gcc.ca/pdf/INT000000012.pdf.

Stenning, Phillip, and Carole LaPrairie. "'Politics by Other Means': The Role of Commissions of Inquiry in Establishing the 'Truth' About 'Aboriginal Justice' in Canada." In *Crime, Truth and Justice: Official Inquiry, Discourse, Knowledge*, edited by John Pratt and George Gilligan, 139–60. Devon, UK: Willan Publishing, 2004.

Stoler, Ann Laura. *Along the Archival Grain: Epistemic Anxieties and Colonial Common Sense*. Princeton: Princeton University Press, 2009.

Storey, Michael L. "Explaining the Unexplainable: Excited Delirium Syndrome and Its Impact on the Objective Reasonableness Standard for Allegations of Excessive Force." *St. Louis University Law Journal* 56, no.2 (Winter 2012): 633–64.

Sullivan, Laura. "Tasers Implicated in Excited Delirium Deaths." *NPR*, 27 February 2007. Accessed 16 December 2013. http://www.npr.org/templates/story/story.php?storyId=7622314.

Talmet, Jacky, Charlotte de Crespigny, Lynette Cusack, and Peter Athanasos. "'Turning a Blind Eye': Denying People Their Right to

Treatment for Acute Alcohol, Drug and Mental Health Conditions – An Act of Discrimination." *Mental Health and Substance Use: Dual Diagnosis* 2, no. 3 (October 2009): 247–54.

Tatz, Colin. *Aboriginal Suicide Is Different: A Portrait of Life and Self-Destruction*. Canberra: Aboriginal Studies Press, 2001.

Taussig, Michael. *Shamanism, Colonialism, and the Wild Man: A Study in Terror and Healing*. Chicago: University of Chicago Press, 1987.

– *Walter Benjamin's Grave*. Chicago: University of Chicago Press, 2006.

Tedmanson, Deidre. "Isle of Exception: Sovereign Power and Palm Island." *Critical Perspectives on International Business* 4, no. 2/3 (2008): 142–65.

Thielen-Wilson, Leslie. "White Terror, Canada's Indian Residential Schools, and the Colonial Present: From Law towards a Pedagogy of Recognition." PhD diss., University of Toronto, 2012.

Thistle, Paul Q. *Trade Relations in the Lower Saskatchewan River Region to 1840*. Winnipeg: University of Manitoba Press, 1986.

U.S. Department Of State, Bureau of Democracy, Human Rights and Labor. "Canada." In *2004 Country Reports on Human Rights*. Washington: Bureau of Public Affairs, 28 February 2005. Accessed 8 November 2013. http://www.state.gov/j/drl/rls/hrrpt/2004/41752.htm.

Valverde, Mariana. *Diseases of the Will: Alcohol and the Dilemma of Freedom*. Cambridge: Cambridge University Press, 1998.

Veracini, Lorenzo. "The Other Shift: Settler Colonialism, Israel, and the Occupation." *Journal of Palestine Studies* 42, no. 2 (Winter 2013): 26–42.

Vilke, Gary M., Jason Payne-James, and Steven B. Karch. "Excited Delirium Syndrome (ExDS): Redefining an Old Diagnosis." *Journal of Forensic and Legal Medicine* 19, no.1 (2012): 7–11.

Wadiwel, Dinesh. "'A Particularly Governmental Form of Warfare': Palm Island and Australian Sovereignty." In *Our Patch: Enacting Australian Sovereignty*, edited by Suvendrini Perera, 149–66. Perth, AU: Network Books, 2007.

Walsh, Christine A., Paula MacDonald, Gayle E. Rutherford, Kerrie Moore, and Brigette Krieg. "Homelessness and Incarceration among Aboriginal Women: An Integrative Literature Review." *Pímatisíwin: A Journal of Aboriginal and Indigenous Community Health* 9, no. 2 (2011): 363–86.

Watson, Joanne. *Palm Island through a Long Lens*. Canberra: Aboriginal Studies Press, 2010.

Wildman, Paul. "The Litany of Death: A Deep Futures Critique of the Australian Royal Commission into Aboriginal Deaths in Custody." *Futures* 34, no. 6 (2002): 571–81.

Wolfe, Patrick. "Settler Colonialism and the Elimination of the Native." *Journal of Genocide Research* 8, no. 4 (2006): 387–409.

Woolford, Andrew John. *Between Justice and Certainty: The British Columbia Treaty Process*. Vancouver: UBC Press, 2005.

– "Negotiating Affirmative Repair: Symbolic Violence in the British Columbia Treaty Process." *Canadian Journal of Sociology* 29, no. 1 (2004): 111–44.

Worme, Donald E. "Submissions on Behalf of Stella Bignell and the Family of Neil Stonechild to the Commission of Inquiry into the Matters Relating to the Death of Neil Stonechild." Saskatoon: Semaganis Worme & Missens, Barristers & Attorneys-At-Law, 2004. Accessed 30 March 2014. http://www.justice.gov.sk.ca/stonechild/finalsubs/Bignell%20-%20Final%20Written%20Submissions.pdf.

Wortley, Scot. *Police Use of Force in Ontario: An Examination of Data from the Special Investigations Unit; Final* Report. Research support from Terry Roswell. Toronto: African Canadian Legal Clinic. Accessed 2 May 2014. http://www.attorneygeneral.jus.gov.on.ca/inquiries/ipperwash/policy_part/projects/pdf/AfricanCanadianClinicIpperwashProject_SIUStudybyScotWortley.pdf.

Wynter, Sylvia. "Unsettling the Coloniality of Being/Power/Truth/Freedom: Towards the Human, After Man, Its Overrepresentation – An Argument." *CR: The New Centennial Review* 3, no. 3 (2003): 257–337.

Yates, Michelle. "The Human-As-Waste, the Labor Theory of Value and Disposability in Contemporary Capitalism." *Antipode* 43, no. 5 (November 2011): 1679–95.

Zieger, Susan. *Inventing the Addict: Drugs, Race, and Sexuality in Nineteenth-Century British and American Literature*. Amherst: University of Massachusetts Press, 2008.

Case Law

Delgamuukw v. British Columbia [1991] BCSC, 79 DLR (4th) 185.

Mabo v. The State of Queensland (No. 2) [1992] 175 CLR 1.

R v. O'Connor [1995] 4 SCR 411.

R. v. S.F.K. [2000] SKCA 28 (CanLII).

Tsilhqot'in Nation v. British Columbia [2007] BCSC 1700 (CanLII).

William v. British Columbia [2012] BCCA 285.

William v. British Columbia [2013] SCC 34986.

Tsilhqot'in Nation v. British Columbia [2014] SCC 44.

Royal Commissions, Commissions of Inquiry, and Task Forces

Australia. Royal Commission into Aboriginal Deaths in Custody (RCIADIC). *National Report Volume 1*. Commissioner Elliott Johnston. Canberra: Australian Government Publishing Service, 1991. http://www.austlii.edu.au/au/other/IndigLRes/rciadic/national/vol1/.

British Columbia. Braidwood Commission on Conducted Energy Weapon Use. *Restoring Public Confidence: Restricting the Use of Conducted Energy Weapons in British Columbia*. Commissioner Thomas R. Braidwood. Vancouver: The Braidwood Commission, 18 June 2009. http://www.ag.gov.bc.ca/public_inquiries/docs/BraidwoodPhase1Report.pdf.

British Columbia. *Coroner's Inquest into the Death of Anthany James Dawson* [Proceeding at Inquest]. Coroner Dianne Olson. Victoria: Coroner's Court of British Columbia, November–December, 2000.

British Columbia. *Coroner's Inquest into the Death of Anthany James Dawson*, vols. 1–3. Coroner Dianne Olson. Victoria: Coroner's Court of British Columbia, 17–25 July 2000.

British Columbia. *Coroner's Report into the Death of C.T.* Coroner Beth Larcombe. Port Alberni: Coroners Service of British Columbia, Ministry of Justice, 19–21 February 2008.

British Columbia. *Coroner's Report into the Death of Paul Alphonse*. Coroner S.A. Cloverdale. Vancouver: Coroners Service of British Columbia, Ministry of Justice, 29 October – 1 November 2001; 4–8 March 2002.

British Columbia. *Coroner's Report into the Death of R.A.W.* Coroner Marj Paonessa. Terrance: Coroners Service of British Columbia, Ministry of Justice, 22–4 September 2008.

British Columbia. *Coroner's Report into the Death of S.Q.* Coroner Tonia Grace. Penticton: Coroners Service of British Columbia, Ministry of Justice, 27–29 May 2008; 3 June, 2008.

British Columbia. Coroners Service of British Columbia. "Statistics 1992 to 2007: BC Custody/Police Involved Deaths." Burnaby: Emergency Management BC, Ministry of Public Safety and Solicitor General, Office of the Chief Coroner, 16 October 2007.

British Columbia. The Davies Commission: Inquiry into the Death of Frank Paul. *Alone and Cold: Interim Report of the Davies Commission Inquiry into the Death of Frank Paul*. Commissioner William H. Davies. Vancouver: The Davies Commission, 12 February 2009. Accessed 7 November 2010. http://frankpaulinquiryca.nationprotect.net/report/Interim/.

British Columbia. The Davies Commission: Inquiry into the Response of the Criminal Justice Branch. *Alone and Cold: Criminal Justice Branch Response; Final Report of the Davies Commission Inquiry into the Response of the Criminal*

Justice Branch. Commissioner William H. Davies. Vancouver: The Davies Commission, 19 May 2011. Accessed 2 September 2011. http://frankpaulinquiryca.nationprotect.net/report/Final/.

British Columbia. Indian Claims Commission. *Williams Lake Indian Band: Village Site Inquiry*. Ottawa: Indian Claims Commission, March 2006. Accessed 30 March 2014. http://iportal.usask.ca/docs/ICC/WilliamsLake_eng.pdf.

British Columbia. *Report on the Cariboo-Chilcotin Justice Inquiry*. Commissioner Anthony Sarich. Victoria: Cariboo-Justice Inquiry, 1993.

British Columbia. "Yvon Gesinghaus (Presentation)." In *Report of Proceedings (Minutes and Hansard): Special Committee to Review the Police Complaint Process*. 37th Parl., 3rd Sess., No. 16. Victoria: Legislative Assembly, 11 April 2002. Accessed 29 April 2014. http://www.leg.bc.ca/cmt/37thparl/session-3/pcp/hansard/l20020411p.htm.

Canada. *Annual Report of the Office of the Correctional Investigator, 2008–2009*, by Howard. Sapers, Correctional Investigator of Canada. Ottawa: Office of the Correctional Investigator, 2009. Accessed 7 November 2010. http://www.oci-bec.gc.ca/cnt/rpt/pdf/annrpt/annrpt20082009-eng.pdf.

Canada. *Annual Report of the Office of the Correctional Investigator, 2009–2010*, by Howard. Sapers, Correctional Investigator of Canada. Ottawa: Office of the Correctional Investigator, 2010. Accessed 2 May 2014. http://www.oci-bec.gc.ca/cnt/rpt/pdf/annrpt/annrpt20092010-eng.pdf.

Canada. *Bridging the Cultural Divide: A Report on Aboriginal People and Criminal Justice in Canada*, by Georges Erasmus and René Dussault. Ottawa: Minister of Supply and Services Canada, 1996.

Canada. *Enhancing the Role of Aboriginal Communities in Federal Corrections*, by Gina Wilson. Ottawa: Correctional Service Canada, 2010. Accessed 10 May 2011. Last modified 15 August 2013. http://www.csc-scc.gc.ca/aboriginal/002003-3003-eng.shtml.

Canada. *A Failure to Respond: Report on the Circumstances Surrounding the Death of a Federal Inmate*, by Howard Sapers, Correctional Investigator of Canada. Ottawa: Office of the Correctional Investigator, Government of Canada, 2008. Last modified 16 September 2013. http://www.oci-bec.gc.ca/cnt/rpt/oth-aut/oth-aut20080521-eng.aspx.

Canada. *Good Intentions, Disappointing Results: A Progress Report on Federal Aboriginal Corrections*, by Michelle M. Mann. Ottawa: Office of the Correctional Investigator, Government of Canada, 2009. Last modified 16 September 2013. http://www.oci-bec.gc.ca/cnt/comm/presentations/presentationsPRAC-RESCFA-eng.aspx.

Canada. Royal Commission on Aboriginal Peoples. Highlights from *People to People, Nation to Nation: Report of the Royal Commission on Aboriginal Peoples*.

Ottawa: Minister of Supply and Services Canada, 1996. Accessed 13 June 2003. http://www.aadnc-aandc.gc.ca/eng/1100100014597/1100100014637.

Manitoba. Public Inquiry into the Administration of Justice and First Nations People. *Report of the Aboriginal Justice Inquiry of Manitoba.* Vol. 1: *The Justice System and Aboriginal People*, by Alvin C. Hamilton and C. Murray Sinclair. Winnipeg: Province of Manitoba, 1991.

Nova Scotia. Department of Justice. *Report of the Panel of Mental Health and Medical Experts Review of Excited Delirium*, by Dr Stan Kutcher, Dr Matt Bowes, Fred Stanford et al. Halifax: Minister of Justice and Attorney General, 30 June 2009. Accessed 13 April 2014. http://novascotia.ca/just/public_safety/_docs/Excited%20Delirium%20Report.pdf.

Nova Scotia. Provincial Court. *Report of the Fatality Inquiry into the Death of Howard Hyde.* Report Pursuant to the *Fatality Investigations Act*, by Anne S. Derrick, Provincial Court Judge. Halifax: Provincial Court, Province of Nova Scotia, 30 November 2010. http://www.courts.ns.ca/Provincial_Court/NSPC_documents/NSPC_Hyde_Inquiry_Report.pdf

Saskatchewan. Commission of Inquiry into the Matters Relating to the Death of Neil Stonechild. *Report of the Commission of Inquiry into Matters Relating to the Death of Neil Stonechild.* Commissioner David H. Wright. Regina: Coroners Service of Saskatchewan, Ministry of Justice for the Government of Saskatchewan, October 2004. Accessed 5 November 2004. http://www.justice.gov.sk.ca/stonechild/finalreport/.

Saskatchewan. *Coroner's Inquest into the Death of A.M.S.* Coroner John Nyssen. Regina: Coroners Service of Saskatchewan, Ministry of Justice for the Government of Saskatchewan, 3–4 June 2003.

Saskatchewan. *Coroner's Inquest into the Death of A.R.C.* Coroner Jeff Grubb. Yorkton: Coroners Service of Saskatchewan, Ministry of Justice for the Government of Saskatchewan, 9–13 February 2004.

Saskatchewan. *Coroner's Inquest into the Death of Lawrence Kim Wegner.* Coroner H.M. Harradence. Saskatoon: Coroners Service of Saskatchewan, Ministry of Justice for the Government of Saskatchewan, 14–18, 21–3 January 2002; 4–8, 11–14 February 2002.

Saskatchewan. *Coroner's Inquest into the Death of Rodney Hank Naistus.* Coroner H.M. Harradence. Saskatoon: Coroners Service of Saskatchewan, Ministry of Justice for the Government of Saskatchewan, 30–1 October 2001; 1–2 November 2001.

Saskatchewan. *Coroner's Report into the Death of A.E.* Coroner Alma Wiebe. Prince Albert: Coroners Service of Saskatchewan, Ministry of Justice for the Government of Saskatchewan, 21–3 March 2005.

Index